D1503647

# Multinational
# Cross-Cultural Management

# Multinational
# Cross-Cultural Management

## AN INTEGRATIVE
## CONTEXT-SPECIFIC PROCESS

Robert J. Mockler
Dorothy G. Dologite

Tennessee Tech Library
Cookeville, TN

**QUORUM BOOKS**
Westport, Connecticut • London

**Library of Congress Cataloging-in-Publication Data**

Mockler, Robert J.
    Multinational cross-cultural management : an integrative context-
specific process / Robert J. Mockler and Dorothy G. Dologite.
        p.   cm.
    Includes bibliographical references and index.
    ISBN 1–56720–010–9 (alk. paper)
    1. International business enterprises—Management—Social aspects.
2. Intercultural communication.   I. Dologite, D. G. (Dorothy G.),
1941–   .   II. Title.
HD62.4.M62   1997
658'.049—dc20          96–26270

British Library Cataloguing in Publication Data is available.

Copyright © 1997 by Robert J. Mockler and Dorothy G. Dologite

All rights reserved. No portion of this book may be
reproduced, by any process or technique, without the
express written consent of the publisher.

Library of Congress Catalog Card Number: 96–26270
ISBN: 1–56720–010–9

First published in 1997

Quorum Books, 88 Post Road West, Westport, CT 06881
An imprint of Greenwood Publishing Group, Inc.

Printed in the United States of America

The paper used in this book complies with the
Permanent Paper Standard issued by the National
Information Standards Organization (Z39.48–1984).

10   9   8   7   6   5   4   3   2   1

*Dedicated to the late Colman M. Mockler,*
*former Chief Executive Officer of the Gillette Company,*
*brother and mentor of one of the authors, one of business's*
*truly great leaders, and an extraordinary human being.*

# Contents

# Figures and Tables

## FIGURES

## TABLES

# Preface

This book is for present and future business managers expecting to face competitive challenges in the multinational cross-cultural market. It is designed to give both a concise introduction to the subject and a perspective to enable working managers and international business students alike to meet these challenges effectively.

## THE PERSPECTIVE OF THE BOOK

This book is primarily an introduction to *managing enterprises that operate across national borders*, whether they be called multinational (operating in many countries), international (operating between nations) or global (operating worldwide). In this book, *multinational enterprise* is used interchangeably with all these terms. Only secondarily is the book an introduction to *how international businesses work*.

Multinational cross-cultural management is viewed from three perspectives:

- global frameworks,
- adaptations to meet local situation needs where appropriate, and
- often, as a creative and innovative tool for handling difficult, unique and unusual situations via situation-specific solutions.

## MEETING THE CHALLENGES OF MANAGING ACROSS CULTURES: THE DISTINGUISHING PURPOSE AND STRUCTURE OF THIS BOOK

This book has several distinguishing features. First, it provides a way to meet the needs of multinational cross-cultural managers, initially by focusing on common frameworks. Chapters 1, 2, and 3 in Part I introduce the reader to the multinational business environment and review contingency and other processes that provide common frameworks for cross-cultural management decision making and action. Putting these common frameworks to work in responding to and managing situational differences is introduced in Chapter 4.

Applications in multinational situations of these common contingency frameworks and other similar structures (such as organizational and behavioral processes, entrepreneurial contingency-thinking processes, global products and services, telecommunications information systems technology and finance/accounting systems) are explored in the chapters in Parts II, III, and IV in a variety of situations at the enterprisewide, business unit, and operational levels.

These chapters explore ways in which common frameworks enable more efficient management and operations, as well as help to rapidly diffuse new knowledge and to reconcile and manage differences. These chapters also explore, within these common frameworks, specific problems involved in managing differences and diversity in different kinds of international situations.

A second distinguishing feature of this book, then, is that it deals with both planning and action. It describes how managers have actually balanced the global aspects (cognitive, organizational, behavioral, product/services and information/telecommunications) of cross-cultural management with responsiveness to the variable situation-dependent aspects in different companies and countries. Acquiring skills in achieving balance (action) is as important as deciding in what way and how to respond (planning).

Carrying out planning and action requires managers to balance disparate skills. First, it requires "having one's head in the air" in order to shape visions and strategic plans. It also requires "having one's feet on the ground" in order to see that visions and strategy are realized in successful day-to-day business operations.

The chapters describe how managers do this, and not only when they are planning and putting in place functional operations (Chapters 5 and 6). They also describe, in Chapters 7 through 9, the processes involved in creating enabling mechanisms for carrying out plans and managing operations (such as telecommunications/information systems, organization culture and structure, and finance/accounting systems) and when managing human resources, which also significantly affect success (Chapters 10 through 13).

A third distinguishing feature is that the book is essentially experience based. While basic theory development and research, as published in the major journals, was important to the book's development, its basic themes and orientation come from the experiences of the authors and others, who have been involved in investing in foreign companies, starting their own multimillion-dollar multinational ventures and joint ventures, engaging in joint studies and research with foreign nationals, consulting, and conducting management development workshops and seminars abroad. To further this experience-based learning orientation, the experiences of companies and individual managers are described throughout the book.

A fourth distinguishing feature of this book is that it deals with the topic from the viewpoint of the individual manager who must engage in decision making and action. In this sense, it presents readers with an opportunity to develop their skills by experiencing a variety of multinational cross-cultural management situations of growing diversity and complexity, in much the same way they would on the job. This means that the book avoids a technical approach, whereby techniques and cultural differences are overly emphasized. Instead, it focuses primarily on situation-by-situation management tasks, decision making, and action.

A fifth distinguishing feature is that the book deals with multinational management on three levels:

- surviving and prospering in the present competitive environment,
- anticipating, adapting to, and generating ideas that manage and exploit change, and
- leading and creating change across industries and markets.

This forward-looking orientation for business management dictates considering new approaches—which must go beyond traditional "Western-style," rational planning. The new approaches involve understanding the multiple perspectives that affect how we view problems, the productive conflicts that will be generated by questioning traditional assumptions about management, the processes by which the conflicts can be reconciled integratively and systematically and the broader systems contexts within which decisions must be made and action taken in today's competitive multinational environment.

## ACKNOWLEDGMENTS

I wish to thank my many associates and friends in business who helped me, especially Warren Buffett (Berkshire Hathaway) and Alfred Zeien (Chairman and CEO, the Gillette Company). I would also like to thank my many professional friends and associates at St. John's University and other educational institutions who contributed to the development of this book. In addition, I want to thank the many graduate students at St. John's University and the many workshop participants around the world who contributed to the book's development.

# Part I

# Basic Processes and Tasks

Chapter 1

# Cross-Cultural Management in a Multinational Context: Introduction

The United Nations has defined *multinational enterprises* as enterprises that own or control production or service facilities outside the country in which they are based. For the purposes of this book, the concept of a multinational enterprise also can include those companies that sell products in international markets, such as mail-order companies selling in countries where they maintain only minimal service facilities or partnerships (WuDunn 1995). The primary difference between a multinational business and domestic businesses is the environment—several countries instead of one—in which the former operates.

Each country in which a multinational enterprise operates can have a distinct economic, political, legal, cultural, industry and competitive market context, to which businesses must be responsive. Since distinct countries are served by multinational companies, these situations present integration challenges to a multinational company that operates in many different countries. Integration is an especially difficult job in a multinational enterprise because it involves maintaining a balance between capturing global efficiencies and being responsive to local country and cultural differences.

*Culture* refers to shared values, beliefs, attitudes, expectations and norms found within countries, regions, social groups, business firms—and even departments and work groups within a business firm. Success in today's highly competitive markets requires effectively and efficiently dealing with the diverse cultures encountered within business firms, as well as within the national and international competitive markets in which businesses operate.

This book focuses on the cross-national and cross-cultural management challenges increasingly faced by business managers in multinational competitive markets. Except in rare instances, multinational business management is essentially cross-cultural management. Managers faced with, or expecting to face, such situations are the intended readers of this book.


## COMMON FRAMEWORKS: BORN OF NECESSITY

This book grew out of the personal experiences of the authors and others in working across cultural boundaries in a multinational business environment.

On one level, surviving and prospering for us has led to a continuing search for common or global frameworks that enabled us to work effectively and efficiently in many countries (both China and Russia, for example). This was necessary in doing strategic management and information systems development work, conducting executive seminars on these subjects in different countries, consulting, and developing and managing multinational businesses. Working tools, perspectives and orientations resulting from this work are all presented here.

As time passed, we discovered that our experiences were similar to those of many business managers who were actively seeking common global links—common frameworks that also enable accommodating national and cultural differences and the rapid transfer of information.

In 1995, Ford was moving forward in its search to develop a global or world automobile (Treece, Kerwin, and Dawley 1995). Coca-Cola, Toyota, McDonald's and Gillette are among the many companies that have built worldwide reputations for their brand names and products. In early 1996, Coca-Cola formally designated itself a "world" company, in which its U.S. operations now comprised only one of six divisions (Collins 1996). Many retailers and mail-order companies, such as Wal-Mart and L. L. Bean; global telecommunications companies, such as AT&T; electronics manufacturers, such as Sony and Hewlett-Packard; advertising agencies, airlines, such as Singapore Airlines and British Airways; accounting firms; and others have all been working to identify and, in many ways, helping to further a growing trend toward a more unified and homogeneous global community. Such a growing global or *whole world* perspective is expected to help multinational managers more easily and cost-effectively capture the efficiencies arising from a global approach. At the same time, it is expected to help them respond to national and cultural differences (Gillooly 1995; Kanter 1995; Nash 1995; Rapoport and Martin 1995; WuDunn 1995; Zeien 1995).

In addition to global or worldwide brands and products, other common global frameworks exist. Advances in technologies for telecommunications and computer information systems are especially serving to stimulate and further this trend, as is seen in such innovations as Cable News Network's worldwide news coverage and the growing worldwide use of the Internet Computer Communications system. Several contingency-thinking processes have proved useful in making moves across national and cultural boundaries easier and more effective, especially when working with individual managers in multinational enterprises. These cognitive processes are also discussed in detail in this book.

While useful, identifiable common frameworks exist across cultures and nations (for instance, global or world products, computer information and tele-communications technologies and common contingency/entrepreneurial thinking processes), on another level, success also depends on creatively working with, and managing, the specific human, business and cultural factors operating within specific situations. When actually trying to get things done in different cultures and different countries, the process is never as simple as it seemed in theory. Look at the situation Anheuser-Busch encountered in mid-1995, for example:

### Tiny Brewer Thwarts Global Push by Budweiser

In 1911, Anheuser-Busch, the world's biggest brewer, signed an agreement with a small Czechoslovakia brewery, Budejovicky Budvar, giving the Czech brewery the right to use the Budweiser name in Europe and the former Soviet Union, where it had used the name for over 100 years. Today, in this age of global markets, this agreement has come back to haunt Anheuser-Busch, which is trying to make its Budweiser a global brand.

Anheuser has tried to buy and/or invest in the Czech brewery and has built a cultural center and given scholarships in the Czech brewery's home town (Ceske Budejovice). So far, however, the Czech company has shown little interest in either selling their company to Anheuser-Busch or in negotiating a new brand agreement. The Czech company realizes it has a very strong strategic position: "We don't need Anheuser-Busch, they need us." The Czech company and its town want no part of a giant Western company that they assume will suck the charm and profits from the brewery—a very real cultural barrier. Besides, many of the Czechs say, Anheuser-Busch makes lousy tasting beer, further reinforcing the different tastes found in different cultures.

So, Anheuser-Busch has for the time being given up efforts to buy into the brewery and is searching for other ways to settle the trademark dispute. The dispute is even more complicated as other European breweries are joining the effort to hinder Anheuser-Busch's international expansion in Europe. (Perlez 1995, pp. A1, D1).

In this situation, figuring out exactly what will work, given the specific people, competitive markets, cultures and other factors, is Anheuser-Busch's immediate multinational cross-cultural problem. The solution, in other words, is *contingent on* effectively and efficiently responding to and managing the specific situation factors. Practical, not theoretical, entrepreneurial solutions appropriate for a situation faced by an individual manager are frequently all that matter to a manager trying to survive and prosper in rapidly changing and competitive multinational cross-cultural markets. These are the managers for whom this book is written.

Management in today's multinational situations involves going beyond traditional analytical and rational processes. It involves thinking more in terms of multiple realities—many perspectives and viewpoints, which are often paradoxical and conflicting. It also involves going beyond conflicts and their resolution in using the dialectics involved in conflict and paradox resolution to more synergistically use human and other resources to deal with future competitive markets. Such a management perspective involves learning to think in the much broader terms of world contexts, while still focusing on the individual managers' need to manage their individual companies.

Finding solutions, therefore, can involve a wide range of creative and entrepreneurial skills. For example, in 1995 Al Zeien, chief executive officer (CEO) of the Gillette Company, described how Gillette had a somewhat atypical experience when expanding into Poland:

Now Gillette had been exporting to Poland for years, but in relatively small quantities until the [Berlin] wall came down. At that time we started to look around to find a joint venture partner there. We found a manufacturing operation in a city called Lodz, which is about a two-hour drive southwest of Warsaw. It is an old textile city.

We negotiated with the management there and gave the employees a piece of the company. This was a blade-manufacturing operation. We now have about 90 percent of the Polish blade business coming out of this plant. During the period of communism there had been very little investment in the plants; the buildings and plant were probably pretty much the same in 1992 as they were in 1946. I remember visiting the operation in Poland during the final negotiations, talking with the general manager there and telling him that he had to get out of those buildings: there were, maybe, 25 small buildings, little brick buildings with back alleys. We knew we couldn't run an operation out of these buildings.

Now they were on their way to putting up a new building. So we put up this new building and moved new machinery in from England. We painted the building "Gillette blue." It looked like a Taj Mahal in the midst of this dusty, dirty city. We wanted to have a celebration for the opening ceremony. We invited the ambassador, governor and others and wanted to have it in a big tent so we could invite all the employees. We couldn't find a tent in all of Poland, so we went all the way down to Athens to get a tent and invited all the employees. We had a big celebration with champagne. Now during the ceremony, what happened? All the bulldozers were brought in and they knocked down all the old buildings.

The employees all stood there gaping, wondering how we could possibly do this. It was the destruction of something that had been there for years. They had never thought about how the place would be a more efficient place without having those buildings there anymore. The buildings were, in effect, an overhead burden, and the best way to get rid of that was to knock them down as soon as possible. After the first shock was over, we all ended up celebrating the destruction of their old factory—actually cheering it on. It was really a thrilling experience. And the plant's been very successful since then. (Zeien 1995)

At times, it is easy to forget how important creative leadership and innovative management thinking and action is to successful multinational cross-cultural management. This omission often occurs in books on the subject that focus on more rational, "Western-style" decision-making processes. As seen from Gillette's experiences in Poland, key roles are also played by charismatic leadership and well-orchestrated dramatic, innovative and aggressive entrepreneurial action that breaks molds and goes beyond existing boundaries. Experience shows that in a multinational environment, it is possible for management thinking and action to be systematic without restricting entrepreneurial initiative and creativity (Mitroff and Lonstone 1993; Suchman 1987).

Individual managers do not need general instructions concerning *what* needs to be done to meet the needs of the ever-changing and diverse competitive environment of the future. Rather, they need to know *how* to effectively and efficiently act in response to their own specific situation (Kanter 1995).

## LEARNING SYSTEMATICALLY FROM EXPERIENCE

The book examines the successes and failures of companies and managers operating internationally across cultures in order to present some useful lessons learned from these trials and errors. For example, Deere & Co., based in Moline, Illinois, is the quintessential American multinational corporation—the world's leading supplier of farming equipment. Deere & Co. operates in all 24 time zones and in more than 50 currencies and languages. Across Deere's global network, a Czech affiliate sells tractors in Mexico, an Argentine factory assembles parts made in Germany, and a plant in Des Moines takes orders for a piece of farming equipment to be customized according to as many as 1.6 million permutations.

The 33-year journey to Deere's present position was not an easy one, however, as shown in a brief review of the company's history, as recorded in company archives and reported in the *Wall Street Journal* (Petzinger 1995). Deere exported products as early as the 1870s. Exports grew more rapidly during the export boom that followed World War II, but the boom soon fizzled. During the 1950s Deere began to build and acquire factories overseas, by 1960 investing more than $50 million in plants in Germany, France, Mexico, Argentina, Australia and South Africa. However, the results were meager and the problems, numerous. For example, technical employees from the United States, with no training in international operations and communications, attempted to improve operations in Germany. However, a "beer strike" resulted when they attempted to prevent workers from taking unscheduled beer breaks. Since Deere's international operations were so small and given so little special attention, its managers proved insensitive to local customer and worker cultural needs.

To correct these problems, in the early 1960s Deere quickly quadrupled its overseas investment in order to be able to build tractors tailored to local markets. In the 1960s, it also took major steps to introduce a global culture into the company headquarters in Moline. Despite $115 million in overseas losses during the 1960s, Deere continued to invest overseas, with total investment exceeding one-half billion dollars by 1970. As grain shortages grew worldwide in 1972, Deere began earning money overseas, and its international sales surged 47 percent in 1973.

Problems continued, however, as the Japanese became more competitive. In addition, there were problems with inflation, terrorism and military coups in

Argentina and with protectionism in Mexico. Political strife forced Deere out of Turkey, and the hostage situation caused it to leave Iran. South Africa also become a sore spot, though Deere decided to remain there, judging it to be the best long-term course of action.

Al Zeien (CEO of the Gillette Company) once noted that a company operating in a multinational environment can expect at least one problem to arise somewhere in the world almost every year (Zeien, 1995). For this reason, crisis and change management, improvisation and innovative leadership—topics covered in Chapters 11 through 14—all are important to success in multinational management.

During the 1980s things began to improve for Deere, as China and the Central European countries began to open their doors to its products. Eventually, even South Africa became a significant growth area. According to a report in the *Wall Street Journal*, by 1995 Deere was exporting from the United States materials worth more than $1 billion a year, most of it in parts destined for assembly overseas. Its foreign plants, in turn, were exporting more than one-half billion dollars of material. In total, one-quarter of Deere's 1994 sales of $7.66 billion were from foreign business (Petzinger 1995).

Not all such ventures have been this successful. For example, investments by many U.S. companies in Russia, Mexico, India and China ran into serious problems during the mid-1990s (Goodman 1995; Liesman 1995; Smith and Brauchle 1995; Stanley 1995; Zeien 1995), and in 1995 Ford's effort to create a global car faced an uncertain future (Treece, Kerwin and Dawley 1995), even though Japanese automakers such as Honda and Toyota have been fairly successful in developing global manufacturing systems (Perlez 1993).

Nor, however, have all such ventures taken as long to succeed as Deere's. However, the experiences of Deere and other companies of all sizes illustrate some of the potential problems, pitfalls and profits of managing multinational operations. These experiences show that money is indeed available to be made overseas but that realizing the profits can often be an extremely difficult task. These competitive market experiences suggest the existence of a rich body of business experience that can be drawn on to help others more effectively and efficiently manage in a multinational and cross-cultural environment. This book presents lessons learned from such experiences.

## A BALANCED PERSPECTIVE: GLOBAL DIVERSITY

This book describes experiences showing that managing multinational enterprises is an essentially context-driven process: there can be important *differences between countries and cultures*, just as many different reasons exist for different companies to expand internationally. Along with such situation-by-situation variations, there also are *common frameworks, perspectives and processes* that affect success. These common (sometimes called ''global'') frameworks can involve:

- global products, services and brands
- information and telecommunications technology
- each firm's core strategic visions and guidelines
- organizational and individual behavioral processes
- financial and accounting systems
- contingency/entrepreneurial and other situation-oriented, cognitive management processes
- the arts and other selected social and cultural areas of concern

This book attempts to balance and integrate both perspectives by focusing on common frameworks useful in managing situational diversity as well as on techniques, practices, and processes that are effective in creatively managing cultural diversity on a *situation-by-situation* and day-by-day basis.

## MANAGING DIVERSITY IN A BALANCED WAY

Because of the wide range of possible situations, the processes and perspectives involved in managing cultural diversity are varied.

Finding fundamental *links or frameworks common to many cultures* and using processes familiar to the cultures involved in a situation provides an effective starting point on which to build successful cross-cultural management solutions. This effort to find and exploit global efficiencies is sometimes referred to as a *global* or *universal perspective*. On the authors' recent trips to Asia and Russia, for example, the intuitive (conceptual and contingency) processes that entrepreneurs followed in starting and investing in new business ventures were very familiar ones, which are encountered worldwide.

As seen from the experiences of Gillette and other companies, *managing differences*—which exist in almost all multinational management situations—within the perspective of common frameworks can make multinational strategic management more effective and efficient.

The well-known phrase, "Think globally; act locally," reflects the integrative perspective of balancing common (global) frameworks and situation-by-situation (local) differences.

For example, a Chinese entrepreneur starting a small conglomerate in Beijing exhibited many basic entrepreneurial skills and thinking patterns familiar and common worldwide, as he developed five different "deals," ranging from a joint venture with a local municipality that was privatizing a small chemical plant to a trucking firm working under long-term supplier contracts. Moreover, in each instance he first focused on studying customer markets (from immediate and longer-term perspectives) and their needs, available financial resources, and other contingent situation requirements in making plans; he then skillfully executed the plans by doing whatever was necessary to make them work in each market.

Without any formal business training, this entrepreneur demonstrated considerable ingenuity in creatively overcoming day-to-day obstacles. For example, he coaxed municipal officials to relinquish control of captive companies, obtained both distribution channels and financing, and closed deals. At the same time, his overall approach to managing and making his diverse enterprises grow was the *common contingency/entrepreneurial process framework* described in Chapter 3 and used throughout this book, a process that is evident worldwide in successful businesses. The approach was supplemented by an equally important mastery of the behavioral skills needed to handle crises as well as the inevitable day-to-day customer and operating problems.

Global products, services and brands, as well as telecommunications/computer information systems technology, also provide common linking frameworks and major operating efficiencies. Airlines have for years provided what is essentially the same transportation services in and through the same types of planes and airports, varying only the minor aspects identified with the country owning the airline. Coca-Cola markets its core products globally, varying distribution and other marketing patterns by country where appropriate. The Gillette Company does the same with its razors and razor blade products, using global products but distributing and manufacturing them in adaptive ways. For example, at times, common computer information systems technology is used to manage the differences. Zeien described with relish how his company's manufacturing operations have been affected by sophisticated computer systems:

Let me give you an example of a global company as it works in the computer age. You are all probably familiar with the Atra cartridge, which is a small razor blade shaving cartridge that we sell. About six months ago our computer optimization program was saying we really shouldn't continue to be suppling those Atra cartridges to the Australian market from our manufacturing operation in Melbourne, Australia. There was a cheaper way the computer identified in just one hour. How are we supplying Atra cartridges to the Australian market today? The steel comes from Yusugi on the west coast of Japan. It goes from there to Rio de Janeiro where it is processed into blade steel. It is then shipped out into the Atlantic Ocean and up the Amazon River 1,200 miles to Manaus [Brazil], where the plastic molding takes place and the blade steel is mounted into the cartridge, what we call a naked cartridge. Back out to sea, it goes to Singapore and there it is packaged and shipped to our Melbourne warehouse. Ladies and gentlemen at this time that is the lowest cost way to supply cartridges to Australia. Believe it. (Zeien 1995)

Gillette's experiences with the global manufacturing of their "Atra" cartridge is an example of how common frameworks (in this case, global products and sophisticated computer information technology that is known and used worldwide) can be used effectively and efficiently to balance, respond to, and make use of differences across national/cultural borders (in this case, capabilities, facilities, costs and needs located in Japan, Brazil, Singapore, Australia). These links have also provided a means of rapidly transferring new technology across cultural boundaries.

Technological advances, such as those in the computer information systems and advanced telecommunications areas, have become critical to management efforts to meet growing and changing business needs. In turn, these advances have changed and integrated business processes, which now cross existing department boundaries and have required the reengineering of older hierarchical organization structures and leadership working patterns in many companies. The following story, reported by *Business Week*, illustrates this point:

It's 7AM Friday in a specially rigged conference room at the head office of GE Appliances in Louisville. CEO J. Richard Stonesifer, a fresh pot of coffee by his side, is ready to roll. The speakerphone hums, and Stonesifer greets his management staff in Asia. Stonesifer and his colleagues chew over sales figures and production glitches and gossip about Whirlpool Corp., their biggest competitor. For the next five hours, Stonesifer follows the sun across the globe, holding phone meetings or videoconferences with aides in Europe and the Americas. These talks "allow us to make immediate adjustments," Stonesifer says. "Customer complaints are never more than seven days from my attention." (Dwyer et al. 1994, p. 80)

International financial systems, which enable the flow of money across borders, went through a major evolution in the 1980s as major cities, such as London, New York and Singapore, attempted to establish themselves as world and regional financial centers. The needs of both businesses and governments necessitated 24–hour business days, international exchange mechanisms and communications systems that treat the world as a single, unified financial exchange system.

Often, such common links are also found in the dramatic and visual arts fields, as with the formation of intercultural acting and dance companies (Holden 1995; Kisselgoff 1995). They are also evident in the areas of worldwide social concerns, such as environmental concern for the rainforests in South America and human rights concerns all over the world. These factors impact business in many ways (Schemo 1995).

As seen from the many company experiences cited in this chapter, multinational strategic managers are continually required to search for ways to balance global approaches and the resulting benefits with the need to take into account and satisfy local needs. Ways of managing these seemingly contradictory tasks—which combine to form a paradoxical situation—are discussed throughout this book. Managing the balance requires understanding and an ability to deal with paradox (Naisbitt 1995; Price Waterhouse 1996).

## GAINING AND SUSTAINING A COMPETITIVE
## ADVANTAGE IN A DIVERSE MULTINATIONAL CROSS-
## CULTURAL ENVIRONMENT

The basic task areas, processes, decisions, and actions involved in multinational strategic management are described in Chapters 2 and 3. Within this
strategic management contingency framework, three aspects of winning in a
competitive multinational market are discussed throughout this book. The first
aspect is *knowing existing markets and managing to meet their needs* in order
to survive and prosper in the present competitive market.

Initially, one needs to plan to meet existing and anticipated near-term competitive market needs. This basic survival process involves traditional analytical
thinking to determine how things work and how the situation can best be handled with available company resources. Since many of the readers of this book
will be students (both graduate and undergraduate) of international business, it
is necessary to emphasize the importance of establishing a thorough knowledge
base of the markets, competition, and company under study.

While it is important to be well grounded in the current situation, however,
it is also necessary to avoid being limited to, or controlled by, it. It is also
important to look to the future and be responsive to changes. A second aspect
of the management process, therefore, involves *anticipating, generating ideas
and adapting* in a way that manages and exploits change over the intermediate
term.

Success may require going beyond the present, envisioning the situation from
multiple perspectives; encouraging the development—and studying the impact—
of differing scenarios, viewpoints and ideas; and studying the situation from a
broader context of all related technical, organization and individual perspectives.
In short, it involves using cognitive techniques that enable a manager to "break
the mold."

Making solutions work in the future requires creating an enabling environment, consisting of the organization structure and culture, leadership and people,
telecommunication and information systems, financial and accounting systems,
functional area operations, and human resources (communications, staffing and
training, and leadership and management). Such an environment is needed to
enable formulating specific operating plans, carrying out plans, and responding
to the changing circumstances that inevitably arise even in the best-planned
situations. Effective day-to-day leadership and management are equally critical
to success. Chapters 5 through 13 concern these critical multinational strategic
management tasks, decisions and actions.

An enabling organization and its leadership has to do more, however, than
simply react to changes and anticipate the company's intermediate-term needs.
Managers and leaders have to look beyond the immediate future and explore
what can be expected to happen—and made to happen—years from now. This
requires *sensing and anticipating the longer-term future*, knowing how to handle

it and, if necessary, creating new markets and industries built on a company's core competencies.

The further into the future one plans, the greater the uncertainty and risk and the more effort will be needed to test assumptions in all areas—competition, customer needs and desires, societal values and political scenarios. Present ways of doing business are questioned. Such thinking requires "breaking of the mold" as one looks further and further into the future (Mitroff and Lonstone 1993; Naisbitt 1995).

During this process, managers and leaders can go further and try to create new markets and industries, even at the cost of making their own company's existing products obsolete. Plans, decisions, solutions and actions must be made with these innovative and creative perspectives in mind in order for a company to prosper over the long-term in rapidly changing, competitive markets.

This book covers all these critical areas for success.

## THE LONGER-TERM FUTURE

Success in a rapidly changing and highly diverse competitive market, then, clearly requires leadership that looks beyond the immediate and intermediate future and explores what can be expected to happen a decade or more in the future in regard to customer/market needs, distribution patterns, technology and competition. By building on the existing plans, operations and enabling organization, moves can be made to anticipate the longer-term future and create an optimal future environment for a company managing cross-cultural situations.

For example, as Alvin Tofler and Heidi Tofler say in their book, *Creating a New Civilization*, the latest technology revolution (which they call "The Third Wave") will lead to an overhaul of everything from family to political systems. Businesses that fail to move aggressively with the wave will "get battered and drowned in the foam" (quoted in Ehrenreich 1995, p. 9). For example, it has been suggested that the global influence of the Cable News Network (CNN) was a major factor in the eventual decline and fall of communism in Russia and Central Europe (Henry 1992; "World View" 1990).

In 1995, there was evidence that information and communication technology were already combining to make major shifts in the way money is transferred and invested (Holland and Cortese 1995; Weiss 1995), how banking is done (O'Brien 1995), how services are delivered and how service employment will gradually be reduced, just as manufacturing employment was reduced earlier (Zachary 1995). It is even affecting the language through which business managers communicate (Pollack 1995).

In addition, other changes are occurring throughout different world cultures, led, to a large degree, by the global dissemination of common information across cultural and country boundaries through both global television and the Internet (Henry 1992; Pollack 1995; "World View" 1990).

In 1995, Hewlett-Packard (H-P) was in the process of constructing a global information infrastructure that would allow consumers worldwide to work digital devices using telephone, fax and printer functions. This global strategy will enable H-P to develop and sell an array of its global computer and communications products. It will also provide customers and other manufacturers with another common framework for developing a wide array of new products and common communications channels. In a sense, H-P is working to create a new market (Gillooly 1995).

Lou Gerstner, CEO of IBM, has developed a similar vision for the longer-term future of his company. Rather than being linked solely to personal computers, IBM's vision is linked to the concept of network computing and electronic commerce. In this new wave of computing, communications, rather than computation, is the key. The vision involves everything from multimedia personal computers (PCs) to the vastness of the Internet. IBM wants to position itself to be a leader in this new market (Sager 1995).

Similarly, Jonathan Newcomb, president of the publishing company Simon & Schuster, invested heavily ($100 million) in multimedia and digital publishing in an effort to anticipate a market that will not make money for several years, and to help give it direction (Landler 1995).

Rosabeth Kanter has studied a number of large and small companies that are strategically positioning themselves to become world-class competitors. These companies are focusing on several areas already discussed here: innovations that lead markets, such as those being developed at Hewlett-Packard and IBM; the ability to use global resources to make and deliver products flexibly at different locations throughout the world, as Gillette has done; and the willingness for both large and small companies to enter into collaborative arrangements of all sorts to obtain global advantages, transfer knowledge quickly, and make the connections needed to adapt to and exploit local differences over the long run, as Mercedes is attempting to do in China (Kanter 1995).

While such ideas about innovation and creative entrepreneurial thinking in managing for the future are important, they are written about frequently, and so are not new. As a result, they are well known to forward-thinking companies. What company executives need to know is not so much *what* needs to be done, but *how* to do it, starting with getting in place the necessary people, enabling structures, telecommunications/information systems, leadership skills and company culture. Companies like Gillette have accomplished the task, while others are in the process of doing it.

This book attempts to deal with the "how-to" aspects of successful multinational strategic management. Essentially, achieving success requires managers to balance disparate skills. It requires having one's "head in the air" in order to shape visions, but it also requires having "one's feet on the ground" in order to see that the vision is realized in successful day-to-day business operations.

## WORKS CITED

Collins, Glenn. "Coke Drops 'Domestic' and Goes One World." *New York Times*, January 13, 1996, pp. 35, 37.

Dwyer, Paula, Pete Engardio, Zachary Schiller, and Stanley Reed. "Tearing Up Today's Organization Chart." *Business Week: Special Issue, 21st Century Capitalism*, November 18, 1994, p. 80.

Ehrenreich, Barbara. Review of *Creating a New Civilization*, by Alvin Toffler and Heidi Toffler. May 7, 1995, Book Review Section, p. 9.

Gillooly, Brian. "H-P's New Course: Hewlett-Packard Wants to Construct a Global Information Infrastructure and Supply All the Equipment That Users Will Need to Access It; The First Step—Converge Its Core Businesses." *InformationWeek*, March 20, 1995, pp. 45–56.

Goodman, Walter. "Crime and Corruption in Russia." Report on Cable News Network TV program. *New York Times*, March 10, 1995, p. D15.

Henry, William A., III. "History As It Happens." *Time*, January 6, 1992, pp. 24–27.

Holden, Joan. "Big Wind Blows across Asia: A Grand-Scale People's Theater Collaboration Tests the Mettle of Artists, Eastern and Western." *American Theater*, September 1995, pp. 17–20, 62–63.

Holland, Kelley, and Amy Cortese. "The Future of Money." *Business Week*, June 12, 1995, pp. 68–78.

Kanter, Rosabeth Moss. *World Class: Thriving Locally in the Global Economy*. New York: Simon and Schuster, 1995.

Kisselgoff, Anna. "In San Francisco, the Latest in Ballet as a Global Link." *New York Times*, May 11, 1995, pp. C13, C18.

Landler, Mark. "A Publishing Empire Takes the Digital Road." *New York Times*, September 11, 1995, pp. D1, D12.

Levy, Steven. "Bill's New Vision." *Newsweek*, November 27, 1995, pp. 54–68.

Liesman, Steve. "High Noon at Russia's Annual Meetings." *New York Times*, April 21, 1995, p. 4.

Mitroff, Ian I., and Harold Lonstone. *The Unbounded Mind: Breaking the Chains of Traditional Business Thinking*. New York: Oxford University Press, 1993.

Naisbitt, John. *Global Paradoxes*. London: Nicholas Brealy Publishing, 1995.

Nash, Nathaniel C. "Coke's Great Rumanian Adventure: In Just Three Years, Coke Has Come from Nowhere to Dominate the Market." *New York Times*, February 26, 1995, Business Section, pp. 1, 10.

O'Brien, Timothy. "Home Banking: Will It Take Off This Time?" *Wall Street Journal*, June 8, 1995, pp. B1, B14.

Perlez, Jane, "Japanese Mix and Match Auto Plants and Markets." *New York Times*, March 26, 1993, pp. A1, D2.

———. "This Bud's Not for You, Anheuser." *New York Times*, June 30, 1995, pp. D1, D4.

Petzinger, Thomas, Jr. "Expanded Horizons: The U.S.'s Rise as an Export Power Took Off after the War, But as Deere & Co. Shows, the Road Was Not Always Smooth." *Wall Street Journal*, April 24, 1995, pp. R1, R7.

Pollack, Andrew W. "A Cyberspace Front in a Multicultural War." *New York Times*, August 7, 1995, pp. D1, D4.

Price Waterhouse Change Integration Team. *The Paradox Principles*. Chicago: Irwin Professional Publishing, 1996.

Rapoport, Carla, with Justin Martin. "Retailers Go Global." *Fortune*, February 20, 1995, pp. 102–108.

Sager, Ira. "The View from IBM." *Business Week*, October 30, 1995, pp. 142–150.

Schemo, Diana Jean. "Amazon Is Burning Again, as Furiously as Ever." *New York Times*, October 12, 1995, p. A3.

Smith, Craig S., and Marcus W. Brauchli. "The Long March: To Invest Successfully in China, Foreigners Find Patience Crucial." *Wall Street Journal*, February 23, 1995, pp. A1, A4.

Stanley, Alexandra. "An American's Bizarre Sit-in in Moscow: Many Western Ventures in Russia Get Messy, But This One Takes the Cake." *New York Times*, May 6, 1995, pp. 35–36.

Suchman, Lucy A. *Plans and Situated Actions*. New York: Cambridge University Press, 1987.

Treece, James B., Kathleen Kerwin, and Heidi Dawley. "Ford: Alex Trotman's Daring Global Strategy." *Business Week*, April 3, 1995, pp. 94–104.

Weiss, Gary. "Online Investing." *Business Week*, June 5, 1995, pp. 64–78.

"World View: Ted Turner's CNN Global Gains Influence." *Wall Street Journal*, February 1, 1990, pp. 4–12, 48.

WuDunn, Sheryl. "Japanese Do Buy American: By Mail and a Lot Cheaper." *New York Times*, July 3, 1995, pp. 1, 43.

Zachary, G. Pascal. "Service Productivity Is Rising Fast—And So Is Fear of Lost Jobs." *Wall Street Journal*, June 8, 1995, pp. A1, A10.

Zeien, Albert. "Gillette's Global Marketing Experiences." Talk given at St. John's University's Annual Colman Mockler Leadership Award Ceremony, New York, February 27, 1995.

# Chapter 2

# Multinational Cross-Cultural Management: Key Tasks, Decisions and Actions

This chapter introduces key overall activities and specific tasks involved in the management of multinational enterprises. They are listed in Figure 2-1.

## THE JOB OF MULTINATIONAL CROSS-CULTURAL MANAGEMENT

As shown in Figure 2-2, key overall multinational cross-cultural leadership/ management activities include:

- Creating an overall strategic framework. This includes a strategic vision and guidelines. Actual plans often emerge over time through the enabling processes and systems.
- Activating, energizing, putting in place and managing enabling systems and processes, such as telecommunications/information systems; organization and business structures, processes and cultures at all functional levels; and accounting and finance systems.
- Leading and managing enabling human resources and processes through understanding cultural diversity, staffing, training and communicating at all levels.

Initial strategic concepts—visions, missions, values, philosophies, strategies, and policy guidelines and principles—can range from very general to very specific (Abraham 1995). Examples of three enterprisewide strategic concept frameworks are given in Figures 2-3 through 2-5. Additional examples are given in Figures 5-2 through 5-4 (in Chapter 5).

Formulating strategies and supporting strategic plans can involve the enterprise as a whole (for example, whether to go international), a business unit (for example, Gillette's operation in Poland), and specific operating functions (for example, marketing or production/operations management). These strategies at-

Figure 2-1
Multinational Strategic Management: Tasks, Decisions and Actions

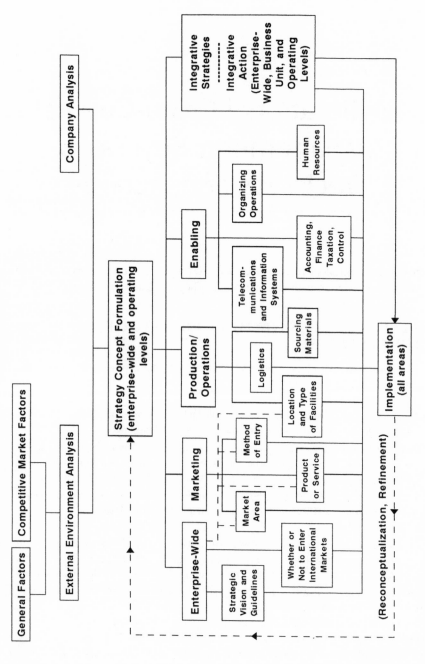

Copyright © 1997 by R. J. Mockler.

**Figure 2-2**
**Strategic Management**

*The Focus: An Emergent Entrepreneurial Leadership Process*

1.  *Strategic Vision and Guidelines*:
    "I knew exactly what kind of company I envisioned; I just didn't know precisely what it would look like." The precise definition, in other words, often emerges over time through experiences in the marketplace.

2.  *Implementation*:
    "Doing whatever was necessary to get the job done, within well-defined general moral, legal, ethical and policy guidelines." This most often involves reconciling and balancing diverse, conflicting, and often paradoxical forces on a continuing basis in a complex rapidly changing competitive market environment.

*The Activities:*

- Creating an overall strategic framework, including strategic vision, guidelines, and values. Specific strategies (enterprise-wide and in business units and functional areas) often emerge over time through the enabling systems and processes.

- Activating, energizing, putting into place, and monitoring enabling systems and processes, such as: functional area operations; telecommunications/information systems; accounting and finance systems; organization and business structures, processes and cultures; and strategic alliances.

- Nurturing enabling human resources and processes through: organization development; understanding cultural diversity; staffing, training, and communicating; and effective flexible leadership and integrative management at all levels.

  -- Ensuring that a core management staff (with appropriate interpersonal, communication, entrepreneurial, and management skills and potential) is in place and functioning to achieve that balance.

  -- Communicating and implementing the strategic framework, as well as cultural benchmarks that are needed to enable the core management staff to translate the desired vision into action. The actual processes involved here will include not only such enablers as telecommunication/information systems, finance and accounting systems and organization redesign, but also the leadership and management appropriate for both the manager and people/groups involved in the situation, as well as for the specific competitive market needs of the situation.

  -- Leaving managers relatively free to manage and pushing decision making as close to the customer as possible, but intervening where appropriate to make certain integrative activities are operating efficiently and effectively to achieve company strategic short- and long-term objectives.

Copyright © 1997 by R. J. Mockler.

tempt to formulate a concept that recognizably differentiates a company from its competition. The process defines the business a company is, or intends to be, engaged in and how that business might be conducted differently. It should be a strategy that can be supported with strong core experience, people or resource competencies. Warren Buffett refers to this differentiation as "brand franchising" (Buffett 1996; see also Hagstrom 1994), since it can involve either a product (the Coke soft drink, for example) or an umbrella concept (such as McDonald's restaurants).

**Figure 2-3**
**Ciba-Geigy Corporation Mission Statement**

### Statement: Our Vision

*By striking a balance between our economic, social, and environmental responsibilities we want to ensure the prosperity of our enterprise beyond the year 2000.*

### Responsibility for long-term economic success
We aim to generate appropriate financial results through sustainable growth and constant renewal of a balanced business structure, so that we justify the confidence of all those who rely on our company- stockholders, employees, business partners and the public.

We will not put our long-term future in danger by taking short-term profits.

### Social Responsibility
Ciba is open and trustworthy toward society. Through our worldwide business activities we wish to make a worthwhile contribution to the solution of global issues and to the progress of mankind. We recognize our responsibility when turning new discoveries in science and technology into commercial reality; we carefully evaluate benefits and risks in all our activities, processes and products.

### Responsibility for the Environment
Respect for the environment must be a part of everything we do.

We design products and processes to fulfill their purpose safely and with as little environmental impact as possible. We use natural resources and energy in the best possible way to reduce waste in all forms. It is our duty to dispose of all unavoidable waste using state of the art technology.

**Industry Category:**  Chemicals

**Corporate Description**

Ciba is a leading worldwide biological and chemical group, based in Switzerland, dedicated to satisfying needs in healthcare, agriculture and industry with innovative value-adding products and services.

**Number of Employees:**      87,480 (worldwide) as of 1993

*Source*: 1993 annual report.

Successfully carrying out strategic visions and strategic plans can involve integrating a wide range of tasks, decisions and actions. This integration is done within the context of immediate-term changes in market requirements, as well as intermediate and longer-term strategic requirements. At the same time, this integration requires balancing the need for global efficiency, local responsiveness and the rapid transfer of innovative knowledge—a difficult balancing act.

While strategic management processes are discussed in this chapter as comprising a discrete application task, the process is rarely a step-by-step, linear one. Each task may have distinct requirements and characteristics, but in most multinational situations, each is also part of a continually emerging integrative

**Figure 2-4**
**Ametek, Inc. Mission Statement**

Statement: Ametek's Mission

*To achieve enhanced, long-term shareholder value by building a strong operating company serving diversified markets to earn a superior return on assets and to generate growth in cash flow.*

- Succeed with the shareholder value enhancement plan, including reducing the cost of capital with debt level consistent with Ametek's strong cash flow.

- Realize over the long term a 30% return on assets (operating profit divided by assets) for all operating businesses.

- Optimize cash flow for investment in growth and debt reduction.

- Build competitive advantages by investing in the growth of current businesses to evolve and extend core products and manufacturing technology into new products, niche markets and new applications.

- Continue to apply Total Quality Management throughout the company to nurture new product development.

- Capitalize on the competitive advantages of floor care, specialty metals and water filtration products. Build on unique advantages in other product lines and other niche markets.

- Multiply the benefit of operational resources with a global market expansion, especially in Europe and the Pacific Rim. Employ strategic alliances and joint ventures to manage risk, especially for international growth.

- Maintain a flat, decentralized organization focused on the customer. Seek business synergies that create strength and reduce costs.

- Link incentive compensation with qualitative and quantitative business performance.

**Industry Category:** Manufacturing

**Corporate Description**

Ametek designs, builds and sells: motors for vacuum cleaners, furnaces, electric lawn tools, computers and business machines; water filtration systems for home, commercial and industrial use; high-purity metal in strip and powder form for the electronics and telecommunications industries; Instruments for the aerospace, automotive, manufacturing, utility and petrochemical industries.

**Size Revenues:** $732 million (net sales) as of 1993

**Number of Employees:** 6,100 (worldwide) as of 1993

*Sources:* 1993 annual report, company representative.

process, as is shown in Figure 2-6. In that emerging process, initial concepts of strategies and strategic visions are formulated, along with policy guidelines. Enablers and enabling systems, such as telecommunications and information systems; accounting, finance and control; organization structure and culture; and human resources are either put into place or strengthened. Plans, projects and programs are initiated continually; appropriate management leadership guides the processes. Refinements and details are developed or emerge continually, as the circular feedback process continues.

The implementation process emerges in ways that are appropriate for the situation. For example, the process at a large, established company such as the

**Figure 2-5**
**Johnson Wax Mission Statement**

### Statement: This We Believe

#### Our Guiding Principles
Our company has been guided by certain basic principles since its founding in 1886. These principles were first summarized in 1927 by H. F. Johnson, Sr., in his Christmas Profit Sharing speech:

*"The goodwill of the people is the only enduring thing in any business. It is the sole substance . . . . The rest is shadow!"*

In 1976, we formally stated these basic principles in **"This We Believe."** Since then, our statement of corporate philosophy has been translated and communicated around the world--not only within the worldwide company, but also to key external audiences. It has served us well by providing all employees with a common statement of the basic principles that guide the company in all the different cultures where we operate. It has also provided people outside the company with an understanding of our fundamental beliefs. It communicates the kind of company we are.

Now, more than ten years after **"This We Believe"** was developed and following the celebration of our 100th anniversary, it is appropriate to restate, clarify and reaffirm our commitment to uphold these principles, because our company, like most others in these highly volatile times, has had to adjust its business strategies worldwide. This restatement and clarification is important to insure that our corporate policies and the actions of our managers and other employees continue to be fully supportive of our beliefs.

**"This We Believe"** states our beliefs in relation to the five groups of people to whom we are responsible and whose trust we have to earn:

#### Employees
We believe that the fundamental vitality and strength of our worldwide company lies in our people.

#### Consumers and Users
We believe in earning the enduring goodwill of consumers and users of our products and services.

#### General Public
We believe in being a responsible leader within a free market economy.

#### Neighbors and Hosts
We believe in contributing to the well-being of the countries and communities where we conduct business.

#### World Community
We believe in improving international standing.

*Our commitment to them is evident in our attitudes to date.*

The sincerity of our beliefs encourages us to act with integrity at all times, to respect the dignity of each person as an individual human being, to assume moral and social responsibilities early as a matter of conscience, to make an extra effort to use our skills and resources where they are most needed, and to strive for excellence in everything we do.

Our way of safeguarding these beliefs is to remain a privately held company. Our way of reinforcing them is to make profits through growth and development, profits that allow us to do more for all the people on whom we depend.

## Figure 2-5 (Continued)

**We believe that the fundamental vitality and strength of our worldwide company lies in our people, and we commit ourselves to:**

*Maintain good relations among all employees, around the world, based on a sense of participation, mutual respect, and an understanding of common objectives, by:*
- Creating a climate whereby all employees freely air their concerns and express their opinions with the assurance that they will be fairly considered.
- Attentively responding to employees' suggestions and problems.
- Fostering open, two-way communications between management and employees.
- Providing employees with opportunities to participate in the process of decision making.
- Encouraging employees at all levels and in all disciplines to work as a team.
- Respecting the dignity and rights of privacy of every employee.

*Manage our business in such a way that we can provide security for regular employees and retirees, by:*
- Pursuing a long-term policy of planned, orderly growth.
- Retaining regular employees, if at all possible, as conditions change. However, this may not always be possible, particularly where major restructuring or reorganization is required to maintain competitiveness.
- Retraining employees who have had acceptable performance records and are in positions no longer needed, provided suitable jobs are available.

*Maintain a high level of effectiveness within the organization, by:*
- Establishing clear standards of job performance.
- Ensuring that the performance of all employees meets required levels by giving appropriate recognition to those whose performance is good and by terminating those whose performance, despite their managers' efforts to help, continues below company standards.

*Provide equal opportunities in employment and advancement, by:*
- Hiring and promoting employees without discrimination, using qualifications, performance, and experience as the principal criteria.

*Remunerate employees at levels that fully reward their performance and recognize their contribution to the success of the company, by:*
- Maintaining base pay and benefit programs both of which are fully competitive with those prevailing within the relevant marketplaces.
- Maintaining, in addition to our fully competitive pay and benefit programs, our long-standing tradition of sharing profits with our employees.

*Protect the health and safety of all employees, by:*
- Providing a clean and safe work environment.
- Providing appropriate safety training and occupational health services.

*Develop the skills and abilities of our people, by*
- Providing on-the-job training and professional development programs.
- Helping employees qualify for opportunities in the company through educational and development programs.

## Figure 2-5 (Continued)

*Creative environments that are conducive to self-expression and personal well-being, by:*
- Fostering and supporting leisure-time programs for employees and retirees.
- Developing job enrichment programs.
- Maintaining the long tradition of high quality and good design in our office and plants.

*Encourage initiative, innovation, and entrepreneurism among all employees, thereby providing opportunities for greater job satisfaction while also helping the worldwide company achieve its objectives.*

**We believe in earning the enduring goodwill of consumers and users of our products and services, and we commit ourselves to:**

*Provide useful products and services throughout the world, by:*
- Monitoring closely the changing wants and needs of consumers and users.
- Developing and maintaining high standards of quality.
- Developing new products and services that are recognized by consumers and users as being significantly superior overall to major competition.
- Maintaining close and effective business relations with the trade to ensure that our products and services are readily available to consumers and users.
- Continuing our research and development commitment to provide a strong technology base for innovative and superior products and services.

*Develop and market products that are environmentally sound and that do not endanger the health and safety of consumers and users, by:*
- Meeting all regulatory requirements or exceeding them where worldwide company standards are higher.
- Providing clear and adequate directions for safe use, together with cautionary statements and/or symbols.
- Incorporating protection against misuse where this is appropriate.
- Researching new technologies for products that favor an improved environment.

*Maintain and develop comprehensive education and service programs for consumers and users, by:*
- Disseminating information to consumers and users which promotes full understanding of the correct use of our products and services.
- Handling all inquiries, complaints, and service needs for consumers and users quickly, thoroughly, and fairly.

**We believe in being a responsible leader in the free-market economy, and we commit ourselves to:**

*Ensure the future of the worldwide company, by:*
- Earning sufficient profits to provide new investment for planned growth and progress.
- Maintaining a worldwide organization of highly competitive, motivated, and dedicated employees.

*Conduct our business in a fair and ethical manner, by:*
- Not engaging in unfair business practices.
- Treating our suppliers and customers both fairly and reasonably, according to sound commercial practice.
- Packaging and labeling our products so that consumers and users can make informed value judgements.
- Maintaining the highest advertising standards of integrity and good taste.
- Not engaging in bribery.

## Figure 2-5 (Continued)

*Share the profits of each local company with those who have contributed to its success, by:*
- Rewarding employees through a profit sharing program.
- Allocating a share of the profits to enhance the well-being of communities where we operate.
- Developing better products and services for the benefit of consumers and users.
- Providing to shareholders a reasonable return on their investment.

*Provide the general public with information about our activities so that they have a better understanding of our worldwide company.*

**We believe in contributing to the well-being of the countries and communities where we conduct business, and we commit ourselves to:**

*Seek actively the counsel and independent judgement of citizens of each country where we conduct business to provide guidance to local and corporate management, by:*
- Selecting independent directors to serve on the board of each of our companies worldwide.
- Retaining distinguished associates and consultants to assist us in conducting our business according to the highest professional standards.

*Contribute to the economic well-being of every country and community where we conduct business, by:*
- Ensuring the new investment fits constructively into the economic development of each host country and local community.
- Encouraging the use of local suppliers and services offering competitive quality and prices.

*Contribute to the social development of every country and community where we conduct business, by:*
- Providing training programs for the development of skills.
- Staffing and managing with nationals from the country wherever practicable.
- Involving ourselves in social, cultural, and educational projects which enhance the quality of life.

*Be a good corporate citizen, by:*
- Complying with and maintaining a due regard for the laws, regulations, and traditions of each country where we conduct business.

**We believe in improving international understanding, and we commit ourselves to:**

*Act with responsible practices in international trade and investment, by:*
- Retaining earnings necessary for reinvestment in our local companies and remitting dividends on a consistent basis.
- Making royalty, licensing, and service agreements that are fair and reasonable and that do not result in any hidden transfer of profits.
- Limiting foreign exchange transactions to normal business requirements and for the protection of our assets.

*Promote the exchange of ideas and techniques, by:*
- Encouraging the rapid diffusion of new technology to our local companies and licensees, while protecting our ownership rights and investment in such technology.
- Organizing worldwide and regional meetings for the dissemination and exchange of information.
- Providing support and assistance, especially in technical and professional fields, to develop skills throughout the organization.
- Following a balanced approach between transferring people to new jobs to gain experience and leaving people on the job long enough to make positive contributions in their assignments.
- Participating actively in non-political national and international activities with the objective of improving the global business climate.

**Figure 2-5 (Continued)**

**Industry Category:**    Consumer Goods and Services

**Corporate Description**
SC Johnson Wax is one of the world's leading manufacturers of chemical specialty products for home, personal care and insect control. It is also a leading supplier of products and services for commercial, industrial and institutional facilities. In the area of financial services, the corporation has interests in venture capital and insurance.

**Number of Employees:**    13,100 (worldwide) as of June 1994

*Sources*: "Profile" company publication; company representative; *This We Believe* (company publication).

Gillette Company, a worldwide personal-care products company that, over the years, has developed a well-defined strategic framework, can be quite different from that at a small international shipping company that may be losing money and in the process of moving from an asset-driven to a market/customer driven enterprise (Hart and Banbury 1994; Priem and Harrison 1994).

Multinational cross-cultural management is, therefore, segmented into discrete tasks (and their related decisions and actions) in this chapter for discussion purposes only. The 12 specific tasks areas outlined in Figure 2-1 in practice can be a continuum of interactive and integrated management activities, which balance internal company requirements with market, cultural, political and other external situation requirements.

## THE BASIC STRATEGIC DECISION TO GO MULTINATIONAL

The first task to be discussed involves deciding whether an enterprise should become multinational. International business, when successful, can have an enormous payoff in increased sales and profits, which has prompted many companies to go multinational. In recent years, companies such as Philips Electronics, IBM, the Gillette Company, Coca-Cola and many large Japanese and European firms obtain 30 to 80 percent of their revenues from production, sales and services outside their home country (Collins, 1996; Zeien, 1995).

Operating successfully in a diverse multinational environment requires managing numerous political, economic, legal, cultural, language and other social situational factors—many of which can create problems. For example, in the early 1990s, Procter & Gamble (P&G) had subsidiaries in nine Latin American countries and sold its products through distributors in ten other Latin American countries. In operating there, the company had battled political meddling, price controls, high inflation, terrorism, massive poverty and poor transportation facilities. However, in spite of these problems, P&G's Latin American division was a $1-billion business and was expected to double its sales in the 1990s (Swasy 1990). Despite the difficulties, therefore, many opportunities for business

Figure 2-6
Strategic Management Process Cycle

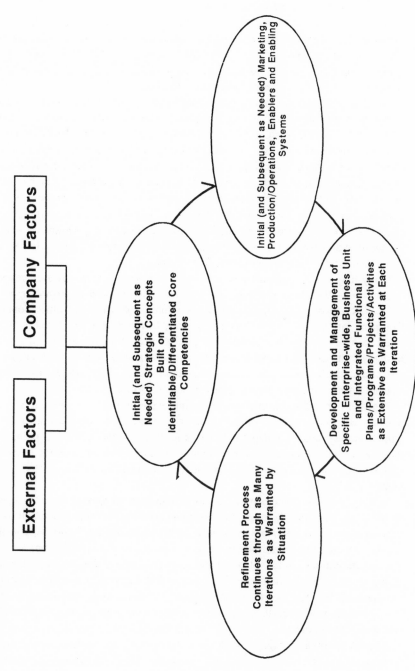

External Factors

Company Factors

Initial (and Subsequent as Needed) Strategic Concepts Built on Identifiable/Differentiated Core Competencies

Initial (and Subsequent as Needed) Marketing, Production/Operations, Enablers and Enabling Systems

Development and Management of Specific Enterprise-wide, Business Unit and Integrated Functional Plans/Programs/Projects/Activities as Extensive as Warranted at Each Iteration

Refinement Process Continues through as Many Iterations as Warranted by Situation

Copyright © 1997 by R. J. Mockler.

growth appear to exist in Latin America (Baker et al. 1992; Brooke 1995), as well as in many other markets worldwide.

Basic strategic decisions about whether to take advantage of multinational opportunities—to commence or expand international operations—and the best way to do so depend on both individual company and market factors. Each company has its own special resources, requirements and method of matching company factors with market opportunity factors.

For example, Hurco Companies, a machine tool maker, fought its way back to solvency in large measure by increasing overseas sales through exporting (Lohr 1991). Air express companies have expanded internationally both to grow and to provide existing customers with extended services in additional countries. Hundreds of companies in Japan, the United States, and other countries established or bought manufacturing facilities in Europe in order to qualify for reduced tariffs in the European Economic Community and so protect their existing markets there. Many international airlines, such as KLM (the Netherlands) and Lufthansa (Germany), have established strong competitive positions by operating worldwide networks through strategic alliances, a means used to limit capital investment and bypass government restrictions.

Many major U.S. retailers and mail-order companies expanded overseas during the mid-1990s when mature U.S. markets offered limited growth opportunities (Rapoport and Martin 1995; WuDunn 1995a). Even the Southern Company, an electric utility, made major moves overseas when faced with mature U.S. markets (Tomkins 1995). Largely because of the maturation of markets in many industrialized nations, multinational companies were expected to invest an estimated $90 billion in developing countries in 1995, while cutting back sharply on new investments in industrialized nations (Bleakley 1995).

Whether expanding internationally for internal (company) or external (market) reasons, or a combination of both, major companies in countries such as the United States, Japan, England and Germany were not alone. For example, three years after the collapse of communism in Eastern Europe, exports from that region rose sharply, from $54.5 billion in 1993 to $64.1 billion in 1994 (Stevenson 1995a).

In turn, the United States presents major international opportunities for foreign companies. As of 1988, foreign companies had a total direct investment in the U.S. of more than $300 billion (Hicks 1989). In 1995 the South Korean firm LG Electronics Inc. purchased a majority interest in Zenith Electronics Corp., the last remaining United States manufacturer of television sets (Holstein and Nakarmi 1995). In the first half of 1995, it was estimated that foreign companies purchased $39 billion worth of interests in U.S. companies, up 43 percent from $27.5 billion a year earlier, in order to take advantage of the comparatively stable and favorable U.S. market (Wysocki 1995).

These experiences suggest that the reasons for a company to go or grow internationally are varied, including attempts to survive, increase sales, acquire resources and expertise, cut costs, diversify into a significant and growing multinational business area, apply expertise to new markets, or sell existing products in new markets.

## SELECTING A MARKET AREA

The next task area discussed, selecting a market area, can involve enterprisewide, business unit, and operational concerns. A wide range of potential overseas markets exist. For example, the unified European market established in 1992 may eventually exceed the United States in both actual and potential opportunities (Prokesch 1990; Wright and Woods 1990). In anticipation of that market's growth, PepsiCo Inc. announced in late 1991 that it would invest more than $1 billion in Spain to build soft drink plants, open fast-food restaurants, and set up an elaborate computerized system to track snack food sales. In the previous three years, Pepsico had already spent a total of $4 billion to expand its presence in Europe (Shapiro 1991).

Newly freed Eastern bloc countries, such as Hungary and Poland, also present major market opportunities. For example, Citibank (New York) opened a branch in Budapest, Hungary, which requires a minimum balance of $250—about a month's salary there—and provides automated teller machines and fast service (Perlez 1995a). In June 1995, A Dutch-Swiss consortium purchased a 27 percent interest in the Czech telephone monopoly for $1.45 billion ("Dutch-Swiss Team" 1995; Perlez 1995b).

Markets in Japan, Australia and other countries in the Pacific Rim also appear to have considerable potential for companies in the United States and Europe. For example, Asia is considered to be the fastest growing air-cargo market: inter-Asian air-cargo traffic grew 15 percent and air-express deliveries grew 25 percent in 1994 (Brady 1995; Overholt 1995). Though politically unstable, China, with a population in excess of 1.2 billion, could eventually become the largest opportunity area in the world.

Latin America also presents major potential opportunities. For example, the News Corporation (England), which owns two satellite services (B Sky B in England and Star TV in Asia), announced in late 1995 that it would form a direct broadcast service in Latin America with three partners: Globo, the leading media company in Brazil; Grupo Televisa, a giant Mexican broadcaster; and Tele-Communications Inc., the U.S.'s largest cable television operator. Although the new service would initially have only 1 million subscribers, in May 1996, Rupert Murdoch, chairman of the News Corporation, identified a potential audience of more than 400 million viewers throughout Central and South America. The partners planned an initial total investment of $500 million in the service, which will transmit 150 channels of entertainment, news and sports programming to homes equipped with satellite dishes and digital receivers (Landler 1995).

Another international growth area of the 1990s, and probably of the 21st century, is expected to be the former Soviet Union. After the nation's breakup in late 1991, however, serious questions were raised as to when and how that potential might be realized and the widespread impact of crime on business (Aslund 1995; Kranz 1995; Powell and McKay 1995; Stanley 1995; Yergin and Gustafson 1995). In addition to the political unrest, two key problems were a lack of contract protection and a lack of guarantees that U.S. companies would be able to repatriate their profits in dollars from the former Soviet republics. When Gillette was negotiating in 1990 to build a $50 million razor-blade plant in Russia, for example, the outcome hinged on Russia's willingness to allow Gillette (the major shareholder in the new company) to find a way to take profits out in hard currency ("Gillette Sets Soviet Venture" 1991; Ramirez 1990). The solution was to allow the firm to import and sell Gillette non-razor products produced elsewhere and to be paid for these products in hard currencies (Zeien 1995).

Along with the United States, Africa, South America and India are other market areas exhibiting enormous potential (Brooke 1995; Burns 1995; French 1995; Fuhrman and Schuman 1994; "International Briefs" 1995; Moshavi et al. 1995; Naisbitt 1994).

Multinational investments are not without risks, however. The purchase of Pebble Beach Resort in California lost its Japanese investors more than $300 million dollars (Carlton and Barsky 1992; Montague 1992). Bridgestone, a Japanese tire company, suffered major loses in the early 1990s at its recently purchased Firestone tire-making subsidiary in the United States (O'Boyle 1991). In late 1994, Sony took a $2.7 billion write-off on its investment in Columbia and TriStar Pictures, and Mitsubishi was having major problems with its investment in Rockefeller Center in New York, eventually losing close to $2 billion on the venture (Landro, Hamilton, and Williams 1994; Rudolph 1994; Strom 1995). Difficulties arising from these losses and from similar problems in the Tokyo real estate market appeared in 1995 to be threatening Japan's entire economy (WuDunn 1995b).

An extensive analysis of the decision situation is required when selecting an overseas market area to serve, as when making the overall strategic decision to go overseas. The situation factors to be analyzed range from general country, area and regional factors such as the political climate, national economy, exchange rates and cultural climate to competitive market and internal company resource factors. These factors and their impact on the decision are discussed in Chapters 4, 5, and 6.

The decision concerning what market area to enter is often made simultaneously with other enterprisewide and operating strategic management decisions in task areas such as determining what product or service to offer, the entry method to use and the location and type of facilities.

## IDENTIFYING PRODUCTS OR SERVICES TO BE OFFERED

This task area, like other marketing areas, can involve enterprisewide, business unit and operational considerations. Enterprisewide and business unit planning decisions involve deciding how to differentiate products, services or brands from those of competitors—and identifying core company competencies that can be used to build competitive advantages in multinational as well as domestic markets. In contrast, a key operating decision in this area might be how to modify a product to meet local differences.

Several overall strategic approaches exist for identifying and marketing existing, new or redesigned products or services when entering and competing in international markets.

When conditions permit, many companies choose a *global* marketing approach to product design, selection, distribution, pricing, packaging and promotion. A global strategy involves using the same products and marketing strategies in all countries served. For example, Coca-Cola uses the same brand name, product design and advertising worldwide (Cohen 1991). In contrast, in 1995 Ford was actively pursuing a new strategy of developing a global car to be sold with modifications in all major markets (Treece, Kerwin, and Dawley 1995).

Due to local circumstances, however, a *multinational* or *market-by-market* approach is required in many situations. For example, accommodating local tastes was a problem in the late 1980s for Scott Paper Company since England, France, and the Mediterranean countries all required different products. In Scott's case, there was much greater concentration on local differentiation in each of the European countries, although considerable regional coordination was also needed (Lampert 1989).

Using U.S. product and marketing strategies in other countries is not always a good approach. For example, in trying to gain a foothold overseas, Federal Express initially attempted to duplicate the services and operations that had made it successful in the United States. Only after investing more than $1.5 billion did the company begin to adapt its approach to local overseas conditions (Pearl 1991). Eventually, it temporarily made substantial cutbacks in European operations in order to reduce its massive losses there and formulate new strategic approaches (Hawkins 1992).

Very often, the choice is a *mixed strategy*, which combines some aspects of the global approach with whatever modifications are necessary to meet local requirements. A company marketing decaffinated coffee, for example, might use a global company name, such as Nestlé, but modify the formula somewhat for each country in order to meet local tastes and government regulations. A wide range of modifications are often necessary because, while it is ideal to think globally, when planning for products, necessity often requires a company to act locally and take into account both general environment and competitive market factors.

## METHOD OF ENTRY

Like the key marketing tasks already discussed—selecting a market area and identifying products or services to be offered—selecting a method of entry can involve enterprisewide, business unit and operating level decisions.

Three major strategies used to enter an overseas market are discussed in this section. Of course, the specific approach used in individual situations will depend on situation requirements, as in other strategy formulation situations.

### Wholly Owned Investment: Buying an Existing Company or Setting up a Wholly Owned Subsidiary

This was the entry method chosen by Compaq in 1984 when it built a computer manufacturing plant in Scotland (Lohr 1989) and by both Toyota and Nissan when they built automobile plants in England in the late 1980s (Sanger 1989). In Compaq's case this method appeared best, since the products and their technology were relatively new, while Toyota and Nissan believed it easier and cheaper to start from scratch, since few English automobile manufacturers were available for purchase. In contrast, in 1989 Pepsico bought two English snack food companies for $1.35 billion (McGill 1989; Shapiro 1991).

### Joint Ventures/Strategic Alliances: Buying a Percentage Interest in an Existing Company or Entering into Cooperative or Partnership Arrangements

This is the entry method chosen by many companies. In 1989, Honda purchased a 20 percent interest—thus entering into a joint venture—in the English automaker Rover Group P.L.C. (Sanger 1989). In 1995, in an effort to extend its penetration of the Japanese market, U.S. automaker Chrysler Corporation entered a joint venture by buying a controlling interest in a Japanese-owned and -based automobile dealership chain (Pollack 1995). While expensive, this method can establish or increase market presence quickly.

Many arrangements, such as codevelopment consortiums, licensing, agency agreements and other contractual agreements, are common in a wide range of industries (Kanter 1989; Lewis 1990). Often referred to by their Japanese name, *Keiretsu*, cooperative arrangements among manufacturers, suppliers, and finance companies also are growing in popularity in the United States, in part because of the successful experiences of companies in countries such as Japan (Kelly et al. 1992; Strom 1992; Treece, Miller, and Melcher 1992). Partnerships are especially popular among airlines, where they allow the partners to function as a single carrier while remaining separate companies (McDowell 1995). Indeed, partnership arrangements are becoming increasingly popular throughout all business areas (Templin 1995).

### Exporting Products to a Country

This entry strategy is often favored by smaller companies exploring the prospects for international expansion. More established companies also find it useful in some situations. For example, Hurco Companies, a machine tool maker, fought its way back to solvency in large measure by increasing its overseas export sales (Lohr 1991). By 1995, major U.S. mail-order companies, such as L.L. Bean and Land's End, had achieved major sales positions and rapid growth in Japan through using catalog selling and mail delivery (WuDunn 1995a). Overall, American-manufactured exports rose 10 percent in 1990, to $316 billion, and jumped 80 percent from 1985 to 1990, with most of the increase coming from mid-sized companies with earnings in the range of $50 to $999 million range (Rose 1991).

## LOCATION AND TYPE OF FACILITIES

A primary decision involved in multinational cross-cultural management involves the location and type of facilities in a chosen international location. This is a key area for production/operations management, business unit, and enterprisewide management decisions and actions.

For example, in 1984 Compaq located a plant in Scotland—to serve the Great Britain market—because of that country's lower labor costs and high unemployment rate. Another factor affecting the decision was the infrastructure, both educational (technical schools) and business (electronics parts supply companies), in the computer industry in Scotland. This location proved to be a wise choice after the formation of the European Community in 1992, as it gave Compaq a low-cost entry to the entire European market. Northern England and Scotland have continued to be a prime location for facilities in the 1990s. In 1995, Siemens of Germany announced that it would build a huge ($1.7 billion) semiconductor plant in northern England, and Fujitsu of Japan planned to double the size of its four-year-old British computer-chip plant (Stevenson 1995b).

At other times companies relocate offices as local circumstances change. For many years, Opel AG, a West German subsidiary of General Motors (GM), coordinated its own European operations. However, in 1986, GM moved its headquarters to Zurich and established a European headquarters there, not so much because it felt that a more centralized location could better control operations, but primarily because West German law required companies headquartered in Germany to have 50 percent of board membership filled by company employees.

## SOURCING MATERIALS

*Sourcing*, another key area for productions/operations management decisions, refers to the means by which a company obtains the raw materials, subcontracted components, and other goods and materials needed to produce goods and services. Basically, firms have two alternatives: sourcing from the country in which they produce (*domestic sourcing*) or sourcing from foreign countries (*outsourcing*).

As the definition implies, outsourcing is an import strategy and, like most import strategies, is influenced by the length of supply lines, production costs, production quality, inventory levels, local import and tariff regulations and currency fluctuations. General Motors has found outsourcing to be very profitable. The company has agreements with Japan's Suzuki Motors, Isuzu Motors Ltd., and Toyota, as well as with South Korea's Daewoo Corp., to procure parts and components for production in its U.S. plants.

However, outsourcing has some disadvantages. IEC Electronics found that sourcing its circuit boards from offshore suppliers created quality problems, with rejects from outside suppliers being substantially higher than from internal production. In addition, since IEC sometimes implemented design changes in less than 24 hours, six to eight weeks' inventory of circuit boards often had to be thrown out by the time engineering changes worked their way through the trans-Pacific supply line (Breskin 1989).

## LOGISTICS

International *logistics*, another key production/operations area, involves the design and management of a business process or system that controls the flow of materials into, through, and out of the corporation. Two major phases of movement are especially important to managers: materials management (the movement of raw materials, parts and supplies through the firm) and physical distribution (the movement of the finished product to the customer).

An international logistics manager considers several factors: transportation (transit time, cost and government regulations); inventory (order-cycle time, customer-service levels and strategic needs of the firm, such as protection against inflation and devaluation); packaging (size, weight and customer specifications); and storage (available space within each country or area, cost and location).

The seven multinational cross-cultural management tasks discussed here are covered in greater detail in Chapters 4 and 5.

## TELECOMMUNICATIONS/INFORMATION SYSTEMS

The telecommunications/information systems task area involves the first of many strategic enablers and enabling systems discussed in this book that affect success in multinational management.

Advances in telecommunications systems worldwide have provided one of the most effective global links in today's multinational environment. They enable:

- communication by voice and television throughout most of the world,
- the electronic exchange of printed information through systems such as the Internet, faxes and e-mail, and
- the instant processing and exchange of computerized information and transactions worldwide.

Advanced technologies in telecommunications and computer information systems have been a major driving force, both in establishing common standards worldwide and in speeding up the transfer of information. They also provide a major resource for responding to local needs and managing cultural differences.

Company information systems need to be coordinated and consolidated globally while at the same time being responsive to local needs. Work is, therefore, needed on developing telecommunications systems links, often using worldwide services such as the Internet, which can support worldwide company information systems architectures and enable local company computer systems to operate effectively and efficiently throughout multinational company operations. These tasks are discussed in Chapter 7.

## FINANCE AND ACCOUNTING

Tasks in the key areas of finance and accounting (which are discussed in Chapter 8) affect almost all multinational operations.

### Finance

In many instances, basic financial strategies are dictated by the entry method, which can involve full or shared ownership, as well as by a company's financial condition and its policy regarding financing expansion through long-term debt, equity, retained earnings, or short-term borrowing. Decisions are also made on financing through local sources, such as government loans and banks, or financing outside the overseas local area.

These tasks have been affected in major ways by the development and expansion of a wide range of global banking and financial services and the use of telecommunications links and computer information support services designed to enable timely delivery of a wide range of financial services (Holland and Dwyer 1994; Javetski and Glasgall 1994).

### Accounting

One problem faced by multinational companies is that accounting standards differ from country to country, making it more complex for a firm to prepare financial statements consistent with the general accounting principles prevalent in the home country. For example, a U.S. firm normally must produce an annual consolidated statement of earnings showing all the operations of the firm in U.S. dollars, converted at current exchange rates. At the same time, statements of earnings are needed in local currencies of international subsidiaries for use in their home countries. Meeting the requirements of consolidated and local reporting for both internal and external purposes is a difficult task.

The development of common accounting standards and software able to function across national boundaries is taking place, but improvements are slow in coming (Dwyer et al. 1994; Gooding 1995).

In addition to exchange rates, several other factors affect the development of accounting strategies and systems. These include: the overall objectives and policies of the firm, the accounting systems of the parent company and subsidiaries, the structure of the enterprise (corporation, proprietorship or partnership), the nature of the industry, the internal and external users of information (management, owners, employees, investors, bankers, tax authorities and creditors), the local government and its policies and regulations, the relationship between parent and subsidiaries, local environmental characteristics (cultural attitudes, the nature and state of the economy and the competitiveness of the market), and international influences, such as global professional accounting standards and auditing practices.

## ORGANIZATION STRUCTURE, PROCESSES (BUSINESS AND HUMAN) AND CULTURE

Enablers or enabling organization systems and processes are needed to carry out enterprisewide and business-unit strategies and to enable marketing, production/operations, and other business processes to function effectively and efficiently.

Several factors affect the task of organizing for multinational business. These factors include geographic distances, language and other cultural differences, rapidly changing and intensely competitive markets, continuing technological advances and changing company strategies.

In the past, three types of organization structures were generally used: *multinational*, in which a company regards overseas operations as a portfolio of independent enterprises; *international*, in which a company regards overseas operations as appendages to a central domestic organization; and *global*, in which a company treats overseas operations as delivery pipelines to a unified global market (Bartlett and Ghoshal 1991). Problems were encountered with all three options.

Changing conditions in competitive markets worldwide and in key drivers of strategic situations have led to a reduced emphasis on organization structure and more emphasis on administrative and business processes and systems, communication channels, and interpersonal relationships and leadership (Bartlett and Ghoshal 1995). Organization structures have become hybrid—with their exact form tailored to meet specific situation needs.

The organizations being developed today balance maintaining global efficiencies, allowing responsiveness to different local needs and enabling the transfer of new knowledge rapidly among divisions (Dwyer et al. 1994). The key is flexibility and adaptability.

Corporate culture has also evolved to meet changing market needs. For example, Deere & Co. worked to change its culture to a global one as the company grew. Similarly, Coca-Cola went so far as to ban the words "domestic" and "foreign" from its corporate vocabulary in order to bolster its image as a single global company—which expects 90 percent of its sales to come from sources outside the United States by the year 2000 (Cohen 1991). Coca-Cola is now formally designated a "worldwide" company (Collins 1996). Organization tasks are discussed in Chapter 9.

## HUMAN RESOURCES (INTERPERSONAL INTERACTION, STAFFING AND TRAINING, COMMUNICATIONS, LEADERSHIP, AND MANAGEMENT)

The roles of leadership and management are changing along with changes in organizations and the international markets in which they compete. Balancing factors such as local responsiveness, global efficiencies and the rapid transfer of new knowledge requires strong leadership and management. As seen in the list of leadership/management tasks discussed at the outset of this chapter, such leadership clearly identifies strategic frameworks, communicates those frameworks and reinforces a corporate culture consistent with them, establishes flexible and adaptive enabling systems (telecommunication/information systems, accounting and finance systems, and organization-operating areas), maintains a core management group that can translate that balance into day-to-day operations, and intervenes where appropriate to ensure that integrative activities are operating effectively and efficiently to achieve strategic short- and long-term objectives.

Many different leadership styles, manager selection and training programs, communication channels and tools, and management processes are employed in effectively managing human resources in multinational cross-cultural management situations. These tasks are discussed in Chapters 10 through 13.

## INTEGRATED STRATEGIES AND INTEGRATIVE IMPLEMENTATION

As in training for a sport or stage-acting career, it is often necessary during the early stages of learning to segment the process into component activities that can be learned and practiced. This is done here and in the following chapters to enable learning the skills of multinational cross-cultural management. In real life, however, one must go beyond segmented techniques, just as the specific skills and techniques that have been learned must be blended creatively when actually playing the sport. Successful players must go beyond merely mastering technique. To perform successfully, they must practice the techniques to create synergy by putting them to work in an integrated way.

In multinational cross-cultural management considerable integrative thinking and action are also needed—at the enterprisewide, business unit and operating levels—when formulating and implementing strategies. In a sense, the tasks outlined in Figure 2-1 are carried out within the integrated context outlined in

Figure 2-6, which shows how the tasks or techniques are put to work in management. This integrated orientation is essential in multinational management, as it is in sports, for several reasons.

First, the tasks in practice are often interrelated: when deciding on method of entry, for example, one would consider financial, marketing, production, logistics, product, and people factors.

Second, in each task area, a manager is involved in both planning and doing, as strategic considerations blend with operating activities, which in turn help give greater definition to strategies.

Third, all of these activities must be carried out with their present and longer-term future implications (Hamel and Prahalad 1994), as well as the requirements of global efficiency, local efficiency, and rapid transfer of knowledge, in mind (Bartlett and Ghoshall 1991). Success depends not only on business plans and their execution, but also on the people and larger global and regional contexts involved in a particular situation (Forester 1965; Mitroff and Linstone 1993).

Clearly, some sense of the concept of an enterprisewide strategy or vision is needed. This involves understanding the ways in which a company's product or service differs from those of competitors. These differences can lie in brand perception; product characteristics, performance, availability or customization; patent protection; service (quality, speed, or proximity); facilities; cost and price; available financing; or any other core competency the company may have to allow it to perform business functions in a superior way. This is the franchise the company holds (or can establish and maintain) in the customer's mind (Buffet 1996; Hagstrom 1994).

Supporting services in a wide range of marketing and production/operations plans, programs, projects and activities are needed to support the strategic objectives.

Especially important are the enablers or enabling systems within four areas: organization structure, processes (business and human) and culture; telecommunications and information systems; accounting, finance and control; and human resource management (communication, staffing and training, leadership and management). Very often, these mechanisms are put in place as strategies are formulated. They are also essential to maintaining the company's abilities to anticipate and adapt and to create future markets.

All these capabilities may evolve over time, as they become more defined (in new companies), change along with market changes (in established companies), or respond to anticipated new markets and trends (in all companies). How the process unfolds in integrating company tasks, decisions and actions can depend on the company, industry and people involved.

The firm 3M provides an example of this integrative process at work. 3M went through a transition in anticipation of the 1992 unification of European markets. In the 1980s, the company brought together representatives of its 23 plants and 40 divisions in Europe, formed teams and developed plans to consolidate its European operations. One of its first moves was to increase research and development. Advertising was to be coordinated, as were other marketing programs. Production was also consolidated. The result was a new, coordinated European effort. For instance, a new product—the "Soft Scour" cleaning sponge—was developed at 3M's French consumer products laboratory, manufactured in its Spanish plant, and marketed across Europe by its British subsidiary. At the same time, local tastes were still being accommodated (Murray 1989; Rose 1991). Many additional examples of integrative multinational management processes at work may be found throughout this book.

This chapter has introduced the key task areas faced by multinational managers. Chapter 3 discusses the integrative processes involved in the task areas, while Chapter 4 discusses implementation.

## WORKS CITED

Abraham, Jeffrey. *The Mission Statement Book*. Oakland, CA: Ten Speed Press, 1995.

Aslund, Anders. *How Russia Became a Market Economy*. Washington, DC: Brookings Institution, 1995.

Baker, Stephen, Geri Smith, Kevin Kelly, and Elizabeth Weiner. "Making a Yanqui Boodle South of the Border." *Business Week*, February 10, 1992, pp. 40, 41.

Bartlett, Christopher A., and Sumantra Ghoshal. *Managing across Borders*. Boston: Harvard Business School Press, 1991.

———. "The Individualized Corporation: New Practical and Theoretical Challenges." Presentation given at the annual Strategic Management Society Conference, Mexico City, October 15–18, 1995.

Bleakley, Fred R. "Developing World Gets More Investment: Multinationals Have Tripled Spending in the Past Seven Years." *Wall Street Journal*, December 15, 1995, p. A9A.

Brady, Diane. "Delivery Giants Race to Provide Overnight Service to Asian Cities." *Wall Street Journal*, August 7, 1995, p. B6A.

Breskin, Ira. "Winning Back the Work That Got Away." *Business Week: Innovation Issue*, 1989, p. 148.

Brooke, James. "U.S. Investors Stampede into Brazil." *New York Times*, April 15, 1995, p. D5.

Buffett, Warren. "A Conversation." Workshop presented through the Colman Mockler Distinguished Leadership Program, St. John's University, New York, March 6, 1996.

Burns, John F. "India Economic Reforms Yield a Measure of Hope." *New York Times*, January 15, 1995, p. 10.

Carlton, Jim, and Neil Barsky. "Japanese Purchases of U.S. Real Estate Fall on Hard Times." *Wall Street Journal*, February 21, 1992, pp. A1, A4.

Cohen, Roger. "For Coke, World Is Its Oyster." *New York Times*, November 21, 1991, pp. D1, D5.

Collins, Glenn. "Coke Drops 'Domestic' and Goes One World." *New York Times*, January 13, 1996, pp. 35–37.

"Dutch-Swiss Team Wins Czech Phone Stake." *New York Times*, June 29, 1995, p. D7.

Dwyer, Paula, Pete Engardio, Zachary Schiller, and Stanley Reed. "Tearing Up Today's

Organization Chart: Tomorrow's Winners Will Use Western-Style Accounting, Japanese-Style Teamwork, Advanced Communications, and Give Entrepreneurial Local Managers a Long Leash.'' *Business Week/21st Century Capitalism; Special 1994 Bonus Issue*, November 18, 1994, pp. 80–90.

Forester, Jay. "A New Corporate Design." *Sloane Management Review*, Fall 1965, pp. 94–112.

French, Howard W. "Out of South Africa, Progress: Apartheid's End Is Helping Revitalize a Continent." *New York Times*, July 6, 1995, pp. D1, D5.

Fuhrman, Peter, and Michael Schuman. "Now We Are Our Own Masters: India Now Has The Look and Feel of the Next China and Latin America." *Forbes*, May 23, 1994, pp. 128–138.

"Gillette Sets Soviet Venture with Terms for Currency." *Wall Street Journal*, March 5, 1991, p. A13.

Gooding, Claire. "Accounting Software: A Challenge to US 'Global' Solutions." *Financial Times* (London), July 5, 1995, p. xi.

Hagstrom, Robert G. *The Warren Buffett Way*. New York: John Wiley and Sons, 1994.

Hamel, Gary, and C. K. Prahalad. *Competing for the Future: Breakthrough Strategies for Seizing Control of Your Industry and Creating the Markets of Tomorrow*. Boston: Harvard Business School Press, 1994.

Hart, S., and C. Banbury. "How Strategy Making Processes Can Make a Difference." *Strategic Management Journal*, May 1994, pp. 251–269.

Hawkins, Chuck. "Fedex: Europe Nearly Killed the Messenger." *Business Week*, May 25, 1992, pp. 124–126.

Hicks, Jonathan P. "The Takeover of American Industry," *New York Times*, May 28, 1989, Business Section, pp. 1, 8.

Holland, Kelley, and Paula Dwyer. "Technobanking Takes Off: The Digital Revolution Is Linking People and Companies around the World with Ever More Sophisticated Services." *Business Week/21st Century Capitalism; Special 1994 Bonus Issue*, November 18, 1994, pp. 52, 53.

Holstein, William J., and Laxmi Nakarmi. "Korea." *Business Week*, July 31, 1995, pp. 56–64.

"International Briefs." *New York Times*, August 11, 1995, p. D2.

Javetski, Bill, and William Glasgall. "Borderless Finance: Fuel for Growth." *Business Week/21st Century Capitalism; Special 1994 Bonus Issue*, November 18, 1994, pp. 40–50.

Kanter, Rosabeth Moss. *When Giants Learn to Dance*. New York: Simon and Schuster, 1989.

Kelly, Kevin, Otis Port, James Treece, Gail DeGeorge, and Zachery Schiller. "Learning from Japan." *Business Week*, January 27, 1992, pp. 52–60.

Kranz, Patricia. "Russia's Really Hostile Takeovers: Organized Crime Is Shooting Its Way into Big Business." *Business Week*, August 14, 1995, pp. 56–57.

Lampert, Hope. "Marketing to Local Tastes." *Business Month*, August 1989, pp. 37–41.

Landler, Mark. "Murdoch and 3 Partners Set Latin Satellite-TV Venture." *New York Times*, November 21, 1995, p. D6.

Landro, Laura, David P. Hamilton, and Michael Williams. "Sony Finally Admits Billion-Dollar Mistake: Its Messed-Up Studio." *Wall Street Journal*, September 18, 1994, pp. A1, A12.

Lewis, Jordan D. *Crafting Strategic Alliances: Corporate Partnerships for Growth and Profit*. New York: Free Press, 1990.

Lewis, Michael. *Pacific Rift: Why Americans and Japanese Don't Understand Each Other*. New York: Norton, 1993.

Lohr, Steve. "Compaq's Conquests in Europe." *New York Times*, July 9, 1989, Business Section, p. 4.

———. "U.S. Industry's New Global Power." *New York Times*, March 4, 1991, pp. D1, D3.

McDowell, Edwin. "Delta Seeks to Expand Its Ties with Three Airlines in Europe: Functioning as One Carrier while Remaining Separate." *New York Times*, September 9, 1995, p. 34.

McGill, Douglas C. "Pepsico, to Aid Europe Sales, Buys 2 British Snack Units." *New York Times*, July 4, 1989, pp. 41–42.

Mitroff, Ian I., and Harold Linstone. *The Unbounded Mind: Breaking the Chains of Traditional Business Thinking*. New York: Oxford University Press, 1993.

Montague, Bill. "Huge Deals Now Look Like Big Mistakes." *USA Today*, March 30, 1992, pp. 1B, 2B.

Moshavi, Sharon, Pete Engardio, Shekhar Hattangadi, and Dave Londorff. "India Shakes Off Its Shackles." *Business Week*, January 30, 1995, pp. 48–49.

Murray, Tom. "From European to Pan-European." *Business Month*, August 1989, pp. 35–37.

Naisbitt, John. *Global Paradoxes*. New York: Avon Books, 1994.

O'Boyle, Thomas F. "Bridgestone Discovers Purchase of U.S. Firm Creates Big Problems." *Wall Street Journal*, April 1, 1991, pp. A1, A4.

Overholt, William H. *The Rise of China: How Economic Reform Is Creating a New Superpower*. Boston: Norton, 1995.

Pearl, Daniel. "Federal Express Finds Its Pioneering Falls Flat Overseas." *Wall Street Journal*, April 15, 1991, pp. A1, A8.

Perlez, Jane. "Citibank in Budapest: A.T.M.'s and Potted Palms." *New York Times*, June 22, 1995a, p. D7.

———. "The Capitalist Pioneers of Prague." *New York Times*, July 29, 1995b, pp. 35, 36.

Pollack, Andrew. "Chrysler to Buy Control of Japanese Dealer Chain." *New York Times*, June 27, 1995, pp. D1, D5.

Powell, Bill, and Betsy McKay. "Cops on the Take—Russia." *Business Week*, August 14, 1995, p. 50.

Priem, R. L., and D. A. Harrison. "Exploring Strategic Judgement: Methods for Testing the Assumptions of Testing Prescriptive Contingency Theories." *Strategic Management Journal* 15 (May 1994): 311–324.

Prokesch, Steven. "Europe Taking a Lead in Growth." *New York Times*, January 15, 1990, pp. D1, D2.

Ramirez, Anthony. "Gillette Is Planning to Open a Plant in the Soviet Union." *New York Times*, February 2, 1990, pp. D1, D2.

Rapoport, Carla, with Justin Martin. "Retailers Go Global." *Fortune*, February 20, 1995, pp. 103–108.

Rose, Robert L. "How 3M, by Tiptoeing into Foreign Markets, Became a Big Exporter." *Wall Street Journal*, March 29, 1991, pp. A1, A5.

Rudolph, Barbara. "So Many Dreams, So Many Losses: Sony's $3 Billion Hollywood

Debacle Is the Latest in a Series of Setbacks for Japanese Firms in the U.S.'' *Time*, November 28, 1994, pp. 42–43.

Sanger, David E. ''Honda Raises Its Stake in Europe.'' *New York Times*, July 14, 1989, pp. D1, D4.

Shapiro, Eben. ''Pepsico Sets Its Sights on Spain.'' *New York Times*, November 7, 1991, pp. D1, D24.

Stanley, Alessandra. ''To the Business Risks in Russia, Add Poisoning.'' *New York Times*, August 9, 1995, p. A4.

Stevenson, Richard W. ''Eastern Europe's Next Round.'' *New York Times*, August 8, 1995a, pp. D1, D6.

———. ''Smitten by Britain: Thatcherism's Industrial Evolution.'' *New York Times*, October 15, 1995b, pp. 1, 10.

Strom, Stephanie. ''More Suppliers Are Helping Stores Push Merchandise.'' *New York Times*, January 20, 1992, D1, D8.

———. ''Japanese Scrap $ Billion Stake in Rockefeller Center.'' *New York Times*, September 12, 1995, pp. A1, D6.

Swasy, Alecia. ''Foreign Formula: Procter & Gamble Fixes Aim on Tough Market: The Latin Americans.'' *Wall Street Journal*, June 15, 1990, pp. A1, A4.

Templin, Neal, ''More and More Firms Enter Joint Ventures with Big Competitors: They Seek To Grow Quickly, Hold Down Rising Costs, Or Even Survive.'' *Wall Street Journal*, November 1, 1995, pp. A1, A8.

Tomkins, Richard. ''Home Discomfort Pushes Southern Abroad.'' *Financial Times* (London), July 12, 1995, p. 17.

Treece, James B., Kathleen Kerwin, and Heidi Dawley. ''Ford: Alex Trotman's Daring Global Strategy.'' *Business Week*, April 3, 1995, pp. 94–104.

Treece, James B., Karen Lowry Miller, and Richard A. Melcher. ''The Partners: Surprise! Ford and Mazda Have Built a Strong Team, Here's How.'' *Business Week*, February 10, 1992, pp. 102–107.

Wright, Diana, and Richard Woods. ''Investors See Europe as Best Market in 1990s.'' *Sunday Times* (London), January 10, 1990, p. E10.

WuDunn, Sheryl. ''Japanese Do Buy American: By Mail and a Lot Cheaper.'' *New York Times*, July 3, 1995a, pp. 1, 43.

———. ''Erosion in Japan's Foundation: Real Estate Crash Threatens the Entire Economy.'' *New York Times*, October 4, 1995b, pp. D1, D3.

Wysocki, Bernard, Jr. ''Outlook.'' *Wall Street Journal*, August 7, 1995, p. A1.

Yergin, Daniel, and Thana Gustafson. *Russia 2010: And What It Means for the World.* New York: Vintage Books, 1995.

Zeien, Albert. ''Gillette's Global Marketing Experiences.'' Talk presented at St. John's University's Annual Colman Mockler Leadership Award Ceremony, New York, February 27, 1995.

# Chapter 3

# Common Frameworks

The tasks described in Chapter 2 involve both strategic planning and strategy implementation at both the enterprise-wide (for example, deciding whether to go international) or functional (for example, marketing or production) levels. From one viewpoint, the management processes described in Chapter 2 reflect a commonsense contingency approach: examine the situation restraints and then creatively formulate alternative solutions, evaluate them, make a decision, and then take action. These actions are taken in phases appropriate for each specific situation, now and over the short-, intermediate-, and long-term future. This decision/action process is shown in Figure 3-1. As described in Chapter 2, it was the process that Siemens and Compaq went through in deciding to locate their plants in northern England (Lohr 1989; Stevenson 1995b).

This chapter describes this adaptive, flexible, commonsense contingency process, which was articulated by John Dewey decades ago (1938), in a more systematic and formal way than in Chapter 2. It also discusses how this process and other common contingency-based management processes have proved to be useful in managing multinational cross-cultural enterprises over the short, intermediate, and long terms.

## COMMON FRAMEWORKS FOR MANAGING
## MULTINATIONAL CROSS-CULTURAL SITUATIONS

The multinational cross-cultural management experiences described in Chapters 1 and 2 describe a basic contingency decision process (such as the one outlined in Figure 3-1) at work. For example, when the Chinese entrepreneur discussed in Chapter 1 was starting his small conglomerate and making his five initial deals, each venture was strategically built on:

**Figure 3-1**
**The Problem-Solving/Decision-Making Process**

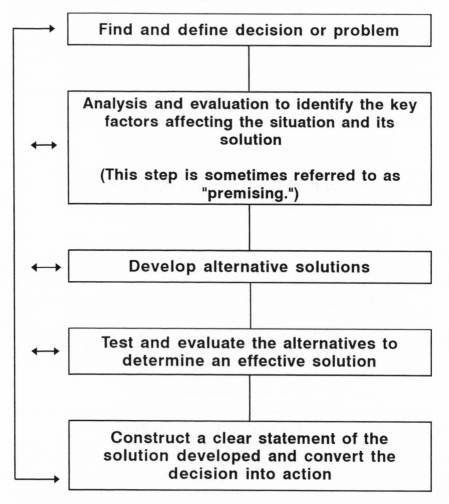

Find and define decision or problem

Analysis and evaluation to identify the key factors affecting the situation and its solution

(This step is sometimes referred to as "premising.")

Develop alternative solutions

Test and evaluate the alternatives to determine an effective solution

Construct a clear statement of the solution developed and convert the decision into action

Copyright © 1997 by R. J. Mockler.

- the analysis of external (market, customer and competition) and internal (financial and other resources) situation factors,
- the evaluation of possible alternatives, given future conditions, and
- the skillful management of making each venture work, given the individuals, organizations and external market conditions involved.

A similar context-specific contingency analysis and alternative exploration done at Gillette was also described in Chapter 1. In that case, the situation

Figure 3-2
The Problem-Solving/Decision-Making Process Including Reconceptualization
Phases

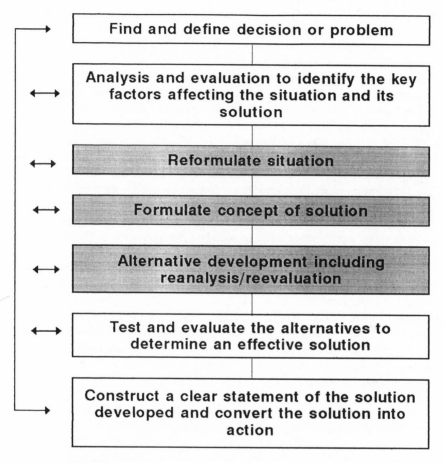

Find and define decision or problem

Analysis and evaluation to identify the key factors affecting the situation and its solution

Reformulate situation

Formulate concept of solution

Alternative development including reanalysis/reevaluation

Test and evaluate the alternatives to determine an effective solution

Construct a clear statement of the solution developed and convert the solution into action

Copyright © 1997 by R. J. Mockler.

involved using a computer and contingent rule-based software to decide from where to source the manufacture and assembly of their "Atra" razor parts.

The problems in practice with generalized contingency-process *outlines* are multifold:

1. Considerable rethinking, reformulating, reconceiving and associative reasoning are involved in the process, as indicated in the boxes added to Figure 3-1 in Figure 3-2.

2. Situations can change often, and sometimes rapidly. The problem lies in finding ways to stay tuned into the marketplace and keep in place an enabling organization structure and culture, people and leadership, and processes and

systems that enable an enterprise and its management to keep learning about, and responding to, messages from the marketplace in a coordinated, consistent and flexible way. This was seen in the experiences of Deere & Co. and of the many companies operating in the former USSR and newly emerging free markets in China (described in Chapters 1 and 2 and throughout the book).

3. As seen from the experiences of L.L. Bean and other U.S. mail-order companies exporting to Japan and those of Chrysler in selling automobiles in Japan, solutions often gradually emerge over time as managers work through a changing, fluid, and turbulent competitive market situation. This is an iterative entrepreneurial process, which can require continually *reconceiving* or reconceptualizing a situation. Such a process is outlined in Figure 3-3.

4. Finding creative practical solutions to achieve success in specific problem situations is often the key, yet very often is difficult to do. This was seen in the example describing how a Czech brewer blocked Anheuser-Busch's international expansion of its Budweiser brand in Europe and Russia in 1995. Solving such problems often requires viewing situations from different perspectives, studying conflicts and, in the conflict resolution process, reconceiving how each planner views a problem in order to stimulate innovative solutions (Mitroff and Linstone 1993).

5. Reliable enabling mechanisms are needed to do more than react to change; they are needed to anticipate change, exploit it and create ways to lead the market into the future.

These and other experiences suggest that the ability to create models or approaches based on contingency-situation factors (Figure 3-3) is more important to business management success than learning universal approaches. For this reason, the figure provides a useful orientation and common framework as a starting point for bridging cultural gaps and managing in many countries, cultures and businesses.

The following sections describe a number of common frameworks that are useful in multinational cross-cultural management:

- contingency/entrepreneurial and other situation-oriented decision processes, which are useful especially in planning basic operations such as marketing and production operations;
- enabling systems, such as organization structure and culture; leadership and people; telecommunications and information systems; and finance and accounting, and
- others, such as global products and services.

## THE UNDERLYING COMMON THINKING (COGNITIVE) PROCESSES

*Basic contingency processes*, such as those described in the preceding section and in Figures 3-1 through 3-3, are called the "it-all-depends" processes since they involve situation-specific decision processes and actions. They are commonly used as a framework in multinational cross-cultural management. One of their applications in the strategic management area in general is outlined in Figure 3-4; its earlier application to multinational cross-cultural management was described in Figure 2-1.

Several examples of these contingency processes at work were discussed in Chapters 1 and 2. For example, 3M went through an in-depth *situation analysis* in the 1980s when it brought together representatives of its 23 plants and 40 divisions in Europe to reevaluate its strategic plans for operating in a unified European Economic Community after 1992 (Murray 1989; Rose 1991). Based on the situation analysis, the company created a new, enabling organization concept, which was designed to prepare it to compete in the intermediate-term future. Under the new plan, research and development and advertising in different areas were coordinated and consolidated. As a result of the new organization, for example, new products could be developed at 3M's French consumer products laboratory, manufactured in its Spanish plant, and marketed across Europe by its British subsidiary. In this instance, an exploratory and open-ended situation analysis led to a flexible, situation-appropriate solution—in the essence of the entrepreneurial contingency process shown in Figure 3-3.

In each situation, managers must create their own approaches (for example, 3M used a "team approach" and organized their analysis around that integrative structure). This is a necessary first step in the iterative emerging process of creating innovative solution concepts appropriate for individual situations.

Different strategic choices for market entry provide another illustration of how specific situation factors can lead individual managers in different companies and industries to formulate different multinational market-entry strategies.

1. Specific situation characteristics of the market in the former Soviet Union, such as crime, the uncertainty of the market and its political environment, the many legal and monetary restrictions, and the need to protect proprietary technology, led Polaroid to formulate a very limited and narrowly defined market-entry strategy there (Greenhouse 1991; Kranz 1995; Stanley 1995).

2. Stanley Works conducted a detailed resource analysis (of the firm's diverse product, technical and production requirements) and market analysis (examining different customer needs in different countries, labor-cost differentials, and tax and tariff considerations). This analysis led the company over the years to formulate a specially tailored, mixed-entry strategy for its multinational manufacturing operations. For example, products requiring sophisticated or precision manufacturing—such as hydraulic tools, made at Stanley's Portland, Oregon, plant—were most effectively shipped throughout the world from a U.S. plant for quality and production efficiency reasons, as well as for tax and tariff considerations. Other products—such as wood planes, made in Sheffield, England—were supplied to the world market from a particular plant because, in this example, Europe has the largest market for wood planes. Stanley's Taiwan plant served the U.S. market with wrenches, partially because of lower labor costs in Taiwan (Uchitelle 1989a, 1989b).

Figure 3-3
Decision Making Involves Reorganizing Reality in a Way That Enables Effective Decision Making

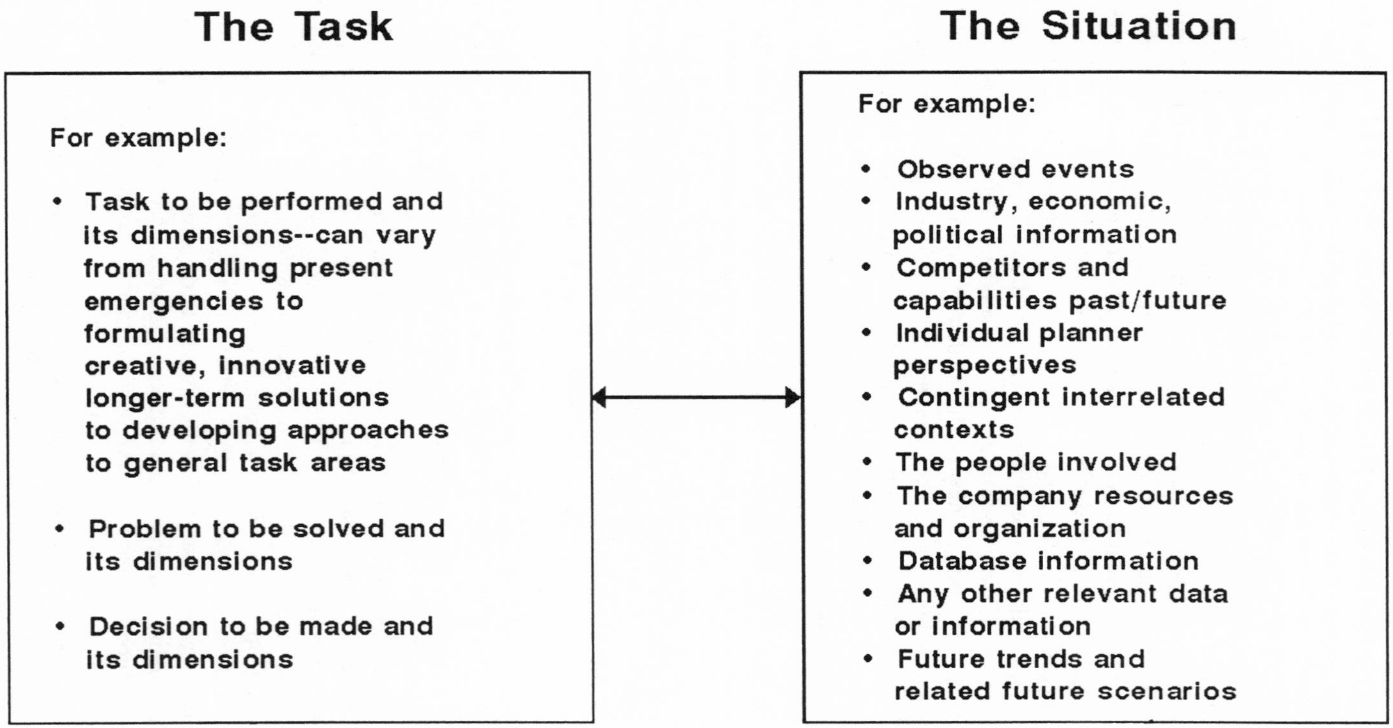

# The Task

For example:

- Task to be performed and its dimensions--can vary from handling present emergencies to formulating creative, innovative longer-term solutions to developing approaches to general task areas

- Problem to be solved and its dimensions

- Decision to be made and its dimensions

# The Situation

For example:

- Observed events
- Industry, economic, political information
- Competitors and capabilities past/future
- Individual planner perspectives
- Contingent interrelated contexts
- The people involved
- The company resources and organization
- Database information
- Any other relevant data or information
- Future trends and related future scenarios

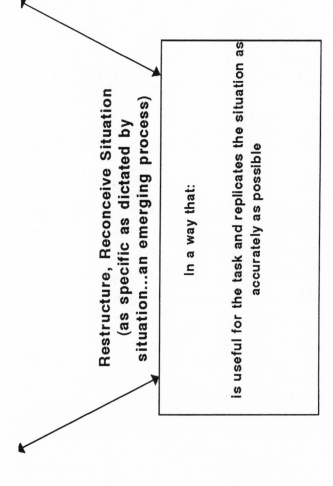

Restructure, Reconceive Situation
(as specific as dictated by
situation...an emerging process)

In a way that:

is useful for the task and replicates the situation as
accurately as possible

Copyright © 1997 by R. J. Mockler.

49

**Figure 3-4**
**Overview of the Strategic Management Process**

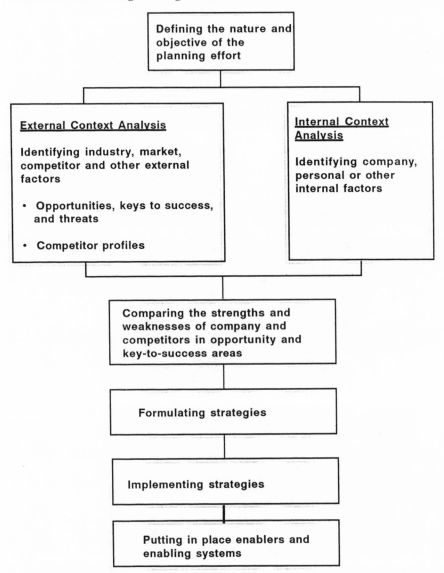

Copyright © 1997 by R. J. Mockler.

3. Using another approach to further penetrate the multinational market, in 1995 Chrysler purchased majority ownership of its Japanese importer and dealership chain, at a cost of around $100 million (Pollack 1995). This was expected to give the company control of a major sales network in Japan, a significant

move stimulated by the many ways in which that nation discriminates against foreign competitors throughout its distribution system (Lewis 1993).

4. In turn, Japanese automobile companies used modified strategies in the United Kingdom. For example, Honda purchased a 20 percent interest in the English automaker Rover Group P.L.C. (Sanger 1989), while Toyota and Nissan believed it easier and cheaper to start from scratch, since few English automakers were available for purchase and the Japanese companies had substantial financial resources and a major worldwide presence in the auto industry.

In these situations, each solution was an outgrowth of the particular company and market factors in each manager's situation. A wide range of situation factors is examined in making market entry decisions. The contingency process outline shown in Figure 3-5 was created using the general conceptualization process shown in Figure 3-3.

The outlines shown in Figures 3-4 and 3-5 are not the only way to reconceive or model the cognitive processes involved in strategic management and multinational market-entry situations. While these outlines are useful for learning purposes, readers are encouraged to ultimately formulate their own cognitive conceptual approaches, as suggested in Figure 3-3.

The following discussion reviews the factors affecting a market-entry decision (outlined in Figure 3-5) and discusses possible decisions and how they are made.

### Situation Factors Affecting the Decision

As shown in Figure 3-5, which extends Figure 3-3, and in the descriptions of company experiences, an initial concept of an entry strategy can be determined by studying several factors:

External factors: Target-country market factors
Target-country general environmental factors
Target-country production factors
Home-country factors
Internal factors: Company product factors
Company resources/commitment factors

The following section gives a brief explanation of how these situation factors can influence decision making.

### How Decisions Are Made

As the factors listed in Figure 3-5 are evaluated in the decision situation under study, an initial entry strategy can be formulated. For this introductory discussion, the possible decisions have been limited to three alternative entry strategies: a wholly owned subsidiary, joint ventures/contractual partnership agreement, and exporting.

**Figure 3-5**
**Decision Situation Diagram: Entry Strategy–International Market Overview Diagram**

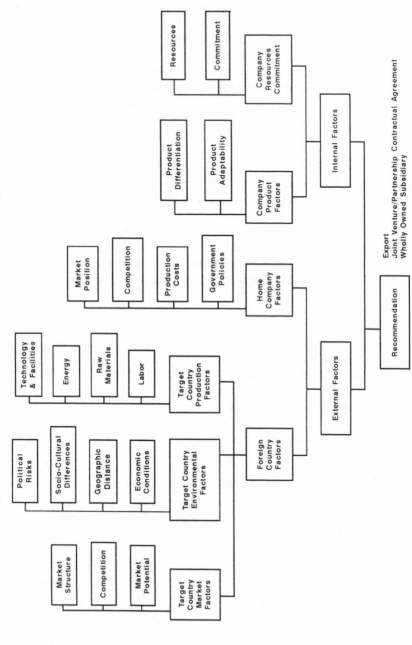

Copyright © 1997 by R. J. Mockler.

To successfully pursue a *wholly owned subsidiary* entry strategy, either through starting one's own subsidiary or buying an existing facility, a firm must have adequate financial resources available to establish the production or service facility. Regardless of the favorable position of other factors—for example, strong sales potential, the availability of technically skilled workers, a low level of political risk, or even favorable responses by the foreign government—a lack of adequate financial resources will constrain the use of this entry strategy. In 1995, Siemens of Germany used this strategy in locating its new $1.7 billion semiconductor plant in northern England. Favorable factors included the firm's strong financial resources, the area's relatively low labor rates and high unemployment, political stability, the availability of skilled labor, and an infrastructure including technical schools and electronics companies, which was favorable for the computer industry (Stevenson 1995b).

Available financial resources do not, however, necessarily mean that an investment strategy involving a wholly owned subsidiary is recommended. For example, in the target market or country under study, political conditions may be unstable, the market infrastructure may be difficult to penetrate, legal restraints may be difficult to overcome or wholly owned investments may not be allowed. In this situation, if it is clearly desirable for other reasons that a company enter this market, the strategy considered might involve *joint venture/ contractual partnership agreements*, two popular types of international strategic alliance.

Joint venture (shared ownership) or contractual (such as licensing) partnership agreements are considered a viable alternative if management is unsure as to the sales potential of the target market, product differentiation or adaptation is high, labor costs are very high, or a firm's level of international expertise is limited. Joint venture/contractual partnership agreements are very often used to limit a company's exposure to risk when entering a new and unfamiliar market. Pepsi-Cola cited such factors as reasons for undertaking its joint venture/contractual arrangements in Romania in the 1990s. Such strategies can have problems, however, as Pepsi-Cola found out in Central Europe, where it failed to maintain adequate control of its joint ventures. Pepsi also failed to keep pace with the massive investment that Coca-Cola made in its own joint ventures—investments and control that enabled Coke to overtake Pepsi over a five-year period. In 1995 Coke was outselling Pepsi two-to-one in Central Europe (Frank 1995; Nashe 1995).

An *exporting* entry strategy is considered a minimum-risk approach. In a joint-venture partnership agreement, a company may have to fund a part of the project and/or give up a substantial portion of the venture's ownership. However, an export strategy eliminates these costs and associated risks. If the sales potential for the target market is high, the estimated production and distribution costs are lower at home than in the foreign location, product adaptability requirements are low, import and export restrictions are favorable, raw materials are relatively more expensive abroad, the political climate abroad is unstable, or the firm has limited financial resources, exporting is a recommended strategy.

U.S. mail-order companies have used exporting to penetrate the Japanese market. They have been successful because they are extremely adept at doing business by mail, it is the easiest and cheapest way to penetrate the market, prices through U.S. mail order companies are much cheaper than through normal retail channels in Japan, and Japanese tastes and buying habits are similar to those of Americans (WuDunn 1995a). In 1994, L.L. Bean's mail-order sales in Japan reached $100 million, up 66 percent from the prior year. Total U.S. mail-order sales to Japan were expected to run around $750 million in 1995—approximately 2 to 3 percent of total retail sales in that country. In response to customer complaints about size and fabric differences, several companies, including Eddie Bauer and L.L. Bean, have opened retail outlets in Japan. These outlets enable customers to examine and try on products before ordering them by mail, in effect constituting a mixed-entry strategy appropriate for their particular businesses (WuDunn 1995a).

In practice, decisions such as these are more complex than this discussion indicates, as it only briefly introduces the basic contingency process at work. A more detailed discussion of this decision and others, and the ways in which key situation factors are taken into account when making decisions and taking action in multinational cross-cultural management situations, follows in Chapters 5 and 6.

## CONTINGENCY PROCESSES: A USEFUL COMMON FRAMEWORK FROM A VARIETY OF PERSPECTIVES

That such a context-specific contingency-based decision process is a useful common framework in managing across cultural boundaries was also evident in executive training workshops.

For instance, during 1990s China was involved in bidding for the summer Olympic Games to be held in 2000 and 2004. In 1993 Sydney, Australia, won the bid for the year 2000 by just two votes, but China was determined to reapply in the future (Longman 1993; Riding 1993).

During dozens of planning/training sessions with a wide range of Chinese managers and executives conducted by the authors between 1993 and 1995, the Olympics decision situation (a familiar, worldwide, future-oriented decision) was used as a basis for an introductory strategic management learning experience. Following the process outlined in Figure 3-3, which was used as an introductory management orientation, the attendees first identified the *nature of the opportunities* presented by having the Summer Olympics in China and the importance of these benefits to China: short-term income; long-term favorable international exposure; incentives to make major infrastructure improvements, such as roads and communication; a significant boost for export trade and tourism; increased transfer of technology and the like.

Second, they identified *key situation components*: including *competitors*; ath-letes; supporting facilities; visitors; reporters and electronic/telecommunications facilities and people; selection committee members; and competitors vying to host the games.

Third, they identified the requirements to be satisfied in each component, that is, the *keys to success* and their implications for plan formulation and imple-mentation. For example, the seminar participants generally agreed that China could realistically develop a new airport with convenient access from downtown Beijing and could meet other success criteria. However, the problems and pitfalls of competing effectively for the games in light of the extensive air pollution in Beijing and the social implications of curing that pollution (in 1993 almost all homes were heated by burning coal) were discussed extensively.

Fourth, *available resources, timing* and *costs* were discussed, both to deter-mine feasibility and to enable a more thorough cost-benefit analysis. Fifth, *spe-cific competitors* for hosting the games were identified—including Africa, which appeared to pose the biggest threat to China for the 2004 Summer Olympics—and comparative competitive position evaluations were performed. Sixth, they discussed possible ways to win the Olympics in later years.

The participants seemed to understand the approach underlying Figure 3-3. At the outset, only basic concepts of cognitive decision-making processes were introduced, such as the one shown in Figure 3-3. The purpose of such a figure was to point out that decision making did not involve learning technical tools, but rather a process familiar to them. Figure 3-3 and the discussions related to it made the point that *any* useful structured technique or device, computer or manual, that seminar participants created or found (that is, the process shown in Figure 3-3) could conceivably be an effective aid in strategic management decision making. Any systematic approach that enabled coordinated systematic evaluation by an interested and informed group and focused on building solu-tions based on a familiar, worldwide, future-oriented situation analysis can be useful.

Introducing Figure 3-3 served four purposes in this case:

- It reoriented seminar participants away from their traditional educational emphasis on learning techniques and technologies and refocused them on common, underlying, con-ceptual contingency-decision processes.
- It drew on a cultural entrepreneurial tradition shared by seminar participants and con-veyed to them the perception that each individual has the natural ability to manage effectively.
- It related the workshop learning experience to their environment and not to something alien, imported from the outside world.
- It provided a common cross-cultural framework for dealing with problem situations.

In Russia, similar exercises were done with groups of banking and insurance executives. Process models and scientific techniques (such as computer simulations) used in the United States were not introduced initially; only Figure 3-3 was discussed.

In both the Chinese and Russian versions of this exercise, the general planning and decision-making processes shown in Figures 3-2 and 3-4 were introduced only after the situation-specific contingency orientation in Figure 3-3 had been explained. This sequence was designed to let a situational orientation prevail over a technical or technique-based learning and thinking focus and to provide a common framework for working together across international boundaries.

A further intent of this exercise was to adapt and use a very general, situation-based (context-specific) orientation, such as the familiar strategic management one shown in Figure 3-4, to build toward a solution appropriate for, and useful in, St. Petersburg, Moscow, or Beijing. The intent was not to mechanically transfer to Russia and Asia the Western business techniques that had worked in the United States, since this is often recognized as a prescription for failure (Erlanger 1994a). Instead, general frameworks were used to provide a common ground for idea development and strategic plan creation appropriate to the countries involved.

Context-specific contingency management processes are common throughout Asia. For example, economists have studied how different Pacific and Asian countries, such as Singapore, Thailand, Malaysia, Korea, Hong Kong, the Philippines, and Taiwan, have developed different strategic economic approaches. Such approaches balance the mix of free-market forces and government control in ways appropriate for each country (Fallows 1994).

Many Russian economists were also familiar with enterprise-specific contingency processes (and their models), since they had been working with similar situation-specific process models and had classified them under the heading, "Theory of the Firm." Essentially, this is another umbrella concept for systematically organizing and developing situation-specific contingency approaches to planning and management.

Other research (for example, Hart and Banbury 1994; Priem and Harrison 1994) reinforces the notion that it is useful to start with the situation and then either create one's own cognitive approaches and success formulas or adapt the formulas of others to one's own special needs. In other words, one starts with the process shown in Figure 3-3, which is a basic contingency management process.

In training session after training session, involving over 1,000 Chinese and Russian executives, enormous untapped capacities to create concepts and conceptual models independent of acquired or learned processes and approaches were in evidence. Participants seemed to rely mostly on their own conceptual and practical skills, either innate or acquired through experience.

For instance, many entrepreneurs described the processes they went through in doing customer research and competitive market planning. A young Chinese entrepreneur who was starting a new beverage company had done both consumer survey mailings and extensive field-testing of a new children's beverage. He had also systemically gathered information on available distribution, promotion channels, and competitors. Another entrepreneur, who had started an advertising agency, was equally alert to the practical aspects of planning for success in new ventures. Their approaches (the cognitive processes they went through) were fairly sophisticated from the strategic management viewpoint written about in the United States (Mockler 1993). However, when questioned, these entrepreneurs indicated that they had developed these very systematic, situation-specific contingency approaches to new business/product development on their own, not from books or management-training programs.

Managers from larger companies also showed ample evidence of an untapped capacity for this kind of situation-oriented contingency thinking as they gradually developed their innate cognitive skills during the training programs.

Evidence exists of a strong entrepreneurial spirit throughout Russia, Central Europe, and China. For example, an article entitled, "A New Breed of Russian Entrepreneur Takes Risks in Stride," describes the experiences of one successful entrepreneur and notes the "millions" of others now in business there. Hundreds of accounts of Russian, Central European, and Chinese entrepreneurs are described in articles with such titles as, "Beijing's Grip Weakens as Free Enterprise Turns into Free-For-All," "A Post-Marxist Hungarian Bus Maker Takes to Capitalist Road," and "A Housing Boom Remakes the Russian Landscape," as well as books such as *Stepping Out: The Making of Chinese Entrepreneurs* (Brauchli 1993, 1994; Bun and Chiang 1994; Engardio, Barnathan, and Glasgall 1993; Erlanger 1994b; Imse 1993a, 1993b; Ingram 1993; Jordan 1993; Milbank 1995; Nelan 1993; Perlez 1993, 1995a, 1995b, 1995c; Reitman 1993).

The breadth and depth of this entrepreneurial spirit is further confirmed in many research studies, especially studies of the Chinese family-based strategic approach to business (Dologite and Mockler 1993; Mockler 1994, 1995).

At the same time, a large number of executives and managers in attendance did not seem to possess an entrepreneurial orientation or even the potential (or the opportunity) for developing it. For example, the manager of a television station in China, himself a contingency-oriented manager, explained that he had little interest in what viewers (consumers) wanted. He claimed that the government believed it knew what was best for viewers, a traditional view in an autocratic, government-controlled country. He explained that the government owned the television station and was likely to retain control of television outlets in China. Unless he adhered to the government's views, he reasoned (in a very logical, contingency-oriented manner), he would be out of a job.

The people we interacted with fell into three categories:

1. Those who have situation-specific contingency modeling and conceptualization skills and can use them in business management situations.
2. Those who have the potential and/or the right work or learning environment to develop this potential for contingency competitive market thinking (a potential that can be identified through skills tests).

3. Those who appear neither to possess these skills or to have the internal potential (or external circumstances) to develop them.

Based on the authors' records of business negotiating and training program contacts, well over two-thirds of the executives and managers dealt with in both Asia and Central Europe fell into the first two categories. Admittedly, these people were not necessarily a representative cross-section of each country's entire population, since they represented only those who were actively seeking to learn about, and exploit, free-market opportunities. Nonetheless, our findings indicated a sizable fertile ground for proceeding with further work in this area based on the common frameworks discussed here. Many people in the training groups seemed to grasp fairly quickly the contingency concepts underlying competitive market thinking. Moreover, models or frameworks depicting contingent situational conceptual thinking, shown in Figures 3-2 through 3-5, seemed clear to them. This provided an easy means of accelerating their learning process and communicating in a common cognitive language.

The experiences and research studies briefly described in this section led to our conclusion that identifying and focusing on common thought processes, attitudes, planning techniques and experiences is *one* effective way to build a working bridge across cultural boundaries and encourage the transfer of technology and other knowledge.

In a practical way, the common framework approaches developed here provided a bridge that enabled work to be done more easily and quickly. They also provided a mechanism for reconciling, handling and putting to good use cultural differences. At the same time, even though it is useful to emphasize common links crossing cultural boundaries, they do not solve all problems, not all people adapt to them, and differences among cultures can have a major impact on a decision situation. Nonetheless normally differences can be handled more effectively if one first focuses on emphasizing common links and establishes a common working framework, such as the one shown in Figure 3-3.

*Contingency theory* has been labeled the "It all depends" theory. It is an emerging theory that involves situation-specific decision and action processes. This section has described some of the more familiar *contingency processes*, which were found to be useful common frameworks when both working and conducting seminars in different cultures. They are useful in making strategic planning decisions at both the enterprisewide and operational levels in a company. Additionally, as shown in Chapters 7 through 12, they are useful in making the decisions involved in implementing strategies, that is, the "doing" part of management.

## ENABLING COMMON FRAMEWORKS

Moving from decisions to actions in multinational cross-cultural management requires having effective enablers and enabling systems in place, four types of which are discussed here and in Chapters 7 through 12: telecommunications and information systems; finance, accounting, taxation and control: organization structure, processes (business and human) and culture; human resources (interpersonal interaction, communication media, staffing and training, leadership and management).

### Telecommunications and Information Systems

Today, telecommunications cable and satellite links enable voice and television communication worldwide, the exchange of printed information stored in databases through systems such as the Internet, communication of messages by computer e-mail, and the instant processing of computer transactions worldwide. These links are rapidly being integrated with ever-more sophisticated computer software and information network services.

Advanced technologies in telecommunications and computer information systems have been a major driving force, both in establishing common standards worldwide and in managing cultural differences.

Satellite dishes were common in the East European countries during the days of the startup of CNN, and these worldwide communication links were a major factor in the breakup of the USSR. They served to expose the mass USSR and Central European population to the many different lifestyles worldwide, as well as the benefits of free-market economies and freedom of speech (Henry 1992; "World View" 1990).

The discussions in other sections of this book (Chapters 7 and 12) describe voice and videoconferencing telecommunications systems used in coordinating and managing worldwide businesses. First Direct, a telephone-only bank in Leeds, England, with a half-million customer accounts and not a single branch office is a dramatic example of the power of the telephone when linked to computer information systems (Hansell 1995).

The Internet, a global, on-line, computer information service, allows worldwide access to information related to business, as well as to any kind of information useful to its estimated 20 to 40 million users. The increasing number of communication sites is an indication of its growth potential: from 1994 to early 1995, China went from 2 sites to 593; Argentina, from 1 to 1,415; and Japan, from 38,267 to 99,034. Language differences have created problems, however. To overcome these problems, a digital coding system with automatic translation capabilities is being developed to allow cross-cultural communication in any language, even Sanskrit and languages using Chinese ideographs or Cyrillic lettering (Pollack 1995). This new system will allow this powerful telecommunication systems framework to adapt to, and integrate, a major culture difference (language) on the Internet and other telecommunications media/software systems.

American Telephone and Telegraph (AT&T), MCI Communications, and Microsoft all plan to offer a variety of services for accessing the Internet (Lewis

1995). Other companies are developing services and software to use sound, animation, and other technologies on the Internet (Rigdon 1995). The spectacular rise in August 1995 of the stock price of Netscape Communications, a small company developing software for Internet access (browsing) and use through modems attached to personal computers, is another indication of the rapid growth in the use of this common multinational framework (Zuckerman 1995).

Many individual companies are developing their own computer information systems that link operations worldwide. During the late 1980s, for example, banks developed systems to create a worldwide around-the-clock financial services network. British Airways has a computerized database system that enables a customer's call at any time of the day or night and from many worldwide locations to be shifted to different locations (for example, a call from the United States might be answered automatically in Scotland). An operator at any of these locations talking with the customer can draw information by satellite from an integrated computerized database, which has records of prior communications with that customer. This telecommunications connection enables the operator to answer questions on an individual, personalized basis and complete many unfinished transactions.

In the production/operations management and services areas, computer systems assist in enabling the mass customization of products and services as well as in balancing the use of diverse resources worldwide. Mass customization of products is another mechanism for balancing the efficiencies of mass production with the ability to meet varying customer needs (Pine 1993). Computer systems like the one employed by British Airways allow for personalized customer service to meet differing customer needs across the world. Gillette's computer system for checking on available manufacturing and supply resources worldwide and calculating the most efficient balanced mix of these differing resources in producing the ''Atra'' razor (described in Chapter 1) is another example.

The standardized accounting software and electronic financial money transfer systems mentioned in this chapter are further examples of how technologies enable the crossing of cultural boundaries and reconciliation of differences that may arise among countries and cultures—in, for example, exchanges rates, accounting standards and the raising of capital (Gooding 1995; Javetski 1994).

In many ways, then, telecommunications/information systems function as a major common framework for achieving the efficiencies of global operations and, at the same time, enabling the effective management of multinational cross-cultural differences. These types of enabling systems are discussed further in Chapter 7.

**Finance and Accounting**

Major developments in global banking, accelerated by advances in communications and information technology, are creating another major common framework for multinational businesses. There are many examples of how these innovations are being used to reconcile differences in multinational cross-cultural management.

Global banks and financial institutions continue to expand their multinational capabilities to provide global banking services. Currency trading is becoming ever faster and easier: for example, Citibank's Hong Kong branches offer customer accounts in ten different currencies, enabling customers to exchange currencies instantly as rates fluctuate (Holland and Dwyer 1994). Banks are building global networks to make the movement of cash among countries easier and quicker, often offering 24–hour service. Debt-financing services have also gone global, thanks in large measure to electronic communications. As increasing numbers of common financial instruments are developed, interest rates are showing increasing signs of merging internationally. The new developments are also making it easier to borrow money across borders worldwide as global standard measures of financial value are developed (Javetski 1994).

This trend is accelerating through mergers and acquisitions in the banking industry. For example, in mid-1995 Dresdner Bank A.G. of Germany agreed to pay $1.6 billion for the Kleinwort Benson Group, a British investment bank, creating the latest in a series of giant multinational financial institutions (Stevenson 1995a). In addition, German bankers have substantially increased their investments in the U.S. stock market (Truell 1995).

These and other developments indicate that accounting and finance are moving toward a more common framework that should help minimize some of the problems encountered in managing business across cultural boundaries. These developments enable individual companies to take advantage of the efficiencies that come from global financing, and at the same time enable more rapid response to local needs for funds to finance day-to-day subsidiary needs.

Many needs have to be balanced in the accounting area. Clearly, data is needed for managing local units. It is also needed at the level of the parent corporation in order to consolidate decision making, management control, and financial accounting. External reporting requirements must also be satisfied on both a consolidated and local level.

The movement toward developing international accounting standards will help firms achieve the proper balance. China is moving quickly toward the adoption of an international accounting standard, and increasingly, large organizations are moving to standardize accounting systems across Europe. Progress elsewhere is slow, however. Efforts are being made to develop computer software that can handle both consolidation and differing local needs, but these common frameworks are still of only marginal value (Dwyer et al. 1994; Gooding 1995; Lieber 1995). In 1996, varying needs in the accounting area seemed to dictate that multinational companies still needed to maintain parallel sets of accounting records for their various operations worldwide. Chapter 8 explores some of the changes occurring in the accounting and finance area and their impact on multinational cross-cultural management.

### Organization Structure, Processes (Business and Human) and Culture

A key problem in multinational organizations is the need to balance three forces:

- the need for local independence in order to be *responsive* to local needs,
- the need to maintain global *efficiency* through coordinating/consolidating worldwide business processes and products, and
- the need to quickly *transfer knowledge* about advances in innovative technology and other areas of company competencies among divisions.

An overreliance on corporate structure can impede this balance, lack of structure can impede coordination/consolidation and the transfer of knowledge. The skills involved in achieving such balance are what make management at times as much an art as a science.

Common organizational concepts are useful in multinational cross-cultural management situations. For example, flat organization structures are replacing hierarchical structures in many worldwide companies, teams are being emphasized, joint ventures and partnerships are being explored, and advanced telecommunications systems are being installed and used. While centralization is useful and global products and services are still emphasized, entrepreneurial local managers are being given more freedom to meet and overcome regional competitive market conditions (Dwyer et al. 1994).

At the same time, a key to achieving the balance seems to be to emphasize business, administrative, and human processes and systems, communication channels, and corporate culture rather than establish a single "best" formal organizational structure. For example, Gillette's organizational approach is generally a matrix organization, but in practice, according to CEO Al Zeien, the structure varies from country to country and is designed to be adaptive and flexible (Zeien 1995).

As in other task areas of multinational cross-cultural management, the final organization concept or form appropriate for an individual company depends on the needs of the company, industry, and markets involved. The form almost always evolves along with changes in leaders and competitive market conditions (Bartlett and Ghoshall 1991). Different ways in which the three strategic driving forces—the needs for global efficiencies, local responsiveness and new knowledge transfer—help shape effective organization structures and enable their management of are explored more fully in Chapters 4 and 8.

### Human Resources: Interpersonal Interaction, Communications, Staffing and Training, Leadership and Management

Given the necessity to have a balanced perspective in multinational cross-cultural management, a balance among making use of common links (such as worldwide technology, focused entrepreneurial contingency decision-making and action skills, and global products); being adaptable and flexible in responding to, and managing, local differences; and enabling the rapid transfer of new knowledge, good leadership is necessarily a key ingredient of success.

A leader is instrumental in creating an adaptive and flexible structure and imbedding a culture that enables an organization to prosper in a rapidly changing, highly competitive international market. Effective leaders do this through:

- Creating an overall strategic-planning framework, including strategic vision and guidelines.

- Stimulating and guiding the emergent development of specific plans (enterprisewide and in functional areas) over time through the enabling systems and processes.

- Putting in place, guiding and energizing the enabling frameworks and systems needed, in light of changing competitive market environments, for achieving success.

- Ensuring that a core management staff, with appropriate interpersonal, communications, and leadership and management skills and potential, is in place and functioning in order to achieve the appropriate balance.

- Communicating and implementing the strategic framework as well as cultural benchmarks that are needed to enable the core management staff to translate the desired balance into action. The actual processes involve leadership and management appropriate for both the manager and people or groups involved in the situation, as well as for the specific competitive market needs of the situation.

- Leaving managers the relative freedom to manage and placing the locus of decision making as close to the customer as possible, yet intervening where appropriate to make certain that integrative activities are operating efficiently and effectively so as to achieve the company's strategic short- and long-term objectives.

Processes leaders go through in formulating enterprisewide and operating-level strategies and organization structures range from top-down directives to bottom-up facilitating, coaching and sponsoring—to some combinations of the two (Hart and Banbury 1994). The strategies themselves are dependent on the strategic driving forces in the situation.

To survive and prosper in international markets, a company needs the effective enabling framework and systems, as well as an enabling core group of managers who:

- know the company, its philosophy, people, processes, and competencies,
- know the country or countries where they are working, and
- are highly skilled at their jobs.

There are several commonly used approaches to staffing international operations so as to achieve balanced strategic objectives:

- Hiring managers who are knowledgeable about specific countries or regions and then having them spend extended periods of time working at company headquarters or in other countries.
- Having existing company managers spend extended periods of time overseas.
- Continuing the integrative process over the years.

The communication channels used, and the way in which they are used, will also vary, as different managers deal with different levels and kinds of situations.

While common frameworks as are described above are available, the ways in which they are put to work and managed will likely differ from situation to situation, as will the management practices and leadership styles useful and appropriate in each situation.

## OTHER BASIC COMMON FRAMEWORKS

Another familiar common link across national borders is global products, services and brands. Coca-Cola, Gillette razor blades, Budweiser beer, Deere tractors, and even the Olympics are familiar names in many countries around the world. They provide a common reference point—when discussing business practices, conducting business training sessions, or establishing a common framework for decision making and attempting to reconcile cultural differences. Global product, services and brand strategies are becoming more common throughout the world.

Increasing numbers of companies are searching for ways to globalize their products and, at the same time, make them adaptable to local customer needs (Kanter 1995). Aided by computer and telecommunications technology, Ford is moving to become a single global company by introducing a worldwide car. This approach is designed to save development and production costs and simplify the coordination of worldwide operations, while still allowing for variations to suit different markets (Treece 1995). Mass customization is another way to combine global product advantages with the ability to meet local requirements.

Even global retailers are attempting to differentiate themselves by transforming their store names into global brands, much like Coke and Pepsi. There has been a massive worldwide expansion of major retailers—for example, Makro (from Holland), Carrefour (from France), Yaohan (from Japan), Marks & Spencer (from the United Kingdom), and Wal-Mart, Kmart, Disney, and Toys "R" Us (from the United States)—in countries including Mexico, Brazil, China, Malaysia and Spain). In 1995 in Europe alone, there were nearly 50 U.S. retailers, up from 14 in 1992. In mid-1995, retailers worldwide were expected to spend a minimum of $5 billion over the next 18 months on new stores in foreign markets (Rapoport 1995). All these retailers are using a global brand umbrella for stores that will stock both global and locally popular items.

Another common link among nations and cultures is social concerns, such as the role of women, human rights, and the environment. For instance, women's positions in business and their rights in general are impacting business decisions worldwide (Faison 1995; WuDunn 1995b). Human rights have also become a common concern, having, for example, impacted business negotiations between the United States and China (Cowell 1995). Inhumane treatment of workers in both Brazil and the State of California have been criticized in major newspapers (Noble 1995; Schemo 1995). Environmental concerns, such as industrial pollution, are additional concerns that are now shared by businesses around the world (Simons 1994, 1995). Cultural events involving different art forms— dance, music and theater, for example, also form a kind of common link across cultures, though their impact on business is much less direct (Holden 1995; Kisselgoff 1995).

An additional common framework (mentioned in Chapter 2) involves core company visions and strategies. As with so many of the common frameworks discussed in this book, this framework as well must often be adapted to local circumstances. For example, several years ago, Coca Cola decided to have its slogan, "Enjoy Coke," adapted into non-Roman alphabets. In Russia, however, the word "enjoy" has a more sensual connotation, so it was changed to "drink." In the Chinese language, Coca-Cola settled on a combination of Chinese characters that means, "A thirst quencher that makes you happy." As an added bonus, those characters are pronounced much like "Coca-Cola." In both markets, the strategic core concept—to encourage consumers to enjoy Coke— was adapted successfully to specific cultures (Radzievsky 1996).

## ESSENTIALLY ENTREPRENEURIAL PROCESSES

What has been discussed in this chapter essentially involves management processes that generally fall under the heading "entrepreneurial". They are ultimately commonsense "street smarts" known well by survivors, who stay constantly tuned to their environment and their own strengths and weaknesses, developing a canny sense of how to work their way successfully through any situation at hand—all within the context of longer-term objectives. The processes described in this chapter are not magic formulas but only systematic descriptions of familiar and commonly known and used contingency ("It all depends") processes.

In other words, the orientation described in this chapter is a context-specific integrated management one, involving processes that make use of global tools and techniques as well as locally appropriate ones in reacting to change and creating longer-term solutions that will work for individual managers in specific companies attempting to operate in different cultures and countries.

The core entrepreneurial contingency process described in Figure 3-3 goes beyond traditional rational/analytical processes that attempt to find a sole solution and obtain consensus based on existing and past situation factors. Rather it provides a disciplined and systematic, yet flexible and adaptive, way to view existing factors from multiple perspectives (''what-if'' scenarios, for example), explore future assumptions, to question and reconceive assumptions and solutions through examining and reconciling differences, and consider broader contexts and longer-term horizons as approaches are tried and solutions formulated (Mitroff and Linstone 1993).

The processes involve both planning and doing. Planning at both the enterprise wide and operating level has been given more emphasis in this chapter, which provides the outlines of common frameworks that are useful in multinational cross-cultural management. Chapter 4 places more emphasis on what some consider to be the more difficult, creative and innovative—''doing''—aspects of multinational cross-cultural management.

## WORKS CITED

Bartlett, Christopher A., and Sumantra Ghoshal. *Managing across Borders*. Boston: Harvard Business School Press, 1991.

Brauchli, Marcus. ''Beijing's Grip Weakens as Free Enterprise Turns into Free-for-All.'' *Wall Street Journal*, August 26, 1993, pp. A1, A5.

———. ''Make Your Fortune in Mainland China; E-Z Terms, No Wait.'' *Wall Street Journal*, March 9, 1994, pp. A1, A7.

Bun, Chan Kwok, and Claire Chiang. *Stepping Out: The Making of Chinese Entrepreneurs*. Singapore: Simon and Schuster (Asia); Englewood Cliffs, NJ: Prentice-Hall, 1994.

Cowell, Alan. ''Bonn Treads Carefully with Beijing, Balancing Rights and Business Deals.'' *International Herald Tribune*, July 13, 1995, pp. 1, 7.

Dewey, John. *Logic: The Structure of Inquiry*. New York: Putnam, 1938.

Dologite, Dorothy G., and Robert J. Mockler. *An Information Systems Plan (Strategic and Operational) for the Malaysian Agricultural Research and Development Institute (MARDI)*. Kuala Lumpur, Malaysia: MARDI, 1993.

Dwyer, Paula, Pete Engardio, Zachary Schiller, and Stanley Reed. ''Tearing up Today's Organization Chart: Tomorrow's Winners Will Use Western-Style Accounting, Japanese-Style Teamwork, Advanced Communications, and Give Entrepreneurial Local Managers a Long Leash.'' *Business Week/21st Century Capitalism: Special 1994 Bonus Issue*, November 18, 1994, pp. 80–90.

Engardio, Bruce, Joyce Barnathan, and William Glasgall. ''Watch Out for China.'' *Business Week*, November 29, 1993, pp. 100–108.

Erlanger, Steven. ''Western Economist Quits Russian Post.'' *New York Times*, January 22, 1994a, p. A4.

———. ''Russia Lurches Further along the Capitalist Road.'' *New York Times*, July 5, 1994b, p. A3.

Faison, Seth. ''Dressing Up for an Unconventional Convention.'' *New York Times*, August 11, 1995, p. A4.

Fallows, James. *Looking at the Sun: The Rise of the New East Asian Economic and Political System*. New York: Pantheon Books, 1994.

Frank, Robert. ''Coca-Cola Is Shedding Its Once-Stodgy Image with Swift Expansion: It Pours into East Europe and Asia.'' *Wall Street Journal*, August 22, 1995, pp. A1, A5.

Gooding, Claire. "Accounting Software: A Challenge to US 'Global' Solutions." *Financial Times* (London), July 5, 1995, p. 11.

Greenhouse, Steven. "Polaroid's Russian Success Story." *New York Times*, November 24, 1991, pp. 1, 6.

Hansell, Saul. "500,000 Clients, No Branches." *New York Times*, September 3, 1995, Business Section, pp. 1, 10.

Hart, Stuart, and Catherine Banbury. "How Strategy-Making Processes Can Make a Difference." *Strategic Management Journal* 15 (May 1994): 251–269.

Henry, William A., III. "History as It Happens." *Time*, January 6, 1992, pp. 24–27.

Holden, Jane. "Big Wind Blows across Asia: A Grand-Scale People's Theater Collaboration Tests the Mettle of Artists, Eastern and Western." *American Theater*, September 1995, pp. 16–20, 62–63.

Holland, Kelley, and Paula Dwyer. "Technobanking Takes Off: The Digital Revolution Is Linking People and Companies around the World with Ever More Sophisticated Services." *Business Week/21st Century Capitalism: Special 1994 Bonus Issue*, November 18, 1994, pp. 52, 53.

Imse, Ann. "A Housing Boom Remakes the Russian Landscape." *New York Times*, August 29, 1993a, Business Section, p. 5.

———. "A New Breed of Russian Entrepreneur Takes Risks in Stride." *New York Times*, December 5, 1993b, Business Section, p. 10.

Ingram, Judith. "On the Revolt's Front Line, Kiosks Feel the Fury." *New York Times*, October 19, 1993, p. A4.

Javetski, Bill, and William Glasgall. "Borderless Finance: Fuel for Growth." *Business Week/21st Century Capitalism*, Special 1994 Bonus Issue, November 18, 1994, pp. 40–50.

Jordan, Miriam. "China's Fledgling Airlines, Flush with Pork, Beef Up Their Fleets." *Asian Wall Street Journal*, July 2–3, 1993, p. 1.

Kanter, Rosabeth Moss. *World Class: Thriving Locally in a Global Economy.* New York: Simon & Schuster, 1995.

Kisseloff, Anna. "In San Francisco, the Latest in Ballet as a Global Link." *New York Times*, May 11, 1995, pp. C13, C18.

Kranz, Patricia. "Russia's Really Hostile Takeovers: Organized Crime Is Shooting Its Way into Big Business." *Business Week*, August 14, 1995, pp. 56, 57.

Lewis, Michael. *Pacific Rift: Why Americans and Japanese Don't Understand Each Other.* New York: W. W. Norton, 1993.

Lewis, Peter H. "AT&T Says It Will Offer Internet Access Service." *New York Times*, August 16, 1995, pp. D1, D2.

Lieber, Ronald B. "Here Comes SAP." *Fortune*, October 2, 1995, pp. 122–124.

Lohr, Steve. "Compaq's Conquests in Europe." *New York Times*, July 9, 1989, Business Section, p. 4.

Longman, Jere. "African Olympics Get a Vote for 2004." *New York Times*, October 31, 1993, Sports Sunday, pp. 1, 2.

Milbank, Dana. "Polish Entrepreneurs Revitalize Economy But Battle Huge Odds." *Wall Street Journal*, March 30, 1995, pp. A1, A6.

Mitroff, Ian I., and Harold A. Linstone. *The Unbounded Mind: Breaking the Chains of Traditional Business Thinking.* New York: Oxford University Press, 1993.

Mockler, Robert J. *Strategic Management: An Integrative Context-Specific Process.* Harrisburg, PA: Idea Group Publishing, 1993.

————. "The Chinese Small-Business Family-Based Strategic Profile." Presentation at Pan-Pacific Conference XI, Bangkok, Thailand, June 2–4, 1994.

————. "Measuring Comparative Entrepreneurial Skills in China, Russia, and the United States." Presentation at the Strategic Management Society, Annual Meeting, Mexico City, October 15–18, 1995.

Murray, Tom. "From European to Pan-European." *Business Month*, August 1989, pp. 35–37.

Nashe, Nathaniel C. "Coke's Great Romanian Adventure: In Just Three Years, Coke Has Come from Nowhere to Dominate the Market." *New York Times*, February 26, 1995, Business Section, pp. 1, 10.

Nelan, Bruce. "Watch Out for China." *Time*, November 29, 1993, pp. 36–40.

Noble, Kenneth B. "Thai Workers Are Set Free in California, from What Agents Called Virtual Slavery." *New York Times*, August 4, 1995, pp. A1, A20.

Perlez, Jane, "In Slovakia, Paper Thrives on Change." *New York Times*, June 28, 1993, p. D6.

————. "In a Polish Shipyard, Signals of Eastern Europe's Revival." *New York Times*, July 4, 1995a, pp. 1, 46.

————. "A Post-Marxist Hungarian Bus Maker Takes to Capitalist Road." *New York Times*, August 10, 1995b, p. D3.

————. "The Capitalist Pioneers of Prague." *New York Times*, July 29, 1995c, pp. 35, 36.

Pine, J. Joseph, II. *Mass Customization: The New Frontier in Business Competition.* Boston: Harvard University Press, 1993.

Pollack, Andrew. "Chrysler to Buy Control of Japanese Dealer Chain." *New York Times*, June 27, 1995, pp. D1, D5.

Priem, Richard L., and David A. Harrison. "Exploring Strategic Judgment: Methods for Testing the Assumptions of Prescriptive Contingency Theories." *Strategic Management Journal* 15 (May 1994): 311–324.

Radzievsky, Anna. "On Trade and Cultures: Multicultural Marketing Means Approaching Consumers through Their Complex Cultural Affinities—Symbols, Core Values, Traditions, Political Nuances, and Passions." *Trade and Culture*, January 1996, pp. 16–17.

Rapoport, Carla, with Justin Martin. "Retailers Go Global." *Fortune*, February 20, 1995, pp. 103–108.

Reitman, Valerie. "To Succeed in Russia, U.S. Retailer Employs Patience and Local Ally." *Wall Street Journal*, May 27, 1993, pp. A1, A6.

Riding, Alan. "2000 Olympics Go to Sydney in Surprise Setback for China." *New York Times*, September 24, 1993, pp. A1, B16.

Rigdon, Joan. "Coming Soon to the Internet: Tools to Add Glitz to the Web's Offering." *Wall Street Journal*, August 16, 1995, pp. B1, B5.

Rose, Robert L. "How 3M, by Tiptoeing into Foreign Markets, Became a Big Exporter." *Wall Street Journal*, March 29, 1991, pp. A1, A5.

Sanger, David E. "Honda Raises Its Stake in Europe." *New York Times*, July 14, 1989, pp. D1, D4.

Schemo, Diana Jean. "Brazilians Chained to Job, and Desperate: Of Modern Bondage." *New York Times*, August 10, 1995, pp. A1, A6.

Simons, Marlise. "East Europe Still Choking on Air of the Past." *New York Times*, November 3, 1994, pp. A1, A14.

————. "Save the City Dump! Home Sweet Home to Birds—in Madrid." *New York Times*, August 10, 1995, p. A4.

Stanley, Alessandra. "To the Business Risks in Russia, Add Poisoning." *New York Times*, August 9, 1995, p. A4.

Stevenson, Richard W. "Dresdner Will Pay $1.6 Billion for Kleinwort Benson." *New York Times*, June 17, 1995a, p. D6.

————. "Smitten by Britain: Thatcherism's Industrial Evolution." *New York Times*, October 15, 1995b, pp. 1, 10, Business section.

Treece, James B., Kathleen Kerwin, and Heidi Dawley. "Ford: Alex Trotman's Daring Global Strategy." *Business Week*, April 3, 1995, pp. 94–104.

Truell, Peter. "Aiming for More U.S. Deals: Three European Banks Get Serious about Wall Street." *New York Times*, September 5, 1995, pp. D1, D7.

Uchitelle, Louis. "The Stanley Works Goes Global." *New York Times*, July 23, 1989a, Business Section, pp. 1, 10.

————."U.S. Businesses Loosen Link to Mother Country." *New York Times*, May 21, 1989b, pp. 1, 30.

"World View: Ted Turner's CNN Global Gains Influence." *Wall Street Journal*, February 1, 1990, pp. A1, A6.

WuDunn, Sheryl. "Japanese Do Buy American: By Mail and a Lot Cheaper." *New York Times*, July 3, 1995a, pp. 1, 43.

————. "Many Japanese Women Are Resisting Servility." *New York Times*, July 9, 1995b, p. 10.

Zeien, Albert. "Gillette's Global Marketing Experiences." Talk given at St. John's University's Annual Colman Mockler Leadership Award Ceremony, New York, February 27, 1995.

Zuckerman, Laurence. "With Internet Cachet, Not Profit, A New Stock Is Wall St.'s Darling." *New York Times*, August 10, 1995, pp. A1, D5.

# Chapter 4

# Managing Cultural Differences

---

The common frameworks developed and described in Chapter 3 provide a practical bridge that enables establishing contact and creating a common environment for easier and more efficient planning for, and working in, situations involving different cultures. At the same time, they also provide a mechanism for reconciling, adapting to, managing and putting to good use cultural differences.

However, using common frameworks to bridge cultural gaps, formulate initial enterprisewide marketing and production/operations plans, and establish enabling environments is only a beginning. While these frameworks serve as a common reference point when managing across cultural boundaries, they do not solve all problems, nor can all people understand and adapt easily to them. Differences among cultures can have a major impact on multinational cross-cultural management situations, and managing these differences requires considerable situation-appropriate, innovative, cooperative, creative and resourceful actions by multinational managers.

This chapter discusses, first, the nature of cultural differences and, second, their diverse impact on multinational cross-cultural management. The third section explains how the common links discussed in Chapter 3 can help in managing cross-cultural differences. The fourth section of the chapter examines other less systematic and disciplined ways to handle a wide range of decisions and actions involved in multinational cross-cultural management situations. This discussion of managing cultural differences in multinational cross-cultural situations continues in Chapters 9 through 13, which cover organization and human resources management.

Many situations require creative, innovative, and resourceful, ad hoc management solutions, which break the mold and go beyond any rational logic framework. The final sections of this chapter discuss these types of situation-by-situation implementation processes.

## CULTURAL FACTORS

One of the key differences faced in multinational management arises from the different cultures found around the world. The term *culture* refers to shared values, beliefs, attitudes, expectations and norms found within countries, regions, social groups, industries, corporations, and even departments and work groups within a business firm. Culture is "that complex whole which includes knowledge, belief, art, morals, customs, and any other capabilities and habits acquired by man as a member of society" (Herskovits 1952, p. 17). It is a distinctive way of life of a group of people—their complete design for living (Kluckhohn 1951, p. 86); it comprises "the behavioral norms that a group of people, at a certain time and place, have agreed upon to survive and coexist (Elashmawi 1993, p. 50).

Culture is acquired and socially enforced. Rather than inheriting culture at birth, an individual learns a set or rules and behavior patterns. For every society, these norms and behavioral responses develop into different cultural patterns that are passed down through the generations with continual embellishment and adaptation.

For many individuals, cultural conditioning is like an iceberg—they are unaware of nine-tenths of it. The subtle process of inculcating culture over time through example, reward and punishment is generally much more powerful than direct instruction, and individuals tend to unwittingly adopt the cultural norms. This process of learning a cultural pattern, called *acculturation*, conditions individuals so that a large portion of their behavior will fit the requirements of their culture and is determined below the level of conscious thought (Herskovits 1963, p. 326; Robock 1993). The depth and breadth of the enculturation process explains in part why it is so difficult to break cultural patterns.

Many dimensions of culture can be identified. A manager's first experience of a new culture is often through exposure to its less esoteric, more concrete components. This is the level of *explicit culture*. Explicit culture is the observable reality of language and communication styles, time and space orientation, work habits and practices, all forms of interpersonal and social relationships, food and eating habits, dress and appearance, fashions and art, public buildings, houses, monuments, agriculture, shrines, and markets (Trompenaars 1994).

Explicit culture can change over time, however. For example, in Argentina, where the production and consumption of beef is an important factor in the economy, people are becoming more health conscious. As a result, Argentines are altering their eating habits and eating less beef (Sims 1995). Similarly, the Japanese are beginning to adopt longer-lasting, Western-style homes to replace traditional, less well-constructed, Japanese-style homes (Andrews 1995), while in London's financial district, traditional British merchant bankers have been gradually replaced by more aggressive European- and American-style bankers (Stevenson 1995). While these changes are evident, significant external cultural differences persist. For example, both Ford and General Motors still find it necessary to manufacture right-hand drive cars for sale in Australia, Japan, New Zealand and Great Britain ("Ford Will Get a Japanese Loan" 1995).

Explicit cultural differences are often symbols of a deeper level of culture which involves norms and values, beliefs and attitudes, and mental processes. *Norms* are a group's collective sense of what is right or wrong. Norms can develop on a formal level as written laws or on an informal level as social control. Norms are sometimes referred to as character traits in educational programs (Johnson 1995). *Values*, on the other hand, define good and bad and are therefore closely related to the beliefs and attitudes shared by the group. In order to understand basic differences in values, beliefs and attitudes, and in the mental processes that reflect them, the history of groups and their struggles for survival need to be examined. Labeled factors of *implicit culture*, these are basic assumptions that are *imbedded* in a culture (Trompenaars 1994).

Deeply imbedded cultural differences can significantly affect society. For example, deep and pervasive differences in Czechoslovakia led to the country's division into two sections, the Czech Republic and Slovakia, after the breakup of the USSR in 1991. This occurred in spite of the country's small size (10,298,731 population and 30,442 square miles—smaller than the state of Maine) and the fact that it created severe political and economic hardships for the new Slovak nation (King 1995). The extensive fighting among the Serbes, Croats, and Muslims in the former Yugoslavia, which necessitated the intervention of the United Nations during 1995, arose in part from deeply imbedded cultural differences (Perlez 1995). In 1995 in Canada, such differences led the Province of Quebec to vote, by only a narrow margin (50.6 to 49.4 percent), to remain part of Canada and not secede to form a new nation. Many wondered whether the bitter election campaign was a harbinger of the eventual disintegration of the Canadian nation (Farnsworth 1995).

The Japanese culture provides another example (Chua-Eaon 1995). Developed over hundreds of years of isolation from the rest of the world, the Japanese culture had evolved in the twentieth century into a very closed society, which was suspicious of the rest of the world. These deep cultural biases have been cited as a major cause of the Japanese aggression during World War II: "Hiroshima was simply the end of a ferocious clash of cultures, fueled by intense hatreds and a history of humiliation" (Chua-Ehon 1995, p. 48). Such biases may also have prompted the subsequent Japanese economic aggressiveness. Even today, considerable distrust, and even hatred, persists among some sectors of the Chinese, United States and Japanese populations, a basic cultural barrier that must be taken into account in business and political dealings among the countries.

The Chinese culture has been influenced significantly by Confucian philosophy, an understanding of which is useful when doing business in China (Kraar 1994). For example, China's long tradition of family-based business draws in many ways on Confucian philosophy (Mockler 1994). The international impact of this tightly controlled, family-based approach has been enormous. For instance, in Malaysia in the early 1990s, the Chinese comprised only 28 percent of the population yet controlled over 50 percent of the wealth (Dologite and Mockler 1993). As described in *Stepping Out: The Making of Chinese Entrepreneurs*, the impact of this family-based approach has also been felt in Singapore (Chan and Chiang 1994). Furthermore, the Chinese have a long tradition of international trade, extending back thousands of years to the ancient "Silk Road," which served as a trading link westward to Europe. This cultural tradition encourages international contacts and exchanges and suggests that China is primed to significantly expand and eventually become a dominant force in international trade.

Clearly, cultural differences can have a major impact on multinational management. Failing to recognize and effectively manage them accounts for many of the blunders committed every day by thousands of international executives around the world.

## THE IMPACT OF CULTURAL DIFFERENCES ON MULTINATIONAL CROSS-CULTURAL MANAGEMENT

The wide range of cultural differences that impact multinational cross-cultural management dictates formulating an overall conceptual framework to help in organizing, understanding and dealing with multinational cross-cultural management situations. The discussion in this section describes one such conceptual framework. This working guideline has proved useful to many managers who wish to become sensitized to cultural differences—a critical first step in adapting to and managing such differences.

Five critical aspects of cultural diversity can be identified as convenient reference points for busy managers:

- social/people relationships factors
- status factors
- language/information flow factors
- time (monochronic versus polychronic) factors
- other factors: corporate culture, institution, business and individual

Before discussing these perspectives, some general guidelines should be reviewed.

1. While it is useful to explore generalities and their implications, individuals do not always conform to general cultural stereotypes—not all Japanese, for example, are "typical" Japanese and "typical" Japanese may vary by age, sex and other demographic categories. For instance, young women in all countries now share many common values, as was demonstrated in the August 1995

United Nations Conference on Women in Beijing, which has led to major differences in Japan between the values of younger and older groups of women (Tyler 1995).

2. Differences are not always culturally based. Some arise from individual personality differences; some from personal, institutional, or business factors. This is true in any country. In addition, any given action may be stimulated by a variety of cultural biases that reinforce each other.

3. Do not assume that because something works in one culture, it will work in another. Sometimes there is communality across cultural boundaries, as with the common frameworks described earlier in this book and the increasing trends toward more global products, services and communications. This is especially true among younger generations in all countries. However, significant differences will always exist.

4. Understand yourself and your own culture first, so that you may be more aware of your own biases or mental set and have a benchmark against which to study others.

5. Study cultural diversity within your own country; it will yield clues to cultural differences and to how to handle diversity. The United States, for example, is known as the melting pot of the world since it has a wide range of cultures within its borders.

6. The following discussion focuses on continuums, that is, as a set of two extremes between which there can be many and varied gradations; try to avoid thinking in terms of extreme black-and-white stereotypes.

7. Ultimately, it is best to learn as much as you can about cultural and personal sensitivities *specific to the situation with which you are dealing*, in much the same way as you would in any situation involving other human beings.

8. The same words often have different connotations in different cultures: for example, the French sense of "individualistic" is very different from a North American's sense of "individualism," and both differ from a Latin American's understanding of either word.

### Social/People Relationships Factors

Two important aspects of culture are covered in this section: the emphasis on personal relationships and the focus on groups versus individuals.

*Personal Relationships.* The social context and human aspects of a situation are given different emphases in different cultures. They are, for example, very important to Asians. For this reason, Asians tend to develop personal relationships with the parties involved before getting to the specifics of a negotiation. This explains why family relationships are frequently so important to doing business in China. At the other end of the continuum (shown in Figure 4-1, section A), Americans are likely to get to the point more quickly and perhaps rely on superficial friendly remarks as a quick way to get things started. In

**Figure 4-1**
**Sample Continuums Representing the Range of Cultural Differences**

A. Importance of Personal Relationships

B. Dealing with Difficult Problems

C. Working in Teams

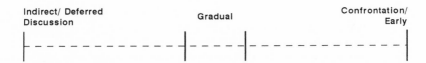

D. Importance of Status and Position

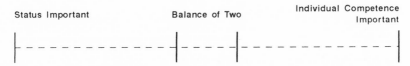

Copyright © 1996 by R. J. Mockler.

general, to Americans, personal relationships are less important than other factors when doing business (Engholm 1991).

Focusing on developing personal relationships in theory is not uncommon among salespeople anywhere in the world when getting to know their customer; the way it is done in different countries, however, can differ. For example, in Egypt it takes significantly more time to develop a relationship that will lead to a sale than it might in North America (Elashmawi 1993).

One implication for business of this varying emphasis on personal relationships is, for example, that a more complex task or negotiation may require more time in order to build a human relationship context in cultures that place more emphasis on personal relationships. As a result, while interpersonal communication media across cultures might in some instances be effective for dealing with simple subjects, face-to-face meetings might be more effective for complex cross-cultural undertakings.

Along another continuum shown in Figure 4-1, section B, at one cultural extreme—for example, in Asia and some Latin American cultures—there can be a tendency to keep relations harmonious by not talking directly about problems. Confrontation is avoided in regions where human relationships are highly valued. In contrast, North Americans, for example, tend to confront problems quickly and directly, in spite of the fact that such an approach might embarrass someone personally and publicly (Foster 1992).

These factors can also affect other business areas, for example, office layouts. Socially oriented people and cultures are more likely to favor open office layouts without office dividers, since this kind of layout promotes interpersonal communications. In contrast, task-oriented people and cultures, such as are found in North America, are more likely to prefer separate, enclosed offices to promote individual effort and concentration.

*Individualism and Groups.* Cultures with a high social conscience, such as in China, tend to favor the belief that "God helps those who help each other," and prefer to work in teams and make decisions by group consensus. As shown in Figure 4-1, section C, at the other extreme there are cultures, such as in North America, that place a high premium on individualism and individualistic reactions, and so believe instead that "God helps those who help themselves." Such people are more likely to be more individualistic and are not inherently team players.

### Status Factors

As shown in Figure 4-1, section D, at one end of the status continuum, some cultures, such as those in Asia, northern Europe, and South America, place great value on social status. This is reflected in, for example, seating arrangements and other protocols based on position. At the other extreme, Americans tend to give more importance to competence (Engholm 1991).

In cultures where status is important, as in Japan and Egypt, talking about problems directly with a person in public tends to be avoided in order not to embarrass him or her or downgrade his or her status (Elashmawi 1993).

### Language and Information Flow Factors

The most immediate and obvious cultural difference is language. Obviously, in multinational cross-cultural management, the more languages one speaks, the better. In practice, except in rare instances, this is almost impossible for most of us. English is the generally accepted language of business, and so most international managers will be using a secondary language, which is not their own.

Problems can arise due to uncertainty, self-consciousness, and hesitancy when using a second language. Sensitivity to this possibility and an appreciation of the enormous effort that has been made by people from non-English-speaking countries to bridge the language gap are important. Others often think Americans arrogant since they expect others to speak English, and this resentment must be overcome when encountered in business dealings.

Even when English is used, misunderstandings and problems can arise. For example, the word "right" can mean "opposite of left," "correct" or "to redo something." Colloquialisms, such as saying, "Run that by me again," instead of, "Please repeat that," are easy to misconstrue. Jargon and idioms—for example, "That idea comes out of left field"—make sense only in a culture that enjoys baseball. Moreover, jokes rarely travel well across cultural borders.

Interpretations of body language can also vary among cultures. Cultural differences can account for misunderstandings about personal space that may arise during conversations. For example, members of socially oriented cultures tend to stand very close while talking, while others, including Americans, prefer to keep a little more distance between speakers during a conversation. Eye contact also has different meanings in different cultures. Not looking directly at someone might be interpreted as a sign of respect in India, where intensely looking someone in the eye is considered disrespectful. Of course, the opposite is the case in many Western cultures. As another example, an American businessperson whose hand is suddenly taken by a Thai associate or who is embraced by a Latin business partner might attribute a sexual meaning to the gesture where in fact there is none. In turn a Thai or Latin associate meeting American resistance to these nonverbal gestures might attribute an attitude of coldness and indifference to the American when this, too, is not the case (Foster 1992).

The way in which information is conveyed also varies by culture. For example, a typical Western trait, especially in Germany and the United States, is to talk about "getting straight to the point." In other cultures, however, both the speed and path of information flow can vary. As seen in the examples, "getting to the point" may first involve "getting to know each other," which paradoxically can take much more time. Moreover, more than one topic (including family affairs), may be a part of the information flow path involved in getting to know each other.

### Time (Monochronic versus Polychronic) Factors

Northern Europeans (strongly) and Americans (moderately) tend to favor treating events in an "orderly" fashion, one at a time. This is a monochronic time perspective. Monochronic time is linear: things are done separately, one after another. Time is compartmentalized, organized and controlled. It is commodity that has value because of its scarcity and its usefulness in defining the context in which activity occurs.

A polychronic time, on the other hand, is more circular. It is endless; there is plenty of it and it has no beginning or end. Most important, many things can happen at once. This cultural perspective is prevalent in Arab countries, Central and Southern Asia, and Latin American countries such as Mexico. At conferences in these regions, many topics, involving both the family and business, may be discussed at once—both because it is part of the ritual of "getting to know each other" and because there is less pressure to stick to an agenda.

Monochronic cultures also tend to focus on the present or immediate future and to believe that an individual can affect future outcomes. Polychronic cultures tend to be more futuristic and fatalistic—as in the dictum, "Whatever will be, will be." This might lead to an attitude that since one cannot control tomorrow, one should make the best of today.

### Other Factors: Corporate Culture, Institution, Business and Individual

It is important not to become so absorbed in cultural differences as to lose sight of the fact that individual actions are influenced by many factors in addition to cultural elements. At times, individual personalities can dominate. Moreover, corporate cultures can influence interpersonal interactions, since a company may impose policy restrictions on employees, for example, in setting limits on their ability to make decisions. Government institutions worldwide may also have these kinds of restrictions. Moreover, business conditions can influence action, as when inflation rates in a particular country are so high that it is impossible to write specific guarantees into contracts. All these factors, as well as cultural elements, can influence the success of interpersonal interactions.

## MANAGING DIFFERENCES WITHIN COMMON FRAMEWORKS: CONTINGENCY PROCESSES

The second aspect of cross-cultural management discussed in this book concerns managing *differences* (or diversity) among cultures and putting them to work effectively in business. In a sense, this is not unlike the management situation faced by any company with a culturally diverse workforce in any country in the world.

Recognition is an important first step toward managing and using cultural differences. Strategic management initially involves enterprisewide planning and planning in functional areas, which requires identifying specific situation requirements. When managing differences, therefore, one can make use of the common contingency frameworks described in Chapter 3.

Figure 4-2 models a contingency decision process involved in introducing a new product into a country served by a large pharmaceutical company. It is a well-defined, context-specific contingency decision process, of which computerized prototypes are available (Mockler 1993).

As seen from the top of the Figure 4-2, country-specific situation information first is systematically gathered on distinctive customer characteristics *in the specific country and business market under study*. This might include information on different tastes, cultural taboos, and local preferences, in addition to demographic information on age, income and other information normally gathered in

**Figure 4-2**
**Diagram of Decision Area to Be Prototyped: New Product Strategy for Local Country Product Proposal**

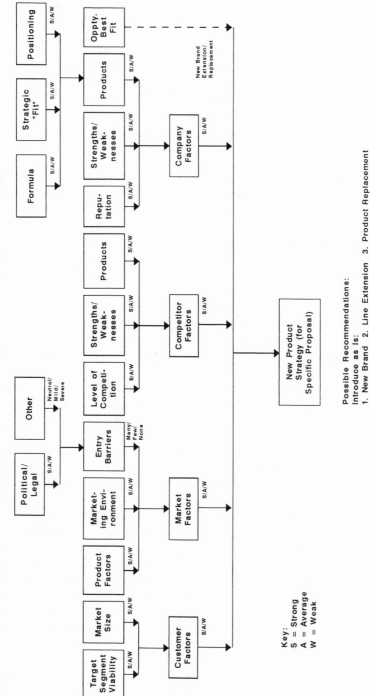

Key:
S = Strong
A = Average
W = Weak

Possible Recommendations:
Introduce as Is:
1. New Brand  2. Line Extension  3. Product Replacement

Adapt/Change before Introducing As:
4. New Brand  5. Line Extension  6. Product Replacement  7. Reject
Proposed Product

Copyright © 1995 by R. J. Mockler.

any free-market study anywhere in the world. The Chinese entrepreneur starting a new children's beverage company whose new venture-planning process was described in Chapter 1 provided an outstanding and sophisticated example of how such a context-specific study is done. In this case, for example, a context analysis led the entrepreneur to develop a soy-based drink which apparently appealed to Chinese children but (based on field taste tests) not American children.

The process modeled in Figure 4-2 also includes analyses of the country's specific distinctive market, product, competitor, legal, political and other relevant situation factors. All this information is situation specific. In that sense, the model itself is a general strategic management contingency process, which can be used to gather and provide the information needed to formulate plans appropriate for the specific country under study and also to implement plans in the same appropriate way. This strategic management contingency process also serves as a basis for accommodating, adapting to and reconciling differences among national cultures in business contexts.

Following the process model in Figure 4-2, modifications may be required. For example, when studying one new product it was found that the formula had to be modified to meet local tastes, the product had to be treated as a line extension because of specific competitive pressures, and local advertising and promotion had to be done through media channels and in formats appropriate to, and available in, the country. Making these changes to suit local cultural differences clearly required considerable local knowledge and information (Mockler 1989, ch. 18). In this case, reconciling differences was a relatively straightforward business planning, marketing and operations task, not unlike those found in new venture situations anywhere in the world. At other times, reconciling differences can involve resolving problems in more creative and innovative ways.

A failure to plan and manage carefully can create problems—even when pursuing culturally sound ventures and managing locally popular enterprises. For example, sorghum beer, the first drink served at any African wedding or funeral, is as important as wine is at the traditional Christian or Jewish wedding. In 1990, as apartheid waned, the franchise to brew sorghum beer, as well as twenty state-owned breweries, was incorporated and returned to black ownership. The new company, National Sorghum Breweries, with many of its 44 million shares held by small shareholders, became the largest black-owned industrial enterprise in South Africa. While successful at first, the brewery—whose beer is as old as the Stone Age, is shipped unrefrigerated and must be drunk within four days—gradually fell on hard times. The beer's deteriorating image (it is considered a "peasant" beer), high interest rates, lack of a niche-marketing plan, fierce competition, an unwise acquisition and construction of an unneeded large brewery all contributed to problems that led to the company's sale in 1995 to a major Indian brewery (McNeil 1995). The experiences of National Sorghum Breweries show that taking cultural differences into account is only one part of a successful multinational business equation. No matter what the culture or country, good planning and management, a common business management framework, are essential for dealing with competitive market conditions.

## OTHER COMMON FRAMEWORKS FOR MANAGING DIFFERENCES

In addition to the situation analysis framework described in the preceding section, other common frameworks are useful in multinational cross-cultural situations. These include the telecommunications/information systems and accounting/finance frameworks described in Chapter 3. While useful in planning and setting up enabling contexts and environments, these frameworks are, in many situations, too analytical and rational to meet situation needs that arise from human resource factors.

Other approaches more oriented to human resource management, such as organization structure, processes and culture, interpersonal interaction, communications, staffing and training, and leadership and management (identified in Chapter 3), are needed in multinational cross-cultural management situations. These are discussed in the following sections of this chapter and in Chapters 9 through 13.

## MANAGING CROSS-CULTURAL DIFFERENCES: SITUATION-BY-SITUATION OVERVIEW

Not all situations can be handled within the common frameworks discussed in Chapter 3. Instead, many must be handled situation by situation, on an ad hoc basis. This section and the next discuss some systematic guidelines for handling such multinational cross-cultural management situations.

As multinational cross-cultural management business experiences show, reconciling and managing differences generally seems to involve five kinds of approaches: modifying one's own behavior and adapting to a situation, taking steps to change the situation environment, abandoning the situation or project (Chatman 1989), exploiting the differences wherever possible, or using any combination of the first four.

### Being Sensitive to, Accepting and Adapting to Differences

Sensitivity, acceptance and adaptation comprise the approach most often written about. Thousands of examples (including the one outlined in Figure 4-2) exist of companies modifying products, reconfiguring manufacturing facilities, adapting advertising and making other moves to accommodate local country situation requirements.

In many situations, a multinational or market-by-market approach is required by local circumstances. Accommodating local tastes was, for example, a problem for Scott Paper Company in Europe. England, France, and the Mediterranean countries each required different products, different product names, and different kinds of advertising approaches. Scott, therefore, concentrated initially on accommodating local differences in each of the European countries, although there was considerable regional coordination as well (Lampert 1989; Mockler 1993, ch. 13).

Many of the cultural differences that must be recognized and adapted to were discussed in the first section of this chapter. Thousands of others exist—including simple things like conference protocols for seating arrangements, the way to address individuals, the order in which they are to be addressed, the time to discuss personal matters and the time to discuss business, what to wear on different occasions, where to go for entertainment, and what to serve for meals. Knowing and adapting to a seemingly unending list of customs and habits is useful in many business and personal dealings.

Many books guide business managers and businesses in adapting to, surviving, and prospering in local cultures. For example, *When Business East Meets Business West* (Engholm 1991) focuses on Asia. Another book, *GlobalWork*, covers worldwide situations (O'Hara-Devereaux and Johansen 1994).

Chapter 10 provides a step-by-step discussion of this cross-cultural management process, as well as specific guidelines for thinking about, organizing, adapting to and managing cross-cultural differences. However, experience has shown that several other contingency approaches exist to managing differences. While adapting to local customers is, at times, effective, it is not always the best approach. Other approaches are discussed in the following paragraphs.

### Not Accepting Differences and Taking Appropriate Steps to Modify the Impact of Cultural Differences or Situation Circumstances

With the growing sophistication of international business managers, a small but noticeable trend toward increasingly sophisticated manipulation of the expectations arising from this growing awareness of cultural differences has emerged. For example, a Japanese negotiator might be aware that sophisticated Americans know negotiations in Japan can take longer because of the cultural need to get to know each other. This can then be exploited, for example, by using this cultural rationale simply to wear down American negotiators and create time-scheduling problems and the need for hasty, last-minute decisions.

As another example, the phrase, "This is the custom (or way we do it) here in my country" may surface during legal negotiations anywhere in the world. Fortunately, those experienced in legal negotiations in the United States know that this phrase often crops up during negotiations there as well. When used by lawyers during many business negotiations in the United States, this phrase invariably is used as a justification for someone else to pay additional expenses not previously agreed on. It is essentially a negotiating ploy used to con someone into paying for something, such as a property transfer fee, that s/he does not have to pay for. An obvious way to handle such a situation in the United States is to keep one's temper and point out that each negotiation is a separate event and each item is open to negotiation, regardless of precedents; past practices are irrelevant. The same can be done in negotiations overseas.

Another commonly encountered exploitive scenario involves depending on a relationship of trust to avoid difficult decisions. For example, during a negotiation someone may try to avoid committing to deadlines by saying, "You can trust me," in an attempt to find an excuse to avoid making a normal business commitment. It is not always necessary to yield or adapt in this or other situations. Professionalism, and not retaliation, is often more appropriate when you sense that someone appears to be trying to exploit you, as he or she may simply be testing your limits.

Ignoring or circumventing alleged and real local differences and customs has proved useful in many areas. Many readers are familiar with the picture of President George Bush becoming ill in Asia, presumably from excessive toasting. In contrast, in over 100 business dinner banquets the authors attended in Asia, no one ever served high-alcohol-content liquor or smoked. This occurred simply because the hosts were informed that someone in the authors' party was highly allergic to smoke and that for health reasons, wine was the only alcohol desired. It was indicated that we realized the impoliteness of refusing to toast with hard liquor and wanted to avoid being impolite, but that if we were served liquor we would politely raise the glass but be unable to actually join in the drinking. If the guests smoked, the person who was allergic to smoke would have to leave the room since her eyes would begin to water and she would begin coughing.

These requests created no problems. Courtesy to guests and hospitality are strongly rooted in the Chinese culture and so made compliance with our requests normal and acceptable. In addition, some cultures, such as the Muslims, do not allow the drinking of any alcohol. Sophisticated executives and managers in Asia apparently are used to accommodating justifiable requests based on cultural differences, providing they are timely and politely introduced.

### Abandoning or Greatly Reducing Involvement in a Project

Gillette threatened to employ this tactic initially when negotiating to build a plant in Russia. The company in part delayed investing until currency regulations restricting repatriation of the dollar had been modified and other guarantees had been worked out.

In another instance, during mid-1995 India experienced a backlash against foreign investments, which was fueled largely by internal political rivalries. A multibillion-dollar electrical power plant project with Envron Corp. of Houston, Texas, was canceled, and an attempt was made to close a Kentucky Fried Chicken outlet and otherwise discredit its multinational parent company,

PepsiCo. While many companies, such as the cereal company Kellogg, were prospering in India, many others adopted a wait-and-see attitude toward investing in India as a result of such incidents (Burns 1995; Greenwald et al. 1995).

### Exploiting the Differences

For example, American Family Corporation Inc. (Aflaco) of Columbus, Georgia, a leading supplier of cancer insurance, was able to use a niche strategy in Japan because of cultural differences and persistence. In the United States there is very little interest in separate insurance policies for individual sicknesses, which accounted for the low sales of cancer insurance policies. In Japan, however, cancer was recognized as a serious concern and regular insurance policies paid minimal cancer benefits, making the culture—and the market—favorable for separate cancer insurance policies. It took the company four years to meet and accommodate all the local legal and regulatory requirements needed to get a license to sell insurance in Japan. However, once licensed, the company received the favorable treatment, which is generally afforded to Japanese companies but denied to most foreign competitors. In 1991, 75 percent of Aflaco's $3.5 billion in revenue came from Japan (Lohr 1992).

In another situation, when selecting projects to invest in China, if the venture is small, the main protection from the impact of unfamiliar differences is a *strong family or personal relationship.* Since contract law is not very enforceable in China and contract terms are frequently modified as circumstances change during the life of the contract, a great deal of mutual trust and respect are needed to do conduct business equitably. Such trust can often be established through strong family or personal relationships.

Large firms have a different kind of protection, since if they complain publicly about abuse, withdraw or otherwise voice dissatisfaction, the attendant publicity can hurt the investment image of the country or local government involved. Since local governments need success stories to attract more investment, this works as an incentive for them to comply with international business contract standards when dealing with large, well-known global companies.

## A BALANCED PERSPECTIVE WHEN MANAGING CROSS-CULTURAL DIFFERENCES

Almost every business management situation anywhere in the world has differences among participating parties that must be reconciled. Taking the time to establish personal relationships has to be balanced with time limitations and situation requirements. At one extreme, General Electric took almost four years to introduce changes into its workforce in its Hungarian light bulb plant, as it gradually introduced its corporatewide programs in which the workers formed teams. Only gradually did Hungarian workers adapt to working together in teams and become receptive to American participative management styles and production efficiency methods (Perlez 1994).

In other situations, overemphasizing culture-based differences can cause a manager to forget the many other factors—individual personalities, institutional and corporate cultures factors, and general business conditions—which can account for differences. In addition, layers of cultural influences can exist, some of which will be deeply imbedded, while others may be external and subject to change.

Indeed, many customs are changing in countries around the world. For example, many Japanese are becoming more thrifty; they are changing their shopping habits and spending less than in the past (WuDunn 1995). An even more surprising generational change seems to be occurring in Mexico. For example, when fears arose in 1995 over possible violence during student demonstrations, it turned out that the students were demonstrating to obtain better access to training for professional careers in business and law. Rather than threatening violence, they were simply young potential professionals demonstrating peacefully and renouncing force, interested instead in very mainstream, traditional, Western-style objectives (Preston 1995).

Even when times are good and businesses are successful, not all the people within a culture will be in agreement. For example, in 1995 Norway was expected to become the second-largest oil exporter in the world, second only to Saudi Arabia. While all the new wealth has benefited many Norwegians through new and expanded social programs, some complain that the money has been misused and misdirected—a common complaint in most democratic countries. A more serious concern is the future. Questions are being asked about whether Norway has gone too far in institutionalizing social programs and created dependency in the culture. While these programs are currently affordable, many worry that as oil prices fluctuate and oil reserves are depleted, cutbacks will be needed, with the potential to cause major social and economic dislocations. These critics are advocating a long-term approach that limits the funding of these longer-term programs and tempers near-term spending (Pope 1995). In this manner, a country's cultural values tend to evolve over the years as such differences are resolved.

In such a rapidly changing and increasingly sophisticated global business environment, overemphasizing differences can often create barriers to building cultural bridges and create a negative, counterproductive atmosphere. It can also, at times, leave one vulnerable to exploitation. Personal experience and a growing body of research literature shows that often too much is made of differences too early in business and business education situations. Rather than draw premature conclusions, the unique requirements of each situation must be studied.

Most often it is necessary to accommodate differences in some ways. It is not necessary to become like a Japanese or Russian in order to deal with one, however. Rather, it is necessary to recognize and adapt to the other's customs in the same way you might reasonably expect him or her to adapt to and accommodate yours. A mutual give-and-take process will help create a balance.

Chapters 9 through 13 discuss further techniques for managing interpersonal relationships, as well as the impact of cultural differences on organization, negotiations, communications, staffing and training, and leadership and management. These chapters also cover the balanced give-and-take required to succeed when interacting with culturally diverse peoples in a wide range of multinational cross-cultural management situations.

## WORKS CITED

Andrews, Edward, "Raise the Roof Beams, Japan: A Boom in 'Imported' Housing Built the Western Way." *New York Times*, September 14, 1995, pp. D1, D6.

Burns, John F. "India Nationalists Oppose Presence of a U.S. Chain." *New York Times*, September 14, 1995, p. D5.

Chan, Kwok Bun, and Claire Chiang. *Stepping Out: The Making of Chinese Entrepreneurs*. New York: Prentice Hall, 1994.

Chatman, Jennifer A. "Improving Interactional Organizational Research: A Model of Person-Organization Fit." *Academy of Management Review* (July 1989): 333–349.

Chua-Eoan, Howard. "War of the Worlds." *Time*, August 7, 1995, pp. 42–53.

Dologite, Dorothy G., and Robert J. Mockler. *An Information Systems Plan (Strategic and Operational) for the Malaysian Agricultural Research and Development Institute (MARDI)*. Kuala Lumpur, Malaysia: MARDI, 1993.

Elashmawi, Fadrid, and Philip R. Harris. *Multicultural Management; New Skills for Global Success*. Houston, TX: Gulf Publishing Company, 1993.

Engholm, Christopher. *When Business East Meets Business West*. New York: Wiley, 1991.

Farnsworth, Clyde H. "Quebec, by Razor-Thin Margin, Votes 'No' on Leaving Canada." *New York Times*, October 31, 1995, pp. A1, A12.

"Ford Will Get a Japanese Loan for Right-Hand-Drive Cars." *New York Times*, September 5, 1995, p. D2.

Foster, Dean Allen, *Bargaining Across Borders: How to Negotiate Business Successfully Anywhere in the World*. New York: McGraw-Hill, 1992.

Greenwald, John, Anita Pretap, Dick Thompson, and Scribala Subramanian. "No Passage to India: American Firms Face an Antiforeign Backlash in the World's Largest Democracy." *Time*, September 18, 1995, pp. 91–92.

Herskovits, Melville J. *Man and His Works*. New York: Knopf, 1952.

———. *Cultural Anthropology*. New York: Knopf, 1963.

Johnson, Kirk. "Character Makes a Comeback." *New York Times*, August 6, 1995, p. 33.

King, Neil, Jr. "Meciar Mounts Hostile Bid for Slovakia: Public Jobs Go to Cronies, as Does Much of Wealth in Suspect Privatization." *Wall Street Journal*, September 20, 1995, p. A13.

Kluckhohn, Clyde. "The Study of Culture." In *The Policy Services*, ed. Daniel Lerner and Harold D. Lasswell. Stanford, CA: Stanford University Press, 1951.

Kraar, Louis. "The Overseas Chinese: Lessons from the World's Most Dynamic Capitalists." *Fortune*, October 31, 1994, pp. 91–114.

Lampert, Hope. "Marketing to Local Tastes." *Business Month*, August 1989, pp. 37–41.

Lohr, Steve. "Under the Wing of Japan Inc., a Fledgling Enterprise Soared." *New York Times*, January 15, 1992, pp. A1, D5.

McNeil, Donald G., Jr. "Not Thriving in Its Homeland: Beer Disappoints as Black South African Business." *New York Times*, October 3, 1995, pp. D1, D4.

Mockler, Robert J. *Knowledge-Based Systems for Strategic Planning*. Englewood Cliffs, NJ: Prentice-Hall, 1989.

———. *Strategic Management: An Integrative Context-Specific Process*. Harrisburg, PA: Idea Group Publishing, 1993.

———. "The Chinese Small-Business Family-Based Strategic Profile." Presentation at Pan-Pacific Conference XI, Bangkok, Thailand, June 2–4, 1994.

O'Hara-Devereaux, Mary, and Robert Johansen. *GlobalWork: Bridging Distance, Culture and Time*. San Francisco: Jossey-Bass, 1994.

Perlez, Jane. "G. E. Finds Tough Going in Hungary." *New York Times*, July 25, 1994, pp. D1, D8.

———. "Serbs Become Latest Victims in Changing Fortunes of War." *New York Times*, August 7, 1995, pp. A1, A6.

Pope, Kyle. "Uneasy Boom: Norway's Oil Bonanza Stirs Fears of a Future When Wells Run Dry; As Output Climbs, Many Say Money Is Being Wasted and Slump Lies Ahead." *Wall Street Journal*, October 3, 1995, pp. A1, A10.

Preston, Julia, "Mexico's New Rebel Students Just Want Careers." *New York Times*, October 3, 1995, p. A3.

Robock, Stefan H. "The Export Myopia of U.S. Multinationals: Overlooked Opportunity for Creating U.S. Manufacturing Jobs." *Columbia Journal of World Business* 22 (Summer 1993): 24–32.

Sims, Calvin. "Will Tofu Replace the T-Bone as a National Dish? Health Issues and Economics Force Argentines to Alter Their Eating Habits." *New York Times*, September 29, 1995, p. A4.

Stevenson, Richard W. "Egos and Loafers on the Rise: British Ways Are Rapidly Disappearing in the City." *New York Times*, August 25, 1995, pp. D1, D17.

Trompenaars, Fons. *Riding the Wave of Culture: Understanding Diversity in Global Business*. Burr Ridge, IL: Irwin Professional Publishing, 1994.

Tyler, Patrick. "Forum on Women Agrees on Goals." *New York Times*, September 15, 1995, pp. A1, A3.

WuDunn, Sheryl. "The Pinched Yen: Freeze Rice and Save Bath Water." *New York Times*, September 15, 1995, p. A3.

Part II

# Decision Making and Action in Multinational Cross-Cultural Management

Chapter 5

# Multinational Cross-Cultural Management: Overview of the Strategic Context

Multinational cross-cultural management is built on, and so starts from, knowledge of the situation. This chapter concerns the context analysis involved in acquiring and structuring the knowledge needed for strategic management decision making and action in multinational situations. The relation of this context analysis process to the strategic management process is shown in Figure 5-1.

This chapter gives an overview of the basic context analysis framework within which one:

- formulates an enterprise's strategic vision; enterprisewide, business unit and functional/operating strategies, plans and programs; and enabling systems, and
- carries them out through leading and managing their implementation, now and in the future, in a balanced and integrated way.

This chapter discusses how the specific external and internal situation factors encountered in multinational cross-cultural management situations are structured and analyzed. The discussion is divided into three sections, covering the general external environment, competitive market environment and internal company environment.

The time and effort required to perform the strategic context study described in this chapter depends, of course, on the knowledge, training and experience of the manager involved. For example, a consultant who was unfamiliar with a company or industry involved in an assignment would need considerably more time in preparing a context study than an experienced executive who had worked for years in the field. A student who was unfamiliar with the industry and company and also lacked extensive business experience would expend even more time and effort in doing a thorough context study.

Figure 5-1
Overall Multinational Operations Approach to Making Strategic Management Decisions

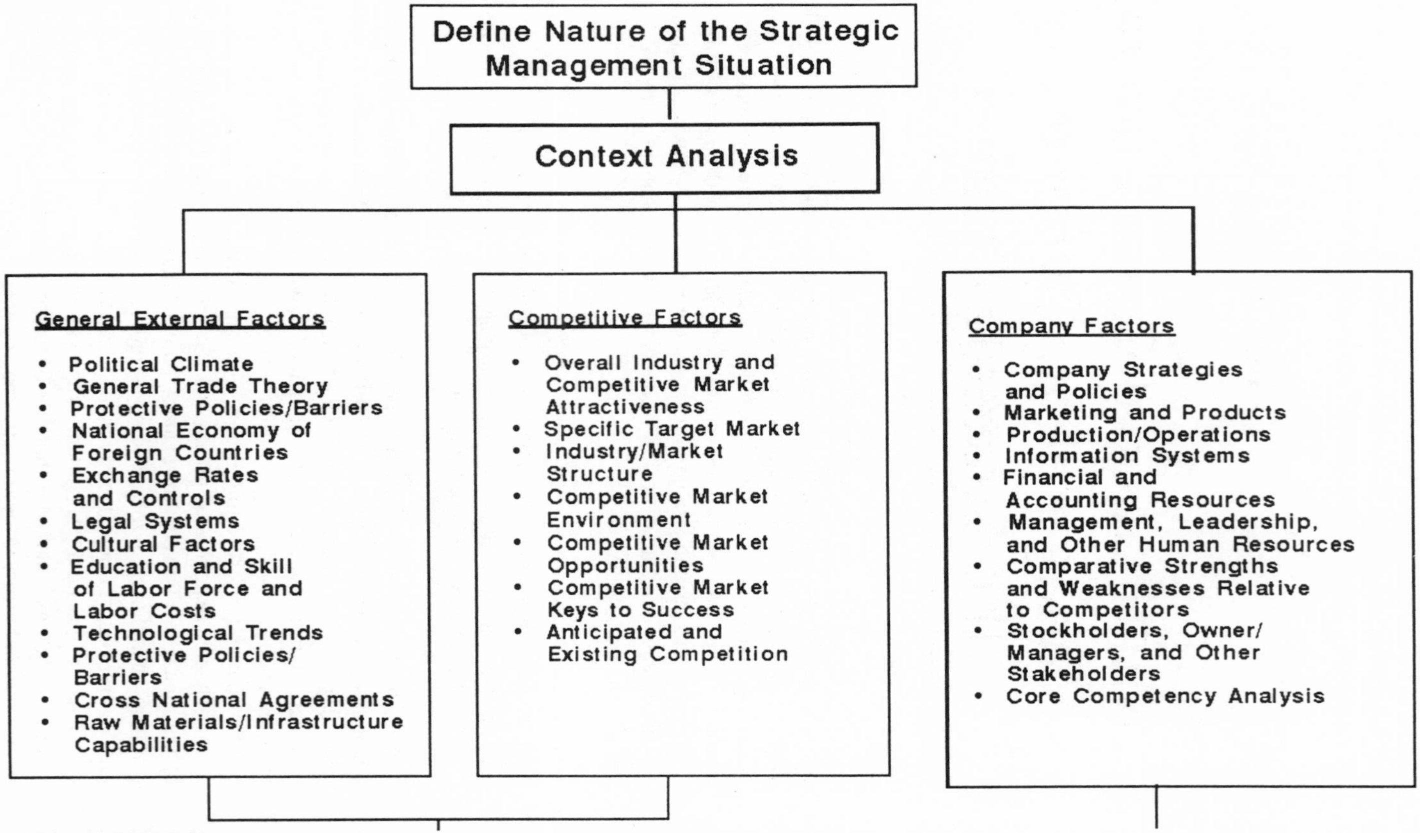

**Define Nature of the Strategic Management Situation**

**Context Analysis**

**General External Factors**

- Political Climate
- General Trade Theory
- Protective Policies/Barriers
- National Economy of Foreign Countries
- Exchange Rates and Controls
- Legal Systems
- Cultural Factors
- Education and Skill of Labor Force and Labor Costs
- Technological Trends
- Protective Policies/Barriers
- Cross National Agreements
- Raw Materials/Infrastructure Capabilities

**Competitive Factors**

- Overall Industry and Competitive Market Attractiveness
- Specific Target Market Industry/Market Structure
- Competitive Market Environment
- Competitive Market Opportunities
- Competitive Market Keys to Success
- Anticipated and Existing Competition

**Company Factors**

- Company Strategies and Policies
- Marketing and Products
- Production/Operations
- Information Systems
- Financial and Accounting Resources
- Management, Leadership, and Other Human Resources
- Comparative Strengths and Weaknesses Relative to Competitors
- Stockholders, Owner/Managers, and Other Stakeholders
- Core Competency Analysis

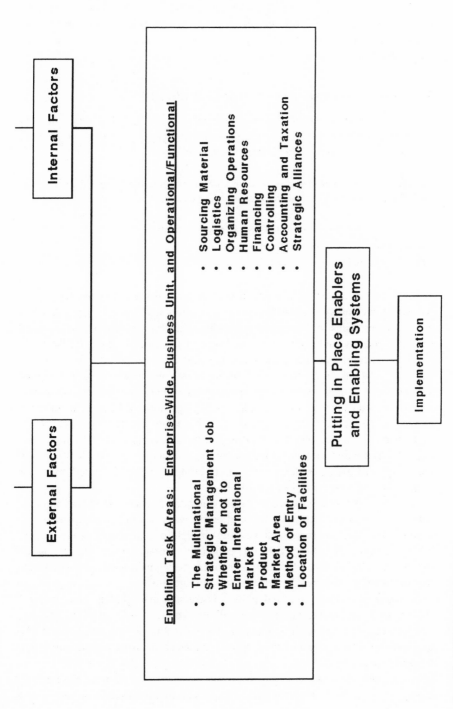

Internal Factors

External Factors

Enabling Task Areas: Enterprise-Wide, Business Unit, and Operational/Functional

- The Multinational
  Strategic Management Job
- Whether or not to
  Enter International
  Market
- Product
- Market Area
- Method of Entry
- Location of Facilities

- Sourcing Material
- Logistics
- Organizing Operations
- Human Resources
- Financing
- Controlling
- Accounting and Taxation
- Strategic Alliances

Putting in Place Enablers
and Enabling Systems

Implementation

Copyright © 1996 by R. J. Mockler.

93

Chapter 6 and the subsequent chapters describe in more detail how specific external and internal factors impact on planning and doing (decisions and actions) at the enterprisewide, business unit and operational levels in a variety of multinational task areas.

## STRATEGIC MANAGEMENT AND LEADERSHIP

In multinational cross-cultural management, the systematic use of situationally oriented common sense serves as a good starting point. According to Colman Mockler, former CEO of the Gillette Company:

Building effective enterprise-wide strategies ultimately involves learning how to systematically listen to what the marketplace is telling us about:

• what is happening now and its impact over the near-term future
• what is anticipated to be likely to happen in the future
• what can be made to happen in the future.

Knowing how a competitive situation works provides a knowledge base without which one cannot manage multinational operations. This indispensable starting point provides a foundation on which innovative visions, appropriate enabling systems, and effective management of the operations can be built.

As the context analysis at the enterprisewide level progresses, for example, one will gradually look increasing distances into the future by using inquiry methods such as looking at the situation from multiple perspectives. These perspectives might include, for example, writing scenarios of how different competitors might view the situation and act on those views or developing scenarios of what might happen when world crises occur. Alternately, one might encourage the questioning of assumption by different managers or request studies of the interrelated global contexts in which the company might find itself operating in the future (Mitroff and Linstone 1993).

The search process often is a gradually emerging and innovative one, through which one seeks to create a vision of effective ways in which a company might position itself (its enterprisewide strategy) in light of anticipated external competitive market conditions and the company's competencies and resources (Abraham 1995). This is the entrepreneurial conceptualization process, which was discussed in Chapter 3 (see especially Figure 3-3).

In addition to the timing and phase of strategic management involved, the context study's structure and context will also be affected by the *level* of decision making and action (enterprisewide, business unit or functional), the *tasks* (discussed in Chapter 2), and the company, manager, industry, country and other *situation variables*.

Three enterprisewide strategic framework concepts are given in Figures 5-2 through 5-4 (three other examples were given in Figures 2-3 through 2-5).

**Figure 5-2**
**Rhône-Poulenc Rorer Inc. Mission Statement**

Statement:  The Rhône-Poulenc Rorer Mission

*Our Mission is to become the BEST pharmaceutical company in the world by dedicating our resources, our talents and our energies to help improve human health and the quality of life of people throughout the world.*

- Being the BEST at satisfying the needs of everyone we serve: patients, healthcare professionals, employees, communities, governments and shareholders;
- Being BETTER AND FASTER than our competitors at discovering and bringing to market important new medicines in selected therapeutic areas;
- Operating with the HIGHEST professional and ethical standards in all our activities, building on the Rhône-Poulenc and Rorer heritage of integrity;
- Being seen as the BEST place to work, attracting and retaining talented people at all levels by creating an environment that encourages them to develop their potential to the full;
- Generating consistently BETTER results than our competitors, through innovation and a total commitment to quality in everything we do.

*Satisfying the needs of our customers*
We will strive for the highest quality and continuous improvement in our products and services for all our customers, external and internal, amintaining the highest standards of integrity in all our relationships.

*Global communication and collaboration*
We will be a global company, fostering open communication, receptivity to new ideas and (worldwide) collaboration on strategies that support the growth and success of the company.

*Being entrepreneurial and acting quickly*
We will be entrepreneurial, working with a great sense of urgency, encouraging teamwork and quick decision-making, rewarding innovation and results at every level of the organization.

*Treating each other fairly and valuing diversity*
We will treat each other fairly, with trust and respect, valuing cultural and individual differences so that our company is strengthened by our diversity.

*Caring for our communities and the environment*
We will will be good neighbors, working to improve the safety of the environment and the vitality of our communities and our workplace.

When we operate according to these principles, Rhone-Poulenc Rorer will grow and prosper as a company and we will as individuals.

Industry Category:            Pharmaceutical/Biotechnology

**Corporate Description**
Rhone-Poulenc Rorer Inc. is a global pharmaceutical company dedicated to the discovery, development, manufacturing, and marketing of human pharmaceuticals.

**Size Revenues:** $4,019,400,00 as of 1993
**Number of Employees:**  22,000 as of 1993

*Source*: 1993 Annual Report.

These strategic concepts, which include general visions, values and strategic guidelines for action, fit the definition that Colman Mockler of Gillette gave for the firm's strategic vision: "I knew exactly the kind of company I envisioned; I just didn't know precisely what it would look like." Such strategic visions are grounded in a thorough knowledge of the competitive market and company involved, as described in this chapter. They also require the kind of futuristic

**Figure 5-3**
**Citicorp Mission Statement**

### STATEMENT: CITICORP'S VISION

To be a global bank, unique in worldwide presence...dedicated to our customers...financially strong...consistent...committed to our staff and its development...delivering sustained superior performance to investors.

#### Unique, Global
Unique in being global, operating both locally and collectively around the world in delivering financial services for the benefit of both individual and corporate customers; unique also in spirit.

#### Customer Dedication
Dedicated to serving the financial needs of customers. Our success depends upon our importance to them. Customer needs define position, product and service offerings. We seek to build sustained relationships and recognize the importance of continuity of people. We are committed to competitive excellence, delivering customer satisfaction, and investing in the business, people and technology required to meet our customer needs.

#### Financially Strong
Our balance sheet and earnings will be a source of strength; recognized internally, by customers, investors, competitors, rating agencies, and regulators. Control, executional excellence and productivity improvements are acknowledged objectives.

#### Consistent
Consistent and dependable: in our commitment to our people, with our customers, in the development and execution of our strategy, and in our risk profile.

#### Staff and Its Development
We seek to recruit, develop and retain the most talented people from around the world. We will reward people based on merit, teamwork, results, and shared values. We are accountable: We will take responsibility for our actions and the exercise of judgment. We treat people with trust, openness and respect, and maintain the highest ethical standards in dealing with customers, the community and each other.

#### Delivering Sustained Superior Performance to our Investors
Our objective is to achieve superior return on shareholders' equity. We seek the reality and reputation of being well-managed, being consistently sound in our risk-taking judgments, and being seen as one of the most respected financial institutions in the world; a unique global bank.

**Industry Category:** Banking

**Corporate Description:** Citicorp, with its subsidiaries and affiliates, is a global financial services organization. Its staff of 81,500 serves individuals, businesses, governments, and financial institutions in over 3,300 locations, including branch banks, representative offices, and subsidiary and affiliate offices in 93 countries throughout the world. Citicorp, a U.S. bank holding company, is the sole shareholder of Citibank, N.A. (Citibank), its major subsidiary.

**Size Revenues:** $16,075,000,000 as of 1993

**Number of Employees:** 81,500 (worldwide) as of 1993

*Source*: 1993 Annual Report.

visionary thinking described at the end of Chapter 1 in the discussions of future planning by IBM, Hewlett-Packard, Simon & Schuster, and Microsoft.

The factors within the situation context that prove useful in formulating such enterprise-wide strategies will necessarily differ from those that are useful in strategic planning at the operational level (with its more immediate time frames) or in strategic management of the major enabling areas, such as telecommunications/computer information systems.

Strategic management also involves "doing what is necessary to get the job done within well-defined general moral, legal, ethical, and policy strategic guidelines,'' as an enterprise implements or carries out the strategic vision. Again varying aspects of the context will be relevant in a particular case, and so will be emphasized and studied. For example, during implementation, major cultural factors will affect interpersonal relationships and therefore be especially important in cross-cultural management. An extensive discussion of these useful factors occurs in Chapters 4 and 10 (on human resource management situations).

In addition, an essential part of the multinational cross-cultural strategic management process is the emerging formulation of specific strategies and plans at all levels. The development phases of the process involved in the situation will also affect the context factors that are studied. An overview of the continuing strategic management process in multinational cross-cultural situations was presented in Figure 2-6.

This chapter and Chapter 6 provide specific exercises to help in learning how to study a competitive market context in a structured way (Chapter 5) and then develop strategies, plans, and actions at all management levels and in many different task areas using the appropriate aspects of the context analysis (Chapter 6).

## CRITICAL FACTORS AFFECTING DECISIONS: GENERAL EXTERNAL ENVIRONMENT

In this section, general external environment situation factors that affect multinational cross-cultural management decisions are grouped into eleven categories for purposes of discussion. This is just a sampling of factors and factor categories that may be analyzed, since the factors will vary by situation and space does not permit complete coverage. The sample factors are listed in the left-hand box of the context analysis section of Figure 5-1.

### Political Climate

*Political climate* refers to the general condition of the governing systems and practices in a country. In Sweden, for example, the political climate is relatively calm and stable, since the population seems to seldom get overly excited about political matters and the government often seeks national referenda before instituting major policy changes. At the other extreme is a country like Lebanon, where mob rule, terrorism and anarchy are prevalent.

Political systems can affect business in many ways. For example, in most countries, various government approvals are needed in order to do business. In some countries, such as England, the process is well established and can be pursued in an orderly fashion. In Japan, where the U.S. insurance company Aflaco spent four years in order to get approval to enter the market (Lohr 1992), the protective system is culturally imbedded and yields to change very slowly. In other countries, especially developing ones, the process of obtaining approval

**Figure 5-4**
**Corning Inc. Mission Statement**

### Our Purpose

Our purpose is to deliver superior, long-range economic benefits to our customers, our employees, our shareholders, and to the communities in which we operate. We accomplish this by living our corporate values.

### Our Strategy

Corning is an evolving network of wholly and jointly owned businesses which owes its continued existence to shared values, a core competence in science and technology, and an unending spirit of innovation in all aspects of our corporate life.

Corning will focus on four strategies that will enable the corporation to reach its long-term financial goals:

Growth Markets. Invest aggressively in growing markets worldwide in which we are or expect to be #1 or #2 and in which we are the high-quality, low-cost supplier. These markets are: Communications, Environment, Life Sciences.

Traditional Businesses. Manage our traditional businesses for cash to support these growth investments.

Core Science and Technology. Nurture our science and technology so that it drives our growth markets and also creates as-yet undefined future opportunities.

Corporate Investments. Hold our investments in Dow Corning and Pittsburgh Corning for optimal growth and cash generation over time.

Our corporate network adds value to its component parts through our company's name and reputation, a common dedication to our core values, a coherent overall strategy, and shared financial and human resources.

## What we value

### Our Values

We have a set of enduring beliefs that are ingrained in the way we think and act. These values guide our choices, defining for us the right courses of action, the clearest directions, the preferred responses. Consistent with these values we set our objectives, formulate our strategies, and judge our results. By living these values we will achieve our purpose.

### Quality

Total Quality is the guiding principle of Corning's business life. It requires each of us, individually and in teams, to understand, anticipate, and surpass the expectations of our customers. Total Quality demands continuous improvement in all our processes, products, and services. Our success depends on our ability to learn from experience, to embrace change, and to achieve the full involvement of all our employees.

### Integrity

Integrity is the foundation of Corning's reputation. We have earned the respect and trust of people around the world through more than a century of behavior that is honest, decent, and fair. Such behavior must continue to characterize all our relationships, both inside and outside the Corning network.

### Performance

Providing Corning shareholders a superior long-term return on their investment is a business imperative. This requires that we allocate our resources to ensure profitable growth, maintain an effective balance between today and tomorrow, deliver what we promise, and tie our own rewards directly to our performance.

**Figure 5-4 (Continued)**

### Leadership

Corning is a leader, not a follower. Our history and our culture impel us to seek a leadership role in our markets, our multiple technologies, our manufacturing processes, our management practices, and our financial performance. The goods and services we produce are never merely ordinary and must always be truly useful.

### Innovation

Corning leads primarily by technical innovation and shares a deep belief in the power of technology. The company has a history of great contributions in science and technology, and it is this same spirit of innovation that has enabled us to create new products and new markets, to introduce new forms of corporate organization, and to seek new levels of employee participation. We embrace the opportunities inherent in change, and we are confident of our ability to help shape the future.

### Independence

Corning cherishes--and will defend--its corporate freedom. That independence is our historic foundation. It fosters the innovation and initiative that has made our company great, and will continue to provide inspiration and energy to all parts of our network in the future.

### The Individual

We know that in the end the commitment and contribution of all our employees will determine our success. Corning believes in the fundamental dignity of the individual. Our network consists of a rich mixture of people of diverse nationality, race, gender, and opinion, and this diversity will continue to be a source of our strength. We value the unique ability of each individual to contribute, and we intend that every employee shall have the opportunity to participate fully, to grow professionally, and to develop to his or her highest potential.

## Where we want to go

### Our Financial Goals

PERFORMANCE

We will consistently be in the top 25 percent of the Fortune 500 in financial performance as measured by return on equity and long-term growth in earnings per share.

CAPITAL STRUCTURE

We will maintain a debt-to-capital ratio of approximately 30 percent and a long-term dividend payout of 33 percent.

We will issue new shares of stock on a limited basis in connection with employee ownership programs and acquisitions with a clear strategic fit, and we will repurchase shares on the open market as appropriate.

**Industry Category:** Manufacturing

**Corporate Description**

Corning Incorporated is a diversified products and services company with a strong tradition of technological innovation. Although historically a glass and specialty materials manufacturer, Corning today concentrates on the three key global markets that account for 60 percent of its revenues: optical communications, life sciences and the environment.

**Size Revenues:** $4,004,800,00 as of 1993
**Number of Employees:** 39,200 as of 1993

*Sources*: 1993 Annual Report, "Our Values" (Corning publication)

Figure 5-5
A U.S. Firm Compared with International Competitors in the Malaysian Market

| Comparison Criteria | A (U.S. MNC) | B (Korean MNC) | C (Local Malaysian Firm) | D (Japanese MNC) | E (Local Malaysian Firm) |
|---|---|---|---|---|---|
| Marketing Capability | 0 | 0 | 0 | 0 | - |
| Manufacturing Capability | 0 | + | 0 | 0 | 0 |
| R&D Capability | 0 | 0 | 0 | - | 0 |
| HRM Capability | + | 0 | 0 | 0 | 0 |
| Financial Capability | + | - | 0 | 0 | - |
| Future Growth of Resource | - | 0 | - | 0 | - |
| Quickness | 0 | 0 | + | 0 | 0 |
| Flexibility/Adaptability | + | + | + | 0 | 0 |
| Sustainability | 0 | 0 | 0 | 0 | - |

*Key:* + = Firm is better than competition; 0 = firm is the same as competition; − = firm is poorer than competition.
HRM = human resources management; MNC = multinational corporation.
Copyright © 1996 by R. J. Mockler.

tends to be less straightforward or clear, and it often requires a considerable knowledge of local customs and the people involved, as well as payoffs to various officials (Millbank and Brauchli 1995).

In India in mid-1995, the Envron Development Corporation was fighting to save a $2.8 billion power plant construction project it had begun. In August 1995, five months after Envron began construction, a newly elected government in Maharastra state "repudiated" the contract Envron had negotiated with the previous government and with the national government in New Dehli; this was a popular political move among nationalistic Indians (Burns 1995; McDowell 1995). Only after Envron threatened to go to court and made major concessions was the problem resolved (McWilliams, Moshavi, and Shari 1996).

In the early 1990s, Procter and Gamble encountered many political problems throughout South America (Swasy 1990), and the American president of the Venezuelan phone company was even jailed for a while (Brooke 1995). Such adverse political climates, in conjunction with other factors, can lead managers to decide not to go into a country, to go into a country in a very limited way, or to institute a host of security measures to protect their operation.

There are two opposite extremes of political systems—democracy and totalitarianism. On the continuum between the two fall many forms of both and many variations or mixed systems.

*Democratic* societies can range from decentralized systems, as in Canada where the provinces have considerable power (for example, over trade treaty decisions), to countries like the United States, where the central government maintains stronger control over the states (which nonetheless often have their own systems for taxing foreign income) and highly centralized nations, such as Japan and France. Each of these kinds of democracies has some form of free-market economy, though in some instances (such as Japan) freedoms are carefully circumscribed and directed in a variety of ways.

*Totalitarian* systems can range from those that are religiously based, such as the Middle Eastern Islamic countries, to those that are secular and dominated (usually) by a military power, such as Cambodia, Haiti and Iraq. Communism, one of the most familiar totalitarian forms of government, is undergoing many changes in the former USSR and China, both of which are experiencing a period of transition from a controlled economy to a hybrid form of free-market system. The impact of the political uncertainty of these transitions can be noted in many of the business examples in this book.

In addition to responding to the political environment by adapting operations to meet its requirements, businesses often have become activists and instituted programs to bring about change, as is done in United States. For example, problems have been encountered in China with piracy, involving music recordings, software and books. During 1994–1995, steps including trade sanctions were taken to force the Chinese government to pass legislation to make businesses in their country comply with international copyright law (Chen 1995).

Lawsuits have also been initiated against Japanese firms to protect proprietary technology.

### Protective Government Policies and Barriers

Governments can raise a wide range of selective nontariff barriers to restrain trade. These include:

- subsidies, including low-interest loans, capital and procurement preferences
- import quotas
- domestic preferences, including buying only domestically manufactured goods, shipping only on domestic flag ships, and preferential treatment in contracting for minority or other socially favored or disadvantaged domestic groups
- customs and administrative procedures, including country-of-origin markings that raise costs, limited ports of entry and arbitrary customs valuations
- technical and regulatory barriers, including license requirements, limited facilities, holding periods for selected goods, excessive standards and testing/inspection procedures, and distribution requirements

Created for a number of reasons, these barriers are sometimes economic, but more often political. Governments may wish to protect infant domestic industries so that these industries can develop or protect domestic monopoly positions. They may be trying to correct a balance-of-payments problem, maintain the domestic supply of goods, assure consumers of lower prices, provide consumer protection, or simply favor politically connected special-interest groups.

Such protective policies can have a reverse effect on multinational decisions. For example, in 1993 a newly formed U.S.-backed manufacturing operation of breast implants opted to move its headquarters from the United States to Nuechatel, Switzerland, because of the regulatory restraints imposed by the U.S. government. In addition, Switzerland provided a new lakeside building, tax incentives and a skilled labor force (Studer 1995).

The General Agreement on Tariffs and Trade (GATT) is the main negotiating body through which countries have multilaterally reduced trade barriers and agreed on simplified mechanisms for conducting international trade. However, recent experience indicates that further trade liberalization on a global basis will be more difficult to achieve.

### Cross-National Agreements

Cross-national agreements affect businesses in many ways, since they regulate commerce among nations. The most familiar cross-national agreements today are the European Union (EU) and the Canadian-U.S. Free Trade Agreement

(FTA), which was expanded to include Mexico and renamed the North American Free Trade Agreement (NAFTA).

As of 1993, the EU was comprised of Belgium, Denmark, France, Germany, Greece, Ireland, Italy, Luxembourg, the Netherlands, Portugal, Spain, and the United Kingdom. Some of the EU's major goals are to abolish intrazonal restrictions on the movement of goods, capital, services and labor; establish a common external tariff; achieve a common agricultural policy; harmonize tax and legal systems; devise a uniform policy concerning antitrust laws; and supersede national currencies.

NAFTA is designed to eliminate tariff barriers and liberalize investment opportunities. The inclusion of other Latin American countries would make this an even more powerful economic bloc.

Another example of a cross-national agreement is the Organization of Petroleum Exporting Countries (OPEC). OPEC was successful as a producers' alliance in the 1970s and effectively forced historic increases in crude oil prices. However, the drop in worldwide demand for crude oil and the increase in supplies from non-OPEC producers have reduced OPEC's influence.

Latin American and African efforts to create regional trading agreements have not been successful, while an Asian group of some form will probably emerge over the next decade (Lewis 1995). International commodity agreements and product alliances among producers have also been created in an effort to stabilize and protect trade.

Multinational managers should study such agreements and their impact when doing business in affected regions.

## General Trade Theory and Related Overall Economic Studies

An understanding of general trade theory can be helpful in identifying the forces that affect a country's major economic choices. Trade theory helps explain what might be produced competitively in a given locale, where a company might go to produce a given product efficiently, and whether governmental practices might interfere with the free flow of international trade.

Adam Smith developed a general trade theory called the theory of absolute advantage, which holds that consumers will be better off if they can buy foreign-made products that are cheaper than domestic ones. According to the theory of absolute advantage, a country may produce goods more efficiently because of a natural advantage (for example, availability of raw materials or a favorable climate) or an acquired advantage (for example, technology or skills).

Many other theories exist concerning what would be the optimum economic configurations given a country's particular circumstances. The factor-proportions theory holds that a country's relative endowments of land, labor and capital determine the relative costs of these factors. These costs, in turn, determine which goods the country can produce most efficiently. The product life cycle (PLC) theory states that many manufactured products are first produced in the countries in which they were researched and developed (usually industrialized nations). Over the product's life cycle, production tends to become more capital intensive and shifts to foreign locations. According to the country-similarity theory, most trade today occurs among industrial countries because they share very similar market segments.

The theory of country holds that countries with large land areas are more apt to have varied climates and natural resources, and thus tend to be generally more self-sufficient than smaller countries. A second reason for greater self-sufficiency is that large countries' production centers are more likely to be located at a greater distance from other countries, thus raising the transportation costs of foreign trade. The comparative advantage theory holds that total output can be increased through foreign trade even though one country may have an absolute advantage in the production of all products. Mercantilist theory proposes that a country should try to achieve a favorable balance of trade (with exports exceeding imports) in order to receive an influx of gold. Finally, neo-mercantilist policy also seeks a favorable balance of trade, but its purpose is to achieve a particular social or political objective.

Understanding the underlying forces affecting a country's economy and their impact on economic configurations is important for several reasons. For example, when Japan was developing a national trade strategy for foreign expansion and Brazil came under consideration, Japanese companies, working with the government, prepared for investing there by giving several top South American economists university appointments in Tokyo. The information that these economists provided helped the Japanese to determine the most promising industries, products and trade strategies to invest in and pursue, given Brazil's structure, resources and other factors affecting the future. In this way, the Japanese were able to target prime investment areas and develop profitable ways to manage investments most profitably from an overall economic perspective.

Large companies (such as steel and automakers) also make use of overall economic studies, since these companies deal in major segments of an economy and so may be directly affected by broader movements. In *The Competitive Advantage of Nations*, Michael Porter focused on the new forces affecting international trading strength, including the ability to support innovation, economies of scale and rapid change (Porter 1990). At times, governments base decisions about national trade policies, including trade barriers, in part on economic trade theory studies such as Porter's, as well as on general trade theories.

These overall economic factors are much less immediately important to most companies, which typically devote most of their energies to responding to, and managing, a wide range of other competitive market factors.

### Exchange Rates and Controls

As inflation fluctuates, so do exchange rates. For companies that report their income in the United States based on current exchange rates, this can cause considerable variations in reported income. In many instances, it can also lead to extraordinary income gains and losses. For example, currency problems in Mexico in 1995 damaged many foreign businesses' profitability there (for instance, automobile sales) and set back growth several years (Preston 1995).

In countries noted for widely fluctuating exchange rates, such as Brazil, particular attention is paid to formulating strategies and tactics, such as dealing in currency futures, that are designed to minimize the potential losses incurred from such fluctuations.

Many countries also have restrictions on how much money can be taken out of the country. For example, the U.S. company GTE experienced many difficulties when heading a consortium that took over management of Venezuela's antiquated telephone company, which was privatized in the early 1990s. At one point, the government of Venezuela refused to allow the company to buy dollars, forcing it to default on millions of dollars in overseas loans (Brooke 1995).

## Legal Systems

Since practically all business activity involves explicit or implied contracts, understanding the differences in legal systems is critical to doing business successfully in foreign countries. Most countries base their laws on civil law (an explicit codified system), as opposed to the common law–basis legal system, which is based on tradition, precedent, custom and usage, as interpretation by the courts. The United States has a mixed civil and common law system. In some countries, for instance, whoever *registered* a brand name first (civil law) is more important under the law than whoever *used* the name first (common law), while the latter prevails in the United States. Labor laws can also be significant multinational planning factors since many countries, such as France and Italy, have strict laws governing such matters as the hiring and firing of workers, which severely limits management flexibility.

Law enforcement is lax in many countries. In the early 1990s, after Gillette opened a new plant in Russia, an attempt was made to kidnap the president of its St. Petersburg operation. The story had a humorous ending, however. As with many old-time gangsters depicted in comedies, the kidnappers bungled the job, kidnapping the chauffeur (who was later released unharmed) instead (Zeien 1995). Although this story is humorous, the criminal element in Russia is a severe problem: killings, payoffs to government officials, and other forms of extortion and violence, as well as government reluctance to prosecute criminals, are common (Handelman 1995; Kranz 1995; Stanley 1995a).

In addition, some countries have a reputation for failing to honor contracts. In Shanghai, China, during the 1990s, leases were frequently canceled as rents rose rapidly and vacancy rates dropped in prime locations (Faison 1995). Apparently, contracts are broken with some regularity in China (Engardio 1994; Loeb 1995).

Russian businesses are frequently controlled by members of organized crime, making contract enforcement difficult and dangerous (Handelman 1995). Many of the former Soviet republics have had little experience with Western contracts and often break and change them, as many oil companies and other investors found out to their regret in the early 1990s (Bonner 1995; Stanley 1995b). In mid-1995, the government of Maharastra, India's most industrialized state, canceled a $2.5-billion power-plant construction project (Burns 1995; "Envron" 1995; McWilliams, Moshavi, and Shari 1995, 1996). The company was forced to threaten to take the government to court and had to make major concessions.

In addition to civil and common law systems, a third type of legal code is based on religion. Islamic law, for example, is based on the Koran, the Sunnah, the writings of Islamic scholars, and the consensus of the Muslim countries' legal communities. Such laws can affect the way in which interest is paid. Under Islamic law, for instance, interest cannot be charged. Consequently, it must be collected or paid indirectly, through, for example, profit sharing—as is done with mutually owned savings banks in other countries.

Bribery is always a problem for U.S. companies operating overseas, since U.S. law forbids it. Unfortunately, U.S. companies have had to develop a number of ways around these restrictions, including donations establishing educational funds that benefit influential institutions and their leaders, "information" junkets to places like Disney World, and "facilitator" payments and "sales service" payments to legitimate third-party intermediaries in countries where bribery is commonplace (Borrus, Toy, and Salz-Trautman 1995; Millbank and Brauchli 1995).

The key international business management issues affected by laws are: trade and investment regulation, intellectual property protection, regulation of financial flows, taxation, reporting requirements, ownership regulation, contractual relationships, international treaties and dispute resolution.

## National Economy of Foreign Countries

Major differences exist among controlled (meaning public ownership of property and controlled resource allocation) and market-driven (with private ownership and a much lesser degree of control) economies. In a market economy, wages and prices are generally set by market forces; labor and product availability are dictated, and resources are allocated, by supply and demand. Consumer sovereignty and freedom to operate are key aspects of a market economy.

In a centrally planned (controlled) economy, such as those of the former USSR and of China until recently, the opposite is true. As noted by the manager of a Chinese television station (see Chapter 3), the government decided what the consumer needed and would get and what resources would be allocated. In most instances, a nation's economic system is closely allied with the political system in place.

In practice, most economies are hybrid mixes of the two extremes, which have developed over the centuries to meet changing needs. In the United States, which is a prime example of a free-market economy, the government runs some utilities and until recently, ran the postal service. In China and Russia, a considerable amount of entrepreneurial business activity exists today, even though neither country has moved fully away from the controlled economy.

Whether countries have controlled, mixed or free-market economies; whether they are developing, developed or emerging countries; the level of inflation; convertibility of currency; unemployment; environmental protection; government spending and debt (external and internal); total economic growth (gross national product); privatization (degree and level of activity); disposable income, infrastructures (for example, transportation, telecommunications and schools) in place; balance of payments and the like all have significant impacts on their business activities.

For example, countries with low per-capita income (so-called emerging or Third World countries), such as Guyana and Rumania, present different opportunities than those countries, such as West Germany, where income levels are closer to, or higher than, those in the United States (so-called developed, industrial, or First World countries). Inflation in countries such as Brazil (the so-called developing or Second World countries), where in 1991 the inflation rate exceeded 1,200 percent, affects how money is invested, since when expanding into areas of high inflation, local borrowing and low cash investment are preferred as a hedge against inflation. One reason why Compaq Computers decided to open a plant in Scotland was that the high unemployment rate there suggested that labor would be plentiful and labor costs would be more controllable.

## Cultural Factors

Cultural attitudes refer to customs, values, beliefs and the behavior of a people. Such attitudes can affect a wide range of business decisions—the colors used in advertising, the handles designed for tools, the texture of toilet paper, the distribution systems used in a foreign country, the way employees are compensated and how business meetings and negotiations are conducted. Subtle, culturally based protocols—for example, the seating at a conference table, the order of introducing people, and the way people are addressed and referred to—can dramatically affect the outcome of negotiations (O'Hara-Devereaux and Johansen 1994).

In the employee relations area in France, the respect given a manager often depends on the university at which the manager studied or ancestral family links to nobility rather than on specific organizational chart relationships. Similarly, in India, the caste system dictates to some degree who can give orders to whom in business situations.

If specific stereotypes, protocols and customs are important in the society of the foreign country under study, the company must be aware of them in order to conform and so operate effectively in that environment. For example, throughout the Muslim world, and specifically on the Arabian Peninsula, women have not yet fully achieved a recognized place in business activity. For this reason, many Saudi-Arabian merchants may be unwilling to deal with a female representative from an overseas exporter.

In 1995, both Ford and General Motors had plans to introduce right-hand-drive vehicles overseas to accommodate driving habits and regulations in Japan, England, New Zealand, and Australia. Responding to political pressure to open up its markets, Japan gave both companies multimillion-dollar loans to do so ("Ford Will Get a Japanese Loan" 1995).

Many of the cultural factors affecting multinational management are discussed specifically in Chapters 4 and 10. Their impact on management decision making and action, as well as the impact of other factors mentioned in this section, are discussed throughout this book.

### Education and Skill of the Labor Force and Labor Costs

The education and skills of a country's workforce can range from superior (in Japan) to very low (in developing countries like Bangladesh). For instance, when planning to manufacture computers, which requires skilled employees, the strategic choice of which country to locate facilities in would, in large measure, be dictated by the education and skills of the labor force. In situations where the planned entry involves the manufacture or delivery of noncomplex products and services, such as McDonald's hamburgers or 3M's "Soft Scour" cleaning sponge, the need for skilled labor will be much less.

Michael Porter's 1990 multinational study concluded that the skill level of a country's workforce is a critical factor in the success of its international trade, since it affects the nation's ability to gain and maintain a competitive advantage through undertaking innovation and change (Porter 1990, ch. 3).

As Porter also pointed out, in a broader sense, the knowledge existing within a country is also extremely important. For example, workers in countries such as Japan are known for their capacity to do applied research. This led a number of companies to set up joint research projects with Japanese research groups, both because of the Japanese knowledge resource and because of the Japanese capacity to carry the research through to completion.

Labor costs also affect planning. For example, German labor costs are the highest in the world, which has led to high unemployment there and the exporting of jobs to other countries (Miller 1996). These problems are compounded by extensive red tape and government regulations and rules, which have discouraged investment in Germany and caused the economy to stagnate (Gumbel 1996).

Where large segments of a workforce are not highly skilled or motivated, companies must be prepared to devote time and effort in order to compensate. For example, at its light bulb factory in Budapest, Hungary, General Electric (GE) found it desirable to use "action workout" sessions, such as those used in its United States plants. These "workouts" involve teams of workers tackling specific problems; they reflect GE's belief in a "borderless" organization culture in which employees remove obstacles in order to work more efficiently. These and other worker and management changes were needed to change work habits carried over from the communist era (Perlez 1994).

## Raw Material and Supporting Supplier Infrastructure Capabilities

As Michael Porter also pointed out in *The Competitive Advantage of Nations* (1990), in addition to labor and knowledge supply, a number of other factors are important in studying the investment attractiveness of a country.

Physical resources might include the abundance, quality, accessibility and cost of the country's land, water, mineral or timber deposits, hydroelectric power sources, fishing grounds and other physical traits. The time zone may even be a relevant factor. For example, London's position between the United State and Japan is often identified as an advantage in financial service industries because London-based firms can do business with both Japan and the United States during a normal working day.

Infrastructure factors that affect competition cover the type, quality and user cost of available infrastructure, including the transportation system, the communications system, mail and parcel delivery, payments and funds transfer, health care and so on. Infrastructure also includes such things as the housing stock and cultural institutions, which affect the quality of life and the attractiveness of the country as a place to live and work. Related infrastructure factors include the availability of supplier networks in industries related to the particular company, as well as the availability of capital resources locally where relevant.

For example, over the last decade, northern Britain has become a popular location for foreign investors. In late 1995, Siemens of Germany announced that it would build a huge $1.7 billion semiconductor plant there, and Fujitsu of Japan planned to double the size of its four-year-old silicon chip plant. Since 1989, the number of foreign projects more than doubled, to 434 in 1995 from 183 in 1980, while the number of jobs that those projects created or kept from moving to other countries rose to 88,000 (from 14,000). Major reasons for this boom included relatively low wages rates, a highly skilled labor force, a supporting supply and parts infrastructure, and Britain's membership location in the European Economic Community (Stevenson 1995).

### Technological Trends

The impact of new technology on future opportunities and threats is evident in many industries. The personal computer industry, for example, was barely ten years old in 1990 and is still experiencing new technological breakthroughs. For one, the development of faster computer chips will likely lead to a whole new generation of super-microcomputers. Computer graphics and communication and information technology are changing entire industries—and even creating new ones, such as desktop publishing and the computer workstation market.

The most dramatic development in 1990 was the introduction of the World Wide Web, which enabled wide access to the Internet network. The impact of the Internet and Web page, as well as of other computer technology, has been far-reaching. (That impact is described in summary in Chapter 3 and at length in Chapter 7.) For example, Internet enables anyone to conduct electronic commerce anywhere in the world. By 1996, major industry leader William Gates, chairman of the computer software giant Microsoft, was forced to reorganize his company to keep up with the rapid changes occurring. According to Gates, "Every effort at the company would be directed at the Internet. . . . Internet is the most development since the PC." The major new division being formed was called the Interactive Media Division and was intended to concentrate both on the growing Internet market and on the next generation of the digital videodisc market (Markoff 1996).

Developments in the related telecommunications area are also expected to produce major changes in the way people think and act. For example, at the end of 1995, almost three dozen satellite development projects, totaling more than 1,500 satellites—five times the number of commercial communications satellites launched since the first, AT&T's Telstar, in 1962—had been announced. Their total cost was estimated to be $43 billion over the next ten years (Lynch 1995). Also in late 1995, Alcatel Cable S.A of France and AT&T Corporation announced that they had reached an agreement to cooperate to design, manufacture, supply and install an underseas cable system which would encircle the continent of Africa; its estimated cost was $2.6 billion ("AT&T Venture" 1995). Developments such as these will open up whole new areas to instant access to major information sources worldwide and in this way influence the way people view the world and respond to it. It was just such a development, the advent of the CNN news service, that reportedly served to increase the pressure leading to the breakup of the Soviet Union (Henry 1992; "World View" 1990).

The costs of the research leading to new technology breakthroughs can be high—for example, hundreds of millions of dollars in the cases of computer chips and high-resolution television. Such enormous costs have led to many new cooperative arrangements between companies that normally compete in these areas. For example, in a surprise move in mid-1991, two major computer industry competitors, IBM and Apple, signed a letter of intent to jointly develop a new operating system, named "Taligent" (Lewis 1992; Pollack 1991). Sun Microsystems was also approached to participate in the venture (Markoff 1992). Of course, not all these partnerships prove effective.

The impact of technological innovations is felt in many industries. Advances in genetic engineering, for example, are creating many new opportunities, as are developments in transportation, medicine, fiber optics, marine biology, micromachines, solar energy, superconductors and metallurgy (Coates 1996; "Most Fascinating Ideas" 1991; Pollack et al. 1991).

In some instances, these developments are market driven. For example, contact lens marketers believed that the aging baby-boom generation would be resistant to wearing bifocal eyeglasses or to wearing reading glasses with their distance contacts. For this reason, a major research effort was begun that led, in 1989, to the introduction of technologically advanced, easy-to-use, and reasonably priced bifocal contact lenses, which had been designed to tap a market estimated to reach close to 30 million people in the coming years (Freudenheim 1989).

Technological developments can also threaten existing products. For example, expected developments in high-definition television may disrupt existing television markets, creating opportunities for some companies and major competitive problems for others (Andrews 1991; Elkus 1989; Fantel 1992).

In the 1970s National Cash Register (NCR) Corp. encountered product problems after insisting on investing in older cash-register technology while competitors turned to computers. Similarly, RCA Corp., which was once synonymous with music, continued to produce vinyl albums while Sony Corp. moved into the now ubiquitous compact disc. (General Electric has since acquired RCA and sold its record business unit.)

However, as Kodak's history shows, predicting the future can be an uncertain business. Early on, for example, Kodak decided not to make 35-millimeter (mm) cameras. Now such cameras are the industry standard, however, and Kodak's Japanese competitors dominate the market while Kodak offers only a few models. More recently, Kodak shied away from camcorders. "[We] missed the opportunity to participate in video," lamented chairman Kay Whitmore (Rigdon 1992, p. B2). Kodak was hoping to handle the new threat of "filmless" photography more effectively by assuming a product-development leadership role and so gaining a measure of control of its impact on Kodak's core film business (Rigdon 1991). So-called cardboard (disposable) cameras represented another competitive threat in which Kodak was also taking a leadership approach (Rigdon 1992).

In addition to creating new product opportunities and threats to existing products, technology developments can also affect how business is done. For example, in the banking business the development of sophisticated computer systems launched 24-hour banking through automated teller machines (ATMs). First Bank, a telephone-only bank in Leeds, England with half a million accounts and not a single branch, is a dramatic example of the power of telecommunications when linked with computer information systems anywhere in the world (Hansell 1995). Similarly, the development of cellular phones allows people to do business while driving or walking and has led to the creation of a billion-dollar industry.

Advances in communications technology enable companies to communicate policy changes to worldwide employees instantly, as well as to lower the costs (and improve the effectiveness) of employee training (Ozley 1991).

Major impacts of technological trends in the computer information/telecommunications area are discussed in the first section of Chapter 6 and in great detail in Chapter 7.

## CRITICAL FACTORS AFFECTING DECISIONS: THE COMPETITIVE MARKET ENVIRONMENT

In addition to the relevant general external factors reviewed in the preceding section, a structured decision situation analysis covers external competitive market forces such as those outlined in the context analysis section of Figure 5-1. They include the target market, market structures, and competitors' capabilities.

### Target Market

The target market study includes, not only the total number of customers, but also their buying habits and motivation, the amount and kinds of purchases expected, present market penetration, and other success factors affecting potential market opportunities. For example, Gillette calculated that over 95 percent of American males shave, making this a relatively saturated market. In Latin America and China, it estimated that currently, less than 25 percent of the males shave, making these attractive emerging markets (Zeien 1995).

Identifying purchasing patterns, customer characteristics (cultural and other) and tastes (buying habits and motivation), income elasticity, legal requirements regarding product composition, comparative pricing and price regulations, anticipated technology advances, market gaps and the like is as important in multinational markets as in domestic markets. These factors affect, not only product design, but also market selection, method of entry, packaging and other marketing programs, type and location of facilities, and other enterprise-wide, business unit and operating-level decisions and actions. For example, an early step taken by a major U.S. advertising firm after the 1992 breakup of the Soviet Union was to conduct a study of the range of target markets in Russia and their buying patterns (Elliot 1992).

Geographic location can also affect decision making because of distribution problems and costs. Other decisions, such as location of facilities, controls needed, entry method, size of product, packaging, and even whether to enter a market, may be based on geographic factors. In many situations, climate is a geographic factor affecting multinational cross-cultural planning.

Changing consumer tastes can have an impact on industry trends emerging from such changing tastes and how companies respond. For example, during the 1990s, stimulated in part by the opening in 1992 of Euro Disneyland just outside Paris, the worldwide theme park idea continued to spread throughout

Europe. In 1995, it was estimated that 60 million people would visit theme parks in Europe. These theme parks reportedly often make use of American theme park consultants and Disney ideas. For example, after the French Parc Asterix (based on Gallic chieftain and antihero Asterix) opened in 1989, it was transformed from a passive form of entertainment, almost like a public park, to a participatory operation, like American theme parks.

Like other areas of multinational management, these theme parks, in their own way, balance universal approaches with the requirements of local country cultures and customers. For example, the two biggest complexes in Europe— Blackpool Pleasure Beach in Blackpool, England, with 7 million visitors a year, and long-famous Tivoli Gardens in Copenhagan, Denmark, with 3.8 million visitors a year, have added rides and other features yet have retained their original character (Tagliabue 1995).

Apparently, consumer tastes in Europe are changing and becoming more like those of American consumers. They were not, however, changing entirely into the American mold. This example makes it clear that multinational management involves balancing common frameworks with adapting to local differences where they exist in all multinational cross-cultural management task areas and situations.

In addition to studying customers, the context analysis also examines aggregrate country markets. For example, considerable interest has developed in China because of its 1.2 billion population, vast untapped natural resources and relatively free market (Barnathan, Crock, and Einhorn 1996; Barnathan et al. 1993; Barnathan, Engardio, and Einhorn 1994; Buruma 1996; Engardio, Barnathan, and Glasgall, 1993; Engardio 1994, 1996; Turcq 1995). For instance, Hoechst AG, a German chemical and pharmaceutical company, announced in March 1996 that it expected to invest more than $1 billion in China by the year 2000. In the words of a company board member, ''China is our key market for investment among developing countries. . . . In terms of growth, the market is very clearly China'' (Associated Press-Dow Jones 1996).

While Russia and other former Soviet republics, along with countries in Central Europe, are also viewed as growing target markets, there are many kinds of problems that need to be identified and considered. Crime, excessive local and national taxes, currency-exchange restrictions and the like all contribute to circumscribing the potential opportunities.

Target markets in many areas of the world appear attractive. In late 1995, Ruppert Murdoch announced a major expansion with two partners (in Mexico and Brazil) of his entertainment, news and sports subscriber-programming satellite/cable TV services into South and Central American, anticipating a rapid expansion of viewer interest in cable and wireless television services (Landler 1996). In 1996, STET S.P.A. of Milan, an Italian government-controlled telecommunications company, invested $270 million for a 10 percent stake in Chile's major telephone company; the company already held shares in telephone companies in Argentina, Bolivia and Cuba (Bloomberg Business News 1996).

During the same period, STET bid for a cellular phone license in Poland, calculating that the market there was ripe for this new technology. In 1996, the U.S. firm Philip Morris announced that it had purchased (for $372 million) a majority interest in Poland's biggest cigarette producer, thus moving to position itself in a market where cigaret consumption is strong—in contrast to the American market, where consumption has fallen (Reuters News Service 1996). Just a few months earlier, Deutsch Telekon and Ameritech Corporation announced that they were buying a controlling interest in the Hungarian phone company Matav for $1 billion (Associated Press 1995), based on their study of the future prospects of the targeted Hungarian market.

In response to market needs in several different overseas target markets, in 1996 Chrysler was developing a very small car (called the BTV, for "basic transportation vehicle") targeted for the needs of developing nation markets in Asia and South America (Updike 1996).

Several extended examples of ways in which marketing decisions are affected by target market factors are discussed in Chapter 6.

### Market Structures

A wide range of other market opportunities and success factors are analyzed during the context study, including distribution and sales channels; advertising and promotion media; suppliers and supplies, including parts and raw materials; industry pricing practices; available equipment and technology; supporting services, such as electricity, gas, transportation, communications and housing; existing manufacturing facilities; and competing products.

As was the case for Chrysler in Japan, access to distribution channels is often severely restricted in practice, a problem that Chrysler resolved partially by buying a controlling interest in a dealership chain (Pollack 1995). U.S. timber companies found similar restrictions when they attempted to bid on timber for the 1998 winter Olympics, to be held in Nagano, Japan. After spending tens of thousands of dollars in preparing bids, they found that the Japanese had specified a type of wood grown only in Japan and so had indirectly cut out all foreign competition (WuDunn 1995).

In many emerging free markets, such as Russia, the country may lack a developed wholesale distribution system that will deliver products to stores on time, consistently, and in good condition. Ben and Jerry's Homemade Inc., an ice cream maker, took more than three years to build its own distribution system in Russia—with tasks ranging from buying its own trucks and freezers to training store personnel in how to scoop ice cream (Banerjee 1995).

The impact of market structures on management decision making and action in a variety of countries and industries is discussed in Chapter 6 and throughout this book.

## Capabilities of Competitors

Potential and existing local and international competitors are studied in all multinational cross-cultural management situations, in much the same way that domestic competition is identified and analyzed.

Aflaco did such a competition study in determining that a niche existed in Japan for its cancer insurance (Lohr 1992). Because Japanese government regulatory agencies believed that Aflaco was likely to fail, they failed to create obstacles (Lewis 1993).

Competition is increasing worldwide in both developing and developed countries. For example, former communist banks in Central Europe have slowly become very competitive by Western standards. In late 1995, Investicni a Postovni Banka A.S. in Prague, Czechoslovakia, was offering cash management, international money transfers, and even on-line banking—prodded in large measure by aggressive competition from foreign banks such as Citicorp (United States), Deutsche (Germany), and ING Bank (Netherlands). Kredyt Bank in Poland was cited as another aggressive new competitor (Bray 1995).

Intel Corp. has invaded computer motherboard markets, which in the past were controlled by Taiwanese companies (four out of five units sold). Intel continued, as it had in the past, to sell chips and microprocessors to the Taiwanese, who use them in the motherboard products they produce. As Intel developed new technologies such as sound and high-tech graphics capabilities to its microprocessors, it moved quickly to compete directly with the Taiwanese by manufacturing its own motherboards. In late 1995, Intel planned to control close to 40 percent of the motherboard market within the next two years as it expanded its production capacity to 15 million units annually (Chang 1995).

An important consideration for firms entering overseas markets is that local competition will almost always have some advantages, since it is more familiar with the market. In addition, firms already operating in the market often pressure their government to protect local business, as was the case with Waste Disposal Inc. when it first tried to enter the French market (Bremner 1989). Local competitors may also benefit from protectionist trade measures (Garsombke 1989). These factors can create substantial market-entry barriers and often lead a company to seek out a well-connected joint-venture partner when entering a market.

It is not always easy to anticipate competitors moves. For example, in Moscow in 1995, a new fast-food restaurant opened across the street from McDonald's, serving the Russian version of the "Beeg Mek" ("Big Mac")—borst, blini and vodka (Specter 1995).

This analysis might also include studying the five forces in a marketplace that tend to predict what future competition will be like: barriers to the entry of new competitors, rivalry among competing firms, the threat of competitive products from other industries, the bargaining power of suppliers and the bargaining power of customers (Porter 1980).

## CRITICAL FACTORS AFFECTING MULTINATIONAL BUSINESS DECISIONS: THE INTERNAL COMPANY ENVIRONMENT

In addition to the external factors, the strategic context analysis in multinational cross-cultural management situations also covers a variety of internal factors involving both the home company and the multinational division operating in the overseas country under study. Eight of these factors, which are listed in the context analysis section of Figure 5-1, are discussed here.

### Company Strategies and Policies

Existing enterprisewide company strategies, as well as specific business strategies affecting a company's multinational operations, are studied in making decisions in the multinational arena. For example, a company may have a policy of always owning subsidiaries completely, as Borden originally did in order to protect its technology in China. However, changing circumstances may dictate that a joint venture is necessary or preferable. General Motors also initially had such a policy, which it later was forced to abandon in favor of a wide range of joint ventures.

The formulation and impact of such strategies at all levels—enterprisewide, business unit and operational—is covered in Chapter 6. The remaining chapters of this book describe their formulation and impact in a wide range of areas: telecommunications and information systems; accounting, finance and control; organization; staffing; leadership; and operating management.

### Marketing and Markets

Marketing factors such as existing customers, products, sales, service, and distribution in the home country, as well as in existing overseas operations, are studied. In the case of Ford's proposed entry into the Soviet Union, the company first considered its existing product line and built its initial entry strategy around importing a product it already was making—its Scorpio model (Galuszka 1989). Survival dictated that Hurco Companies, a machine tool maker, fight its way back to solvency largely by increasing overseas sales through exporting because its competitive position in the United States was so poor (Lohr 1991).

It is especially important to identify core competencies on which competitive advantages can be built, sustained or extended. For example, the company/product brand strength has been effectively exploited by Coca Cola, extended by Gillette to a family of personal care products, and used by McDonald's in the retail franchise area to gain worldwide competitive advantages.

### Operations and Production

The review of operations/production capabilities covers factors such as facilities, workforce, quality, flexibility, inventory management, and research and development. For example, Stanley decided that the production know-how required to produce some of the company's precision tools, which was a core competency that gave the company a worldwide competitive advantage, dictated manufacturing them in a single facility that firm controlled and from which it would supply the worldwide market.

As shown in Chapter 6, the Southern Company, a U.S. electric utility company, determined that its core competency in effectively producing and delivering low-cost electricity services was a major competitive advantage. It proceeded to exploit that perceived advantage by buying electric utilities in a wide range of international areas.

As shown in the example of Gillette's decision about where and how to manufacture and supply its "Atra" shaver (in Chapter 1), company availability of supply in different countries, as well as transportation costs, duties, costs of raw material, foreign-exchange risk, tariffs and production economies of scale, can vary over time and by country. This information is needed to make decisions about where to purchase raw materials, where to manufacture or purchase components and parts, where to assemble or manufacturer products, how to provide services, and what is the appropriate mix of these production/operations functions. Solutions involve using internal company facilities and supply sources in some combination with external sources of supply.

## Information Systems

Information systems are likely to be included in most present-day company internal analyses because of their importance to both survival and gaining competitive edges in marketing, production/operations, management decision making, human resource management, and finance and accounting. In multinational corporations in general, telecommunications and related computer information systems are important due to the problems involved in managing geographically dispersed and diversified organizations, rapidly transferring information among divisions, reconciling differences and achieving global efficiencies.

As seen in the experiences of Gillette, using information systems to gain a competitive advantage in the operations area is only one example of the use of information systems as a competitive weapon. Chapter 7 gives many examples of their significant and widespread strategic impact in both manufacturing and service industries.

## Financial and Accounting Resources

In analyzing a company's financial situation, the obvious and necessary factors examined are the income statement, balance sheet, and cash flow, using financial ratios, computer simulations of projected scenarios and other analytical tools. These analyses provide a basis for estimating the financial resources available for overseas operations—overall, country by country, or target market by target market. The more creative task is to go beyond these ratios and tools to uncover hidden resources and opportunities. Disney's use of possible future income from its movies to obtain favorable terms when financing its European ventures is only one of the many ways in which core competencies in this area can be used to gain a competitive advantage (described in Chapter 8).

Imaginative financing arrangements, preferably involving local money sources, are especially important in countries with high inflation rates. The applicability of existing company accounting systems and practices in each overseas market and the need to develop new approaches appropriate for the market being studied, as well as the kinds of systems and practices needed, are factors considered during this phase.

### Management and Other Human Resources

The availability of personnel who are experienced in international operations is critical to success, since international operations are, in many ways, quite different from domestic operations. Such knowledge and experience are needed, not only to deal with the many special local factors affecting success (including political, legal, custom, cultural, personal and attitude factors), but also to establish the contacts needed to open up and exploit opportunities in target markets. Chapters 10 through 12 discuss the human resources management aspects of multinational cross-cultural management—how to analyze existing resources and shape strategies, plans and programs for acquiring and developing human resources, and how to lead and manage them effectively.

### Comparative Strengths and Weaknesses Relative to Competitors: Core Competency Analysis

A key element of the structured industry analysis is to determine how the capabilities of the company under study compare with competitors' capabilities in the targeted market. Figure 5-5 shows a comparative competitive analysis summary for a U.S. specialty seafood firm's position in the Malaysian market (Garsombke 1989).

One key ultimate focal point of such a study is to identify and then strategically exploit—or acquire and exploit—core competencies in light of the competition's core competencies. For example, Chapter 6 described how Mitsubishi Motors Corp. used a comparative analysis to build a strategy around its potential strengths in new markets, which at the same time realistically assessed its comparative weaknesses in its home country market, Japan. Chapter 6 also describes the experiences of Aflaco Inc., which analyzed weaknesses in the area of cancer insurance among potential competitors in Japan to build a successful strategy in what was its core competency, cancer insurance.

Hamel and Prahalad's *Competing for the Future* (1994) gives extensive examples of companies that created competitive edges through comparative competitive analysis that built on the identification of core competencies. Their book also provides guidance on how to construct the analysis.

Since competitive success in the marketplace requires differentiation—doing something better, and thus differently from the competition—a major piece of knowledge needed from this analysis is what core competences the company now has or can be developed. Emphasizing these, and in some way realizing their potential and marketing them, should be a key priority in a company's enterprise-wide and business unit strategy (see Chapter 6).

### Stockholders, Owner/Managers and Other Company Stakeholders

Interest groups that impact on multinational cross-cultural management include owners (stockholders), customers, suppliers, creditors and lending institutions, unions, franchise holders, government agencies, society (local or in general), and company managers, professional staff and hourly workers. Interest groups can impact on company strategy, as was shown by the number of companies that sold their South African operations during the 1970s and 1980s as a result of shareholder pressure.

Studies of stakeholder relations also can lead to finding new strategic opportunities. For example, *When Giants Learn to Dance* (Kanter 1989) presents studies of a number of multinational companies that benefited from forming international alliances, not only with other firms operating in overseas markets, but also with unions, customers and suppliers.

## CONCLUSION

This chapter has focused on the factors in the international business environment that affect planning and doing in multinational cross-cultural management situations. Some company experiences that illustrated the effect of these factors on management were briefly described.

The context analysis described in this chapter is, of course, just a beginning in developing a knowledge base. This initial introductory discussion was necessarily segmented and simplified, just as with the introductory phases in learning a sport or a profession.

The following chapter discusses the impact of the many factors discussed in this chapter, as well as other factors critical in the situation under study, in a variety of multinational cross-cultural management task areas.

## WORKS CITED

Abraham, Jeffrey. *The Mission Statement Book*. Oakland, CA: Ten Speed Press, 1995.
Andrews, Edmund L. "Six Systems in Search of Approval as HDTV Moves to the Testing Lab." *New York Times*, August 18, 1991, Business Section, p. 7.

Associated Press. "Hungary Stake Grows for Ameritech Venture." *New York Times*, December 21, 1995, p. D8.

Associated Press–Dow Jones News Service. "Hoechst Expects Outlays in China to Top $1 Billion." *Wall Street Journal*, March 8, 1996, p. A5A.

"AT&T Venture to Lay Cable for Africa." *New York Times*, December 21, 1995, p. D8.

Banerjee, Neela. "Ben & Jerry's Is Trying to Smooth Out Distribution in Russia." *Wall Street Journal*, September 19, 1995, p. A18.

Barnathan, Joyce, Stan Crock, and Bruce Einhorn. "Rethinking China." *Business Week*, March 4, 1996, pp. 57, 58.

Barnathan, Joyce, Pete Engardio, Lynne Curry, and Bruce Einhorn. "China: The Emerging Economic Powerhouse of the 21st Century." *Business Week*, November 17, 1993, pp. 54–69.

Barnathan, Joyce, Pete Engardio, and Bruce Einhorn. "China: Birth of a New Economy." *Business Week*, January 31, 1994, pp. 42–48.

Bloomberg Business News. "STET Will Acquire Chile Phone Stake." *New York Times*, January 27, 1996, p. 34.

Bonner, Raymond. "Getting This Oil Takes Drilling and Diplomacy." *New York Times*, February 15, 1995, pp. D1, D2.

Borrus, Amy, Stewart Toy, and Peggy Salz-Trautman. "A World of Greased Palms: Inside the Dirty World of Global Business." *Business Week*, November 6, 1995, pp. 36–38.

Bray, Nicholas. "Ex-Communist Banks Learn to Compete." *Wall Street Journal*, October 31, 1995, p. A14.

Bremner, Brian. "Europe's Garbage Smells Sweet to Waste Management." *Business Week*, May 29, 1989, p. 33.

Brooke, James, "Yankees, Phone Home! GTE Role in Venezuela Is Warning on Privatization." *New York Times*, June 21, 1995, pp. D1, D7.

Burns, John F. "India Project in the Balance: Envron's Last-Ditch Effort to Save a Power Plant." *New York Times*, September 6, 1995, pp. D1, D3.

Buruma, Ian. "China On the Edge . . . Of What? The 21st Century Starts Here." *New York Times*, February 18, 1996, Magazine Section, pp. 25–46.

Chang, Leslie. "Intel Challenges Taiwan on Its Own Turf." *Wall Street Journal*, October 31, 1995, p. A14.

Chen, Kathy. "China Is Faulted by U.S. Group on Piracy Pact." *Wall Street Journal*, October 13, 1995, p. A40.

Coates, Joseph F. "Science, Technology and American Business: 2025." Speech presented at the Strategic Leadership Forum, New York, February 13, 1996.

Elkus, Richard J. "The Fast Track to New Markets." *New York Times*, May 28, 1989, Business Section, p. 2.

Elliot, Stuart. "Sampling Tastes of a Changing Russia." *New York Times*, April 1, 1992, pp. D1, D5.

Engardio, Pete. "Why Sweet Deals Are Going Sour in China." *Business Week*, December 19, 1994, pp. 50–51.

Engardio, Pete, Joyce Barnathan, and William Glasgall. "Asia's Wealth: It's Creating a Massive Shift in Global Economic Power." *Business Week*, November 29, 1993, pp. 100–108.

Engardio, Pete, and Dexter Roberts. "Global Tremors from an Unruly Giant." *Business Week*, March 4, 1996, pp. 59–65.

"Envron to Halt India Project." *New York Times*, August 8, 1995, p. D19.

Faison, Seth. "Shanghai's Neo-Capitalists Find Real Estate." *New York Times*, June 24, 1995, pp. 1, 2.

Fantel, Hans. "HDTV Faces Its Future." *New York Times*, February 2, 1992, p. H17.

"Ford Will Get a Japanese Loan for Right-Hand-Drive Cars." *New York Times*, September 5, 1995, p. D2.

Freudenheim, Milt. "Race On for Bifocal Contact Lens." *New York Times*, May 24, 1989, pp. D1, D6.

Galuszka, Peter. "The Deal of the Decade May Get Done in Moscow." *Business Week*, February 5, 1989, pp. 54–55.

Garsombke, Diane J. "International Competitor Analysis." *Planning Review*, May–June 1989, pp. 42–47.

Gumbel, Peter. "Job Losses Soar While Germans Fumble Real Reform." *Wall Street Journal*, February 2, 1996, p. A6.

Hamel, Gary, and C. K. Prahalad. *Competing for the Future*. Boston: Harvard Business School Press, 1994.

Handelman, Stephen. *Russian Wise Guys: Russia's New Mafia*. New Haven: Yale University Press, 1995.

Hansell, Saul. "500,000 Clients, No Branches." *New York Times*, September 3, 1995, Business Section, pp. 1, 10.

Henry, William A., III. "History as It Happens." *Time*, January 6, 1992, pp. 24–27.

Kanter, Rosabeth Moss. *When Giants Learn to Dance*. New York: Simon and Schuster, 1989.

Kranz, Patricia. "Russia's Really Hostile Takeovers: Organized Crime Is Shooting Its Way into Big Business." *Business Week*, August 14, 1995, pp. 56, 57.

Landler, Mark. "Murdoch and 3 Partners Set Latin Satellite-TV Venture." *New York Times*, November 21, 1996, p. D10.

Lewis, Michael. *Pacific Rift: Why Americans and Japanese Don't Understand Each Other*. New York: W. W. Norton, 1993.

Lewis, Paul. "Asia-Pacific Regional Trade Group Is Showing Signs of Life." *New York Times*, August 31, 1995, p. D5.

Lewis, Peter. "Apple IBM Venture, with New Leaders, Searches for Soul." *New York Times*, March 8, 1992, Business Section, p. 8.

Loeb, Marshall. "China: A Time for Caution." *Fortune*, February 20, 1995, p. 129.

Lohr, Steve. "U.S. Industry's New Global Power." *New York Times*, March 4, 1991, pp. D1, D3.

———. "Under the Wing of Japan Inc., a Fledging Enterprise Soared." *New York Times*, January 15, 1992, pp. A1, D5.

Lynch, David J. "Telecom Giants Enter Crowded, High-Cost Race." *USA Today*, November 21, 1995, pp. 1B, 2B.

Markoff, John. "Sun Link Is Sought by IBM." *New York Times*, March 13, 1992, pp. D1, D2.

———. "Microsoft Sets a Revamping to Gain Edge on the Internet." *New York Times*, February 20, 1996, pp. D1, D7.

McDowell, Edwin. "Delta Seeks to Expand Its Ties with Three Airlines in Europe: Functioning as One Carrier while Remaining Separate." *New York Times*, September 9, 1995, p. 34.

McWilliams, Gary, and Sharon Moshavi. "More Power to India: Why Enron Renegotiated Its Deal—on Maharashtra's Terms.'' *Business Week*, January 22, 1996, p. 62.

McWilliams, Gary, Sharon Moshavi, and Michael Shari. ''Enron: Maybe Megadeals Mean Megarisk.'' *Business Week*, September 4, 1995, pp. 52–53.

Millbank, Dana, and Marcus W. Brauchli. ''Greasing Wheels: How U.S. Concerns Compete in Countries Where Bribes Flourish; Foreign Travel, Donations, and Use of Middlemen, Help Them Win Business.'' *Wall Street Journal*, September 29, 1995, pp. A1, A16.

Miller, Karen Lowry. ''Are the Easy Times Gone for Good?'' *Business Week*, January 29, 1996, pp. 48, 49.

Mitroff, Ian I., and Harold A. Linstone. *The Unbounded Mind: Breaking the Chains of Traditional Business Thinking*. New York: Oxford University Press, 1993.

''Most Fascinating Ideas for 1991, The.'' *Fortune*, January 14, 1991, pp. 30–62.

O'Hara-Deveraux, Mary, and Robert Johansen. *Global Work: Bridging Distance, Culture and Time*. San Francisco: Jossey-Bass, 1994.

Ozley, Dan. ''Reaching People through Satellite Communications.'' Presented at the Society for the Advancement of Management, Conference on Management in the Information Age, Auburn, Alabama, April 4–6, 1991.

Perlez, Jane. ''G.E. Finds Tough Going in Hungary.'' *New York Times*, July 25, 1994, pp. D1, D8.

Pollack, Andrew. ''A Quirky Loner Goes Mainstream.'' *New York Times*, July 14, 1991, Business Section, pp. 1, 6.

———. ''Chrysler to Buy Control of Japanese Dealer Chain.'' *New York Times*, June 27, 1995, pp. D1, D5.

Pollack, Andrew et al. ''Transforming the Decade: 10 Critical Technologies.'' *New York Times*, January 1, 1991, Science Times Section, pp. 35, 38.

Porter, Michael. *Competitive Strategy*. New York: Free Press, 1980.

———. *The Competitive Advantage of Nations*. New York: Free Press, 1990.

Preston, Julia. ''Mexico Peso Fall Leads to Auto-Sales Standstill.'' *New York Times*, August 10, 1995, p. D3.

Reuters New Service. ''Philip Morris Takes a Big Polish Stake.'' *New York Times*, January 31, 1996, p. D6.

Rigdon, Joan E. ''Kodak Tries to Prepare for Filmless Era without Inviting Demise of Core Business.'' *Wall Street Journal*, April 18, 1991, pp. B1, B7.

———. ''For Cardboard Cameras, Sales Picture Enlarges and Seems Brighter Than Ever.'' *Wall Street Journal*, February 11, 1992, pp. B1, B2.

Specter, Michael. ''Borscht and Blini to Go: From Russian Capitalists, an Answer to McDonald's.'' *New York Times*, August 9, 1995, pp. D1. D3.

Stanley, Alessandra. ''An American's Bizarre Sit-In in Moscow: Many Western Ventures in Russia Get Messy, But This One Takes the Cake.'' *New York Times*, May 6, 1995a, pp. 35–36.

———. ''To the Business Risks in Russia, Add Poisoning.'' *New York Times*, August 9, 1995b, p. A4.

Stevenson, Richard W. ''Smitten by Britain: Thatcherism's Industrial Evolution.'' *New York Times*, October 15, 1995, Business Section, pp. 1, 10.

Stern, Gabriella. ''GM Executive's Ties to Native Country Help Auto Maker Clinch Deal in China.'' *Wall Street Journal*, November 2, 1995, p. B5.

Studer, Margaret. "Breast-Implant Maker LipoMatrix Relishes Its New Home in Europe." *Wall Street Journal*, August 11, 1995, p. A6B.

Swasy, Alecia. "Foreign Formula: Procter & Gamble Fixes Aim on Tough Market: The Latin Americans." *Wall Street Journal*, June 15, 1990, pp. A1, A4.

Tagliabue, John. "Step Right Up, Monsieur! Growing Disneyfication of Europe's Theme Parks." *New York Times*, August 23, 1995, pp. D1, D8.

Templeman, John, David Woodruff, Dexter Roberts, and Pete Engardio. "How Mercedes Trumped Chrysler in China." *Business Week*, July 31, 1995, pp. 50–51.

Turcq, Dominique. "India and China: Asia's Non-Identical Twins." *McKinsey Quarterly*, no 2 (1995): 5–19.

Updike, Edith Hill, and Bill Vlasic. "Will the Neon Be the Little Car That Could? Chrysler Takes a Serious Crack at Japan's Toughest Market." *Business Week*, June 10, 1996, p. 56.

"World View: Ted Turner's CNN Global Gains Influence." *Wall Street Journal*, February 1, 1990, pp. A1, A6.

WuDunn, Sheryl. "U.S. Companies Slip on Way to Winter Olympics." *New York Times*, March 10, 1995, p. A4.

Zeien, Albert. "Gillette's Global Marketing Experiences." Talk presented at St. John's University's Annual Colman Mockler Leadership Award Ceremony, New York, February 27, 1995.

Chapter 6

# Making Decisions and Taking Action in Selected Enterprisewide, Business Unit and Operational Task Areas

Within the strategic context framework described in Chapter 5, this chapter describes a number of multinational cross-cultural decision and action situations:

- the basic decision to go multinational
- selecting a marketing area
- identifying products or services to be offered
- method of entry
- sourcing materials
- location and type of facilities
- international financing

This chapter differs from earlier ones in that it also includes reader self-learning exercises, which allow readers practice decision making.

The situations discussed in this chapter involve enterprisewide and operating-level strategic management. The tasks involve both formulating plans (strategic and operational) and implementing them, and range from reacting to immediate market needs, to meeting anticipated changes, to responding to, and creating, new, long-term markets. They require balancing global efficiencies with local responsiveness and the rapid transfer of new knowledge. They focus mainly on the planning aspects of strategic management; the enabling and doing aspects are given more emphasis in Chapters 7 through 13.

## THE BASIC DECISION TO GO MULTINATIONAL

Many reasons can stimulate an enterprise to go multinational. A prime motivator is the search for new outlets for products and services that face a highly competitive, mature home market, with only modest growth prospects. For example, because of mature home markets, U.S. retailers were expected to spend a minimum of $5 billion in late 1995 and 1996 on new stores in foreign countries (Rapoport and Martin 1995).

During the early 1990s the pharmaceutical industry witnessed many mergers of large international companies. For example, in mid-1995 the Upjohn Company (United States) and Pharmacia A.B. (Sweden) announced a $13-billion merger. A major reason for the merger was competition—most of the eight pharmaceutical companies that were larger—for example, Merck & Company, Bristol-Meyers Squibb, and American Home Products—had grown through mergers over the preceding two years. This trend was stimulated by customer market trends in the United States and elsewhere. For example, in pharmaceutical customer markets, buying is now concentrated in very large health maintenance organizations, hospital chains, and preferred-provider groups (most of which grew through mega-mergers), which respond best to large companies offering diverse, up-to-date product lines. The Upjohn/Pharmacia merger provided the new company with a $1-billion war chest for developing new drugs and a diverse product line, two factors that will make it more competitive.

The merger also provided access to new markets, with Upjohn benefiting from Pharmacia's very strong distribution network in Europe and Pharmacia benefiting from Upjohn's equally strong distribution position in the United States. The control of large networks of goods and services distribution, as well as information networks, had become a major strategic key to success (Naughton and Hawley 1995; Wysocki 1995). Since the combined company would be able to consolidate and strengthen operations in many countries and so reduce staff by about 10 percent, there were cost-saving reasons as well. Both specific, external, competitive market and internal, company factors, therefore, seem to have been among the deciding strategic situation factors in the merger (Uchitelle 1995).

The desire to go multinational has also been a strategic driver in the electric utility industry. In August 1995, Southern Company, one of the largest U.S. electric utilities, sought to purchase an interest in South Western Electricity, an electric utility in the United Kingdom. Southern Company was initially motivated to expand internationally because of the potential increased competition and consequent price pressures in the home market. This competitive market condition arose in large part from increased federal and expected state deregulation, starting with passage of the U.S. Energy Policy Act of 1992. Strategic internal factors also influenced the company's decision to go international. In the company's own statement: "We are looking for electric utility investments where we can supply the Southern Company's core competencies of efficient utility operations, low-cost production, and innovative customer services, which we believe is a winning combination for the electric utility business in any marketplace" (Tomkins 1995, p. 17). Other U.S. utilities have made similar moves ("Bidders for Power Plants" 1995; "Two Texas Utilities" 1995).

Because of competitive conditions in the United States, Southern looked overseas, investing initially in South America and the Caribbean. In an effort to increase diversity, Southern made the offer for South Western (England) and indicated that it intended to diversify further into other European and Pacific Rim countries. The Southern Company's experience was primarily strategically driven and shaped by company core competencies (including available financial resources) and competitive market conditions arising directly from political action. This is a commonly encountered motivator for overseas expansion, though not necessarily the sole one.

## SELECTING A MARKETING AREA

Selecting a market area, which is a second critical enterprisewide strategy decision, is based on a variety of strategic factors, depending on the situation.

During the early 1980s, Mitsubishi Motors Corp., Japan's youngest automaker, faced heavy competition in Japan. However, Mitsubishi was at a severe disadvantage when considering expansion into Europe or the United States, where experienced companies such as Honda and Toyota had strong market positions. Necessity dictated that the company focus on a newly emerging market where competition was less severe—Asia. Though born out of necessity, this strategy proved to be very successful for Mitsubishi. Throughout Asia in mid-1995, auto sales were booming along with the local economies. Since 1989, South Korea's gross domestic product had soared 300 percent and car ownership had jumped 500 percent, to 74 million. Some 500 new cars were hitting Bangkok's traffic-choked streets every day, and the Asian market was expected eventually to become as big as the total European or North American markets (Updike and Nakarmi 1995).

Few companies were as well situated to ride the surge as Mitsubishi, which had already established a huge network of relationships in Asia. The company also had a wide mix of products designed to match the varied tastes of Asian car buyers, giving it a major core competency tailored to meet market needs.

Even smaller firms can succeed in difficult overseas markets, such as Japan, where opportunities can be staggering. For example, American Family Life Assurance Corporation (Aflaco) Inc. of Columbus, Georgia, a leading supplier of cancer insurance, used its niche product strategy successfully in Japan, where insurance spending per capita is the highest in the world (Holman 1995) and concern over cancer is high. Since Japanese insurance companies were reluctant to provide cancer coverage, Japan was an ideal market in which to promote Aflaco's product. Although it took the company four years to initially get a license to sell its insurance in Japan, its persistence paid off. Once licensed, the company received the favorable treatment afforded other Japanese companies

(Lohr 1992), and by 1991, 75 percent of its $3.5 billion in revenues came from Japan. Paradoxically, one reason given for Aflaco's success was that Japanese regulators thought Aflaco's product had little chance of success and so its application was allowed to slip through the highly protective regulatory and economic structure. Again, a unique combination of strategic external and internal situation factors led to a successful multinational cross-cultural management initiative (Lewis 1993).

In contrast, as Chrysler moved to expand in China by negotiating a deal to participate in a major joint venture (60,000 vans and 100,000 gas and diesel engines yearly) in Guangdon province, the Chinese demanded a number of changes in the initial agreement at the last minute. The demand included provisions for Chrysler to invest $1 billion up front, rather than in phases as originally agreed; that the Chinese be permitted to export Chrysler vans and components—even in markets where Chrysler had its own distribution—without paying licensing fees; and that a clause guaranteeing intellectual-property protections be deleted. These changes would have permitted knockoff artists to copy Chrysler's components with impunity. Because Chrysler was already very strong in the minivan market worldwide, the company felt it had a lot to lose by the changes and refused to meet the demands. The automaker Daimler-Benz (Mercedes) in Germany, however, agreed to a somewhat modified version of the terms since it was not strong in the minivan market and so had much less to lose by the deal. In mid-1995 it was still unclear whether the final deal would go through or just how good the deal was for Mercedes (Templeman et al. 1995).

Over the last decade, northern Britain has become a popular location for foreign investors. In late 1995, Siemens of Germany announced that it would build a huge, $1.7-billion semiconductor plant there, and Fujitsu of Japan planned to double the size of its four-year-old silicon chip plant. Since 1989, the number of foreign projects in northern Britain had more than doubled, to 434 in 1995 from 183 in 1980, while the number of jobs those projects created or kept from moving to other countries rose to 88,000 (from 14,000). Major reasons for the attractiveness of the location included relatively low wage rates, a highly skilled labor force, and its location in the European Economic Community (Stevenson 1995).

These experiences show that selecting a market is a decision that is highly dependent on specific situation factors—both internal company and external competitive market factors.

## IDENTIFYING PRODUCTS OR SERVICES TO BE OFFERED

Decision and action situations involved in the key task area of identifying products or services to be offered include:

- long-term enterprisewide decisions
- intermediate-term decisions

• operational decisions, such as product modification decisions involved in adapting a product to meet local country requirements

### Creating Future Markets: Long-Term Planning Decisions

Hewlett-Packard (H-P) provides an example of how a company can look ahead and attempt to create markets and initiate changes that promise to have a long-term impact on the marketplace.

H-P's visionary new product strategy was to create an "information utility," an infrastructure that would allow workers and consumers worldwide to link digital devices as easily as they can plug in electrical appliances. H-P hoped to supply the utility's building blocks, as well as to equip its users with an array of hand-held communicators, specialized computers and other futuristic machines. In the summer of 1995 the company introduced the first such product—a $300, hand-held organizer that marries telephone, fax and printed functions. This new product/service vision brought together H-P's three core businesses: computers, communications, and test and measurement equipment.

Such a strategy makes sense today, given the worldwide telecommunications networks either in place (such as the Internet) or being considered. H-P could help build these new networks or information utilities by supplying network managers and computers, test and measurement equipment to design and troubleshoot them, and other products to help make the high-speed networks a reality.

In addition, H-P could build the information appliances to plug into these information networks or utilities. The new products include the desktop and laptop PCs, as well as an entire range of projected new products that will be hand-held and wireless in many cases, and highly customized for a particular job. They should not necessarily be thought of as just computers: they could be measurement, medical or analytical appliances as well—for example, a hand-held gas chromatograph or a PC that has videoconferencing capabilities (Clark and Templin 1995).

According to H-P's chairman, Lewis Platte:

We're in the very early stages of computers. Most computers are generic. But why should we all use the same type of computer? Today, the world of electronic appliances is characterized by highly specialized, single-purpose, relatively inexpensive, very easy-to-use devices. In the future, my lawyer will have one computer, my doctor will have another. These have to be intuitive products. Think about it: Have you ever read a toaster manual? Growth, of course, will be an incremental business in this market environment. (Gillooly 1995, p. 49)

H-P's three global core competencies gave it the technological basis it needed to both create and enter this market. The market was expected to move in a favorable direction, since enabling telecommunications capabilities were expanding rapidly. The lack of user-friendly products and easy access to using products blocked faster new product development. H-P saw this as one of its product missions: to create ease of use by being responsive to individual market needs. The strategic situation factors were, therefore, to some degree in place for H-P to build a long-term product and service vision (Gillooly 1995).

Lou Gerstner, CEO of IBM, has developed a similar vision for the longer-term future of his company. Rather than being linked solely to personal computers, his new vision revolves around the concept of network computing and electronic commerce. In this new wave of computing, communications, rather than computation, is the key. IBM wants to position itself to be a leader in this new market, which involves everything from multimedia PCs to the vast Internet (Sager 1995).

An even more massive move to control the future is being made by Bill Gates at Microsoft Corporation, the world's largest and most powerful software company (in 1995, nearly half the world's total PC software revenue went directly to Microsoft). The company is developing "wallet computers" that carry digital signatures, money, and theater or airplane tickets; new generations of fax machines, telephones with screens, and car navigation systems; interactive television boxes, office networks, and wireless networks; and, most importan, an aggressive Microsoft role on the Internet itself, focusing on the processing of electronic financial transactions. By making connections among all these levels of modern computing and exerting control over the architectures that govern their connections through the all-pervasive PC operating systems, Microsoft is in the process of attempting to transform the very structure of the world's computer businesses (Gates 1995; Gleck 1995; Levy 1995).

### Anticipating and Exploiting Global Trends Over the Intermediate-Term Future

Many decisions and actions in the product identification area involve the intermediate-term future. For example, Volkswagen AG had for years been producing limited quantities of its old "Beetle" automobile (fondly referred to as the "Bug") at its plant in Mexico. The car was sold mainly in Mexico and in limited export markets.

In 1995, because of the evidence of demand for the Beetle worldwide, and especially in the United States, Volkswagen announced that within four years it would begin producing a new model of the "Beetle" at its plant in Mexico, which was already producing the old-style "Beetle" and where exchange rates and manufacturing costs were very favorable. Its major target market outside Mexico was to be the United States, a receptive and nearby market. In keeping with modern marketing trends, the company also announced that it would retain the essentials of the original model but would adapt its design to suit the tastes of modern-day customers (Simison 1995).

In the mid-1990s, Ford Motor Co.'s chairman, Alex Trotman, launched a much bolder move—to produce a global car and consolidate its worldwide product design and development facilities. The newly consolidated product design units were expected to take into account the needs of diverse markets, as well as to reap the benefits of coordinated operation in terms of lower costs and faster development time. Ford had long been the new product developer with the highest cost and longest lead time in the industry.

Design teams would now be organized around product (for example, the "Escort" car), and not function (for example, brake, engine or structural design engineers; marketing and financial experts; and purchasing groups). These teams would wrestle with differences such as different fabric bolt sizes in different countries and come up with ways to save money and speed development worldwide. In a sense, this was a massive effort to globalize the world as the design process interacted with the need to reconcile the many cultural differences in a coordinated, integrated way.

This global move was also designed to speed Ford's entry into new markets. For example, in 1995 Ford was behind other companies in opening operations in China and other Asian countries. This was evident from GM's late-1995 luxury car deal in Shanghai, where it reportedly beat out Ford for $1-billion joint venture (Naughton et al. 1995). Ford hoped that through the consolidation of product development and other company operations, it would be able to better realize the advantages of product globalization while retaining the flexibility to reconcile local differences and transfer new knowledge rapidly.

Major obstacles stood in the way of Ford's global initiative, which was especially daring since its major competitor, General Motors, did not believe in such heavy global coordination. The move was a major product strategy change designed to anticipate expected dominant market trends over the next several years. However, outcome of this daring move to globalize Ford's major product was still uncertain as of early 1996.

In contrast to these global, intermediate-term strategies, some companies pursue mixed-product strategies. For example, Interbrew S.A. pursued a global beer-label strategy (its "Labatt" label) at the same time it used its extensive distribution networks to distribute its many smaller beer labels ("Stella Artois," "Hoegaarden"). When it bought into a Hungarian brewer, it continued to promote that brewer's local brand, "Borsodi Vilagos," at the same time that it used the distribution system in Hungary to promote Interbrew premium brands that were popular in other countries (Munk 1995).

### An Introductory Learning Exercise: Responding to Today's Market Needs

Many of the decisions involved in identifying a product or service to be offered are much narrower in scope than the intermediate- and long-term decision situations described in the two preceding sections. This section differs from the two preceding it in that it describes a smaller operational decision in great detail and then develops a contingency framework for making such a decision. It is basically an introductory for decision-making exercise. Actual multinational cross-cultural management decision making and action can often be much more complex, requiring initiative, creative insight and associative leaps.

The following paragraphs describe how expert managers (at a local foreign affiliate of an international manufacturer of health-care products) evaluate new-product proposals generated by the international company headquarters. There are three alternative strategies considered in the situation described here:

- Introduce the product (without change to the formula) as a new brand, as a line extension to an existing brand, or as a replacement of an existing brand.

- Change one or more elements of the proposed product and introduce it as a new brand, as a line extension to an existing brand, or as a replacement of an existing brand.

- Reject (do not introduce) the proposed product.

In this study, it is assumed that corporate management had already developed the product formula and recommended overall marketing strategies for the product. These strategies were based on preliminary research in other countries where the product has demonstrated significant international sales potential. International company headquarters has requested input from the local affiliate manager as to the feasibility and strategic ''fit'' of the new product in the local manager's country.

The new product proposal received from international headquarters will normally include:

- Complete information on the product—its formula and manufacturing (or other important) specifications.

- Full details (and necessary supporting documentation) of its medicinal purpose—that is, what it is designed to do.

- The basic costs of raw materials and manufacturing or of importing the product.

- The product's proposed consumer promise, brand name and suggested promotional strategy (for local adaptation); an identification of the suggested target market segment or segments for which the product was designed; and the product's recommended positioning versus that of competitive products.

- Summaries of experiences (both positive and negative) to date in other international markets, covering: consumers, competitors and trade reactions; initial levels of product sampling and purchase; likelihood of ''me too'' copies or generic competition; and regulatory barriers.

- Other information pertinent to local product decisions, such as the strategic importance to the parent company of introducing the product in as many countries and as soon as possible in order to preempt competition.

### Examining Critical Factors Affecting the Decision

The proposal is evaluated in light of key customer, market, competitor and company factors, as shown in Figure 4-2.

*Customer Factors.* In the local country, it is first determined if there is a sufficiently large, definable and potentially viable market—or market segment—to which the product can be sold. The determination involves comparing the target market, as defined in the proposal, with local demographics and conditions. In evaluating the *viability of a target-market segment*, such factors as income and appropriateness of the product are considered. A general evaluation of the market size, including estimates of total country population and per capita income, is also required.

*Market Factors.* Market factors are conditions faced in marketing products in a particular country and can be grouped into three categories. *Product factors* require judgments, based on market research, of such product factors as awareness, usage, brand loyalty, purchase frequency and overall consumer involvement levels. Evaluating the *marketing environment* involves determining the strengths and weaknesses of the existing marketing structure in the local country. Key considerations here are the availability of distribution channels and advertising media. *Entry barriers* may include:

- *Product* regulations, which can hinder a company's ability to register or distribute a product or formula.
- *Price* regulations, in the form of either price freezes or direct profit constraints on manufacturers or retailers.
- *Promotion* and advertising regulations, which can hinder a company's ability to communicate information about a new product to a specific target population.
- *Place/distribution* regulations, such as those restricting sales of nonprescription drugs to pharmacies.
- *Foreign-exchange controls*, which can hinder the efficient purchase of raw materials or finished products from international sources.
- *Cultural factors*, such as those in Middle Eastern countries concerning women's dress and behavior, that could prohibit the introduction of, for example, certain personal-care products.
- *Inflation*, which in some Latin American markets can exceed 1,000 percent a year.
- *Market saturation levels*, which could indicate diminishing returns for investments in new products.

*Competitor Factors.* Analyzing competitor factors involves examining the level of competition, the specific strengths and weakness of competitors in the industry and competing products. The *level of competition* measures the number, size and effectiveness of the competitors. *Competitor strengths and weaknesses* include measures of the overall strength of competitors' financial, distribution, manufacturing, promotional, and pricing resources. *Competing products* are examined for their similarity to the product under consideration, market position, and brand strength; assessments must be made of the likelihood of copycat products subsequently entering the market.

*Company Factors.* A firm's reputation or standing in a country is considered, along with its operating strengths and weaknesses. The evaluation also weighs the specific attributes of the proposed product and the product's relation to the company's existing product line. *Reputation* is measured by examining the company's relations with three key groups (industry trade groups, the medical community and consumers) and assessing the strength of the company's sales force. The *company strengths and weaknesses* examined include the firm's distribution, manufacturing, and promotion capabilities, its flexibility in pricing, and the resources available to support the introduction of a new product. A company's strengths and weaknesses are then compared with those of competitors.

*Product Evaluation.* Product evaluation involves examining the proposed product's formula and positioning, as described in the new product proposal, and weighing its strategic "fit," in terms of both the local company and its international parent. In evaluating the product, the degree to which the proposed *formula* conforms to locally accepted medical practice is determined, as well as whether some aspect of the formula (for example, an ingredient) needs to be changed before the product is introduced. The need for change can arise from regulations, accepted local norms for self-treatment, the availability of raw materials and other factors. Whether the product can be made in the country or must be imported is also studied. Formula considerations include estimates of the new product's value to the market. Is it unique? Does it present a significant and valuable improvement over existing product offerings in the market? The absence of any such advantages would mean that the parent is a "me-too" product—usually a weak competitive position.

*Judging Strategic Fit.* Judging strategic fit requires evaluating how well a proposed product would blend with, or improve, a company's existing product mix. It also involves studying a company's international enterprisewide strategy to determine if such an introduction is consistent with the firm's broader strategy of market penetration or positioning. Three separate, though related, evaluations are made of a proposed *product's positioning.* These determine whether the positioning, or "consumer promise," is: clear and understandable to the consumers in a local country, relevant to their wants, needs, and lifestyles and believable to potential product customers.

*Opportunity: Best Fit.* A number of other strategic factors, which are classified as "Opportunity: Best Fit," are considered. For example, if a company has no existing brand in the proposed product category, the product would be introduced as a new brand provided other factors are favorable. If the company already has a strong brand in the category, it is usually advisable to incorporate the new product into the existing line as a line extension rather than introducing a new brand. An example was Sterling Drug's "Midol 200," a pain-killing product introduced as a line extension to the existing Midol line, rather than as a new brand. This was a strategically sound move because the company lacked the resources to compete head-on with similar products such as Johnson & Johnson's "Tylenol" and "Medipren."

When a company has an existing brand in the new product's category and that is currently strong but the declining stages of its life cycle, it is often advisable to introduce the new product into the market as a new, improved (replacement) version of the existing brand rather than an entirely new brand. Where existing brands are weak and declining, introduction as a new brand would be preferable provided the other factors are favorable.

### Possible Recommendations and How They Are Made in Light of the Identified Critical Factors

After evaluating the impact of the major factors, seven possible strategic recommendations can be identified as possible responses a local manager might make to the new product proposal. These decisions can be grouped into three basic categories:

- Introduce the product (without change to the formula) as a new brand; as a line extension to an existing brand, or a replacement of an existing brand.
- Change one or more elements of the proposed product and introduce it as a new brand, as a line extension to an existing brand, or as a replacement of an existing brand.
- Reject (do not introduce) the proposed product.

The ideal situation is one in which the customer, market and company factors all strongly favor the company, and where competitor factors are weak. In this case, the final strategy choice is made by combining the appropriate "best-opportunity-fit" values—the new brand, line extension, or replacement—with information as to whether changes are needed. For example, if the best-opportunity-fit analysis concludes that the proposed product should be introduced as a new brand and that changes in the product are not needed, that would be the recommendation. If changes in the formula *are* needed, the recommendation would be to adapt or change the proposed product before introducing it as a new brand. If the best-opportunity-fit analysis indicates that the product would be best as a *line extension*, this would be the recommended strategy, depending on whether changes were needed.

Rarely, however, are conditions so totally favorable. Rather, more complex judgments are required in most situations. For example, in cases where customer and market factors are either average or strong (indicating that the market could support the introduction of a new product), but the competitors' position factors are stronger than the company's position factors, a new brand introduction would not be recommended under any circumstances. Instead, assuming the company had a strong existing brand in the category, the recommendation would be to introduce the product as a line extension or replacement. This strategy relies on the company's existing brands' strengths where all other factors are poor. If a strong existing company brand does not exist and there are no other special strategic corporate considerations, the proposed product would be rejected.

If competitor factors are strong and customer, market and company factors are weak, the recommendation would be not to introduce the proposed product—at least until conditions change. Other factors that should also trigger an automatic rejection include the presence of severe political, legal or other entry barriers, a combination of weak formula and weak positioning, and weak customer and marketing environment factors.

## METHOD OF ENTRY

The next multinational cross-cultural management decision area discussed here, market entry, is another critical enterprisewide and operational marketing planning decision. Three commonly used methods of entry are discussed in the following sections: export, wholly owned subsidiary and strategic alliances, such as joint ventures and contractual partnership arrangements.

### Exporting

Deere & Co. (whose experiences were described at the beginning of Chapter 1) first entered the international market through exporting, which is a common way to initially test an unfamiliar market.

Mail-order companies, such as L.L. Bean and Lands' End, also initially used exporting, both because it was a natural outgrowth of their business—selling through catalogs by mail—and because it was the least costly and risky way to initiate overseas operations. Japan, a country familiar with U.S. fashions and with a population of upscale, affluent shopping consumers, was chosen, and in this instance the export strategy has been very successful.

Mitsubishi Motors Corp. uses a variety of export strategies within its overall mixed multinational strategy. Its plant in Thailand exports parts to Canada, Malaysia and the Philippines; its Taiwan facility exports small parts to Japan; its Indonesian plant exports truck frames to Japan; its Malaysian plant exports cars to Britain and Asia and car doors to Thailand; and its South Korean plant exports parts to Taiwan and Japan (Updike and Nakarmi 1995). The method used by Mitsubishi is clearly a contingent one—each deal was tailored to the particular country's and business's situation requirements.

Overall exporting has been increasing rapidly: Eastern Europe's exports have increased at an annual rate of 25 percent, consumer good exports to Latin American rose 46 percent from 1991 to 1993, and sales of capital goods to Asia grew 19 percent in 1993 (Norton 1995). Overall, American-manufactured exports rose

10 percent in 1990 to $316 billion and jumped 80 percent from 1985 to 1990, with most of the increase coming from mid-sized companies in the $50 million to under $1 billion range (Rose 1991).

### Wholly Owned Subsidiary

The Drummond Company of Birmingham, Alabama, chose to invest $1 billion over 30 years in a coal-mining operation (including a port from which to ship the coal) in Columbia. Drummond is the owner and sole investor in the project. The company made the investment because of the high quality, magnitude (6.9 billion tons) and accessibility of the coal reserves in Columbia, in spite of the fact that Columbian taxes are high, there are no clear ground rules for investors and the threat of left-wing rebel sabotage is ever-present. To reduce the risks arising from these factors, the company established major security measures at its sites and received government guarantees that it need not share its profits (something Columbia requires of other firms).

The company expected to be producing 13 million tons of coal by 1999, most of which it planned to sell in Europe. Drummond's wholly owned investment and the investments made by other companies in coal-mining operations were expected to make Columbia the third-largest coal exporter by the year 2000. Competition is expected from both Venezuela and Chile, both of which were encouraging foreign investment in mining operations (Mercer 1995).

Many companies vary their approach, as seen from the discussions of Mitsubishi's mixed strategy—which varies, country by country, as dictated by the particular circumstances. For example, Blockbuster Entertainment, the biggest global video retail chain, planned to have 4,000 stores outside the United States by the year 2000, up from 1,400 in 1995. This was considered necessary for growth, since the U.S. video rental markets are saturated. In late 1995, the company owned 686 stores in Britain, an English-speaking country that permits such ownership. In contrast, in non-English-speaking countries, such as Italy, the company often uses joint ventures with local partners (Fabrikant 1995).

### Strategic Alliances: Joint Ventures and Contractual Partnership Arrangements

*Strategic alliances* is a general term referring to a wide range of cooperative ventures among different firms. They may involve a wide range of actitities, including the sharing of production facilities, cofunding of research projects and marketing of one another's products. Two common types are discussed here: joint ventures and marketing partnerships.

*Joint Ventures.* When entering the Asian market, Mitsubishi Motors used a variety of entry strategies as dictated by the various situations. For example, besides building a dozen parts and assembly plants throughout Asia, it also had ten joint ventures in Asia and others in Australia and New Zealand. These investments ranged from a 6.7 percent stake in Korea's Hyundai Motor Co. and a 16 percent stake in Taiwan China Motor to a 32 percent stake in Indonesia's Mitsubishi Krama Yudka and its latest prize—Vina Star Motors, a three-way venture with the Vietnamese government and Malaysia's state-owned Perisajaam Otomobil Nasional (Proton), which started selling vans in Vietnam in May 1995. Mitsubishi provides a model for the design of a mixed-entry strategy approach to Asia, where different kinds of deals are needed to meet varying situation requirements. Overall formula prescriptions appear to be no more effective in this task area than in other multinational cross-cultural management areas.

Mitsubishi's approach to overseas investment also provides a guide to success in the international auto market in the 1990s. Between 1990 and 1995, Japan had poured almost $20 billion—almost double the expenditures of its competitors—of direct investment into members of the Association of Southeast Asian Nations (ASEAN), a seven-member trading block (Updike and Nakarmi 1995).

The competitive impact of heavy investment in new markets was also evident in Poland in 1995 when Daewoo Motor Corp. of South Korea signed a letter of intent to invest $1.1 billion for a 60 percent stake in Poland's state-owned FSO car factory, thus throwing a wrench into General Motors Corp.'s plans to invest in Poland, as General Motors was unwilling to invest that much in FSO. Earlier, Fiat SpA (Italy) had invested $1.36 billion in another auto plant in Poland (Michaels and Marshall 1995).

Coca-Cola outspent its closest competitor, Pepsi-Cola, and won higher market shares in Eastern Europe, budgeting $700 million (mostly for joint venture investments), compared to Pepsi's $300 million in 1995 (Nash 1995).

In contrast, when faced with the uncertainty and difficulties caused by the breakup of the Soviet Union (Bohlen 1991), Polaroid developed a very conservative entry strategy for that region. Because of the turbulent environment, Polaroid wisely started small to test the waters and build a base for expanding later, if and when the Russian economy grew in a way that favored foreign firms. Using this entry strategy, Polaroid was able to operate one of the few successful manufacturing plants in Russia at that time—turning out 70,000 circuit boards a month (Greenhouse 1991).

*Partnerships.* In addition to its many investments, Mitsubishi also used an extensive marketing partnership with Chrysler to help raise its presence in the United States. Beside selling through its own modest network, Mitsubishi made cars for Chrysler (Updike and Nakarmi 1995).

Partnerships are common among international airlines. For example, in September 1995, Delta Air Lines applied for approval and antitrust immunity in order to expand its partnerships with Austrian Airlines, Sabena (Belgium), and Swissair (of Switzerland). Such immunity would allow the airlines to go beyond integrating passengers on selected flights, as they already did; it would also allow them to integrate flight schedules, marketing plans and sales promotions. In short, it would allow the partners to function as one carrier while not investing in one another and therefore remaining separate companies (McDowell 1995).

A comparison of the approaches used by Pepsi-Cola and Coca-Cola in Eastern Europe provides an example of the problems that can arise from partnerships. Pepsi initially made arrangements with state-owned company plants to bottle and sell its products; at the time when this was arranged, in the 1960s, it was realistically the only way available to penetrate the market. Many problems arose: inconsistent carbonation, hygiene (the bottles were often not washed), and delivery (small shops had to go to the bottler to get supplies). Still, Pepsi continued with the relationship after the breakup of the USSR. Six months after Coke started its own joint-venture plant in Bucharest, its sales surpassed Pepsi's in that city (Nash 1995).

### A Second Introductory Decision Learning Exercise: An Initial Entry Method Decision

The following is a second introductory learning exercise designed to let the reader use structured outlines of contingency decision processes to explore decision making in more depth. The decision process involved in making market-entry decisions is outlined in summary form in Figure 3-5.

Figure 3-5 represents a very simplified version of the decision, since it is intended for introductory learning purposes only. A more detailed overall outline of the decision is given in Figure 6-1a; some details of selected segments of the decision are given in Figures 6-1 (b, c, and d).

The exercise involves taking the description of The Drummond Company's wholly-owned investment decision described above and using the critical factors given there and the decision model representing the decision (Figures 6-1 and 6-1 [b, c, and d]). For introductory purposes, the possible recommendations are limited to: Export, Wholly-Owned Subsidiary, or Joint Venture/Contractual Partnership Arrangement. The reader should compare how the decision was made at Drummon with the process outline and study how closely Drummond's decision process followed the processes outlined in the figures.

### OTHER TASK AREAS: ADDITIONAL INTRODUCTORY LEARNING EXERCISES

This section briefly reviews a number of other contingency decision structures that the reader might wish to review. The objective of these exercises is to let the reader review the contingency processes involved in different task areas, practice using key factors to guide decision making, and perhaps even make some preliminary decisions that can be investigated further.

#### Sourcing Materials

These decisions involve determining the source used to supply products sold by a company. A sophisticated example of this type of decision and the use of

Figure 6-1a
Overall Dependency Diagram: Entry Mode Decision in the International Markets

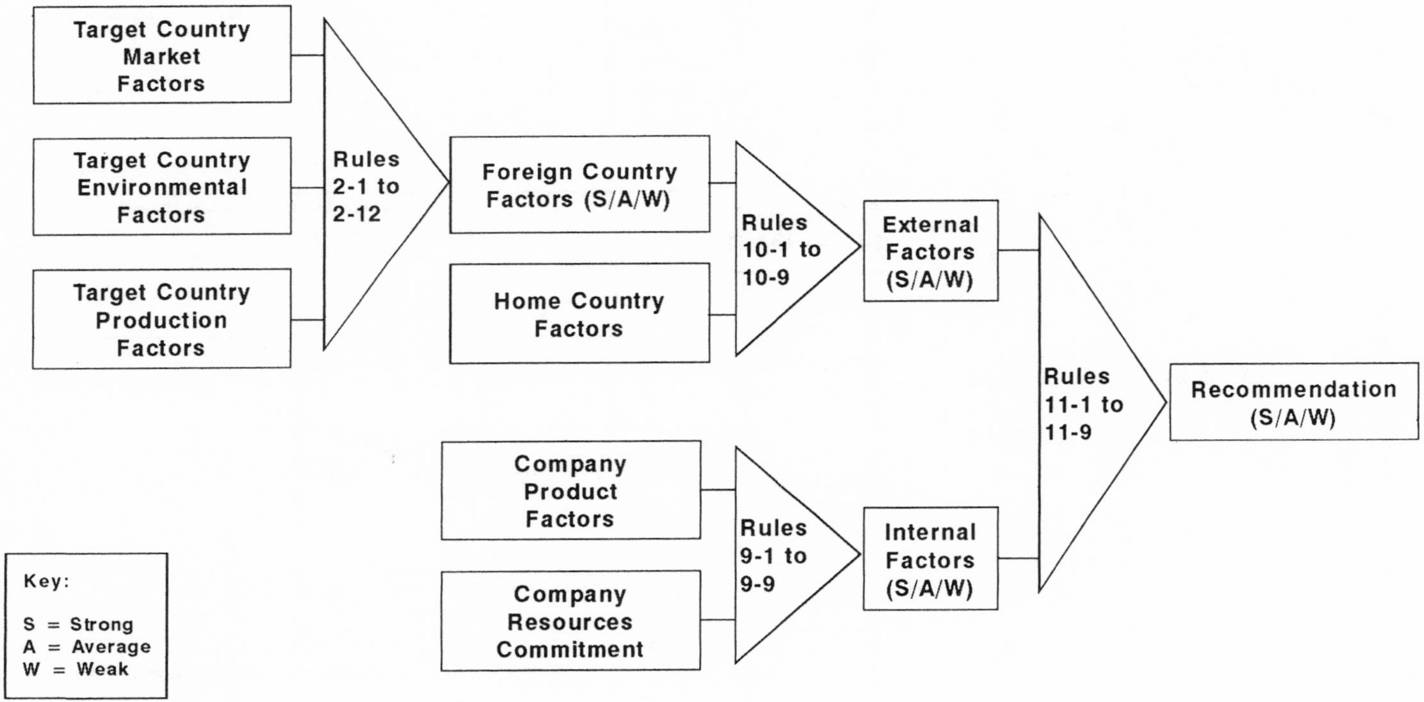

Key:

S = Strong
A = Average
W = Weak

Copyright © 1997 by R. J. Mockler.

Figure 6-1b
Dependency Diagram for Home Country Factors

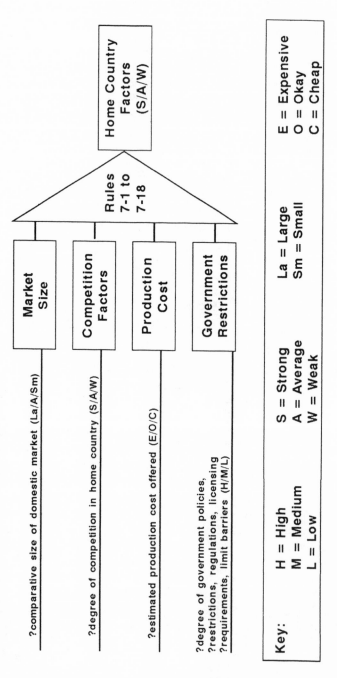

Copyright © 1997 by R. J. Mockler.

140

Figure 6-1c
Dependency Diagram for Company Product Factors

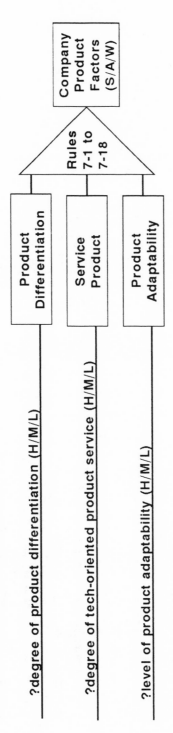

Copyright © 1997 by R. J. Mockler.

141

**Figure 6-1d**
**Dependency Diagram for Commitment of Company Resources**

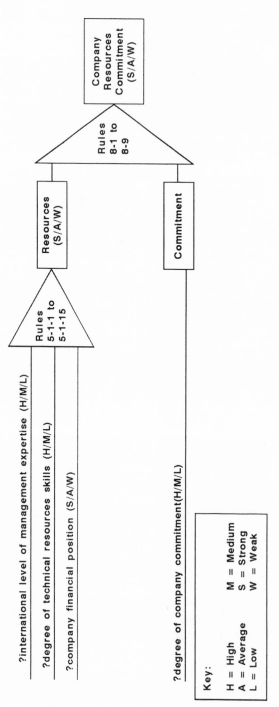

?international level of management expertise  (H/M/L)

?degree of technical resources skills  (H/M/L)

?company financial position  (S/A/W)

Rules
5-1-1 to
5-1-15

Resources
(S/A/W)

Rules
8-1 to
8-9

Company
Resources
Commitment
(S/A/W)

Commitment

?degree of company commitment(H/M/L)

Key:

| | |
|---|---|
| H = High | M = Medium |
| A = Average | S = Strong |
| L = Low | W = Weak |

Copyright © 1997 by R. J. Mockler.

computers to make them is given in Chapter 1, which describes the sourcing decision made and implemented for Gillette's "Atra" razor cartridge.

Figure 6-2 outlines a less complex kind of decision in this area, involving operations in Asia.

The following is an example of how a sourcing situation was handled in an actual test-case scenario. The process described here is outlined in Figure 6-2.

The RXC Company in Malaysia sent a sourcing request to its headquarters for a pharmaceutical product: "Feldene" 25 milligrams (mg) in bottles of 50 capsules, packaged in boxes of 100 bottles per box. RXC needed 100 boxes per month for six months, starting on September 1, 1995.

The materials analyst at headquarters first determined Malaysia's potential geographical supply area to be Asia. The supply point, according to the Asia sourcing guidelines, was located in Hong Kong. The analyst then determined if the requested product was available in the Hong Kong supply point.

Two reports were used to determine availability: the Hong Kong Supply Point inventory report and the shipment forecast report (from the manufacturing area). The inventory report showed that Feldene 25 mg in bottles of 50 capsules was not in inventory. The next step was to determine if Feldene 25 mg, regardless of the number of capsules per bottle, was in inventory at all. If this were the case, the manufacturer could repackage Feldene 25 mg in bottles of 50 capsules as requested by Malaysia. In this scenario, there was no inventory for Feldene 25 mg in Hong Kong.

The shipments forecast report was studied next to verify if there would be future shipments to the Hong Kong Supply Point of Feldene 25 mg. A review revealed that no shipment of the product was forecasted. At this point, the analyst concluded that the Hong Kong Supply Point could not be used as a supplier of the requested product.

The analyst next determined which Asian manufacturers were producing Feldene 25 mg in bottles of 50 capsules. This search produced two prospective sources: Australia and the Philippines. The sourcing guidelines indicated that Australia had a capacity problem and was currently manufacturing Feldene 25 mg for domestic consumption only. Australia was therefore eliminated as a candidate for sourcing. The materials analyst next examined the Philippines. The financial factors that the analyst studied showed that the standard product cost was average, the product markup was low, and the percentage of profits that could be sent back to the parent company in the United States was high. Therefore, overall, the financial factors were favorable.

The manufacturing factors studied show that actual product cost is average, product quality is high and plant capacity is good, as is materials availability. Overall, manufacturing factors are also favorable.

The legal factors studied reveal that import laws are flexible (low), and the need to export is high, as is ownership status. Overall, legal factors are, therefore, favorable.

The political factors analyzed show that the government is not stable (low),

Figure 6-2
Overall Decision Area: Determining the Source of Finished Goods, International Operations

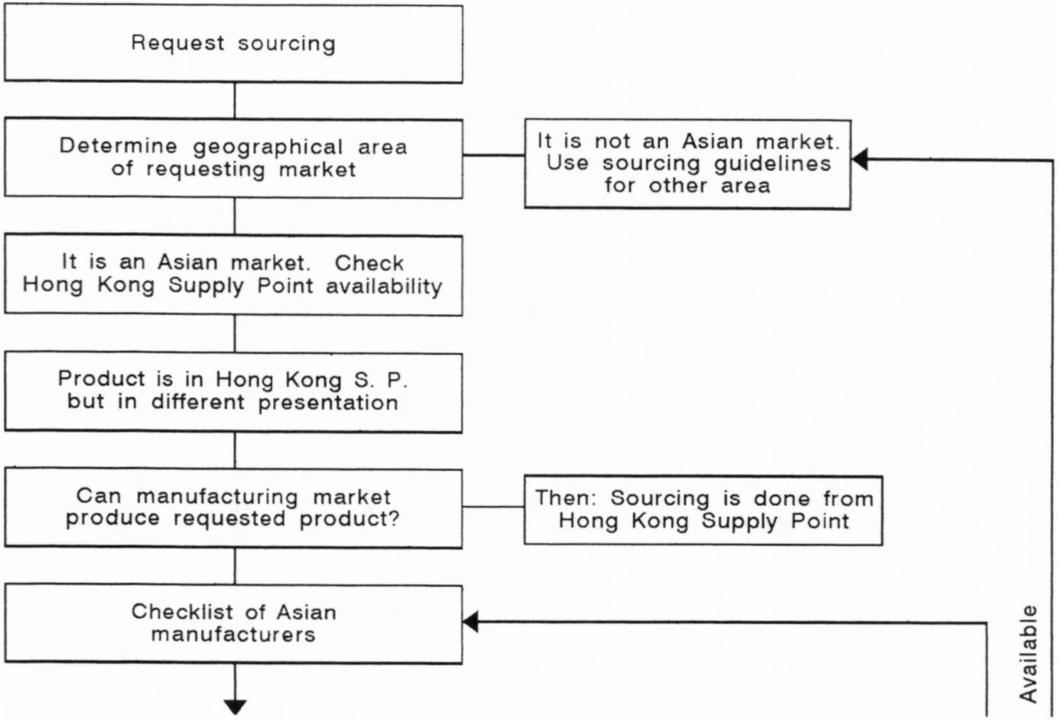

144

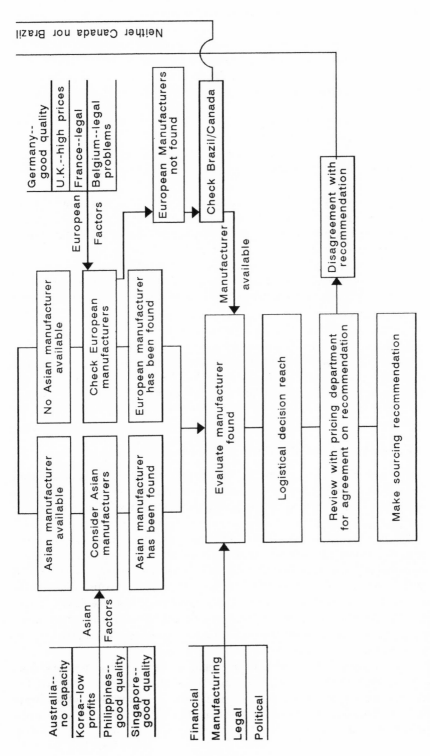

Copyright © 1996 by R. J. Mockler.

145

relations with the United States are good (high), and the economic situation is low. In this case, overall political factors are average.

At this point, the materials analyst assesses the outcome of this evaluation of the Philippines supply point:

Financial factors        = favorable
Manufacturing factors = favorable
Legal factors            = favorable
Political factors        = average

Based on the analysis, a recommendation is made to use the Philippines to supply Malaysia with Feldene 25 mg in bottles of 50 capsules. This decision is taken to the Pricing/Cost Department, which, after a study of all the factors, agrees to use the Philippines as a source.

In this situation, an Asian manufacturer was found. There are, however, cases where viable sourcing candidates are not available in Asia. The analyst would then check European manufacturers. Germany is considered first because it has favorable export laws. The United Kingdom has products of excellent quality but its prices are high, while France and Belgium have excessive import/export restrictions. If the search for a European source fails, Brazil is considered next because it has excess capacity, and Canada next, due to its high quality and reasonable prices. Once a country outside Asia has been found, the source will be submitted to the tests for financial, manufacturing, legal and political factors analysis.

### Location and Type of Facility

The following is another introductory learning exercise using structured outlines of contingency decision processes in another multinational task area—determining the location and type of facility. The decision process is outlined in Figure 6-3.

The Plastixx Corporation, a multinational manufacturer of plastic goods, has built two new plants in South Korea and Malaysia in addition to the two it has operating in Japan and plants in Hong Kong and Singapore. In the summer of 1989, the company has to consider setting up a regional Plastixx warehouse to reduce shipping costs for Plastixx goods being shipped from the Pacific Rim to Europe and the United States. The goods are plastic containers and plastic seals, packaged in lots of 1,000 onto standard packing crates. The items need no special storage conditions.

The vice-president in charge of international operations has made an initial survey of available sites and screened the list down to four locations. The choices are a shoreside lot in Seoul, South Korea; a downtown lot in Taipei, Taiwan; a warehouse just outside Kowloon, Hong Kong; and a lot in an industrial park in Manila, the Philippines.

**Figure 6-3**
**Factors Affecting an International Warehousing Decision**

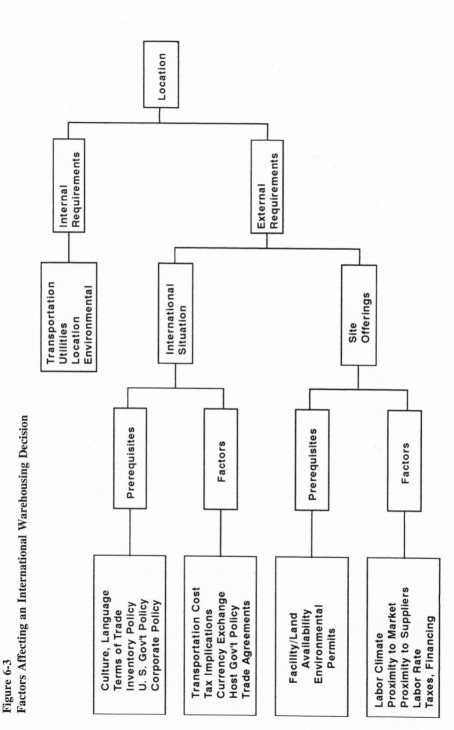

Copyright © 1996 by R. J. Mockler.

The vice-president starts the evaluation process by examining those elements that are considered prerequisites for the new warehouse. For each country he determines whether special U.S. laws govern the relationship between the United States and that nation. In a similar manner, he checks the corporate policies of the Plastixx Corp. The vice-president finds no obstacles to operating in any of the countries considered. Since each of the sites has been identified, he does not exclude any of the alternative countries due to a lack of available land, and he checks to make sure that the plastic products to be stored meet the health and environmental standards in force at each location. Since the Plastixx Corporation will take delivery of the goods, the terms of trade will not be a factor with this warehouse, nor will inventory policy, since the need for the warehouse has already been established. The final consideration is culture and language. Since a warehouse is needed in the Orient and the company has set no particular requirements as to language and culture, after analyzing the prerequisites, none of the four alternate locations are excluded.

The vice-president then evaluates other factors at each location. He observes that the United States has trade agreements with several Pacific Rim countries but discovers that none of the agreements pertain to the storing or moving of plastic containers. He then checks to see whether any of the governments in question have policies favorable toward a company like Plastixx; he finds that none do.

He then does a financial analysis. First, he examines the local costs of transportation in each country and calculates transportation costs from the production sites to the potential warehouse locations, and then on to the United States and Europe. He calculates labor costs and evaluates the overall labor environment in each country. He calculates the costs of taxes and financing at each location and the effects of each on the U.S. tax obligations of Plastixx. He factors in the effects of currency-exchange problems and the costs of currency transactions in each of the four locations.

Since all the nonfinancial factors at all locations are favorable, he picks the site that is most favorable to Plastixx from the perspective of the financial analysis as the location for the new warehouse.

In a similar instance, situation factors led Toyota to announce in 1995 that it would build a pickup truck plant in the United States. Toyota already owned and operated North American plants in Kentucky and Cambridge, Canada, and had established a joint-venture plant with General Motors in Fremont, California ("Toyota Plans" 1995). Favorable market factors, as well as transportation costs, tariffs, import restrictions, labor rates, construction and land costs, tax concessions, and consumer perceptions all contributed to Toyota's decision.

Similarly, situation factors such as low labor costs, European Economic Community regulations, the availability of an experienced labor force, and supporting manufacturing and parts supply infrastructures led both Siemens of Germany and Fujitsu of Japan to make billion-dollar investments in facilities in northern England (Stevenson 1995).

## THE COMPLEXITIES INVOLVED IN BALANCING DIVERSE SITUATION FACTORS

The situations discussed in this chapter involve enterprisewide and operating-level strategic management. They include reacting to immediate market needs, meeting anticipated changes, and responding to, and creating, new, long-term markets. Such situations require balancing global efficiencies with local responsiveness and the rapid transfer of new knowledge. They focus mainly on the planning aspects of strategic management; the enabling and doing aspects are given more emphasis in Chapters 7 through 13. In that sense they give a feel for the range of multinational management decisions.

A common framework—contingency processes—provided the structure for the decision making discussed in this chapter. That framework is an extension of the outlines discussed in Chapters 2, 3, and 5.

The examples discussed in this chapter were, however, relatively simple ones, having been designed as workshop examples of basic aspects of decision making in multinational cross-cultural management. They were also designed to provide some introductory learning exercises. As a result, they were segmented and somewhat simplified; therefore, they may not fully replicate reality.

For example, while it is useful to segregate tasks areas for discussion and learning purposes, and while many operational decisions are task specific, decisions in each area are often interrelated. Mitsubishi Motor Corp.'s decisions concerning the method of entry, market selection and product offered were inherently part of one decision involving all three task areas. Because of its introductory purpose, the discussion in this chapter did not explore these synergistic complexities in great detail.

In addition, while a systematic discipline, such as the contingency process, is useful—and needed—it is not enough. Like an actor or skier training to learn his or her chosen field, mastering the techniques of the profession is only a beginning. Using the techniques integratively, flexibly and creatively is the key to finding good solutions and getting the job done. Learning to synergistically put to work the different aspects of a discipline such as multinational cross-cultural management in order to ensure a positive real-life outcome goes beyond book learning. It requires real-world experience.

For example, in response to a soft world market for its jetliners, the Boeing Co. turned to China, a fast-growing market for its products (and the world's biggest market for jetliners), where it had already sold 100 planes, valued at $4.5 billion. In exchange, Boeing gave China parts-making contracts, manufacturing expertise and assistance with safety problems. A state-owned Chinese factory was to make as many as 1,500 tail assemblies for the Seattle-based Boeing manufacturing operations. Such exchanges are necessary because China is a very competitive market. Consequently, to compete with Airbus Industrie of Europe and McDonnell Douglas Corp., Boeing has had to make concessions. While such a move has done much for Boeing's overall longer-term prosperity, it has created local labor and political problems, which have to be balanced with its longer-term strategic moves in China. For example, in October, Boeing's machinists' union (representing 33,000 workers) went on strike, demanding, among other things, that Boeing cease or at least reduce its subcontracting. Boeing cutbacks have reduced its workforce by over 30,000 since 1989. The union was also pressing the U.S. government and President Bill Clinton to halt the exportation of jetliner production and technology to China, which was trying to build its own airliner industry. The press referred to Boeing's position as a high-wire balancing act, as it is forced to compete against much-lower-cost foreign manufacturers in worldwide markets that are growing much faster than the U.S. market for jetliners. Unless it can institute effective cost control and establish new joint market/manufacturing ventures, the company's long-term future seems bleak (Cole, Grauchli, and Smith 1995; Egan 1995).

The paradox that must be resolved affects the unions, the company, and the U.S. government. The unions want Boeing to compete globally, because without foreign sales, employment will drop substantially. At the same time, in order to obtain foreign sales, Boeing must subcontract at least half its production overseas to compete with other multinationals enjoying that region's dramatically lower labor costs. Boeing is the leading U.S. exporter—over 70 percent of its sales are overseas. In addition, when a foreign nation agrees to buy planes from Boeing, it typically does so on the condition that some of the work will be done in that country. No clear resolution of this difficult problem was in sight as of late 1995.

Also in late 1995, Fruit of the Loom Inc. announced that it was closing six of its U.S. plants and laying off 12 percent of its U.S. workforce. It cited as the cause the impact of the North American Free Trade Agreement (NAFTA) and the General Agreement on Tariffs and Trade (GATT), two trade agreements that are alleged to have led to the loss of over 100,000 textile jobs (out of a total of 1.6 million) in the United States. Originally, Fruit of the Loom's chairman, William F. Farley, had supported NAFTA, arguing that the expected resulting increased foreign sales would offset any production losses. As it turned out, however, in order to be competitive, the company had initiated a drive to move a high percentage of its operations to cheaper plants abroad (Feder 1995).

Situations involving the loss of jobs to plants overseas are only one aspect of the overall problem faced in the United States of a growing gap between the rich and the poor. Lower trade barriers are causing the loss of high-paying jobs across industries. Other factors contributing to the increasing gap and the resultant increasing pressure that companies are experiencing include an increased influx of legal and illegal, low-paid immigrants, increasing numbers of middle-level and management jobs lost due to the spread of computer information systems technology in business, and the huge influx of women into the work force (Wright 1995).

The situations faced by Boeing and Fruit of the Loom, like the problem faced by Anheuser-Busch over use of the Budweiser brand name in Czechoslovakia (see Chapter 1) and other difficult conflict situations described in this book, illustrate how multinational business situations can, in practice, be much more complex than the ones described in this chapter, which must therefore be considered only as an initial introduction to the fundamentals of multinational cross-cultural management in practice. The complexities involved in resolving paradoxes and other differences in multinational cross-cultural management are explored in more detail in the following chapters.

## WORKS CITED

"Bidders for Power Plants." *New York Times*, October 4, 1995, p. D3.

Bohlen, Celestine. "The Union Buried: What's Being Born?" *New York Times*, December 9, 1991, pp. A1, A9.

Clark, Don, and Neal Templin. "Compaq to Unveil Plan To Include Intel's Videoconferencing Technology in PCs." *Wall Street Journal*, October 26, 1995, p. B8.

Cole, Jeff, Marcus W. Grauchli, and Craig S. Smith. "Boeing Flies into Flap over Technology Shift in Dealings with China: Its Striking Machinists Urge White House to Limit Subcontracting Abroad; Developing an Asian Plane." *Wall Street Journal*, October 13, 1995, pp. A1, A11.

Egan, Timothy. "At Boeing, a War over Job Exodus: Strikers Try to Stem a Flow of Work to Outside Contractors." *New York Times*, October 14, 1995, p. 7.

Fabrikant, Geraldine. "Blockbuster Seeks to Flex Its Muscle Abroad." *New York Times*, October 23, 1995, p. D7.

Feder, Barnaby J. "Fruit of the Loom to Close 6 U.S. Plants." *New York Times*, October 31, 1995, p. D6.

Gates, Bill. *The Road Ahead.* New York: Viking/Penguin Books USA, 1995.

Gillooly, Brian. "H-P's New Course: Hewlett-Packard Wants to Construct a Global Information Infrastructure and Supply All the Equipment That Users Will Need to Access It; The First Step—Converge Its Core Businesses." *InformationWeek*, March 20, 1995, pp. 45–56.

Gleck, James. "Making Microsoft Safe for Capitalism." *New York Times*, November 5, 1995, Magazine Section, pp. 50–57, 64.

Greenhouse, Steven. "Polaroid's Russian Success Story." *New York Times*, November 24, 1991, Business Section, pp. 1, 6.

Holman, Richard L. "Postscripts. . . ." *Wall Street Journal*, August 18, 1995, p. A8.

Levy, Steven. "Bill's New Vision." *Newsweek*, November 27, 1995, pp. 54–57.

Lewis, Michael. *Pacific Rift: Why Americans and Japanese Don't Understand Each Other.* New York: W. W. Norton, 1993.

Lohr, Steve. "Under the Wing of Japan Inc., a Fledging Enterprise Soared." *New York Times*, January 15, 1992, pp. A1, D5.

McDowell, Edwin. "Delta Seeks to Expand Its Ties with Three Airlines in Europe: Functioning as One Carrier while Remaining Separate." *New York Times*, September 9, 1995, p. 34.

Mercer, Pamela. "U.S. Venture Bets on Colombian Coal." *New York Times*, July 27, 1995, p. D7.

Michaels, Daniel, and Matt Marshall. "Daewoo to Invest $1.1 Billion in Factory in Poland, Setting Back GM There." *Wall Street Journal*, August 17, 1995, p. A8.

Munk, Nina. "Make Mine Hoegaarden: Countering Anheuser-Busch's Drive to Make Bud a Global Brand, Belgium's Giant Interbrew Has Adopted a Multibrand Strategy That It Hopes Will Make It a Force in the U.S. Market." *Forbes*, December 18, 1995, pp. 124–125.

Nash, Nathaniel C. "Coke's Great Romanian Adventure." *New York Times*, February 26, 1995, Business Section, pp. 1, 10.

Naughton, Keith, Pete Engardio, Katie Kerwin, and Dexter Roberts. "How GM Got the Inside Track in China: A Relentless Push and Clever Strategy Seem to Have Won the Auto Maker a Huge Joint Venture." *Business Week*, November 6, 1995, pp. 56–57.

Naughton, Keith, and Heidi Hawley. "Upjohn Finally Makes It to the Big Leagues." *Business Week*, September 4, 1995, p. 35.

Norton, Rob. "Strategies for the New Export Boom: America's Big Exporters Are Striking It Rich Overseas—And So Are Thousands of Smaller Companies." *Fortune*, August 22, 1995, pp. 124–130.

Rapoport, Carla, with Justin Martin. "Retailers Go Global." *Fortune*, February 20, 1995, pp. 103–108.

Rose, Robert L. "How 3M, by Tiptoeing into Foreign Markets, Got to Be a Big Exporter." *Wall Street Journal*, March 21, 1991, pp 41, 45.

Sager, Ira. "The View from IBM." *Business Week*, October 30, 1995, pp. 142–150.

Simison, Robert L. "Volkswagen to Build New Beetle Model by End of Decade." *Wall Street Journal*, October 26, 1995, p. A4.

Stevenson, Richard W. "Smitten by Britain: Thatcherism's Industrial Evolution." *New York Times*, October 15, 1995, Business Section, pp. 1, 10.

Templeman, John, David Woodruff, Dexter Roberts, and Pete Engardio. "How Mercedes Trumped Chrysler in China." *Business Week*, July 31, 1995, pp. 50–51.

Tomkins, Richard. "Home Discomfort Pushes Southern Abroad." *Financial Times* (London), July 12, 1995, p. 17.

"Toyota Plans North American Truck Plant." *New York Times*, September 13, 1995, p. D23.

"Two Texas Utilities Seek a British Acquisition." *New York Times*, September 29, 1995, p. D3.

Uchitelle, Louis. "Aiming at H.M.O.s, Upjohn Agrees to $13 Billion Merger." *New York Times*, August 21, 1995, pp. A1, D2.

Updike, Edith, and Laxmi Nakarmi. "A Movable Feast for Mitsubishi." *Business Week*, August 28, 1995, pp. 50, 51.

Wright, Robert. "Who's to Blame? Job-Stealing Aliens and Job-Exploiting CEOs Are Easy Targets, But Growing Income Inequality Has Deeper Roots." *Time*, November 6, 1995, pp. 33–37.

Wysocki, Bernard, Jr. "Improved Distribution, Not Better Production, Is Key Goal in Mergers: The Kind of Service Developed by Wal-Mart Is Becoming Crucial in Many Industries." *Wall Street Journal*, August 29, 1995, pp. A1, A2.

**Part III**

# Supporting Enabling Systems

Chapter 7

# Telecommunications and Information Systems

This chapter covers both telecommunications worldwide and the information systems that make use of telecommunication links when used in enabling multinational cross-cultural management.

*Telecommunications* are defined as any transmission, emission or reception of signs, signals, writing, images or sound, as well as intelligence of any nature carried by wire, radio, optical, or other electrical or electromagnetic systems (Akwule 1992, p. 2). The impact of telecommunications on worldwide businesses is substantial. According to the *1995 World Telecommunications Development Report*, the information/communication industry, consisting of telecommunications, computing, and audiovisual sectors, saw revenues worldwide grow to $1.4 trillion in 1994. Out of every $1,000 spent worldwide, $59 goes to this industry (cited in Egolf 1995b, p. 5). In Europe alone, the 100 top companies (with assets of $5.5 trillion) were expected to spend some $41.7 billion on information systems in 1995 (Tate 1995, p. 34).

The growth and impact of this industry is expected to continue to be a major contributor to the creation of a truly global village. Because of its perceived role as a stimulator of economic growth and prosperity and a bridge across diverse cultures, the industry's impact is being felt in all kinds of nations, emerging and mature, in many different areas. For example, the introduction of the Cable News Network (CNN) is considered to have been a major factor in the breakup of the USSR (Henry 1992; "World View" 1990). This chapter focuses on the impact of telecommunications on multinational cross-cultural management.

A wide range of business information systems use worldwide telecommunications capabilities. Many are proprietary company (*intracompany*) information systems, such as the globally linked production/operations computer systems at

Gillette (described in Chapter 1) that determined the best locations in which the "Atra" razor could be most economically manufactured.

*Business-to-business* systems include the electronic data-interchange systems established between companies and their suppliers, which allow, for example, hand-held computers in a retail store to generate information that can be automatically used to check inventory, order replacement goods from warehouses or generate orders to suppliers for replacement goods—all without human intervention. An example of a *business-to-customer* system is the British Airways reservation system (described in Chapter 3), which handles customer reservations worldwide.

This chapter discusses telecommunications and computer information systems and their impact on multinational cross-cultural management. It also discusses some of the problems encountered in diffusing technology worldwide, especially in developing countries.

## TELECOMMUNICATIONS

Telecommunications systems provide the access and speed needed for global business information systems to function effectively. The following sections review the basic aspects of telecommunications systems one should understand when planning, developing, and using worldwide information systems: types of transmissions and connecting links, types of systems and expected future technological developments.

The impact of advances in telecommunications on the world is significant. Theoretically, over the next ten years it will be possible to link every home (and thus, every person) in the world through any one of a number of telephone, video, radio, computer and facsimile devices. The implications of development for globalization, information exchange and business are vast, since it will provide total and instantaneous communication among the world's population. Therefore, it is useful to understand the basics of telecommunications linkages, as well as the computer systems that make use of these linkages being used to create sophisticated business information networks.

### Transmission Systems: Wire and Wireless

Telecommunications systems use electrical or electromagnetic energy to transmit information, in the form of sound, light or mechanical energy, between two or more points. The information is first converted into energy and transmitted directly over wires or radiated through space to a receiver, where it is then reconverted into its original form or another form that is understandable to the person or machine involved (Akwule 1992, p. 30). The signals can be either *analog* (electronic frequency sound or acoustical waves) or *digital* (a series of electronic signals representing discrete numeric values, represented by the binary numbers (0 or 1) that are used by a computer) (McDaniel 1994, pp. 24, 198).

Digital signals are more commonly used today, since they are more efficient for business purposes.

Telecommunication transmission systems can be either wireline or wireless (or some combination of the two).

*Wireline Transmission Systems.* Three wireline systems are commonly used. *Copper wire* is used for basic telephone systems. For efficient long-distance communication, several acoustical signals can be combined, or multiplexed, over copper wire so that they may be carried simultaneously by a single wire cable as opposed to a large bundle of wires. *Optical fiber,* which transmits light waves and so permits much faster communication (186,000 miles per second), and which enables carrying many more conversations over a narrower cable (making it cheaper), is replacing copper wire as an essential component of telephone transmission systems. Another major advantage of optical fibers is that they can carry, not only voice and data, but video as well. *Coaxial cable* uses two conductors, a hollow metal tube about the diameter of a pencil and wires inside the metal tube wrapped in insulation. It is used especially for long-distance communication since it can carry a much larger number of channels than ordinary wire.

*Wireless Transmission Systems.* Current global communication networks are made possible by the use of two properties of nature: electromagnetic energy and orbital space. Long-distance wireless communication systems—telephone systems, television networks (CNN, for example) and computer networks (the Internet, for example)—function by converting information into energy, which is then radiated through space. The electromagnetic spectrum—the range of available natural energy resources that make possible the transmission of different kinds of telecommunications signals—and the available orbital space for satellites are limited natural resources. Since demand for these resources is increasing as they are being harnessed for a rapidly growing number of practical ends, future problems could arise involving their allocation (Akwule 1992, pp. 33–34). The transmission of wireless signals over the airwaves uses the radio portion of the electromagnetic spectrum. Other portions of the spectrum include infrared rays, visible light, ultraviolet rays, x-rays, gamma rays and cosmic rays. The following paragraphs discussed several familiar wireless transmission systems.

*Mobile radio communication* networks are now widely available to the general public, thanks largely to developments in cellular radio, which now make the limited number of frequencies available to many more subscribers. Cellular radio functions by dividing an area geographically into cells, with each cell having its own base station; each mobile terminal communicates with a base station (cell site) using specially allocated ultra-high-frequency (UHF) channels. Advances in the integration of cellular technology with satellites and computer-assisted technology signifies endless possibilities for the individual subscriber. Modern-day cellular networks were first developed in 1981 in Scandinavia, then in 1984 in the United States, and in 1986 in the United Kingdom. By 1992, mobile cellular networks in the United States alone had about 9 million sub-scribers. In China, cellular phones are one of the fastest-growing products. In developing countries, wireless communication is a substitute for nonexistent communications infrastructures (Budway 1992, p. 22).

*Microwaves* use a frequency band of 3,000-12,000 megahertz (MHz) for line-of-sight microwave relay links in which signals are transmitted from antennas mounted on tall towers. Repeater stations, which pick up, amplify and retransmit the signal, are also tower-like structures, which are placed at 25- to 30-mile intervals, usually on the tops of hills. The microwaves are very useful for con-necting large population centers and can carry thousands of telephone channels on a single microwave carrier.

*Satellites* operate in the microwave band. In fact, a satellite is simply a giant microwave relay up in the geostationary earth orbit (a nearly circular orbit 22,300 miles over the equator). A satellite can, at any one point, view 40 percent of the earth's surface. Its antennas can be designed to send a weak signal to this entire area or to concentrate stronger signals from an earth station in one country to several different stations located in the same, or different, continents or countries. This technology enabled 3.4 billion television viewers to watch the Worldcup soccer matches in 1994, 34 times the number of people who watch the Superbowl football game (Akwule 1992, p. 38; Zeien 1995).

Since satellites have to be separated in order to avoid radio interference, a limited number of orbital positions in geosynchronous orbit can be used for communication. Nonetheless, satellite transmission capabilities are developing quickly. For example, Hughes Electronics launched three satellites to supply "Direct TV," a digital service for the home. In 1995, "Direct TV" antennas were the fastest-selling consumer electronics product in history and had become available eighteen months ahead of cable companies' efforts to use digital proc-essing to create hundreds of television channels (Dolinar 1995, p. 23). A major advantage of "Direct TV" installations is their size—they are only eighteen inches in circumference and easily attached to the side of a house, which en-hances their portability and ease of installation.

The most popular types of transmission systems feature a combination of optical fiber, coaxial cable, mobile communications and satellite systems. At this time, optical fiber is probably the most valuable because it can transmit larger amounts of voice, data, and video at more efficient costs. Coaxial and mobile communications lack the capabilities of optical fiber, while satellites have im-mense capabilities but are much more expensive.

### Types of Telecommunication Transmissions and Connecting Devices

The most commonly used types of telecommunication transmissions are voice, data and video.

*Voice.* The ability to transmit voice over systems is accomplished using different kinds of equipment. The *basic telephone* uses a microphone to convert speech or sound into electric signals, which are transmitted over various wireline and wireless systems. *Cellular phones*, which are now small enough to fit into one's pocket, use wireless systems.

*Data.* Cables were laid in 1858 for the *telegraph*, the original transoceanic data communication link. One of the most popular forms of data transmission today is the *facsimile (fax) machine*, which can transmit printed matter and still pictures by telephone, telegraph or radio for reproduction by another facsimile machine. *Computers* are another popular means of communicating data, which can be stored in memory, processed by processor components, and sent and received through input/output components. The networking of computers through such global communication systems as the Internet has greatly increased their capability to create worldwide linkages, especially in the area of computer information systems. Modern computers also have video capabilities.

*Video. Videophones* were introduced 25 years ago by AT&T. They were not successful because of the fuzzy picture and the fact that while people like to see others while phoning, apparently they do not like to *be* seen (Samuelson 1995, p. 210). New versions have recently been introduced for use in health-care services and a wide range of businesses. In the future, *"VideoDialtone"* will allow a dialtone to be activated directly through a television set, thus enabling and enhancing video-on-demand services and other interactive on-line services. *Videoconferencing* utilizes a video camera to capture the activity of a group at one location while using a television monitor to view another group located elsewhere. Each location has a similar setup. Many companies now use such conferencing worldwide. For example, one division of General Electric reported using videoconferencing as many as 1,000 times a year. *Desktop videoconferencing*, which makes use of computers and computer screens, is an emerging technology. Johnson Controls Inc. was exploring this technology and expected to have each its fifteen worldwide sites connected in 1996 in order to provide international training and technical support (Brandel 1995, p. 81).

### Expected Future Technological Developments in Telecommunications

A number of new developments promise to make telecommunications even more effective and efficient for multinational management. The integrated services digital network (ISDN) provides a means of combining high-quality voice and high-speed data transmission in a single, simple and very economical line. ISDN will help improve any communication that requires voice, data, image or video, whether together or separately. Ansynchrous transfer mode (ATM) broadcasting is another form of technology capable of offering users high bandwidth for sending and receiving mixed video, data and voice transmissions. Efforts are even being made to meet the needs of small businesses by putting together such services as ISDN, voice-mail capabilities, and long-distance telephone. This is being done by GTE Telephone Operations, among others (Egolf 1995a, p. 34).

Major trends in telecommunications technology are also affecting competitive positions in the telecommunications industry and stimulating international mergers, expansion and partnerships among many large companies. Cable and telephone companies are forming joint ventures: for example, U.S. West, Tele-Communications Inc. (TCI) and Time-Warner formed a full-service public cable company in England. Telecommunications companies are also merging with media and entertainment companies ($16 billion Time-Warner now has cable programming and cable operating systems divisions, as well as publishing, music, and television production divisions) in order to create synergistic competitive advantages arising from combining communications links with programming development capabilities.

Even NYNEX, a regional telecommunications/telephone service provider in the northeastern United States, is expanding overseas and into related telecommunications areas—largely because of the legal limitations on expansion in the home country. For example, NYNEX bought seventeen cable franchises in the United Kingdom (NYNEX CableComms) and formed a joint venture in Thailand (TelecomAsia) to offer telephone services there (Arnst, Jackson, and Shari 1995a; "Meeting" 1994; "NYNEX" 1993; Sylvester 1994, 1995a, 1995b; Williamson 1992).

By the end of 1995, plans had been announced for almost 36 satellite development projects totaling more than 1,500 satellites—five times the number of commercial communications satellites launched since the first, AT&T's Telstar in 1962. Their total cost was estimated to amount to $43 billion over the next ten years (Lynch 1995). Also in late 1995, Alcatel Cable S.A of France and AT&T Corporation of Morristown, New Jersey, announced that they had reached an agreement to cooperate on the design, manufacture, supply and installation of an underseas cable system that would encircle the continent of Africa; its estimated cost was $2.6 billion ("AT&T" 1995). On the same day, Deutsch Telekon and Ameritech Corporation announced that they were buying a controlling interest in the Hungarian phone company, Matav, for $1 billion (Associated Press 1995).

## WORLDWIDE INFORMATION SYSTEMS

Information systems are the organized transmission and dissemination of information in accordance with defined procedures, whether automated or manual (Longley and Shain 1989, p. 261). These worldwide computer and other information systems make use of, and so are enabled by, telecommunications superstructures, which serve as common frameworks.

There are many ways to create and use information systems to meet different needs. Prior to Johannes Gutenberg's invention of the movable type printing press, people had to rely on town criers; Irish monks, who copied books by hand (Cahill 1995); smoke signals; carrier pigeons; strolling troubadours and similar means for the latest news and information. Toward the end of the nineteenth century, electronic information media were introduced. In 1893 in Budapest, Hungary, the *Budapest Messenger*, a local newspaper, offered the first electronic news service—via a five-inch telephone speaker connected to two receivers, thus accommodating two listeners (Ferrarini 1985, p. 1). It has taken more than 100 years and many technological advances to reach the computer information age of today, which gives people an overabundance of information through a wide range of media. In 1995, for example, a weekday edition of the *New York Times* contained more information than the average person in seventeenth-century England was likely to come across in a lifetime (Wurman 1989, p. 31).

Technology, the proliferation of media, the increase in the number of people and companies involved in data production and processing, and the low cost of collecting data all contributed to the explosion of information, the total amount of which is now estimated to double every four years. The following sections discuss the worldwide information systems that have been, and are being, developed to both increase the proliferation of information and, at the same time, harness it in the service of multinational cross-cultural management. These sections cover four types of worldwide computer informations systems: *networks; intrabusiness* computer information systems; *business-to-business* systems; and *business-to-customer* systems.

## Worldwide Computer Information Networks: Information Superpaths

Telecommunications systems provide the superstructure along which information superroadways may be built and information systems can flow. In this sense, telecommunications systems are only one aspect of the superstructure: they serve as the electronic or electromagnetic wireline and wireless rails or roadbeds along which the information systems travel.

Many of the connecting links that enable people to use the telecommunications systems superstructure have already been discussed: computers and processors, telephones and cellular phones, telegraph and telefax machines, facsimile machines, videocameras and video phones, satellite dishes, and other sending and receiving devices, all of which are only a part of a much larger information superstructure.

The world's largest and most dramatic network developed along the information telecommunications superstructure has been the Internet, network of procedures, protocols and other computer-based software mechanisms that enables the instantaneous worldwide transmission of information. It is a wide-area network that connects thousands of smaller, disparate networks in industry, education, government and research.

The forerunner of the Internet was the Advanced Research Projects Administration Network (ARPANET), a project created by the U.S. Department of Defense (DOD) in 1969, both as an experiment in reliable networking and to link DOD to military contractors. It grew quickly since many universities joined the network, and it eventually split into two networks, one military and one nonmilitary. These two networks were connected through the International Protocol (IP), a system of internationally accepted transmission protocols. All networks in the Internet are connected by IP, which enables traffic to be routed from one network to another (McDaniel 1994, p. 354). Additional networks, both government (National Science Foundation, for example) and commercial (IBM and Sprint, for example) networks have been established.

During 1990–1991, Tim Berners-Lee created the multimedia software for the World Wide Web and put it on the Internet without charge. A major technological breakthrough, the Web enables anyone to use the Internet to access and establish a *home page*, on which an individual or company can advertise, sell products, publish notices and generally communicate throughout the world. This capability is now known as the World Wide Web. Berners-Lee has refused to license the software to any commercial interest, since he believes it should be available to everyone (Lohr 1995). Today, anyone can create a Web page or site, and many already have: college professors (for their students), businesses (to advertise and sell products), news media (for readers to locate information), and individuals (people with special interests, for example). Anyone in turn is free to consult these Web pages, either on their own or using one of the many available *browsers* (in 1996, "Netscape" was the most well-known).

The introduction of the World Wide Web and graphical interface software, such as "Mosaic" and, later, "Netscape," led to an explosion in the use of the Internet. Between 1993 and 1994, the Internet as a whole doubled in size, as it had done every year since 1988. It now reaches 5 million "host" computers, which are connected to a total of well over 20 million users (Anderson 1995). Based on the 1995 worldwide increase in communications sites (for example, China went from 2 sites to 593; Argentina, from 1 to 1,415; and Japan, from 38,267 to 99,034), it appears that future growth will be even faster. The Internet (and the World Wide Web) have forever changed the way business is done on an international scale. The Internet's open accessibility has also led to major strategic changes at companies such as Microsoft, which can no longer control markets as they did in the past (with such products as their DOS operating software).

Many ways exist to make use of the worldwide telecommunications superstructure, of which the Internet is only one. The following section discusses many of the computer information systems that businesses have developed and use to communicate information along the telecommunications superstructure. Some systems make use of the Internet, while others were in existence long before its creation. Many companies are, however, beginning to switch to the Internet to save money, especially when security is not a concern.

**Intrabusiness Systems**

Many different kinds of global information systems have been developed by companies to enable managing and running the company. For example, Westinghouse developed its own "Westinghouse Information Network," an information network that links more than 600 locations across Europe, Asia, and the Americas and that, as of 1990, was used daily by more than 90,000 people (Ruffin 1990). In the manufacturing area, thanks largely to the ability of the computer information network to speed data around the world, for example, parts for circuit breakers can be made in the Dominican Republic and fitted neatly into finished products in North Carolina. Orders are placed, parts configured, and shipments confirmed, all machine-to-machine over the network. From a monitoring point in Orlando, Florida, technicians use the network to keep tabs on the performance of Westinghouse turbine generators in the United States and three foreign countries, as well as to spot small glitches before they become big ones.

Westinghouse's network also helps the sales process with such innovations as the "EDGE" advanced negotiations system, which automates pricing and order engineering. As complex negotiations progress, they involve far more than face-to-face interchanges; they also involve the people who sell the product, as well as those who will price it, make it and deliver it. EDGE creates a database containing product information that all these groups can access over the network, ensuring that information flows quickly and smoothly from all points to the people who are actually closing the deal.

Westinghouse's network also includes an internal electronic-mail (e-mail) system, which makes virtually every employee around the world instantly reachable. If desired, employees can even tie their home phones into the network. Managers on the road can tap into the network from laptop computers, and a global voice-mail system helps travelers keep track of messages. Leading-edge digital technology can carry massive amounts of data, including technical drawings. A videoconferencing system ties operations together with the most advanced and flexible technologies.

All of these interactive decision support systems within the network are in addition to the normal finance, accounting and financial control systems. In addition, Westinghouse Information Network also has links with business customers.

Exxon Corporation's worldwide (nontechnical) computer information systems are handled by Exxon Computing Services Company (ECSC) in Houston, Texas. With a staff of 500, the organization handles customer-order processing, customer invoicing, marketing terminal operations, refinery maintenance information, U.S. retail credit card operations, accounting, inventory tracking, payroll processing and human resource records. The center operates extensive telecommunications networks at Exxon locations around the world and helps coordinate the networks' use in doing business in more than 80 countries. The center is a large operation that provides computing services for more than 30,000 Exxon employees and has sufficient capacity for 8,000 or more employees to use the center's computers concurrently, at peak hours. The center can process more than 800 million computer instructions per second (Zwicker 1993).

Festo (a medium-sized company headquartered in Esslingen, Germany), with 3,500 employees worldwide and branches in 187 countries, provides another example. Festo is a world market leader in pneumatics and device control. One of its four major product groups is Festo Pneumatic, which manufactures valves and cylinders and provides complete solutions for device control, offering 35,000 components and 4,000 products by catalog. All products are manufactured in Germany, and 55 percent of the products are exported through one of the company's 35 subsidiaries and more than 100 branches. Between 200 and 300 orders, with an average of four items each, are received daily from each of the major subsidiaries.

In general, customers order from a branch office by fax or phone. The branch sends orders by microcomputer to the subsidiary headquarters. If the component is unavailable in the country's warehouse, the order is sent by computer to the German headquarters where it is entered into the central computer, which checks inventories and production schedules, confirms the order and sends a delivery date to the subsidiary. As appropriate, the computer system then issues either warehouse or production instructions. The system is an integrated worldwide order-processing system linked to both manufacturing and warehouse management systems (Loudon and Loudon 1996, pp. ICS 19–22).

Levi Strauss and Co. uses personal computers to enable employees to join electronic discussion groups with colleagues around the world. They can even watch Levi's latest commercial or comment on marketing pitches. This system was to be available to 10,000 workers by the end of 1996. Interestingly, Levi does not use Lotus Notes (a group software product). Instead of paying IBM to install Lotus Notes software on thousands of desktop computers at $150 a computer, it uses the Internet's World Wide Web, which can be used free of charge, except for a $20 charge for the browsing software (Zeigler 1995).

Europcar, a rental car operation headquartered in Paris, created a new information system to match a company reorganization in the early 1990s. The new system replaced 55 different systems that had been in use in nine countries in Europe. It integrated reservations, billing, fleet management, cost control and corporate finance across all rental car stations and administrative offices (Greenbaum 1994).

Many problems can be encountered in developing global informations systems, since each country works within its own context and so, as in other multinational management task areas, their development requires being responsive to local differences (Madnick 1995). In many cases, it is difficult to transfer systems from one country to another. Esprit de Corp in California attempted to use a manufacturing system developed at a Far East affiliate. The Asian computer software system tracked where an item of clothing was manufactured, sewn, pressed, finished and washed. Unfortunately, work habits are different around the world: for instance, in the Far East, the shop doing the sewing customarily handled pressing and washing, whereas in the United States, these tasks were contracted out. Such context differences prevented the transfer of the software, so the company elected to develop new software rather than to redesign the Asian version (Ambrosio 1993). In another instance, Federal Express, an express package/mail delivery service, had to redesign its billing system for Britain and Japan because local customers used different invoicing procedures. Similarly, Europcar encountered substantial problems in adjusting to foreign currency fluctuations and diversity and to the different languages in each location. This chapter's final section, on technology diffusion, discusses additional aspects of the impact of context differences on systems development globally.

Systems like the ones here are proprietary systems; that is, they are developed and owned by a particular company. There are also worldwide information systems that link proprietary company systems with other systems worldwide. For example, GrandMet of Britain has turned its entire global voice and data network over to Concert, a joint venture of British Telecommunications (BT) and MCI. GrandMet, owner of the Pillsbury, Burger King, Paddington, Pearl Vision and Heublin consumer brands, now has the ability to share information worldwide. For instance, Burger King of Japan is able to get the same information about the global supply of ground beef or hamburger rolls as the U.S. Burger King by computer—and from the same database, at the same time (Thyfault 1995).

Worldwide information systems within multinational organizations are made up of a variety of different kinds of systems—from highly integrated global corporate systems and industry networks to individual systems for accounting and finance, manufacturing planning and control, sales support and marketing management, information exchanges through the Internet, e-mail, video conferencing, voice mail, human resources management and group/team work. Worldwide business information systems that link companies to other companies and to customers are covered in the following sections.

### Business-to-Business Systems

Electronic data interchange (EDI)—the computer-to-computer exchange of business documents and data, such as that needed for invoices, purchase orders, letters of credit, solicitations and proposals—is one of the most widely used forms of business-to-business information systems. Over 500 of the "Fortune 1,000" firms were involved in EDI in the early 1990s, a number that was expected to increase by 50 percent during the mid-1990s.

EDI links a business's internal computer systems with those of other businesses. The function of EDI is to use electronic transactions to replace the manual flow of paper, faxes, and verbal communications involved in processing orders. The Harper Group, an international freight-shipping company, uses EDI technology to support its deliveries around the world (Turban, McLean, and

Wetherbe 1996, p. 384). Harper has an EDI connection with 500 of its larger business customers, including Honda Motor Company of Japan. Honda ships more than 300,000 cars and trucks to the United States each year, and Harper handles all the required arrangements including those involving U.S. Customs.

The process involves the following steps. To initiate the process, Honda sends its commercial invoices electronically from Japan to the U.S. Honda office in Los Angeles. The information—details of the cars and parts being shipped, tariff numbers and the value of each item—is then transferred electronically to Harper's mainframe computer in San Francisco, where Harper supplements this data with antidumping (below-cost pricing) information, visas for floor mats and other textiles used in the car, and the freight carrier's name. The complete order file—consisting of as much as 100 pages—is transferred electronically to U.S. Customs several days before the ship docks in the U.S. port. Customs calculates and sends to Harper the amount of payments due on each shipment, and Honda's duty payments are then transferred electronically from a bank designated by Harper's mainframe to customs. Finally, Harper bills Honda electronically for its services and is paid via the electronic transfer of funds.

Commercial EDI software packages are widely available. In the health-care industry, OnCall EDI, which was developed by the EDI software vendor TSI International, runs on desktop computers, with "Microsoft Windows" as the user interface. It includes a built-in database for tracking transactions and interfaces to materials management computer information systems, and provides communications support for direct links between hospitals and suppliers (Betts 1994).

One integrated part of the international Westinghouse Information Network is a business-to-business customer subsystem. Through this integrated subsystem, customers can shop on their own personal computer (PC) using software supplied by Westinghouse. For example, if they need a part for a turbine, they dial into the network and fill out the appropriate form on their computer screen. Business customers can examine a detail schematic of the part on the same system. The electronic purchase order goes into the system, which locates the equipment and issue an order to move it out.

To provide fast maintenance and technical service, Westinghouse tracks the whereabouts of key support staff in a constantly updated database. If a customer needs a rush repair on a generator, Westinghouse can track down and dispatch the right technician via the network. The company also uses the network to maintain communications links to its power equipment so that it can monitor performance and spot potential problems in the United States and three foreign countries (Ruffin 1990).

Systems like these require a considerable amount of security, and so, like so many of the internal company computer information systems discussed in this section, they make only infrequent use of the Internet for recording and handling actual business transactions, such as financial transactions, which need the authentication of parties involved to protect against fraud (Gambon and Maddox 1995).

Business-to-business systems are also found in the media industry, where the Internet is used. In the past, many creators and users of photographs, such as news agencies like United Press International (UPI), newspapers and magazine publishers, and stock photo houses, did not have automated access to photos, nor the means for their distribution. A new Internet software application developed by Phrasea has done this. Like World Wide Web applications, Phrasea's archiving or authoring software can be set up on one workstation. Clients seeking photos can then dial in and browse through the available photos, select the ones they want, and instantly download the high-resolution (digital) photos they have selected. Prior to this, a company like UPI in Washington used to do a daily analog broadcast of 400 to 600 poor-quality news photos that were available that day. Business clients would select the ones they wanted, and the originals would be couriered to them or delivered via satellite (Olmsted 1995).

### Business-to-Customer Systems

The preceding section contained a variety of examples of businesses dealing with other businesses. This section deals with systems that involve businesses dealing with individual customers, who may lack a sophisticated knowledge of computers.

Chapter 3 described the British Airways system, which used satellites to link a sophisticated customer database with customers throughout the world via telephone operators and through service representatives in British Airways offices.

Today, many companies have developed computer links with their customers. Citibank in New York, for example, offers its customers free computer software to enable them to bank wherever and whenever they like, using their computer modem and a telephone line. Once customers are connected with their accounts, they can move money between accounts, check balances, see whether checks have cleared, and review 90 days' of transactions on both their bank accounts and Citibank credit card accounts. This service also allows the customer to pay most bills on-line, obtain free stock quotes, and place orders to buy and sell securities (Citibank 1996). Citibank's Hong Kong branches offer automated teller machines and accounts in ten different currencies, which enable customers to exchange currencies instantly as rates change (Holland and Dwyer 1994). First Direct, a telephone-only bank in Leeds, England, has one-half million accounts without having to operate a single branch. This is another dramatic example of the power of telecommunications when linked to computer information systems anywhere in the world (Hansell 1995).

DHL Worldwide Express, a package delivery service, is now offering free software to its customers to enable them to instantly get information about the delivery status of their packages. This software links customers' shipping processes to DHL's internal information system, enabling them to track packages, order supplies and arrange pickups. It can also be integrated with customers' internal systems such as order entry and inventory control (Heichler 1995).

The ability to deal directly with customers is growing rapidly with the expansion of the Internet and Web pages. For example, Federal Express (FedEx), another express package/mail delivery service, has a Web site (Web server) on the Internet that allows both business and home customers to enter their waybill number to make an inquiry; FedEx's Web server then automatically sends a query to the FedEx shipment tracking system. The results of this query are returned to the Web server, formatted, and then returned to the customer. The answer is available to the requester or anyone in his/her organization at any time; one does not have to call or be placed in a service queue. The Internet Web page enables FedEx to provide better service at a cheaper cost (Little 1995, p. 32).

In 1995, a number of Internet services for small businesses were introduced through the Web sites. For example, a small business owner trying to sell products in China can use one of these services to find reams of market research on China for a fraction of what it might cost from traditional sources. Or a toy maker, lacking Mattel's power to make expensive sales calls, can use another service to advertise its wares around the world for $10 an ad. The Small Business Administration introduced a new Web page in November 1995 for international trade (Siwolop 1995).

Andrew Grove, president and chief executive of Intel, at a South African conference in 1995 demonstrated what he called "Smart Connections," one of the information-application software packages being developed by Intel. In live demonstrations, Grove linked into a live conference between two doctors in different cities in South Africa, helped a Japanese designer decorate a room by wireless PC, and introduced a teenager to his international pen pals through virtual reality ("Mandela" 1995, p. 10).

While there are many exciting developments in the area of computer information systems, and many systems now in existence are truly global, many companies do not yet have such systems in place, even in industrialized countries. For example, Nestlé (a Swiss company) has a policy of decentralizing authority, and as a result, its systems are essentially different all around the world. Only in the mid-1990s did the parent company begin to develop global standards for its information systems, but the size and diversity of the subsidiaries worldwide and the differences in the systems then in place made integration an extremely expensive and slow process, especially given Nestlé's policy of allowing the subsidiaries considerable autonomy (Loudon and Loudon 1996, p. 747).

The problems that Europcar, Esprit de Corp, and Federal Express encountered and eventually overcame in order to develop coordinated global information systems involved not only language, foreign exchange, and business practice differences. They also involved differences in organization cultures and local customs, which can create resistance to change. Obstacles to diffusing technology and creating integrated global systems which make use of state-of-the-art computer information systems and telecommunications technology are substantially greater in cases where developing or emerging countries are involved.

## DIFFUSION OF TECHNOLOGY IN DEVELOPING COUNTRIES

Creating integrated information systems in developing countries is more difficult for several reasons:

• lack of advanced telecommunication systems infrastructures
• lower level of technical skills
• lower education levels, making training more difficult
• lack of substantial financial resources
• lack of technology, technology infrastructures and related equipment in place
• lack of business support services (Davis 1992)

One of the key infrastructures needed in the developing countries is one for the gathering and disseminating news. The following describes the experiences of one organization in trying to set up the telecommunications and information systems structures, processes and facilities needed to run a technologically up-to-date integrated news service in Africa.

The continent of Africa has 54 separate countries. Most of the population lives in cities, which usually have local papers and local publications to fill basic information needs. Within Africa, news does not flow quickly and smoothly among countries or to the outside world. News of epidemics, floods or other events is often supplied by the leaders of one government to the leaders of other governments. The general public and outside world often find out about a situation only weeks or months after it occurs. Clearly, there is a need for speedier information flows in Africa.

Telecommunications are a major problem in Africa, where the entire continent has fewer telephones than the borough of Manhattan in New York City. Africans who signed up for phone service in 1995 were put on a waiting list 3.6 million customers long; in the sub-Saharian regions, the wait was currently nine years (Gibbs 1995). Only 12 of Africa's 54 countries are linked to the Internet (French 1995). In early 1996, AT&T and Alcatel (a French company) announced plans to build, over the next five years, a multibillion dollar fiber-optic underseas cable encircling Africa, a project which, if successfully carried out, would be a major enabler for improving telecommunications there (Gibbs 1995).

The education levels of Africans are low by international standards, due to political, economic and cultural reasons. This has created a society in which it is difficult for any great number of people to be trained for jobs requiring basic skills such as math, writing or complicated thinking processes—jobs such as those involved in operating advanced telecommunications and computer information systems.

The Pan African News Agency (PANA), which is funded through the United Nations and the government of Senegal, was launched in 1979 and published its first report in 1983. PANA's objective was to gather information about and around the continent and distribute it to all African countries as well as to anyone one else who wanted the information. Financial and political control problems arose during PANA's early years of operation, and it was reorganized in 1991 with three objectives: develop state-of-the-art international telecommunications, privatization, and independence. As of early 1995, most internal African communications were still done by radio or telephone. While this is faster than by mail, it can still take several hours to get to a radio or telephone when a newsworthy event occurs; in rural locations, it can take days or weeks.

A start has been made, however, in bringing PANA's operation up to international standards. PANA was connected to the Internet in 1994 through a very-small-aperture satellite terminal (VAST) system at its main office in Senegal (Greenwald 1994).

Problems at the home office in introducing the new Internet satellite systems were typical of those encountered in technology diffusion situations. A VAST representative and a United Nations Educational, Scientific, and Cultural Organization (UNESCO) representative spent several days installing the system and getting it running. PANA lacked the funds to hire an expert to operate and maintain the system, and no staff members had the needed expertise. As a result, a two-week intensive training program with periodic refresher courses was needed. Many staff members resisted learning how to use the new equipment or were unable to adapt to or learn the new system. Many new people were hired; some left very quickly due to the level of work or personality conflicts. Some of the trainees left during the year for better-paying jobs after they had learned to operate the new equipment. The need for parts and repairs also caused problems, since repairpersons were hard to find in Africa.

Gradually, the problems were solved, and by early 1996 the headquarter's international communication system was functioning. PANA now had the capability to send, receive and search for information worldwide. The next phase planned was to upgrade all the major local news bureaus throughout Africa, a task that, based on experiences to date, was expected to be very difficult and lengthy.

Compelling circumstances can at times lead to dramatic breakthroughs, even in less-developed countries such as Bosnia and Herzegovina (the former Yugoslavia). During the war in Bosnia in the mid-1990s, medical care was needed immediately to save lives. The extension of telemedicine capabilities to the United Nations and its coalition partners was considered prudent and humane. Through telemedicine, wounded and sick personnel could not only have care at the front line, they could also have optimal care in real time from attending specialists and physicians in the continental United States.

For example, a wounded peacekeeper might be brought into a frontline hospital in Bosnia with a bullet wound in the leg. The physician on call in the Bosnian hospital would evaluate the injury and might decide that he needs an expert opinion from an orthopedic specialist. The Bosnian doctor would go to his or her PC and sign on to obtain this advice from an orthopedic specialist at the Veterans Administration Hospital in Washington, D.C., selecting the physician from a schedule of available specialists who have access to viewing workstations. The physician in Bosnia would x-ray the patient's leg and use the computer-imaging software package (GPACS) to transmit the x-ray to the specialist in Washington. After a couple of seconds, the specialist in Washington would see the image at his or her workstation and diagnose the patient as being a surgical or nonsurgical candidate.

The doctors "talk" to each other during this session using real-time voice interaction (Richards 1996). The physician in Bosnia will probably agree with the diagnosis, and the two physicians will consent to a course of treatment using stitches to close the wound and drugs to fight off infection. Such a system can be built using available off-the-shelf software. This new battlefield telemedicine capability was reportedly introduced at a field hospital in Zagreb (Engel 1994, 1995). A much more limited satellite system, called Healthnet, is now in operation. It allows written requests for help to be made by satellite and diagnostic replies to be returned by satellite (fourteen times a day) (Rifkin 1996).

The Bosnia situation is an exception, however. Even in emerging countries that have already made considerable progress in developing market economies, progress in developing computer information systems does not come easily. For example, a study of four large companies located in Beijing, China, showed that the enterprises still owned by the state (a general hospital and a petrochemical company) were very slow in changing and adopting new technologies. The two enterprises moving away from state control, a steel company and a harbor port authority, were making substantial progress, motivated, it would seem, by competitive market pressures, especially from overseas companies entering China and trading with the nation.

The steel company's technological profile was especially impressive, as might be expected of a competitive growth company. Computer resources at company headquarters included an IBM mainframe computer that housed the corporate (so-called public) data. This included summaries of daily products, sales, orders and inventory, as well as financial and statistical data. While old applications were developed in COBOL, newer ones used "PowerBuilder."

The branch operations also have IBM mainframes, which are used for local applications and for maintaining networks for 2,000 personal computers (PCs). An additional 5,000 PCs are not connected to the network. The PCs use modern software, such as Windows, Sybase, FoxPro, and Access. Management information systems applications on these networks include contract management, sales management, production planning, raw material management, spare parts management, inventory control and personnel management. A decision support system (DSS) focuses on cost analysis and forecasting, as well as production forecasting. Every company "leader" has a PC on his or her desk that functions as a terminal to access management information systems. Every morning, the first thing leaders generally read on their PC screen is a top-level briefing report (Dologite et al. 1996).

While impressive, the steel company is an exception, probably because of its global interfaces. Generally, not only are resources very restricted because money is needed for other business uses, but considerable human resistance to change normally occurs where new technologies are concerned. For example, in general, although it is far ahead of countries such as Africa, China has a long way to go to catch up with the technological level of the industrialized countries. The study described here was a comparative one, which showed that overall, very little progress in introducing computer information systems was made in selected businesses in China between 1991 and 1994.

## CONCLUSION

Telecommunications and computer information systems are, in many businesses, critical enablers—necessary factors in order to be competitive. While a well-developed telecommunications structure is in place internationally, access to and use of it is still developing. Here, as in other task areas, multinational enterprises are required to manage the elusive balance between global efficiencies and local responsiveness. Many examples of how this balance was achieved were described in this chapter. The precise solution will be contingent on specific situation requirements.

One thing is clear: many of the cross-cultural barriers discussed elsewhere in this book have to be bridged when developing integrated and adaptive computer information systems. This is most apparent when introducing technology into developing countries, such as Africa. At the same time, developing integrated and adaptive computer information systems in industrialized countries also means overcoming barriers. Language, customs, technological developments, established working procedures, cultural barriers, government regulations, available funds, geographical distances, available human resources and workforce skills and education levels—all of the multinational cross-cultural factors discussed in this book—can impact on systems development, and so must be taken into account. Given the advances expected in these technologies, a manager can expect the pressures for change and adaptation to continue in what is becoming an increasingly competitive global market.

## WORKS CITED

Akwule, Raymond. *Global Telecommunications: The Technology, Administration, and Policies.* Stoneham, MA: Butterworth-Heinemann, 1992.
Ambrosio, Johanna. "Global Softwhere?" *Computerworld*, August 2, 1993, pp. 74, 75.

Anderson, Christopher. "The Accidental Superhighway." *Economist*, July 1, 1995, pp. 13–16.

Arnst, Catherine, Susan Jackson, and Michael Shari. "NYNEX' Excellent Adventure in Thailand." *Business Week*, September 18, 1995a.

———. "Special Report: The Last Frontier." *Business Week*, September 18, 1995b.

Associated Press. "Hungary Stake Grows for Ameritech Venture." *New York Times*. December 21, 1995, p. D8.

"AT&T Venture to Lay Cable for Africa." *New York Times*, December 21, 1995, p. D8.

Betts, Mitch. "EDI Cures Ills of Hospital Supply Procurement." *Computerworld*, May 16, 1994, pp. 63–66.

Brandel, Mary. "Creative Sparks Fly." *Computerworld*, February 20, 1995, p. 81.

Budway, James N. "A Metamorphosis in Communications: 25 Years in the Making." *Telecommunications*, June 1992, pp. 21–22.

Cahill, Thomas. *How the Irish Saved Civilization*. New York: Doubleday, 1995.

Citibank. "Advertisement." *New York Times*, January 21, 1996, p. 34.

Davis, Gordon B. "A Model for Adoption and Diffusion of Information Systems in Less Developed Countries." In *The Global Issues of Information Technology Management*, ed. Shailendra Palvia, Prashant Palvia, and Ronald M. Zigli. Harrisburg, PA: Idea Group Publishing, 1992, pp. 384–402.

Dolinar, Lou. "The Information Superskyway." *Newsday*, October 24, 1995, Health and Discovery Section, pp. B23–B29.

Dologite, Dorothy G., Robert J. Mockler, Yu Chen, and Meiqi Fang. "The Changing Role of Information Systems in Chinese State-Owned Businesses." In *Presentation: 29th Annual International Conference on Systems Sciences (HICSS)*. Maui, Hawaii, January 3–6, 1996.

Egolf, Karen. "Beyond the Basics." *Telephony*, March 13, 1995a, pp. 30–36.

———. "Reaching the Global Village." *Telephony*, October 16, 1995b, p. 5.

Engel, Wilson F. "Global Telemedicine Report: International Telemedicine Markets and Business Opportunities." *Internet* http://opal.vcu.edu/html/biomede/i_9vch.htm (April 1994): 1–8.

———. "Evolving a Multinational Telemedicine Capability for Bosnia: Towards Global Telemedicine for Coalition Peacekeepers." *Internet* http://opal.vcu.edu/html/biomede/im_10vch.htm (May–June 1995): 1–2.

Ferrarini, Elizabeth. *Informania: The Guide to Essential Electronic Services*. Boston, MA: Houghton Mifflin, 1985.

French, Howard W. "In the Internet, Most of Africa Is Getting Off to a Slow Start." *New York Times*, November 17, 1995, p. A5.

Gambon, Jill, and Kate Maddox. "Another Web Hole." *InformationWeek*, October 30, 1995, p. 80.

Gibbs, W. Wayt. "Trends in Scientific Communications: Lost Science in the Third World, Parts 1 and 2." *Scientific American*, August 1995, pp. 92–99.

Greenbaum, J. "A Bumpy Road for Europcar." *InformationWeek*, February 7, 1994, pp. 64–67.

Greenwald, Jeff. "Wiring Africa." *Wired*. Los Angeles, CA: Ventures Ltd., 1994, p. 12.

Hansell, Saul. "500,000 Clients, No Branches." *New York Times*, September 3, 1995, Business Section, pp. 1, 10.

Heichler, Elizabeth. "DHL to Roll Out Info Delivery Software Tailored to Customers." *Computerworld*, June 16, 1995, p. 4.

Henry, William A., III. "History as It Happens." *Time*, January 6, 1992, pp. 24–27.

Holland, Kelley, and Paula Dwyer. "Technobanking Takes Off: The Digital Revolution Is Linking People and Companies around the World With Ever More Sophisticated Services." *Business Week/21st Century Capitalism; Special 1994 Bonus Issue*, November 18, 1994, pp. 52, 53.

Little, Dave. "Internet @ Work." *Information Highways*, June 1995, pp. 32–33.

Lohr, Steve. "His Goal: Keeping the Web Worldwide." *New York Times*, December 18, 1995, pp. D1, D4.

Longley, Dennis, and Michael Shain. *Van Nostrand Reinhold Dictionary of Information Technology*. 3rd ed. London: Macmillan, 1989.

Loudon, Kenneth C., and Jane P. Loudon. *Management Information Systems*. Upper Saddle River, NJ: Prentice-Hall, 1996.

Lynch, David J. "Telecom Giants Enter Crowded, High-Cost Race." *USA Today*, November 21, 1995, pp. 1B, 2B.

Madnick, Stuart E. "Integrating Information From Global Systems: Dealing With the On- and Off-Ramps of the Information Superhighway." *Journal of Organizational Computing* 5, no 2 (1995): 69–82.

"Mandela: Bridge the Information Gap." *Telephony*, October 9, 1995, pp. 8–10.

McDaniel, George, ed. *IBM Dictionary of Computing*. 10th ed. New York: McGraw-Hill, 1994.

"Meeting Future Needs—A Special Report by NYNEX." *AsiaMoney*, October 1994, pp. 65–69.

"NYNEX Buys PacTel UK Franchise." *Telephony*, March 29, 1993, pp. 7–10.

Olmsted, Marcia. "A Picture's Worth a Thousand Words." *Information Superhighways*, June 1995, pp. 7–10.

Richards, Bill. "Doctors Can Diagnose Illnesses Long Distance to the Dismay of Some: 'Telemedicine.' " *New York Times*. January 17, 1996, pp. A1, A8.

Rifkin, Glenn. "Bringing Advanced Medical Expertise to the World's Poorest Regions." *New York Times*, January 22, 1996, p. D5.

Ruffin, William R. "Wired for Speed." *Business Month*, January 1990, pp. 56–58.

Samuelson, James. "Voyeurs vs. Exhibitionists." *Forbes*, May 23, 1995, p. 210.

Siwolop, Sana. "For Small Businesses, Beacons in Cyberspace." *New York Times*, December 10, 1995, p. A10.

Sylvester, Kevin, ed. "Global Strategy Outlines." *NYNEX* (published by the NYNEX Corporation), June 3, 1994, p. 1.

———. "Group Created to Build and Grow Asian Market." *NYNEX* (published by the NYNEX Corporation), October 2, 1995a, p. 1.

———. "NYNEX Earnings Up 13.6%." *NYNEX* (published by the NYNEX Corporation), October 30, 1995b, p. 1.

Tate, Paul. "European 100: As the Shift to Distributed Systems Continues to Grow, Europe's IS Leaders Go on a Spending Spree." *InformationWeek*, December 11, 1995, pp. 33–49.

Thyfault, Mary E. "Global Communications Get Real." *InformationWeek*, October 20, 1995, pp. 43–45.

Turban, Efraim, Ephraim McLean, and James Wetherbe. *Information Technology for Management*. New York: John Wiley, 1996.

Williamson, John. "UK Cable Industry: A Window on the Future." *Telephony*, October 5, 1992, pp. 6–13.

"World View: Ted Turner's CNN Global Gains Influence." *Wall Street Journal*, February 1, 1990, pp. A1, A6.

Wurman, Richard Saul. *Information Anxiety: The Black-Hole between Data and Knowledge, and It Happens When Information Doesn't Tell Us What We Want or Need to Know*. New York: Doubleday, 1989.

Zeien, Albert. "Gillette's Global Marketing Experiences." Talk given at St. John's University's Annual Colman Mockler Leadership Award Ceremony, New York, February 27, 1995.

Zeigler, Bart. "The 'Intranet': Internet Software Poses Big Threat to Notes, IBM's Stake in Lotus." *Wall Street Journal*, November 7, 1995, pp. A1, A5.

Zwicker, D. A. *The Lamp* (Exxon Corporation), Winter 1993, pp. 9–12.

# Chapter 8

# Finance and Accounting

This chapter concerns two traditional business enabling areas, finance (managing the sources and uses of funds) and accounting (recording and reporting economic information).

First, finance and accounting are defined and their relationships are defined. Finance and accounting management tasks and processes are then discussed from the perspective of a multinational situation context. Finally, this chapter discusses the combined, integrative role of finance and accounting in enabling an enterprise to more effectively realize its strategic vision through directing and stimulating innovation and controlling performance.

## FINANCE AND ACCOUNTING

Finance is the means by which funds are obtained and the methods by which these funds are managed, allocated and used (Brealey, Meyers, and Marcus 1995, p. 8). Accounting is defined by the American Accounting Association as "the process of identifying, measuring, and communicating economic information to permit informed judgments and decisions by users of that information" (quoted in Needles 1995, p. 4). In essence, accounting measures financial transactions, while finance *manages* financial transactions as well as the firm's underlying financial position.

Although accounting and finance are distinct functions, the two are closely related, especially when doing business across national boundaries. For example, a financial manager deciding whether to invest in a joint venture with an existing company in China examines accounting reports on the financial condition of the potential partner—reports that, in China, are prepared by other standards and so are not always reliable. Investors in Russia also face a series of obstacles in obtaining accurate information on potential investments. This is the case, not only because the financial statements may be unreliable, but also because business managers there face many political and criminal pressures, which can influence the disposition of a company's funds.

## FINANCE: MANAGEMENT TASKS AND PROCESSES

Financial management in a multinational environment presents many challenges since it requires balancing a variety of factors worldwide. For instance, exchange rates can vary from hour to hour, as they did during Mexico's 1994 peso crisis. Each country has its own reporting requirements and regulations, as, for example, in the securities area, where inadequate financial reporting laws make it difficult to evaluate equity investments in newly privatized Russian and Chinese companies. Inflation rates vary by country and over time: over the past decade, several South American countries had annual rates over 1,000 percent. Political instability can create problems, as in India during 1995 when a Kentucky Fried Chicken outlet was temporarily closed and when Enron's power plant project was temporarily stopped. Chapter 5 covered these and other situation factors affecting the finance tasks discussed in this section.

At the same time, many developments in the finance area are making the job both more challenging and more efficient. For example, banking services are becoming more global, stimulated in part by worldwide information systems developments. Many developments in the financial area are helping to reconcile cultural and national differences and enable a more global approach:

- the ability to exchange money more quickly through global networks
- the increasingly wider range of financial instruments available
- the continuing merger of major investment banks in different countries—making competitive international financial services more readily available within worldwide megabanks

The tasks involved in managing a multinational company's finances are:

- obtaining the funds needed to start and run a multinational enterprise, including internal and external sources of funds
- determining capital structure
- global working capital management
- financial risk management: foreign currency
- financial management of business transactions
- capital budgeting and foreign investment

### Global Sources of Funds

International operations are financed either from external sources, such as local or international borrowing and equity financing, or internal sources, such as funds generated by the parent company, subsidiary operations locally, or other subsidiaries (Eiteman, Stonehill, and Moffett 1995; Eng, Lees, and Mauer 1995; Gates 1994; Madura 1995; Rose 1994).

*External.* The major external sources of funds in the international area include the following.

1. *Local capital markets*: When borrowing money (short or long term) in the home, host, or another country, many sources can be explored to obtain the best interest rates. A company may decide, as did LSI Logic Corp., that using a joint venture in which LSI retained a majority interest had several benefits. First, the company gained access to local marketing expertise. Second, by setting up a local company, a firm gains easier access to local financing—both long-term bonds and equity and short-term lines of credit—a major help in raising much-needed capital for expansion (Daniels and Radebaugh 1994, pp. 740–743). Local capital market sources include commercial banks, investment banks, securities firms, insurance companies, pension institutions, savings banks, equity (stock) markets and large individual investors. Borrowing locally on occasion will help protect the home country multinational corporation, as it did the Disney Company when its 49 percent–owned Euro Disney operation, which had borrowed heavily from local French banks, ran into financial problems in the 1992–1994 period. Both Ford and General Motors announced in 1995 that they would borrow substantial sums from Japan's Export-Import Bank to convert car models to right-hand drive in order to expand their export sales to Japan ("Ford Will Get a Japanese Loan" 1995).

2. *International capital markets*: Money can be borrowed through several types of international bonds. *Foreign bonds* are sold outside the borrower's country, in the currency of the issuer's country, to residents of the issuing country (British bankers issue bonds in pounds to residents of the United Kingdom). *Eurobonds* are taken to market normally by a syndicate of banks from different countries. They are borrowed by a company in one country in that country's currency (for example, Italy and lira), and sold in countries (for example, Japan, France, and England) other than the one in whose currency the bond is denominated. Eurobonds are the most widely used type of international bonds. A *global bond*, which combines domestic and Eurobond configurations, is registered and issued in different national markets (usually in Europe, Asia, and North America).

A variety of underwriting arrangements have been, and are being, developed by investment banks (for instance, Goldman Sachs) and securities firms (for example, Nomura). A company may issue a dual-currency bond, through which one pays interest in one currency and repays principal in a second currency. Bond swaps are sometimes used by a company to balance its obligations (both principal and interest) in different currencies, as company and market requirements change (a company, for example, may want to reduce risks by spreading its obligations over many different currencies). In one instance, the Walt Disney Company borrowed $400 million on which the minimum guaranteed interest rate was 3 percent. Interest could rise to 13.5 percent, however, depending on the success of a package of 13 Disney movies (comparable rates at the time were around 8 percent).

Major international banks, such as the Bank of China, Mitsubishi Bank, Deutsche Bank, National Westminster Bank, Credit Lyonnais, and Citicorp, are also a source of funds. These banks provide worldwide commercial banking services (for example, short-term trade financing, currency exchange and electronic funds transfer) and outside the United States investment banking services (for example, packaging long-term debt, mergers and acquisitions arrangements, and equity funding). Due to U.S. government regulations, investment banking services in the United States are supplied by securities firms.

3. *Equities capital markets*: The equity capital market is another major source of funds for multinational companies. To make it easier to raise money this way, many companies list their stock on several stock exchanges, even though it is expensive to do. In addition to the three major exchanges—the New York Stock Exchange (NYSE), the Tokyo Stock Exchange, and the London Stock Exchange (LSE)—there are several other developed countries that have established exchanges (Canada, the Netherlands, Germany, France, Switzerland, Belgium, South Africa), as well as Hong Kong. Markets are emerging in many developing countries, notably, Russia, Mexico, Brazil, Chili, Argentina, Singapore, Malaysia, Korea, Taiwan, India, Thailand and several Central European countries. Many differences exist in how exchanges operate, from the hours of operation to settlement times (in Russia, an average of two weeks; in the United States, three days) and transaction execution (in Russia all executions are made in person and by hand; in the United States, they are made electronically or over the phone) (Clark 1994; Liley 1994; Zausner 1995).

4. *Eurocurrencies. Eurocurrencies* are any currencies on deposit outside the country of origin or issue. They may involve Eurodollars, Euroyen, Eurosterling, Euromarks, Asiadollars or other currencies. The deposits may be made by governments, individual multinational corporations, or banks that have excess cash or wish to maintain local currency deposits outside their home country. Internationally, some $6 trillion is available through Eurocurrencies (Krugman and Obstfeld 1994, p. 642). Eurocurrencies are a very inexpensive way to borrow, since the risks are low (large transactions, fewer government regulations, and the most creditworthy borrowers make them less costly). Most of the transactions are interbank, but over $1 billion involves multinational corporations.

5. *Offshore financial centers*: These centers are located on island states such as the Cayman Islands, Bermuda, Bahamas, Bahrain, and the Netherlands Antilles, and in countries or major cities such as Switzerland, London, New York, Hong Kong, Singapore, and Luxembourg. These centers offer banking and fi-

nancial services to nonresidents and are often used by multinational corporations to obtain Eurocurrency loans. The larger ones perform a wide range of banking activities, while the smaller island locations function mainly as booking centers where transactions are recorded to take advantage of secrecy and low (or no) taxes.

*Internal: Parent Company, Other Divisions or Local Operations.* One source of funds is internal company cash flows generated from operations. The complexity of moving such funds among subsidiaries depends on the number of the subsidiaries, needs of the host- and home-country enterprises, legal regulations, exchange rates, differing inflation rates and ownership status. For example, if a subsidiary in a foreign country is only partially owned, then partner or other shareholder interests and restrictions on the movement of money may have an impact. The amounts of cash available and needed are also related to the capital structure of each enterprise. Capital structuring and cash-flow management in multinational companies are discussed in the following sections.

Excess funds available in either the host or home country company can be put to work in many ways. Money can be transferred by buying or increasing equity investment or by granting a loan, as was and is now being done by parent companies for three subsidiaries in England (Stevenson 1995). Dividends and licensing fees are another way: for example, in 1993, U.S. companies received more than $20 billion in licensing fees and royalties from their foreign subsidiaries. Another way to meet working-capital needs is to adjust the transfer price between units, though this has to be done in such a way as to avoid tax problems and allow for the continuing evaluation of individual unit performance.

While many options are available, in each instance the specific situation requirements dictate the financial management approach used to raise initial capital and meet working-capital needs.

### Determining Capital Structure

Financial, as well as other company, political, and competitive market factors, play a key role in deciding on the capital structure of new and expanded operations in other countries (Eiteman, Stonehill, and Moffett 1995).

For example, in 1990 Rally Dawson Sports (with $29 million in sales) was making a decision about opening a manufacturing plant in Pakistan and marketing its sports products (tennis, cricket, golf, soccer, baseball, skiing, football, badminton and field hockey) in and from that part of the world. Labor and material costs were very low there, and the government encouraged foreign investments. Rally first wanted to make a direct investment in a wholly owned subsidiary, as it had done in other countries in the past. In Pakistan, however, Rally decided to take on a joint-venture partner in order to overcome the many political, supply, distribution and marketing problems.

Rally Dawson Sports obtained its potential joint-venture partner, Hamid Sports of Pakistan, through the Pakistani Trade Office in Washington, D.C. As negotiations progressed, it was decided that Rally would own 60 percent of the $4 million joint venture (called Ampak International, Ltd.), and would purchase its interest with machinery and cash borrowed in the United States. The reason Rally did not use Pakistani sources to finance the purchase was that the Pakistani government did not want to tap its foreign exchange reserves. Instead, local banks were to be used for borrowing working capital. The government limited the taking of profits out of the country to the amount originally invested ($2.4 million) plus half of all cumulative profits. Detailed financial forecasts of profits, costs, return on investment and cash flows were prepared (Fatehi 1996; Springate 1990). As in other multinational cross-cultural management situations, then, decisions in the finance area are not isolated. Many situation factors have to balanced with financial considerations in making the final decisions about financial structure.

As a general guideline, it is best to finance through debt rather than equity in countries that have strict limits on profit repatriation and dividends but not on the repayment of loans. In countries with high inflation, the equity investment of cash should be limited, local borrowing should be used as much as possible, technology or know-how investment should be substituted where possible for cash-equity investment, and licensing and management fees should be explored.

In general, the overall financial structure of the parent multinational and the objective of minimizing costs worldwide should be major focuses in creating capital structures for subsidiaries. For example, LSI Logic Corp. needed capital from as many sources as possible, and so local capital was an important source when structuring ventures. On the other hand, Rally Dawson Sports had financing sources outside Pakistan that were available and cheaper, so in that case, local financing was used mainly for short-term operating needs. Whether a multinational parent enterprise invests through equity, debt, or machinery/services may depend as much on other situation factors as on finance factors. Further, as shown by Disney, the parent can, at times, leverage worldwide strengths in unusual ways. As is seen from these experiences, then, the best choice depends on a wide range of factors and has to be balanced with feasibility when making the final capital structure decision.

## Global Management of Working Capital

Managing the flow of capital within and among units of a multinational company has three objectives: to minimize working capital balances, currency conversion costs and foreign-exchange risks. Achieving these objectives is affected by local and corporate cash needs and the way in which cash is transferred. A fourth objective is to earn as much as possible on the excess cash held, which can depend on the amount, where it is located and how long it is available.

Cash budgets and forecasts, which are discussed below, are used to estimate the minimum level of cash or liquid assets (such as instantly marketable securities) needed. Once the need level is determined, decisions can be made concerning whether to invest the cash locally or centrally, and if centrally, how to transmit it. This is another instance of the intricate balancing decisions and actions that multinational management face.

Dividends are the most straightforward way to transfer (or repatriate) cash from a subsidiary or partially owned overseas unit. However, such transfers are often limited by law or taxed heavily (for example, Russia or Brazil) in order for the host country to control its overall balance of payments (inflow and outflow of cash). Repayment of loan principal, management fees, and payment for technology transfer are other useful, but limited, ways to repatriate funds.

Licensing fees and royalties are used extensively to transfer cash. Where this is not possible, devices such as fees on imports or fixed import prices can be used. Gillette does this in Russia, where all the fund repatriation is done through sales of imported Gillette personal-care products and appliances, while all profits from the sale of razor blades manufactured at a jointly owned plant in Russia are kept for reinvestment within Russia.

A coordinated finance center (whether regional or international) is one device used to handle balancing cash needs and investing excess cash. Such a center determines varying cash needs in different locations and the best means of transferring cash to each location from central reserves built up with cash inflows from units with excess cash on a daily basis.

Where there are transfers among divisions of parts, supplies and other services, such as at Ford Motor Company, *multilateral* or *bilateral netting* is used to minimize currency-conversion costs. *Netting* involves the recording of all transactions at a finance center. The monies owed among the different units are then, where possible, netted and settled by book transfers instead of by actual multiple payments for each separate transaction. For example, if two parts transactions occurred between a French and a Spanish unit of a multinational company (a bilateral netting situation), the two transactions would be netted, and only the difference actually paid. Where three units or more are involved (a multilateral netting situation), the payments among all units during a specified time period would be netted, and only the remaining differences actually transferred. Companies such as the Dutch airline KLM deal in as many as 180 different currencies, so the coordination job requires constant attention and is normally enabled by complex computer-decision support systems.

In making these transactions, an effort is also made to minimize foreign-exchange risks.

### Financial Risk Management: Foreign Currency

Foreign-exchange risks are generally categorized as transaction, translation and economic (including inflation) exposure.

*Transaction exposure* arises when the receivables or payables of a multinational company change in value as the exchange rate changes (Eng, Lees, and Mauer 1995, p. 515). For example, suppose a German manufacturer is due to pay $1 million for imports in three months at a fixed U.S. dollar price. If the manufacturer expects the deutsche mark to weaken in relation to the dollar, it has several choices:

- Purchase an option to buy U.S. dollars three months from now at today's exchange rate to protect itself should a drop occur: if the mark gains in value, the manufacturer can allow the option to lapse and pay for the imports with the resultant cheaper dollars.
- Buy U.S. dollars on a forward contract, collect the dollars in three months, and pay the bill with them: if the dollar weakens in relation to the mark, then as the price of the protection, the manufacturer will have lost an opportunity to profit from the exchange fluctuation and will have paid a contract fee.
- Buy an offsetting asset (such as a three-month U.S. treasury note), earn interest on the note and pay the bill with the proceeds of the note.
- Do nothing and bear the risk.

Each alternative has a cost and a risk contingent on the specific situation factors at hand—and both of which must be weighed in making the final decision.

*Translation exposure* occurs when subsidiary balance sheets are translated into home-country currency to consolidate accounting records. For example, when a U.S.-owned multinational corporation issues its annual income and balance-sheet statements, it must translate the statements from foreign currencies into U.S. dollars. Fluctuations in exchange rates will impact, whether favorably or unfavorably, on the final consolidated statements. Balance sheet hedges can be used, as when a company which has $50 million at the year's fiscal closing (an asset) borrows Eurodollars to make plant additions outside the United States in the coming year (a liability) as a means of protecting itself against possible unfavorable exchange fluctuations of the dollar in relation to its own currency.

*Economic exposure* arises from possible exchange fluctuations that could affect pricing, which in turn may affect sales. For example, such an economic impact led both German and Japanese automakers to build plants in the United States to protect their sales positions there. They did so because the value of the Japanese yen and German mark had risen substantially in relation to the U.S. dollar. The move was also stimulated by the desire to avoid government import regulations and consumer resistance to so-called foreign-made products. Since exchange rates generally follow inflation rates, estimates of inflation affect the amount of risk expected from exchange fluctuations and the steps that may be taken to reduce or avoid risks—each of which has a price.

This is only a brief introduction to financial risk management. With the introduction of a variety of financial instruments, many ways now exist for hedging risks. As described in this chapter, the Disney Company created bonds tied to its future revenues from thirteen movies, in one example of an imaginative financial-hedging strategy.

## Financial Management of Business Transactions

When buying and selling in the international market, several financial management decisions arise, such as which currency should be used for the transaction, when and how credit should be checked, which form of payments should be used, and how financing should be arranged (Griffin and Pustay 1996).

*Currency Choice.* Both parties will prefer to be paid in their home currency in order to avoid risks. Where two weak currencies are involved, a compromise is to have payment in a stable currency, such as Eurodollars. Each country and many industries have their own customs, though ultimately the choice of currency is a negotiated item whose solution will depend on individual company and country factors.

*Credit Checking.* Checking on a purchaser's creditworthiness, although difficult, is necessary, especially when doing business in a developing country. Simple and inexpensive mechanisms for checking credit are available in many countries; these are similar to the Dun & Bradstreet credit-checking service provided in the United States. International banks are a good source for locating these public and private services, as are the country desk officers of the U.S. and foreign commercial services.

*Methods of Payment.* These include:

- payment in advance (a rare but negotiable method),
- open account (best limited to well-established, long-term customers with very good credit ratings),
- documentary collection (commercial banks handle the paperwork and facilitate payment using such documents as bills of exchange and bills of lading, along with acceptances with and without recourse),
- letter of credit (a document issued by a bank that promises to pay an exporter on receipt of proof of fulfillment of the obligation from the exporter),
- credit cards, and
- countertrade (including barter, counterpurchase, buyback and offset purchase).

*Financing Trade.* For large contracts, exporters from industrialized countries should develop access to low-cost loans to support their exports, since local sources may be expensive and difficult to obtain. In many countries, government agencies (such as the Export-Import Bank of the United States) help guarantee payment of major percentages of contracts in instances where the exporter finances the purchase in some way, depending on the terms of downpayments and subsequent payments.

## Capital Budgeting and Foreign Investment

International finance management involves several areas of planning and action, including funds acquisition from global sources, capital structures, cash flow and working capital, foreign currency transactions and business transactions. Managing these areas requires making decisions on how funds should be allocated or budgeted and invested (Eiteman, Stonehill, and Moffett 1994).

For example, in the Rally Dawson/Ampak situation, financial management assisted in making the investment decision by preparing estimates of costs, profits and losses, cash flows and return on investment. These decisions involve *determining the value of an investment* to an international company. This value was studied from both the viewpoint of the parent corporation (Rally Dawson) from a consolidated, enterprise-wide perspective and from the viewpoint of the subsidiary business unit (Ampak), as an independent venture, just as it would be viewed by the joint-venture partner.

Decisions were also needed on the *financial structure* of the subsidiary. This was determined again in part by the needs of the local subsidiary (Ampak) and its local competitive environment, in part by the financial resources and structure of the two joint-venture partners, and in part by the availability of funds worldwide. As an example of the complexities involved in such decisions, in the Ampak situation, an *allocation* problem arose. Rally had a subsidiary in Spain that needed additional capital investment, which forced the company to secure an external source of financing—the Export-Import Bank—and to structure the joint venture in a way that kept cash investment low in order to have funds available for Spain.

Business investment decisions such as Ampak's, then, involve many *planning and budgeting* steps. First, they involve screening and selecting projects based on financial forecasts and analysis. As seen from the experiences described in this book, many factors affect the decision. Once the situation has been structured, the funds allocated to the project must be obtained, often from a wide range of sources.

Furthermore, budgeting requires that the future flow of funds be projected and decisions made about how the funds can be maximized and how the funds generated will be put to other use. These decisions help determine the payback period of the investment.

Throughout the budgeting process, attention is paid to the risks that may arise from changes in government regulations, policies, and parties; changes in competitive market conditions; fluctuations in foreign currency rates; local and global factors affecting all areas of costs; and many other aspects that require assumptions to be made about what is likely to happen in the future.

The Ampak study is a small, integrated example of the complexities of the financial management job at work in just one area: capital budgeting for investments in foreign subsidiaries. The decisions and actions in this task area, like those in other multinational management task areas, involve balancing many business factors to arrive at what appears to be the best compromise decision, given one's assumptions about the future and understanding of the financial options available internationally.

## ACCOUNTING AND TAXATION: MANAGEMENT TASKS
## AND PROCESSES

Accounting is the process of collecting, identifying, measuring and communicating economic information (primarily financial in nature), about economic entities (in this case, international businesses), which can be used to enable informed decisions by information users (Choi and Mueller 1992; Gray 1995; McNair 1993).

The process of accounting involves observing or being informed of some economic event (for example, a sale or purchase of some product or service) and then determining whether the event needs an accounting entry. If the event qualifies, the accounting system will measure the economic changes that took place and record them in the form of an accounting entry, which is used to update the financial records. This information is then reported in forms needed by different end users. Examples of these reports are tax forms, income statements, balance sheets, cash-flow statements, and management control and decision support reports.

The processes, and the reports produced through them, vary depending on the intended uses of the financial statements as well as on applicable accounting standards. Accounting information is used for different purposes by many people, including managers and proprietors of businesses; creditors, suppliers, customers and lending institutions; government bodies; employees; financial analysts, potential investors, stockholders and investment advisers; and reporting agencies (Needles 1995, p. 7).

Business managers use accounting information as a *diagnostic* tool to determine how different operations are performing. These information reports, which are both financial and management accounting reports, can be used to spot problems and opportunities—to take corrective action (*control*) or *plan* new initiatives. Management-accounting reports, such as *forecasts*, are needed for planning. For example, Rally Dawson used detailed financial forecasts of profits, costs, return on investment and cash flows in making its decision to enter into a joint venture in Pakistan (Fatehi 1996; Springate 1990). *Budgets* of sales, costs, production and any other performance outcomes are also produced and then used as standards in management-accounting reports to measure performance against and then take corrective action.

Creditors, suppliers, customers, lending institutions and other external users examine financial-accounting statements (annual balance sheets and income statements, for example) of a company—before lending money, negotiating payment for supplies, making large purchases that require delivering on commitments or extending credit on purchases.

Government agencies use financial accounting information for tax purposes. For example, because of the tight government control over taxation, accounting records and reports in Germany are created and used as a basis for tax reporting and auditing. In the United States, in contrast, two sets of books may be kept—

one for tax purposes and one for reporting to external users of company financial information, in compliance with U.S. Securities and Exchange Commission (SEC) regulations, Generally Accepted Accounting Principles (GAAP) and the U.S. Financial Accounting Standards Board (FASB). Financial advisers use accounting information to make investment decisions for their clients, as do individuals investing on their own behalf (Needles 1995, p. 8).

The types of accounting and reporting required by external users is generally classified as management accounting, financial accounting and tax accounting.

## Management Accounting

Management accounting is the process of identification, measurement, accumulation, analysis, preparation, interpretation, and communication of financial information which is used by management to plan, evaluate, and control within the organization. Because this information, along with related diagnostic, forecasting, and budget reports, is used internally by business managers, management accounting—unlike financial accounting—is not required to follow generally accepted accounting standards.

Cost accounting is one example of management accounting. It is a systematic set of procedures for recording and reporting measurements of the cost of manufacturing goods and performing services in the aggregate and in detail. It includes methods for recognizing, classifying, allocating, aggregating, and reporting such costs and comparing them with standard costs. The major purpose of cost accounting is to accumulate data for inventory valuation (Shim and Siegel 1989, 1990). Like the other accounting systems described above, these are used mostly for internal management purposes.

## Financial Accounting

Financial accounting is the gathering and reporting of historical financial information required by groups that are interested in a company's financial position—especially profits, losses, cash liquidity, debt and assets. These reports, which are generally concerned with overall business operations, are used by stockholders, customers, creditors, suppliers, financial analysts, potential investors, and government and regulatory bodies, as well as by business managers.

Basically, financial accounting supplies information to people who generally do not have an interest in the day-to-day operations of the company—the external users of accounting information and reports. To keep financial statements uniform and prevent the statements from being misleading, financial accounting in industrialized countries is governed by accounting standards (in the United States, these standards are referred to as Generally Accepted Accounting Principles [GAAP]). Different countries have different accounting standards and practices, which can create problems for managers.

### Different Financial Accounting Standards and Practices: A Multinational Perspective

The major differences in the way reports are prepared from country to country can create huge differences in the assumed profitability of an operation overseas. For example, three accounting professors developed a computer model of an imaginary enterprise's financial reports in four countries. Starting with the same gross operating profit—$1.5 million—the enterprise had a net profit, after the adjustments and entries required in each country, of $260,000 in the United Kingdom; $240,000 in Australia; $34,600 in the United States; and $10,402 in Germany (Breton 1989).

The lack of a strong enforcement body outside of North America permits overseas companies to be less than forthright about disclosures. Only companies in the United States and Canada, for example, issue quarterly profit reports, and Germany does not require that financial data from majority-owned subsidiaries be consolidated. Where stock exchanges are relatively small, as in Holland, Spain and France, the government regulation and oversight of company disclosures are not very strong. Insider trading overseas, for instance, is often greeted with a wink by government regulators (Breton 1989).

Because of such differences, the German automaker Daimler-Benz, best known for its Mercedes-Benz luxury car, was not initially permitted to list its stock on the U.S. exchanges. This was because the New York Stock Exchange and the Securities and Exchange Commission lacked the appropriate accounting information (according GAAP) to properly monitor the business for regulatory compliance (Daniels and Radebaugh 1994, p. 706). Many less-developed countries, such as Russia and Rumania, have not yet developed such accounting standards.

The differences in financial-accounting standards and practices have developed for many reasons. First, the basis of law in countries differ. The United States, Canada, the United Kingdom, New Zealand and Australia have accounting standards that are common-law–based, that is, they evolved from decisions and practice. In contrast, countries relying on code law, such as France and Germany, are likely to codify their national accounting procedures and standards. In these countries, accounting practices are determined by the law rather than by the collective wisdom of professional accounting groups based on experience (common law). Enforcement also is influenced by the legal origins, with private enforcement through lawsuits more common in the United States and public oversight more common in France and Germany. The U.S. Securities and Exchange Commission adds a major government legal dimension to enforcement in the United States.

Second, there are cultural differences, with countries like France being more statist, and so more inclined to favor state intervention. France also requires social balance sheets, which detail the treatment and composition of workforces. Australia, on the other hand, has a more frontier, individualistic culture, and consequently has far less government intervention in setting accounting standards and practices.

Third, economic differences exist. For example, in countries with high inflation, such as those in South America, financial-accounting statements are adjusted for inflation. (Financial accounting in most other countries is based on the historical cost principle; that is, values are entered at the cost price and are not adjusted subsequently for inflation.)

These are only a few of the differences which have to be considered in international accounting—when consolidating statements or when comparing, judging, planning and controlling subsidiary performance in different countries. Other differences include (Mueller, Gernon, and Meek 1994):

*Pensions.* Along procedural lines, the United States is the only country that requires an annual revaluation of all pension plan obligations. Revaluations every three years are the international norm. Moreover, U.S. pension accruals are high by international comparisons, which means that comparative net earnings reported by U.S. companies are relatively lower.

*Goodwill.* A firm that acquires a second firm often pays more than the book value of the acquired firm's stock. The excess payment is called a *goodwill* payment. In the Netherlands, firms typically amortize goodwill over a five-year period, although they may write it off instantaneously or over a period of up to ten years. French firms may amortize goodwill over five to twenty years. Japan, however, severely limits the ability of firms to write off goodwill (Griffin and Pustay 1996, p. 567).

*Capitalization of financial leases.* U.S., British and Swedish firms must capitalize financial leases, while French and Swiss firms may, but are not required, to do so.

*Capitalization of R&D expenses.* Most countries permit firms to capitalize R&D expenses, but this practice is forbidden except in limited circumstances, in the United States.

The differences among accounting systems, practices, principles and reports in different countries create problems for both financial and management accounting. For example, comparative financial analysis across cultural borders is very difficult and time-consuming, since adjustments have to made for the different factors unless the financial statements have been converted to a single currency and accounting system. Management accounting also requires reconciling different viewpoints in order to compare results, evaluate and measure performance, and adjust and plan operations based on these analyses.

### Global Efforts to Reconcile Differences

Steps are being taken to make accounting systems more global and easier to deal with across national boundaries and cultures. An International Accounting Standards Committee (IASC) was created in 1973 and today has over 100 members from professional societies in more than 80 countries. One of its goals is to make the comparability of financial statements in different countries easier by establishing standards for inventory valuation, deferred income taxes, depreciation, improved disclosure and the like. The committee is slowly starting to have an impact.

The United Nations (UN) has issued some guidelines, but because of the composition of that body and pressures from Third World countries, social, as well as financial, performance is a major reporting consideration. The Organization for Economic Cooperation and Development (OECD), an organization of 24 governments representing nearly all the industrialized countries, has issued guidelines for the voluntary disclosure of financial information. More recently, it has been studying accounting principles in different countries with a view toward encouraging greater harmonization and comparability of accounting and financial reporting.

The European Union (EU) also has taken steps to harmonize the accounting systems of its member states. Other regional organizations interested in regularizing accounting practices are the African Accounting Council, the Confederation of Asian and Pacific Accountants, the Federation of Accountants of the Association of Southeast Asian Nations (ASEAN), and the Federation of European Accountants. However, because of competition for international business among accounting firms in different countries, it appears unlikely that consistent global standards for accounting will be adopted.

SAP, a computer software package developed by a German company, coordinates information reporting borders. While its main function is to link different departments within a company—for example, sales, manufacturing, warehousing, and accounting—it also has the capacity to work across borders. One company linked order processing information across borders using SAP, since SAP can automatically calculate exchange rates and translate foreign languages.

Other forces creating pressure for change include the global integration of capital markets, which deals in comparative evaluations across borders and so needs comparable statements, and regional and political forces, such as China's efforts to adopt U.S. accounting standards to make trade and investment between the two countries easier. Progress is slow, however, and many serious obstacles to establishing global accounting standards remain.

### Reconciling Differences: A Management Perspective on Financial Reporting

Until international accounting standards have been created, multinational cross-cultural managers must deal with differences when meeting their own reporting and management needs.

*Overall approach.* When faced with conciliation problems, a multinational company has several choices (Mueller, Gernon, and Meek 1994):

*Do nothing.* This is the best choice if a multinational company is not listed on worldwide stock exchanges, uses a language and currency that are widely known and understood, and raises little capital outside its home country, since the cost of the other alternatives can be very high.

*Prepare convenience translations and statements.* Convenience translations are financial statements that are translated into English but use the home country's accounting standards. Convenience statements translate the monetary amount into the reader's currency. They are low-cost alternatives to doing nothing.

*Restate the information to a limited extent.* These statements usually contain footnotes which reconcile the net income amounts and shareholders' equity from the home country to the reader's country accounting standards.

*Prepare a secondary financial statement.* This is a complete restatement of financial statements in the reader's language, currency and accounting principles. This statement can be very expensive to prepare and so is used only when the investment and investor needs justify the cost.

Other problems that a multinational manager might have to consider include disclosure, foreign-currency translation and international financial statement analysis.

*Disclosure.* Disclosure refers to the information in an annual report that supplements the financial statements. Disclosures can cover both financial and nonfinancial information. Depending on local laws, disclosures may be mandatory, suggested or voluntary. Samples of disclosures might include information on breakdowns of sales by geographic area or product line, share and shareholder distribution, social benefits and contributions or the company, employee data (such as age and seniority, training, fringe benefits and absenteeism), and environmental aspects of a company's operations around the world.

*Foreign Currency: Accounting for Transactions and the Translation of Statements.* Accounting for transactions in different foreign currencies and reporting on operating results of foreign subsidiaries in consolidated parent-company financial statements are two additional problems encountered in multinational business accounting reporting, which managers must resolve (Choi and Mueller 1992).

One problem that arises concerning *transactions in foreign currencies* is that one exchange rate may be in effect on the date a sale is made and recorded, and another exchange rate on the day the payment is received. For example, according to FASB statement no. 52, on the day a sale of $1,600 is made, the accounting entry should be:

| | | |
|---|---|---|
| Accounts receivable | $1,600 | |
| Sales | | $1,600 |

On the day the account is paid, the exchange rate is taken into account. For instance, if the sale was made by a U.S. firm to an English firm that paid in English pounds (say, 1,000 pounds) and the exchange rate dropped from $1.60 per English pound to $1.50 per pound between the day the purchase was made and the bill was paid, the American manufacturer would lose $100. The entry would be as follows:


| | | |
|---|---|---|
| Cash | $1,500 | |
| Foreign exchange loss | $100 | |
|    Accounts receivable | | $1,600 |


The American firm's income statement would show, as a separate item, the cumulative profit and loss from foreign exchange. If the firm had anticipated such a loss, it doubtless would have considered some of the protective steps discussed earlier in the chapter, such as buying currency options or using forward contracts.

*Foreign-currency translation*, another multinational financial accounting management decision, involves the process of restating foreign-currency statements in the currency of the parent's home country (Choi and Mueller 1992). Translation is needed to create consolidated multinational company statements.

In the United States, three methods of translation are allowed under FASB statement no. 52: figures can be shown as cost (if less than a 10-percent ownership stake), shown as equity (if a 10- to 50-percent ownership stake), or consolidated (if over a 50-percent ownership stake). Under the cost method, the historical exchange rate is used to enter the cost in accounting records, while the current rate is used to enter current earnings. Under the equity method, the initial cost-accounting entry is at the historical exchange rate, and each reporting period, this figure is adjusted for dividends at current exchange rates. Profits and losses are also recorded at the current exchange rate.

For U.S. firms, consolidation requires restating a subsidiary's financial statements using U.S. GAAP. One first determines the subsidiary's functional currency, which is the currency of the primary economic environment in which the subsidiary operates. If most of a French subsidiary's business is done using French francs, then the franc is its functional language; if the subsidiary supplies a global market through the parent company and does most of its transactions in U.S. dollars, then its functional currency is dollars.

Three methods are allowed for translation. The *current-rate method*, which is used where the functional currency is the host country's currency, requires that all assets and liabilities be translated at the spot exchange rate on the date of the balance sheet. All income items can be translated at the *weighted-average exchange rate* for the period or the exchange rate on the day each transaction took place. The owner's equity is translated at the rate in effect when capital stock was issued and retained earnings were accumulated. If the functional currency is the parent's currency, the *temporal method* is used. The temporal method requires that only monetary assets and liabilities be translated at the current exchange rate; inventory and property, plant and equipment must be translated at the rate in effect when the assets were acquired. In general, net income is translated at the *average exchange rate*, but the cost of goods sold and depreciation are translated at the appropriate historical exchange rate.

An accumulated translation adjustment is made for foreign-exchange losses and gains. Under the temporal method, the gain or loss is taken directly to the income statement; under the current-rate method, the gain or loss is taken directly to the balance sheet as a separate line item.

## Tax Accounting

Tax accounting deals with the processes, records and reports needed to determine the taxable income to be reported to tax authorities. This type of accounting is primarily governed by laws or regulations of the accepted tax authorities in the countries in which a multinational enterprise operates. These authorities are the primary users of this information.

Because this type of accounting is normally governed by local regulations, major differences exist across national boundaries. Because of these differences, an expert is needed to deal with tax planning. A number of multinational management decisions affected by tax considerations include:

*Market selection.* Tax rates and concessions can impact on the choice of market. For example, a U.S. breast implant company (described in Chapter 5) moved its headquarters to Switzerland, in large measure because of the tax incentives that nation offered it.

*Method of entry.* The method used and the venture's structure can change the tax costs considerably. For example, during the early 1990s China had a policy that gave tax concessions to foreign investors if they had a Chinese joint-venture partner. These concessions were related to both import taxes and taxes on income.

*Method of financing.* In some situations, it is desirable to finance a new overseas venture with high debt. This enables repatriating the investment without paying taxes on repatriated profits, though the parent would then be liable for taxes on the interest earned.

*Transfer pricing.* Taxes have a major impact in the area of transfer pricing.

Tax planning can impact both profits and cash flow. For example, a parent company can chose to set up a foreign operation as a branch or a subsidiary. If losses are expected in the early years, a branch may often be advised during those years to allow the parent to deduct these loses. However, there are exceptions, as seen in the Rally Dawson experiences described in this chapter, since other factors besides taxes are important in making these decisions.

Loans may be used instead of equity where this makes it easier to repatriate capital, as in the experiences of Rally Sports. The interest on loans is generally deductible by the subsidiary but taxable to the parent company; dividends are not a deductible expense by the subsidiary, but they are taxable to the parent.

Tax havens are also considered where appropriate to the situation at hand. However, as in other tax-planning areas, a careful situation analysis is required to balance all the relevant factors.

**Figure 8-1**
**Enabling Accounting and Finance Control Systems**

*Source*: Adapted from Simons (1995), p. 7.

## STIMULATING INNOVATION AND CONTROLLING PERFORMANCE: INTEGRATIVE MANAGEMENT PLANNING AND CONTROL SYSTEMS

Managing tomorrow's multinational enterprise requires balancing *control* with *stimulation of the innovations* needed to realize an enterprise's strategic vision, while *meeting the strategic challenges* of making timely changes and continually reducing costs, while at the same time improving quality, delivery time and customer service.

Achieving this balance requires management guidance and control systems, which are the *formal, information-based* routines, guidelines and systems that managers use to maintain or alter patterns in organizational activities (Simons 1995). Four key guidance-and-control systems are shown in Figure 8-1.

A balance of control systems is needed to manage the complexity, paradoxical contradictions and chaos encountered in today's business environment (Price Waterhouse 1996). The paradoxical forces that must be balanced include motivation and coercion, reward and punishment, guidance and proscription, stimulation and control, self-interest and the desire to contribute, and intended and emergent strategies. The four guidance-and-control systems discussed in the following sections are used to create a dynamic tension between specific goal achievement and creative innovation.

### Strategic Guidance and Control Systems

A belief system is an explicit set of organizational definitions, which senior managers communicate formally and systematically reinforce in order to provide subordinates with the core values, shared purpose and common direction that they want them to adopt. Used to inspire and focus the search for new opportunities, these core values are linked to the business strategy. A formal belief system is communicated through such documents as credos, mission and vision statements, and statements of purpose (like those given in Tables 2-1 through 2-3 and 5-1 through 5-3), which show the vision, mission, and belief statements of Ametek Inc., Ciba-Geigy Corporation, Rhône-Poulenc Rorer Inc., and Corning Inc.

### Strategic Boundary Systems

The second kind of strategic guidance-and-control systems is referred to as the *boundary system*. These systems involve policy and other guidelines that are used to set—based on defined business risks—limits for organizational participants on opportunity-seeking behavior designed to achieve the enterprise's shared vision. Tables 2-1 through 2-3 and 5-1 through 5-3 provide both general (Rhône-Poulenc Rorer Inc., and Ametek Inc.) and specific (Johnson Wax) examples of boundary system definitions within the context of belief systems. Belief systems and boundary systems transform unbounded opportunity space into a focused domain that organizational participants can be encouraged to exploit. In the sense that they provide direction and necessary benchmarks or standards against which performance can be measured, these two types of information frameworks function as guidance-and-control systems. These systems are generally nonquantitative.

### Diagnostic Guidance and Control Systems

Two types of systems are discussed in this chapter: diagnostic control systems and diagnostic guidance and control processes.

*Diagnostic control systems.* Diagnostic control systems are comparative-performance feedback-reporting systems, which are the backbone of traditional management control and are designed to ensure predictable goal achievement. Diagnostic control systems, many of which were described in the accounting section, are the formal information systems that managers use to motivate em-

**Table 8-1**
**Comparative Sales Control Report, United Kingdom Subsidiary (in English pounds)**

|  | Actual Unit Sales | Budget | Deviation |
|---|---|---|---|
| Product A | 14,000 | 15,000 | −1,000 |
| Product B | 8,000 | 8,500 | + 500 |

ployees, monitor organizational outcomes, correct deviations from standards and reward achievements.

Three features distinguish diagnostic control systems:

• the ability to measure outputs of a process,

• the existence of predetermined standards against which actual results can be compared, and

• the ability to correct deviations from standards.

The standards, which are the key element of control systems, may include: budgets, performance benchmarks from industry competitors, adjusted historical figures, spending limits, financial ratios, agreed-upon objectives and even financial forecasts. Cost-accounting reports are an example of control-reporting systems, since they report on cost results and compare them to established standard costs. The simplest form of control report is a comparative sales report, such as the one shown in Table 8-1.

Since standards must be appropriate for the specific situations being controlled, and since variations occur from country to country (variations in labor costs, materials costs, transportation times, and exchange rates are common), international control systems are difficult to establish.

For example, in Table 8-1, if, for consolidation purposes, the sales results were translated into dollars in order to make the comparison meaningful, both the budget and the results would have to be converted at the same rate when evaluating the performance of the subsidiary management. In addition, if the performance of this subsidiary is to be compared with a similar one in another country, then local circumstances—such as whether a recession or labor problems existed in one country, new competitors entered the market, or other circumstances or events affected the results—would have to be noted and factored into the evaluation.

Because of differences encountered from country to country, comparative statements across boundaries are contingency based and so must be constructed carefully in order to meet individual situation requirements. Transfer pricing provides a typical example (Mueller, Gernon, and Meek 1994). The need for determining a transfer price arises when goods or services are exchanged between international subsidiaries. When goods are transferred, the price set is not a market price. While the current market price may influence the transfer, the transfer price is determined by many other situation restraints: minimizing taxes and worldwide import duties, winning host government approval, taking into account financial and other government restrictions and regulations, covering product costs, meeting competitive market conditions, enabling profit evaluations of subsidiaries and managing currency fluctuations.

Some ground rules have been developed for subsidiaries in light of these restrictions. If a country has a low tariff on imports, a higher transfer price is recommended. If a country has a high corporate tax rate, then a high export transfer price is recommended (to minimize profits, and thus, taxes on profits). If the expatriation of profits is restricted, setting a high export transfer price is one way to take profits out of a country. If devaluation is continual, a high price is also a way to minimize currency losses. If a subsidiary needs to boost profits or sales by lowering its costs and selling prices, on the other hand, a low import transfer price is one way to do this. If a government has a preference for either a cost-based or market-based price or strictly controls transfer prices, any decision must take these limits into consideration.

It is unusual to find situations where all these conditions can be met. For this reason, the decision should strive for the most advantageous overall solution— that is, the best balance—as in other multinational cross-cultural management situations. Given the complexity of the balancing of factors, computer-analysis systems are useful in these situations.

A manager exercising control over transfer-pricing transactions must also weigh the impact of these prices on the profitability performance of the units involved. While such transfer adjustments are best overall for the multinational parent company, care must be taken to adjust for the impact of nonperformance factors when evaluating the performance of a unit and its managers, so that they are not penalized for generating improved overall profits at the expense of lowering their unit's reported profits.

Comparative control systems cover many areas in addition to finance and accounting: quality, productivity, sales (dollars and units), costs, unit output, inventory turnover (days or weeks), debt-to-equity ratios, customer satisfaction (monthly comparisons of customer complaints, for example), on-time performance (airlines, for example), employee turnover, compliance with government regulations (racial mix of the workforce, for example), supplier performance (meeting just-in-time schedules, for example), manager performance, and compliance with policies (limits on speculative currency trading, for example).

In addition to actual diagnostic control *reporting systems*, other kinds of diagnostic control *systematic processes* exist. It is important to distinguish between actual control systems, that is, systems that *compare performance to standards and report on deviations* (such as cost-accounting reports and the sales reports shown in Table 8-1), and the wide range of systems that *only report information* and are used by managers as part of planning-and-control management processes.

*Diagnostic Guidance and Control Processes.* Many management-information systems do not contain standards or generate comparisons to standard measures; instead, they provide analytic information that can be used for planning-and-control decision making. For example, financial-accounting statements provide historical information that is useful in planning stock-investment decisions. In the broadest sense, any operating report that analyzes or decomposes operating aggregates can be considered a management guidance-and-control system. For instance, the cost breakdowns by category of expense on profit-and-loss statements (contained in a company's annual report) are analytical tools that can help an investor *diagnose* how healthy a company is. In an international situation, such analyses are much more difficult to do if a company chooses not to translate its annual reports into the language or accounting standards familiar to the user. For this reason, an expert is often needed to interpret them.

In an operational situation, reports on competitors' sales, for example, can be sufficient to trigger action by executives who know their comparable company sales. This was the case at Pepsi, where top managers carried in their wallets little charts with the latest key Nielsen industry sales figures by product in order to stimulate their drive to top Coke in all products and all markets (Simons 1995, p. 96). The weekly telephone and videoconferences at General Electric (described in the next section) are another example.

### Interactive Planning and Control Systems

Managing and balancing the tension between stimulating creative innovation and controlling predictable goal achievement is the essence of management control. Diagnostic control systems (such as the example in Table 8-1) can constrain innovation and opportunity seeking in trying to ensure that outcomes are kept in line with the intended strategies. Interactive control systems are designed to produce the opposite effect. They stimulate search and learning, allowing new strategies to emerge as participants throughout an organization respond to perceived opportunities and threats.

An interactive control system is *not* a unique type of control system. Many types of control systems that are generally referred to as decision support systems can be used interactively. For example, a computer-based spreadsheet that allows a manager to enter different price assumptions and then calculate the effect on profits of each assumed price change is a basic interactive tool, which enables a manager to plan and to forecast. The system that Gillette used to determine the best way to manufacture and supply products (described in Chapter 1) is a good example of an international decision support system:

You are all probably familiar with the Atra cartridge, which is a small razor blade shaving cartridge that we sell. About six months ago our computer optimization program was saying we really shouldn't continue to be supplying those Atra cartridges to the Australian market from our manufacturing operation in Melbourne, Australia. There was a cheaper way the computer identified in just one hour. How are we supplying Atra cartridges to the Australian market today? The steel comes from Usugi on the west coast of Japan. It goes from there to Rio de Janeiro where it is processed into blade steel. It is then shipped out into the Atlantic ocean and up the Amazon River 1,200 miles to Menaus where the plastic molding takes place and the blade steel is mounted into the cartridge, what we call a naked cartridge. Back out to sea, it goes to Singapore and there it is packaged and shipped to our Melbourne warehouse. Ladies and gentlemen, at this time that is the lowest-cost way to supply cartridges to Australia. Believe it. (Zeien 1995)

Such systems enable a manager to input different sets of future circumstances, for example, assumptions about the future competitive market in a given country, and to receive a recommendation on what kinds of product strategies would be appropriate under each set of simulated assumptions. Mathematical-based forecasting software packages that permit a manager to forecast economic environments (for example, gross national product) under different sets of assumptions are another example of interactive systems.

Interactive and diagnostic systems can involve any kind of systematic use of information to stimulate thinking about new directions (planning) or correcting problems (control). General Electric's (GE) weekly video conferences and phone meetings are a good example of a systematic interactive and diagnostic exchange of information:

It's 7AM Friday in a specially rigged conference room at the head office of GE Appliances in Louisville. CEO J. Richard Stonesifer, a fresh pot of coffee by his side, is ready to roll. The speakerphone hums, and Stonesifer greets his management staff in Asia. Stonesifer and his colleagues chew over sales figures and production glitches and gossip about Whirlpool Corp., their biggest competitor. For the next five hours, Stonesifer follows the sun across the globe, holding phone meetings or videoconferences with aides in Europe and the Americas. These talks "allow us to make immediate adjustments," Stonesifer says. "Customer complaints are never more than seven days from my attention." (Dwyer et al., 1994, p. 80)

Interactive management planning and control are found in many areas. (Several types of interactive decision-support systems were described in Chapter 7.) In the development area, brainstorming sessions can be used to stimulate the free-flowing generation of ideas; they should be structured so as to avoid critical judgments. Such group-based interactive structures are described in Chapters 9 (on organization) and 12 (on leading and managing teams). Groupware (computer software) and Internet exchanges are described in Chapters 7 (on information systems) and 11 (on communications).

## MANAGEMENT PLANNING AND CONTROL SYSTEMS: A BROADER PERSPECTIVE

Finance and accounting systems are extremely important enablers in multinational cross-cultural management. However, management control and planning systems are not limited to those found in the finance and accounting areas.

Based on the experiences described in this book, the human resources and their management described in Chapters 10 through 13 can be considered equally essential enabling planning and control systems, as can the organization structures, cultures and processes discussed in Chapter 9.

## WORKS CITED

Brealey, Richard A., Stewart C. Meyers, and Alan J. Marcus. *Fundamentals of Corporate Finance*. New York: McGraw-Hill, 1995.

Breton, Lee. "No Comparisons." *Wall Street Journal*, Septmber 22, 1989, p. R30.

Choi, Frederick D. S., and Gerhard G. Mueller. *International Accounting*. 2nd ed. Englewood Cliffs, NJ: Prentice-Hall, 1992.

Clark, Robert A. "ASEAN Equity Markets: The Role of ASEAN Securities Markets in Development." *Journal of Asian Business* 10, no. 1 (1994): 26–41.

Daniels, John D., and Lee H. Radebaugh. *International Business*. Reading, MA: Addison-Wesley, 1994.

Dwyer, Paula, Pete Engardio, Zachary Schiller, and Stanley Reed. "Tearing Up Today's Organization Chart." *Business Week: Special Issue, 21st Century Capitalism*, November 18, 1994, p. 80.

Eiteman, David K., Arthur I. Stonehill, and Michael H. Moffett. *Multinational Business Finance*. 7th ed. Reading, MA: Addison-Wesley, 1995.

Eng, Maximo V., Francis Lees, and Lawrence J. Mauer. *Global Finance*. New York: Harper-Collins College Publishers, 1995.

Fatehi, Kamal. *International Management*. Upper Saddle River, NJ: Prentice-Hall, 1996.

"Ford Will Get a Japanese Loan for Right-Hand-Drive Cars." *New York Times*, September 5, 1995, p. D2.

Gates, Stephen. *The Changing Global Role of the Finance Function*. New York: Conference Board, 1994.

Gray, Sidney J. *International Financial and Accounting Reporting*. New York: McGraw-Hill, 1995.

Griffin, Ricky W., and Michael W. Pustay. *International Business*. Reading, MA: Addison-Wesley, 1996.

Krugman, Paul R., and Maurice Obstfeld. *International Economics*. New York: Harper-Collins, 1994.

Liley, Jeffrey. "Fleece Street." *Far Eastern Economic Review*, October 1994, pp. 80, 82.

Madura, Jeff. *International Financial Management*. St. Paul, MN: West Publishing Company, 1995.

McNair, C. J. *World Class Accounting and Finance*. Homewood, IL: Business One Irwin, 1993.

Mockler, Robert J. *The Management Control Process*. Englewood Cliffs, NJ: Prentice-Hall, 1973.

Mueller, Gerhard G., Helen Gernon, and Gary K. Meek. *Accounting: An International Perspective*. 3rd ed. Burr Ridge, IL: Irwin, 1994.

Needles, Belverd. *Financial Accounting*. Boston: Arthur Andersen and Co. Alumni, 1995.

Price Waterhouse Change Integration Team. *The Paradox Principles: How High-*

*Performance Companies Manage Chaos, Complexity, and Contradiction to Achieve Superior Results*. Chicago, IL: Irwin Professional Publishing, 1996.

Rose, Peter S. *Money and Capital Markets*. 5th ed. Homewood, IL: Irwin, 1994.

Shim, Jae K., and Joel G. Siegel. *Encyclopedic Dictionary of Accounting and Finance*. Englewood Cliffs, NJ: Prentice-Hall, 1989.

———. *Barron's Accounting Handbook*. Happauge, NY: Barron's Educational Series, 1990.

Simons, Robert. *Levers of Control: How Managers Use Innovative Control Systems to Drive Strategic Renewal*. Boston: Harvard Business School Press, 1995.

Springate, David J. *Ampak International, Ltd*. Rev. ed. Dallas: University of Texas at Dallas, 1990.

Stevenson, Richard W. "Smitten by Britain: Thatcherism's Industrial Evolution." *New York Times*, October 15, 1995, Business Section, pp. 1, 10.

Zausner, Steven. "Russian Roulette." *Central European Studies*, January 1995, pp. 28–30.

Zeien, Albert. "Gillette's Global Marketing Experiences." Talk given at St. John's University's Annual Colman Mockler Leadership Award Ceremony, New York, February 27, 1995.

Chapter 9

# Organizing for Multinational Operations: Structure, Processes (Business and Human) and Culture

Organization is another key enabler in multinational cross-cultural management. Three aspects of organization are discussed in this chapter: structure, process and culture. The chapter concludes with a discussion of the contingency processes involved in the organization task.

While organization *structure* provides an important enabling environment, probably more important is the *process*, the way the organization works: the business and administrative processes, cooperative activities, interpersonal relationships and frequency and quality of the communications—what might be called the human and business processes. These processes are supported by an enabling corporate *culture*, which is the lubricant that helps make the processes work. Structure, then, is only one part of the equation. What happens within the structure is often more important than the structure itself.

As in the earlier chapters on enablers and enabling systems, the company experiences described in this chapter involve all three levels of multinational management—enterprisewide, business unit, and functional/operational. These experiences also involve a wide range of company and industry situations. The final section of the chapter discusses the underlying framework of this and other chapters—the basic contingency process and its usefulness in helping understand and structure the organization processes at work in a multinational environment.

## ORGANIZATION: THE NEW EQUATION

Over the next several decades, according to both business and academic studies, successful companies will be those that take advantage of global economies of scale by selling similar products worldwide and offering the same services in dozens of countries. However, they also must make sure that their operations blend in locally. This is necessary in order to gain acceptance as well as to find out what their customers want and to gain access to new ideas, tactics and technologies. They must also encourage information sharing and innovation throughout their companies and make sure they are not bypassed by competitors—as IBM was for a time when the company continued to focus on mainframes instead of listening closely to, and responding quickly to, actual and anticipated market changes.

The task of creating a flexible, opportunistic organization that is appropriate for the countries, product, competition and company involved is difficult. All organization structural forms—centralized, decentralized, matrix, hierarchical, and collaborative—can work in some combination, depending on the situation (Bartlett and Ghoshal 1991; Dwyer et al. 1994, pp. 80–90).

The concept of organizations has changed substantially as companies have come to place more emphasis on flexible collaborative structures. Perceptions about how organizations actually work have also changed as managers realized that organizations at work do not always conform exactly with organization charts.

For example, when asked about Gillette's worldwide organization, CEO Al Zeien gave this equivocal answer:

My answer to the question "How do you organize our type of company?" is that if you look at our company there is no fully definable pattern. Gillette has at least six different kinds of organization structures. People ask me why we organize the blade business one way, the Braun appliance business another way, and the Oral-B business a third way. The answer to that is simple. There is no ideal way to structure because with time things change and because different products, countries, and companies have different needs. But, at the same time one thing is consistent. Throughout all those structures, all those organizations, they are matricized in three ways: by function, by product and by job. It's often just a question of reporting relationships varying.

People ask, how can you operate with a three-way matrix? Who's responsible, who makes decisions when you have a three-way matrix, who has the authority? The answer is that the first rule you learn in business school—responsibility should equal authority—is wrong. The answer is everybody's responsibility is far greater than the authority they can exercise. So you have in effect overlapping responsibilities. But who makes decisions when you have this three-way matrix, who has the authority to make decisions? The answer is usually the person who best did his or her homework most often tends to have their way. (Zeien 1995)

This somewhat paradoxical view of organization structure—that the formal structure at the same time is, and is not, important—is only one of the many paradoxes of multinational cross-cultural management. However, this paradox exists only if one insists on too formal and fixed a solution. When viewed from a contingency perspective, the solution to organization structure, as in other task areas, is that the preferred final decision and action will be the one that best balances situation factors: the core company competencies, country, changing competitive market, and available people, systems and communications. As a result, organization structures very often change over time.

This view was confirmed by Bartlett and Ghoshal (1991) in their research study of twenty multinational corporations, which concluded that creating and changing organizations successfully resulted from the following steps:

First, the successful companies did not use a zero-based approach, that is starting from scratch. Rather they built on what they had, defending and reinforcing their existing capabilities, resources and competencies and adding new ones where appropriate to the situation.

Second, in creating new capabilities or overcoming existing problems, these companies did not try to imitate competitors' physical organization structures but looked for ways to compensate for their deficiencies or approximate a competitor's source of advantage—in a form appropriate for their own operations and company situation.

Third, these companies treated organizations as adaptive environments, able to respond to and restructure and reprocess as situation requirements change. (Bartlett and Ghoshal 1991)

## STRUCTURE: THE NECESSARY EVIL

Some organization structure is obviously needed. The best kinds of structures are those that are appropriate for the specific company and competitive market involved and can quickly respond to, and adapt to, change. It is possible, for example, that both a highly centralized and a highly decentralized multinational organization can prosper. The key to success, then, is not the structure, but the hybrid functioning organization processes within the structure that enable a balanced approach and the capacity to change appropriately.

For example, changing competitive market conditions forced Alcatel Alsthom, the giant French telecommunications equipment manufacturer, to change its organization structure. The company encountered major problems after a rapid drop in prices for its wide range of products, including network switches, fiber-optic lines and wireless communications devices. As a result, it lost $250 million in the first half of 1995. In the past, Alcatel had prospered by designing, manufacturing and selling a full line of communications products for each of its major clients, including France Telecom and Belgacom, the Belgian phone-service provider.

That market changed, however, as telecommunication equipment was increasingly designed according to uniform worldwide standards—a growing common framework (discussed in Chapter 7). In late 1995, Alcatel announced a sweeping reorganization, to be based around product lines instead of countries.

The old organization structure had made sense in the past when Alcatel got the bulk of its business from European, state-owned telephone companies, such as France Telecom. However, as the European phone monopolies were privatized and challenged by new competitors, these companies began demanding lower prices for equipment and instituting competitive bidding for contracts. The new structure was designed to enable Alcatel to compete more effectively in Western Europe with slimmed-down competitors such as AT&T (United States), Siemens (Germany), and Northern Telecom.

Under the new structure, the company was able to standardize its product development process across markets to meet competitive needs. The new structure was also expected to lead to a change in corporate culture, which in the past had been based on tightly controlled national fiefdoms, which communicated very little with each other concerning innovative new information. Moreover, the move also was expected to reduce the company's workforce by around 30,000, thus sharply reducing costs (Landler 1995b).

In late 1995, AT&T Corporation also announced a major reorganization, which split the company into three parts: long distance and other communications services ($49 billion in annual sales); communications equipment, such as telephones ($20 billion); and global information solutions, involving the manufacture and sale of computer systems to business ($8 billion). A company spokesperson said that the firm was responding to changes in technology and government regulations, which had turned the communications world upside down. According to the company, "the vertical [hierarchal] integration organization model was good for its time, but shifts in the market suggested it was time for a change" (Keller 1995; Landler 1995a).

Al Zeien of Gillette believes that an organization's structure has to be appropriate for the business involved, as well as flexible and capable of change. Furthermore, he explains, people make the organization work, which happens only with cultural imbedding, leadership, and training and selection processes that create well functioning internal administrative processes and a value-based entrepreneurial spirit. Gillette's greatest core competency, according to Zeien, is its group of more than 300 expatriate managers, who have an average of twenty years of experience. These managers know both Gillette's core global culture and how to manage different country operations within that perspective. The way in which Gillette creates this culture through its selection and training processes and through leadership is described in Chapters 11 and 12 (see also Zeien 1995).

Depending on human, administrative and business processes, the activities and attitudes intended to enable an organization to achieve a balance among global efficiencies, local responsiveness and the rapid transfer of knowledge is consistent with the strategic management philosophy of Gillette's prior president, Colman Mockler. He defined strategy implementation as doing whatever is necessary to get a job done, within well-defined legal, moral, ethical and policy restraints. Success depends on having, throughout the company, managers who know the firm's core culture—who can talk freely with other managers in the firm and also have the entrepreneurial instincts to respond creatively to local conditions.

## CREATING A BALANCED ORGANIZATION

As seen from the experiences of Deere & Co. (described in Chapter 1), organization change does not come easily for existing companies that are either considering going international or have already done so. As with the organization structure itself, the way in which change is managed does not follow some universal theoretical formula, but only general contingency guidelines that are situation based.

Not all companies have the luxury of creating adaptive organizations over an extended period of time, as Gillette did. For example, Alcatel had to move quickly to create a new structure to suit its specific needs and overcome its specific problems. In the mid-1990s, Ford Motor Company attempted a daring structural change over a short period of time. This change did not imitate normal decentralized industry patterns, such as those then prevailing at General Motors (Treece, Kerwin, and Dawley 1995).

In January 1995, CEO Alex Trotman formally introduced a new organization structure at Ford Motor Co. With completely independent geographic auto subsidiaries designing and selling their own vehicles on each side of the Atlantic, Ford had long paid a price in duplicated effort, waste and high product-development costs. Top-heavy and bureaucratic, the organization spent far too much time and money in designing new cars. Since Ford was having a good year in sales and profits, a trend it expected to continue for the next few years, 1995 seemed a good time to make changes in preparation for the next market downturn or alteration.

By combining the North American and European units, Trotman hoped to transform Ford into a far more nimble, efficient competitor. In particular, global product teams would now design cars to be sold throughout the world. However, Trotman's ambitions went well beyond cost cutting. He also wanted to position Ford to compete better in emerging markets. Clearly, he was strategically positioning his firm to compete in a more coordinated way in order to take advantage of global efficiencies.

The merger of Ford of Europe and Ford North America—to form a $94–billion company—was one of the largest mergers in history, and the planned merger with Ford's South American and Asian units will make the firm even more immense.

Ford was forced to make such a major move because its competitors were more efficient (and faster) in getting new car models to market. Ford's Taurus, for example, took 5 years to redesign, while Japanese competitors redesigned competing models in less than 4 years, and Chrysler developed its Neon subcompact in just 31 months. Chrysler was also more profitable, earning $2,110 operating profit per vehicle, while Ford made $877 in 1994; Chrysler's pretax profit was 11.6 percent against Ford's 5.4 percent. Toyota was also more efficient, turning out 37 vehicles per worker to Ford's 20.

Many questioned whether Ford could maintain its ability to respond locally within the new global structural framework. For example, under the new, combined, product-development organization design engineers were asked to take into account the needs of diverse markets, which could slow new-car development processes rather than speed them up. Moreover, cars designed to satisfy drivers around the world might end up pleasing no one. In addition, vast numbers of Ford employees found themselves in new jobs with new bosses, creating management and morale problems.

The new-product development function was organized in centers by vehicle type (for example, the Taurus), not by function (for example, structural design engineers) as before. Hundreds of personnel were transferred around the world to the new centers. To facilitate this transition, managers from around the world went through nine months of reengineering sessions to help ease the cultural disputes and integration problems. Work had already begun on reconciling the many differences in parts specifications while drawing on, and integrating, the best manufacturing and tooling procedures from around the world. Work was also being done on the most efficient way to adapt different car components and models to local needs, adding, for example, heaters in Scandinavian cars and air conditioners in the Singapore models. In theory, the savings could be enormous, provided the newly integrated product design units could capture global efficiencies while at the same time allowing for responsiveness to local market conditions. Ford estimated that the new organization structure would save the company $1 billion yearly. Ford's first venture into a global car, the Mondeo, sold well in Europe but not in the United States, since the design variations for Europe (for example, small back seats and powerful motors) either were not popular in the United States or led to higher-than-competitive market prices.

What makes the strategy even more daring and the case more interesting is that General Motors was using an opposite structural approach, with decentralized, separate regional units, which develop distinctly different autos for their own markets. The units subsequently examine crossover potential among countries and make minor design adjustments. GM claimed that such ad hoc efforts were cheaper, more effective and more flexible.

The outcome of the initiative to globalize Ford through major changes in structure organization was still uncertain in 1996 since the change was being made during a time of profitable operations rather than crisis (Treece, Kerwin, and Dawley 1995). Ford's Taurus was America's best-selling car; it (along with its twin, the Mercury Sable) accounted for close to 10 percent of Ford's sales. Ford hoped to sell the Taurus, with minor modifications, in many countries. In preparation for the strategic shift to its world car, Ford hoped to sell 47,000 Taurus vehicles overseas each year, including 15,000 with right-hand drive for markets such as Japan (Krebs 1995).

The success of Hewlett-Packard Co.'s inkjet printer provides an example of how a balanced organization approach and the ability to adapt and change quickly benefits a company. In 1984, H-P did not make printers, while twelve years later, in 1996, it was expected to have over $8 billion in printer revenue, even in the face of major foreign competition, especially from the Japanese (Yoder 1994). In 1994 H-P held 55 percent of the world inkjet printer market, and its success in printers (both laser and inkjet) made H-P one of the two fastest-growing major U.S. multinationals (along with Motorola Inc.).

According to Richard Hackborn, the H-P executive who led the successful printer effort;

If you're going to leverage American culture to compete globally, you need a balance of entrepreneurship and central leverage. The rugged individualism of our cowboy culture alone doesn't work; but to be centrally directed doesn't either, because you lose the tremendous contribution of local innovation and accountability. (Yoder 1994, p. A9)

While H-P headquarters was becoming increasingly more bureaucratic, in the 1980s, its individual business units were set up as fiefs, each having great autonomy. Each unit had the resources of a large company but was separate, and so was able to make decisions rapidly. For example, the teams involved in the printer business were in outposts like Boise, Idaho—far from H-P's increasingly bureaucratic Palo Alto, California, headquarters—where they were permitted, though sometimes reluctantly, to go their own way.

During the early 1980s H-P developed its inkjet technology, which was cheaper and better than that of its Japanese competitors, such as Epson, the king of the dot-matrix printers. H-P took out a blizzard of patents on its new technology and developed a family of products. H-P also borrowed another Japanese tactic; continually improving its existing products, an approach referred to by the Japanese as "eating your young," since it involves making one's current products obsolete.

In 1989 H-P reexamined its target market (it had initially presented the inkjet printer as a low-cost alternative to its own high-quality, commercial laser printer) and decided instead to focus on the consumer dot-matrix printer market, which was dominated by the Japanese. The strategic decision was made in the autumn of 1989, and within only a few weeks, the company had made major moves at all levels to target primarily Epson products and customers. H-P used every available mass-marketing technique, including price adjustments, store positioning, and cost cutting. It even adopted a Japanese strategy of issuing rapid-fire product variations.

Consistent with H-P's forward-looking market-creation strategy, inkjet mechanisms were expected to find their way into facsimile machines and color copiers. Sales could explode if, as expected, the inkjet becomes the technology of choice inside television-top printers used for interactive-TV services. If this hap-

**Figure 9-1a**
**Traditional Hierarchical Organization**

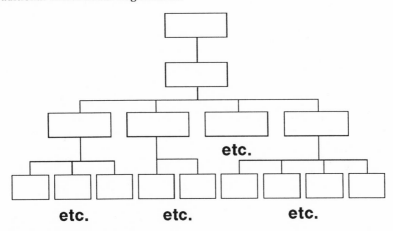

Copyright © 1997 by R. J. Mockler.

pens, ''Printers will be like toilets, they'll play a central role in the home,'' according to Hackborn (Yoder 1994, p. A9).

In these situations, the key to successful restructuring was to develop a flexible, adaptive structural organization appropriate for the situations at hand. One formal organization tool used to encourage the development and use of collaborative infrastructures, promote individual effort and help create a learning organization is the *flattened hierarchy*, a formal organization structure that has many segments reporting to a single person (as shown in Figures 9-1a and 9-1b). Within such structures, survival depends on increased delegation and entrepreneurial initiative, instead of formal bureaucratic hierarchical channels, to overcome the boundaries among different working functions. In other words, success depends on developing more interactive, collaborative business and human processes within the organization structure.

## THE HUMAN AND BUSINESS SYSTEMS: COLLABORATIVE INFRASTRUCTURES

The company experiences described in this book clearly establish that human and business systems and processes can be as critical to success as the organization and administrative processes and the organization structure.

An organization can be viewed from two alternate perspectives. First, it can be viewed as a structure of tasks, functions and reporting relationships. This is the organization and administrative structure. Second, an organization can be viewed as a set of day-to-day working processes, which include both integrated *business* work-flow processes as well as *human* activities, communications prac-

**Figure 9-1b**
**The Flatter Network Organization**

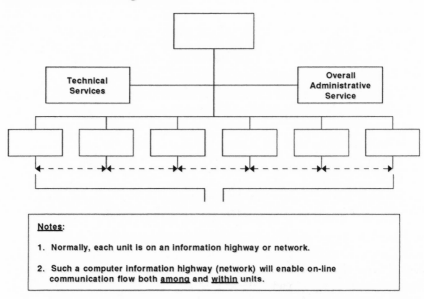

Notes:

1. Normally, each unit is on an information highway or network.

2. Such a computer information highway (network) will enable on-line communication flow both <u>among</u> and <u>within</u> units.

tices, working relationships, teamwork and coordination. Making sure that these business and human working processes are tuned to market and business needs will compensate for deficiencies and imbalances in the structure. Some writers have referred to the human processes as the "human system" (Sachs 1995, p. 44). The time and effort required to realign these other systems to meet competitive market needs is the reason why Philips needed fifteen years to do its reorganization; similarly, Gillette needed twenty years to train its core of expatriate managers to function at this level. For this reason, it is often easier for a new company to develop the system from scratch.

Initiating and maintaining these systems within the overall organization structure in order to achieve global and local balance is done in a variety of ways. The collaborative team structure is one familiar way to maintain balance at either the parent, global level or within the local unit structure (Zenger 1994). These structures can range from formal ones initiated from the top to structures that form in response to daily working needs.

Special company "SWAT" teams are an example of a more formal task team structure at the multinational parent level. Many multinational companies have developed such teams to actively promote integrative action, respond to local needs, and rapidly transfer technology across cultural boundaries. For instance, in 1994, Texas Instruments had some 200 professionals—dubbed the "Nomads"—who had set up chip-fabricating plants in Italy, Taiwan, Japan, and Singapore in the past four years, while U.S. West's CEO Callahan boasted that he could "put a team into South Africa by Friday" to begin setting up a cellular-phone system. "We're faster than any telephone company in the world," he added. Similarly, when opening up and expanding operations in China, along with hiring experienced local Chinese professionals, Unilever dispatched a team of Chinese-speaking troubleshooters from the company's 100-country operation. They helped build detergent plants, market shampoo and other personal-care products, and even sell Lipton Tea to the world's largest tea-drinking population in China (Dwyer et al. 1994, pp. 84–86).

Because of its specific situation requirements, General Electric used a very different approach at its light-bulb factory in Budapest, Hungary. GE uses "action workout" sessions, similar to those it uses in its United States plants. These "workouts" involve teams of workers tackling specific problems; they reflect GE's belief in a "borderless" organization culture in which employees remove obstacles in order to work more efficiently. These and other worker management changes were needed to change work habits left over from the communist era (Perlez 1994).

During its wrenching realignment during the early 1990s, Honda Motor Company made extensive use of teams to cut down on excess costs, shorten product development times, and make the company more flexible and market-oriented. Teams working at local units and extensive global teams working in Japan played a role in the revitalization program, which is described in Chapter 12 (See Miller, Armstrong, and Woodruff 1993; Updike, Woodruff, and Armstrong, 1995).

Many metaphors exist for describing and initiating an infrastructure of different relationships within a formal organization structure (Bartlett and Ghoshal 1995). A relatively new metaphor is called the "web" (an obvious play on the idea behind the World Wide Web), which is described in *The Web of Inclusion: A New Architecture for Building a Great Organization* (Helgesen 1995). Webs of inclusion are flexible units that can adapt, contract or expand in accord with what needs to be done. They are not necessarily as stringently configured as the corporate "SWAT" teams, and people's responsibilities in webs can alter over time, since the webs evolve through a process of trial and error. They are not always conceived of as a formal, enterprisewide strategy but rather often arise out of learning during tactical implementation. They are examples of the human processes that can develop within a learning organization in response to business-process needs.

Webs function as open channels across divisions and within the organization. People who work side-by-side often possess different skill levels, and thus are encouraged to share expertise, knowledge and access to certain resources. In this way, webs act to subvert the hierarchy in the organizations of which they are a part.

Webs are permeable around the edges, which makes them open to the world outside the organization. They are not necessarily internally focused, which makes them particularly useful in working beyond the firm's borders to forge strategic alliances and create joint ventures.

A key characteristic of webs is that although they are firmly task focused, they do not completely dissolve once a task is done. They develop innovative processes that affect the organization as a whole by creating new networks that may redistribute power and resources throughout an organization. In webs of inclusion there often is no difference between the decision makers and the people who implement the tasks. In contrast, other task forces (such as the corporate "SWAT" teams) are conceived and initiated at the top, where the mission is firmly set, and then called in to execute.

"Partnerships" is another working metaphor for cross-functional infrastructures within formal organization structures. In one company, the entire strategic plan was summarized on small cards that employees could carry in their pockets. The plan pointed out that the company's strategy was built on partnerships—between company employees and their customers, company employees and their suppliers, and the company and its financial backers, and among company employees in different divisions. The company employees' mission was to work together in the most efficient and effective way possible in order to keep all the partners satisfied. This partnering strategy worked, but it required an active CEO who translated these concepts into working guidelines on a day-to-day basis (Castello 1992). Today's successful international companies tend to think of national subsidiaries as strategic partners whose knowledge and local entrepreneurial capabilities are vital to the international corporation's ability to maintain a long-term, global competitive advantage.

Going further, as part of this partnership companies are giving more attention to creating an organizational environment in which individuals can learn, grow and contribute. General Electric went through just such a revitalization. It was led by then-CEO Jack Welsh, who continually visited the operations in order to personally communicate the need to take responsibility, initiate, question and challenge (Hurst 1995). One metaphor for this approach is the *individualized corporation*, which is a corporation that promotes maximum individual contribution, both through more flexible organization structures and by more supportive, task- and people-oriented leadership.

As suggested in this chapter, a multinational company can make use of multiple organizational and leadership linkages to maintain global efficiencies, respond to local needs and transfer knowledge rapidly. These linkages are especially important to helping new-product developers understand local market needs and obtain an enthusiastic commitment from those responsible for introducing new products. In 1995 Ford was wrestling with this job linkage problem by making use of cross-training assignments, permanent transfers of international researchers to new locations, dual assignments, communication links and product-oriented teams. Gillette, for example, has made use of a variety of formal and informal linkages, including frequent assignment changes; computer-aided decision making; a loosely defined three-way matrix organization; distributed decision-making power; and multifaceted, cross-functional, cross-national border-training programs.

One formal organization tool—the use of flattened hierarchies—was discussed earlier in this chapter. Another tool that encourages the development of collaborative human and administrative systems is an innovative office layout. One such layout, which has no walls or separate offices, and which links all workers by computers, has been used at several companies, especially those that use laptop computers to link widely dispersed sales forces (Macht 1995).

Each of these working metaphors (and similar ones such as learning organizations, rejuvenation through individualized corporations, flexible or collaborative workplaces, collaborative team organizations, strategic alliances, and organizational transformation), the organizational concepts underlying them, and the formal structures devised to support them can be used to inspire, initiate and guide the development of organization infrastructure. Infrastructures can be useful within any formal structure (hierarchical or flat, centralized or decentralized, or matrix, or structures based on product, division, geographic region or function) and can enable learning, adaptability, cooperation, and the balancing of many diverse objectives. It is a concept that GE adopted when it began to emphasize quick response rather than planning, as described in *The Boundaryless Organization: Breaking the Chains of Organization Structure* (Kerr and Ulrick 1995).

Variations on this human, administrative and business process infrastructure approach are described in books such as *The Fifth Discipline: The Art and Practice of the Learning Organization* (Senge 1990), *Designing Team-Based Organizations* (Mohrman, Cohen, and Mohrman 1995), *Designing Organizations* (Galbraith 1995), *Crisis and Renewal: Meeting the Challenge of Organizational Change* (Hurst 1995), *Creating a Flexible Workplace* (Olmstead 1995), *Creative Destruction: A Six Stage Process for Transforming Organizations* (Nolan and Croson 1995), *Transforming the Way We Work: The Power of the Collaborative Workplace* (Marshall 1995), and *The Global Learning Organization* (Marquardt and Reynolds 1994).

The key to success lies in developing a hybrid organization concept or pattern and a metaphor to describe it that works in one's own organization. It is usually unwise to adapt someone else's metaphor and conceptual pattern, since rarely will such a tool exactly match the new set of situation requirements.

As noted here and in Chapter 12, these human, administrative, and business processes need active leadership to ensure that the concepts are translated into working guidelines and that the company culture which emerges is sustained and supports this infrastructure.

## CREATING AN ENABLING, SUPPORTIVE, ENTERPRISEWIDE CORPORATE CULTURE

Not only are there national cultures that must be bridged when doing business internationally, there are also internal company cultures (religious, ethnic and professional) that must be integrated, as well as an enterprise-wide corporate culture, which must be developed and sustained.

An enterprise-wide corporate culture needs a special kind of entrepreneurial character to encourage individual initiative that meets local requirements and leads to innovations that are useful at both the local and global levels. At the same time, however, individual entrepreneurial initiative must take into account the limits, interconnections and global perspectives of the international company environment within which it works. It is, above all, a culture dedicated to purposeful change.

The approach to strategy implementation discussed in Chapter 1 encourages people to do whatever is necessary to get a job done, within well-defined legal, moral, ethical and policy restraints, a guiding principle set forth at Gillette by Colman Mockler during his seventeen years as CEO. Obviously there are risks to such a loosely defined entrepreneurial working environment. Leadership, therefore, first requires creating a culture 'that accepts failure. More than that, however, it requires defining these general guidelines (or boundaries) through daily leadership actions, such as those of CEOs Jack Welsh at General Electric and Al Zeien at Gillette. This aspect of creating an enabling cultural environment is discussed in Chapter 12.

The *organizational* enabling environment for fostering such a controlled entrepreneurial culture is covered in this chapter. Chapters 10 through 13 discuss the *human resource* enablers—both the *leadership* aspects and the *staffing and training* tools—that are useful in creating an organization culture/environment that balances global efficiency, local responsiveness and rapid knowledge transfer.

## AN INTEGRATIVE CONTINGENCY PROCESS

The management process shown at work in this chapter is, in general, the contingency process described in Chapter 3 (see Figure 3-2): moving from the task and the relevant situation requirements through concept formulation to putting in place the actual working organizations and other enablers. This process is essentially one of entrepreneurial management, as discussed in Chapter 3 (see Figure 3-3).

Figure 9-2 outlines the specific enabler formulation process at work in the chapters in Parts II, III, and IV. What occurs, as is shown in Figure 9-2, is that situation factors—the competitive market, all existing systems and the extent of changes occurring—are constantly monitored and solution concepts are formulated in an ongoing fashion. Some may be immediate solutions, such as the flattened organization structures, computer systems, facility location, product strategies, and financial analysis tools described in Chapters 7, 8, and 9. Others require more time to formulate. This emerging process is described in Figures 3-2, 3-3, and 9-2.

This common cognitive framework was evident in the company experiences

**Figure 9.2**
**Strategy Implementation: The Enabling Processes**

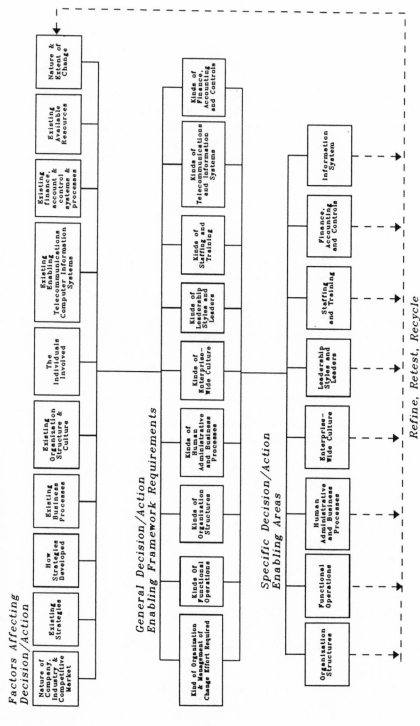

*Factors Affecting
Decision/Action*

| Nature of Company, Industry & Competitive Market | Existing Strategies | How Strategies Developed | Existing Business Processes | Existing Organization Structure & Culture | The Individuals Involved | Existing Enabling Telecommunications Computer Information Systems | Existing finance, account & control systems & processes | Existing Available Resources | Nature & Extent of Change |

*General Decision/Action
Enabling Framework Requirements*

| Kind of Organization & Management of Change Effort Required | Kinds Of Functional Operations | Kinds of Organization Structures | Kinds of Human Administrative and Business Processes | Kinds of Enterprise-Wide Culture | Kinds of Leadership Styles and Leaders | Kinds of Staffing and Training | Kinds of Telecommunications and Information Systems | Kinds of Finance, Accounting and Controls |

*Specific Decision/Action
Enabling Areas*

| Organization Structures | Functional Operations | Human Administrative and Business Processes | Enterprise-Wide Culture | Leadership Styles and Leaders | Staffing and Training | Finance, Accounting and Controls | Information System |

*Refine, Retest, Recycle*

Copyright © 1996 by R. J. Mockler.

described in this chapter, where it was used to formulate a useful enabling organization environment for balancing and integrating the three perspectives affecting successful multinational cross-cultural management: global efficiency, local responsiveness and the rapid transfer of knowledge at both the enterprise-wide and operational planning and action areas.

Such integrative management processes and enabling environments are necessary when managing across national cultures and borders. Change and rebirth in light of changing environments require this type of contingency framework, both at the planning and implementation levels in order to continually respond to, anticipate and create new ways to deal with continually changing competitive market forces.

## WORKS CITED

Bartlett, Christopher, and Sumantra Ghoshal. *Managing across Borders: The Transnational Solution.* Boston: Harvard Business School Press, 1991.

———. "The Individualized Corporation: New Practical and Theoretical Challenges." Presentation at the Strategic Management Society annual conference, Mexico City, October 15–18, 1995.

Castello, Robert. "Taking the Big Plunge—Ownership." Talk given at the Planning Forum Distinguished Speaker Luncheon, New York, September 17, 1992.

Dwyer, Paula, Pete Engardio, Zachary Schiller, and Stanley Reed. "The New Model: Tearing Up Today's Organization Chart." *Business Week, Special Issue: 21st Century Capitalism,* November 1994, pp. 80–90.

Galbraith, Jay R. *Designing Organizations.* San Francisco: Jossey-Bass, 1995.

Helgesen, Sally. *The Web of Inclusion: A New Architecture for Building a Great Organization.* New York: Doubleday/Currency, 1995.

Hurst, David K. *Crisis and Renewal: Meeting the Challenge of Organizational Change.* Boston: Harvard Business School Press, 1995.

Keller, John J. " 'New' AT&T Bets on Long Distance, But Its Competitors Are Fleet of Foot." *Wall Street Journal,* September 22, 1995, pp. A3, A8.

Kerr, Steven, and David Ulrick. *The Boundaryless Organization: Breaking the Chains of Organization Structure.* San Francisco: Jossey-Bass, 1995.

Krebs, Michelle. "Ford Presents the Importance of Being Taurus, Act III." *New York Times,* September 3, 1995, Automobiles Section, p. 1.

Landler, Mark. "AT&T, Reversing Strategy, Announces a Plan to Split into 3 Separate Companies." *New York Times,* September 21, 1995a, pp. A1, D8.

———. "Alcatel to Be Reorganized along Product Lines." *New York Times,* October 6, 1995b, p. D6.

Macht, Joshua. "When the Walls Come Tumbling Down." *Inc. Technology,* no. 2 (1995): 70–72.

Marquardt, Michael, and Angus Reynolds. *The Global Learning Organization: Gaining Competitive Advantage through Continuous Learning.* Burr Ridge, IL: Irwin Professional Publishing, 1994.

Marshall, Edward W. *Transforming the Way We Work: The Power of the Collaborative Workplace.* New York: Amacom, 1995.

Miller, Karen Lowry, Larry Armstrong, and David Woodruff. "Honda. New Car. New Culture. Can It Get Back on Top?" *Business Week*, September 13, 1993, pp. 63–72.

Mohrman, Susan Albers, Susan G. Cohen, and Allan M. Mohrman, Jr. *Designing Team-Based Organizations*, San Francisco: Jossey-Bass, 1995.

Nolan, Richard, and David C. Croson. *Creative Destruction: A Six Stage Process for Transforming Organizations*. Boston: Harvard Business School Press, 1995.

Olmstead, Barney. *Creative a Flexible Workplace*. New York: Amacom, 1995.

Perlez, Jane. "G.E. Finds Tough Going in Hungary." *New York Times*, July 25, 1994, pp. D1, D8.

Sachs, Patricia. "Transforming Work: Collaboration, Learning, and Design." *Communications of the ACM*, September 1995, pp. 36–44.

Senge, Peter. *The Fifth Discipline: The Art and Practice of the Learning Organization.* New York: Doubleday/Currency, 1990.

Treece, James B., Kathleen Kerwin, and Heidi Dawley. "Ford: Alex Trotman's Daring Global Strategy." *Business Week*, April 3, 1995, pp. 94–104.

Updike, Edith, David Woodruff, and Larry Armstrong. "Honda's Civic Lesson: The Carmaker Learned to Listen to the Troops When a Key Model Faced a Cost Squeeze." *Business Week*, September 18, 1995, pp. 71–76.

Yoder, Stephen Kreider. "How H-P Used Tactics of the Japanese to Beat Them at Their Game: It Hogged Patents, Cut Costs and Pared Prices to Grab Market in Inkjet Printers." *Wall Street Journal*, September 8, 1994, pp. A1, A9.

Zeien, Albert. "Gillette's Global Marketing Experiences." Talk given at St. John's University's Annual Colman Mockler Leadership Award Ceremony, New York, February 27, 1995.

Zenger, John H., Ed Musselwhite, Kathleen Hurson, and Craig Perrin. *Leading Teams.* Burr Ridge, IL: Irwin Professional Publishing, 1994.

# Part IV

# Enabling Human Resources

# Chapter 10

# Interpersonal Interaction

---

Human resources—the people working in an enterprise—is a key strategic driver that profoundly affects the success of a multinational cross-cultural enterprise.

This chapter builds on the description in Chapter 4 of a five-dimensional perspective for becoming sensitive to, and thinking about, cultural differences. Chapter 4 provided a framework and vocabulary for the discussion in this chapter, which describes ways to understand, adapt to and more effectively manage cultural differences that affect multinational cross-cultural management.

## UNDERSTANDING AND MANAGING CULTURAL AND PERSONAL BIASES AND MENTAL SETS

One useful way to become sensitive to, understand and acquire a facility to manage cultural differences is first to understand one's own cultural and personal biases. Since this book is published in the United States, the North American stereotype model is used as a reference point in the following discussion. The same concept would work as well using any (preferably, the reader's own) national culture as the reference point. Like the five-perspective framework developed in Chapter 4, it is simply a conceptual perspective that is useful for discussion purposes. It is not to be taken literally as a recommendation to "think American" in interpersonal interactions.

Not all North Americans, or people of any other nationality, are like the people described in the following examples. Before going on, therefore, it is useful to review the guidelines articulated in Chapter 4:

1. While it is useful to explore generalities and their implications, individuals do not always conform to general cultural stereotypes.

2. Differences are not always culturally based. Some arise from individual personality differences and some from personal, institutional or business factors.

3. Do not assume that because something works in one culture, it will work in another.

4. Understand yourself and your own culture first, so that you may be more aware of your own biases or mental set and have a benchmark against which to study others.

5. Study cultural diversity within your own country, since such a study yields clues to cultural differences and how to handle diversity.

6. The following discussion focuses on continuums, that is, on two extremes between which there can be many, varied gradations; try to avoid thinking in terms of extreme black-and-white stereotypes.

7. Ultimately it is best to learn as much as you can about cultural and personal sensitivities *specific to the situation you are dealing with.*

8. The same words often have different connotations in different cultures.

The following discussion covers five key characteristics that are considered benchmark areas for measuring differences among cultures and have proven in the past to impact cross-cultural relationships:

• The role of personal relationships: business or people first?
• Focus on the individual or on the group?
• Status: is everyone created equal?
• The question of priorities: what is the value of time?
• Other factors: Corporate culture, Institutional, Business and Individual

This has proved to be a useful framework against which to measure one's own profile, but it is important to remember that these categories are for discussion and understanding purposes only. In practice, actions and motivation do not always fall into such clearly defined categories.

Others may judge North Americans against reference points such as are discussed in the following pages. For example, many French think North Americans are naive, shallow, uninteresting and unaware, while managers in the United States at times cite such typical French traits as arrogance, self-congratulation, stubbornness and unwillingness to compromise. Both views are most often exaggerated and wrong, since each person can differ from a typical preconceived national personality profile, depending on personality, age and upbringing.

Often it is useful to view differences as possible opportunities. For example, the Japanese are noted for their concern for cleanliness. This has inspired such products as automated teller machines that iron and sanitize the dispensed bills, germ-free pens and pencils whose barrels are impregnated with an antiseptic chemical to kill bacteria, and antibacterial stationery, origami paper, bicycle handles, and even maracas and tambourines (Pollack 1995).

When faced with multinational cross-cultural management situations, it is also useful to draw on one's experience with other nationalities (in one's own country or when traveling overseas) and write scenarios of impressions of the key typical characteristics of each of the nationalities encountered or dealt with. Such national profiles are, of course, only benchmarks that serve as a starting point. Any person may differ from this typical personality profile, and in each situation a variety of other noncultural factors may influence individual behavior.

## THE ROLE OF PERSONAL RELATIONSHIPS: BUSINESS OR PEOPLE FIRST?

American businesspeople reputedly like to get to the point quickly and handle business first, before establishing personal relationships. This cultural bias is reflected in such phrases as, ''I don't have to like someone I do business with.'' Like most cultural biases, this statement is true, and the bias can be useful in a culture similar to that in the United States. Such an attitude can, however, create problems in other cultures. Two aspects of this cultural trait can affect managing cultural differences: the importance of developing personal relationships in the culture being dealt with and the way people in that culture form relationships.

For example, a multinational company with a subsidiary in Mexico, a culture in which personal relationships are important, might think very carefully about whom they send to Mexico City to replace a male sales manager from the United States who had long-term personal relationships with Mexican customers. The selection of a business-like woman from New England might work against the company, given the machismo and culture of male camaraderie in Mexico. At a minimum, one would need to carefully plan an extended transition period, to be managed in a very personal way by both the new and former sales managers (Foster 1995).

The notion of a personal relationship in the United States can be quite different from the view of other, more ''relationship-oriented'' cultures. For Americans, relationships are often casual and do not require deep commitments, especially in business situations. Americans often seem to lack the time and inclination to pursue the one-on-one learning about each other that is necessary to form deep friendships. In their breezy style, they are informal and friendly, and they often have difficulty cultivating friends in business situations involving cultures with opposite traditions, where deep, long-lasting relationships are required (relationships that, by necessity, take time).

For example, a Chinese firm wishing to purchase papermaking machinery negotiated with two suppliers, one French and one American. The American firm had superior technology yet lost the contract. During the negotiations, the American business negotiation style was seen as disrespectful by the Chinese, and the Chinese style was seen as confusing, time-consuming and not getting to the point. The American firm lost the deal because of insensitivity to the importance of personal relationships in the Chinese culture (Mu 1995). This and numerous similar incidents make the point that during intercultural exchanges one should communicate mutual respect, be nonjudgmental, realize that perceptions are personal, show personal empathy, and tolerate ambiguity (Kraar 1995).

The way in which business relationships are formed in different cultures also varies. Americans often build a relationship with informality, cheeriness, a playful disrespect for status and position, breezy hospitality, and an expectation that everyone will find this attitude charming and friendly. It is friendliness—but not necessarily friendship. Europeans, on the other hand, are less open, especially in England, where respect for differences and status is particularly important. In the European cultural context, the casual, informal American approach appears shallow, superficial and insensitive.

The French especially enjoy highlighting differences as a way to define their individualistic character and to ascertain another person's true nature, an approach that may seem unfriendly to members of other cultures. They are often perplexed by Americans who search for similarities among cultures as a means of establishing a relationship. To the French, such an approach seems to lack the depth that develops from getting to know the distinctive character of a person from another culture.

The French traits combine a kind of personal individualism and a natural suspicion of strangers. This individualism seems to generate a resistance to adapting to anyone's needs and has led to the French reputation for rudeness. This is especially true of salespeople in Paris, who are known for their surliness and not for smiling or being accommodating (Riding 1995).

Considerable cultural variations exist in regard to the display of emotions. For example, during negotiations in business occurring at the upper management level between individuals just getting to know each other, the range of emotional expression considered acceptable is greater for Americans than it is for the British, and greater still for the Latin Americans. In contrast, for the Japanese and most Asians, the display of emotions is more restricted than for the British. These relationships change, of course, in other settings, such as social events.

Since the history of pioneer America instilled in its citizens the belief that hard work and persistence can make things happen, Americans are likely to insist on receiving specific information that will enable them to plan. For example, an Arab negotiating with an American was puzzled by the insistence on specific information about future delivery dates and available quantities, as he believed that, having built a relationship, they would have established enough trust to make such detailed information unnecessary. After discussing the matter and explaining the need, the solution in this instance was for the Arab to understand the American's need and take the time to supply more information as requested, even though he initially felt that being asked for that information was unnecessary and showed a lack of trust. Such a solution is common in these situations: first understand the cultural difference and its basis, and then, based on one's own or others' experiences, take the steps necessary to accommodate a sensitive human situation.

Before proceeding overseas to negotiate, it is important to understand that the very purpose of a negotiation may vary by culture (Moran and Stripp 1991). Often, the purpose is *not* to accomplish a task and arrive at a deal, as it is in the United States. In many other cultures, negotiations may be a process of getting to know the other parties and of establishing a long-term personal relationship to serve as the basis of many future deals. This is one reason why so little often seems to be accomplished during early stages of negotiations in China, Japan and South America and why negotiations there seem to take so long.

In fact, the most important key to success in cross-cultural negotiations or any other task of multicultural management is to first establish a strong personal relationship. Often, of course, an uncomplicated deal can be written or a simple matter can be handled quickly among different cultures. Nonetheless, building relationships is a significant means of doing business over a long period of time among different cultures.

## FOCUS ON THE INDIVIDUAL OR THE GROUP?

Success in managing cultural differences does not depend on becoming or acting like the nationality being dealt with. Generally, it simply requires adapting or bending to some degree.

Relative to other cultures, Americans as a whole are very extreme in the value they place on individualism. U.S. history and the educational system support an individualistic culture. For example, children are taught to be self-reliant and are rewarded for individual achievement. In contrast, in the past, young Japanese children often worked in groups, with the pride of achievement and reward going to the collective output. This accounts in part for why such extensive training is needed in U.S. companies as they move toward organization structures that are free of hierarchy and toward a reliance on interactive teams.

This trait can cause problems during negotiations. For example, Americans often expect the Japanese to make decisions at the negotiating table, while the Japanese are continually surprised to find individuals on the American side advancing their own opinions and ideas and, on occasion, contradicting one another. This creates a cultural gap that must be bridged by one side or the other through initiating a dialogue about the gap and reaching an understanding of how to bridge it. Again, this usually requires more time than Americans originally were prepared to spend on negotiations.

An American expatriate in Malaysia who managed Motorola Penang's Research and Development operation for several years reflected on his experiences there in these words:

When I was transferred to Penang it was a cultural shock. I remember when I tried to publicly reward some people for exceptional effort, how embarrassed they were. Rewards such as free time or free lunch for the team as whole were more appropriate. I didn't realize that teamwork is more important there than standing out as an individual. In the states we fight for recognition (quoted in Gogan, Zuboff, and Schuck 1994, p. 6).

Another Malaysian manager described what he learned in this way: "Australians are taught to be strong and speak their minds. Italians are more emotional. I had to role-play an American. I cannot act like Americans; they are more aggressive and individualistic" (quoted in Gogan, Zuboff, and Schuck 1994, p. 7).

Cultures of the United Kingdom, the Netherlands, France, and the Nordic countries also have strong individualistic tendencies. More collectivist cultures, in addition to the Japan, include many Asian and Latin American countries. Guatemala is considered the most group-oriented culture, due to its Mayan tribal heritage (Foster 1995).

Cultural values are changing, however. For example, in Japan a system of competitive "cram" schools has been developed to train children (two years and older) to compete for positions in better grammar schools—which leads to entrance into better universities and subsequently, better jobs at graduation. This is creating a generation of "kids like in America," who are being nurtured in a more "individualistic and independent thinking" mold (WuDunn 1996, p. A3).

At times, the origin of the collectivist cultural values lies, not in historical traditions, but in traditions acquired during communist rule. For example, when doing business in Russia or Central Europe, one often encounters situations such as:

• the inability to negotiate individually and make decisions during meetings because approval is needed from higher authorities;
• final arrangements may have to be worked out with labor groups, which still control many of the decision processes;
• many constituents still must be paid off with bribes and under-the-table payments, raising serious ethical questions for U.S. executives.

While it is easier to make decisions and take action in an individualistic frame (it takes longer to reach decisions and act in collective contexts), and while Americans are noted for being action oriented, group-oriented cultures can be action oriented as well. For example, in Hong Kong, Singapore and China, small, family-based businesses have been very successful throughout Asia, often growing into major conglomerates (Gargan 1995)—though that may be changing as the family sons and daughters take command (Barnathan, Engardio, and Winzenburg 1995).

In the United States, one hears the phrase, "The squeaky wheel gets the grease." In collectivist cultures, the opposite may be true: the outspoken individualist may be viewed as disharmonious and a danger to the group, and so be ostracized. In collectivist, group-centered cultures, harmony is an important goal—harmony with groups and society and also with traditions that may have developed over many hundreds of years. This dictates some careful judgment and restraint as to the timing of outspoken criticism and objections during business negotiations. Where appropriate, businesspeople should resist the urge to prematurely attempt to get down to business and into the task of establishing bargaining positions.

In light of these cultural and historical differences, it is necessary to be contingency oriented. First, the situation context should be examined: both the individual and culture, as well as the tasks being dealt with. Some factors to look at and be sensitive to have been discussed in this section (see also Chapter 4). Other factors exist as well. Being sensitive to these differences is a major first step in adapting to, and managing, perceived differences. Above all, when in doubt, ask questions gently to find out what situation context is being dealt with.

## STATUS: IS EVERYONE CREATED EQUAL?

The United States has an egalitarian culture, which asserts that all men are created equal. Next to Australia, it is probably the world's most informal culture.

In many cultures, formal protocols are important, however. Early in business relationships, people are referred to by their formal titles (Mr., Mrs.), not by first names, as in the United States. Business cards are treated seriously, from the titles printed on them (corporate rank, title, and educational degrees) to the way they are exchanged (start with the highest-ranking person) and stored. Gift-giving practices also vary by culture. Gifts are common in Asia, and usually given in relation to some specific service, such as presenting a talk. Businesspeople should be aware that customs in regard to dinner invitations and appropriate host or hostess gifts vary widely, as do the timing and length of meals. You can expect to be invited to a business associate's home in Australia, though rarely in China or Japan. If you are invited to a home in France, bring flowers—but never roses. In Spain, dinners are much later—close to 11:00 P.M.; look for three-hour lunches in Buenos Aires. It is important to learn these such protocols as quickly as possible.

Embracing egalitarianism, in contrast, leads to a willingness to speak frankly as an equal to anyone, which is a very direct approach. Businesspeople from the United States tend to speak frankly, no matter what the rank of the listener. Protocols based on status or custom dictate a somewhat different approach, however. In cultures where rank and position are considered more important—such as Mexico, Italy, and even France—such directness can appear vulgar, harsh and impersonal. Many other cultural values dictate ambiguity and indirectness in order to maintain harmony, respect status, elaborate points within larger contexts, and save face. The status values also dictate that it is prudent to praise contributions to increase a listener's status before offering any criticism; this is a good idea in any culture.

The desire to avoid diminishing another's status in public leads to considerable confusion (Mu 1995). In Asia especially, people have difficulty saying "no" directly. Instead, they may equivocate, as by saying, "We must study the question further," or "We will try to solve the problem or overcome the difficulty." However, in Asia "yes" means no more than "I heard you"; it is not to be taken as an affirmative reply. In its extreme, at many stores when you are dissatisfied or want something changed, the clerks will say "no problem." However, what they mean is that there is no problem for them but a big problem for you, as you will discover later when you find nothing has been done.

North Americans have always had trouble dealing with bureaucracies. They prefer to seek out the person making the decision to get a direct answer as quickly as possible. This is not possible in many cultures. In the United States there has recently been considerable talk about changing (reengineering) systems in government, education and business systems. The feeling is that in order to be competitive with the rest of the world, U.S. institutional systems should be more efficient in delivering services and performing functions.

Hierarchies for their own sake are common in many cultures, based on history and past practice. They require time to work through, and are often manipulated (as in Japan) to exploit or win concessions. They are also the source of much crime and bribery. They can be especially troublesome when trying to introduce change in business, such as when empowering workers to make decisions. For example, Moroccan teams can have trouble with empowerment because they are used to a hierarchical religious, social and political environment (Hatch 1995).

North Americans are often at a loss to explain why contracts are ignored so often in Asian, Latin American, and Russian and Central European countries. An egalitarian system is built on the assumption that laws and standards (ethical and moral) permit all people to be treated equally. Other countries are more pragmatic and judge each new event based on the existing circumstances. In China, for example, the latter seems to generally hold true. American contracts tend to be lengthy because the parties try to anticipate and cover all contingencies. For the Chinese, the contract is the beginning of the negotiation rather than the end, since they may depend on the trust and relationship with their Western partner to help resolve difficulties that arise. This is why it helps a great deal to work through family ties when doing business in China.

While women are viewed as equal to men in many cultures (such as in Scandinavia), many other cultures do not believe in such equality. In very masculine-oriented countries, such as Japan, women may have trouble negotiating and interacting with Japanese business people. The same may also be true in some of the Arab states. These attitudes are changing, but only very slowly (WuDunn 1995).

The direct approach is also a problem during employee performance evaluations. While desirable in egalitarian cultures such as in the United States, being honest, frank and open—or working with objective standards fairly developed during management by objectives programs—is not as effective in nonegalitarian societies. First, such behavior is perceived as a threat to the status of the person being evaluated and usually violates associated cultural values related to avoiding unpleasant subjects and confrontations. Second, working with a person to set work objectives, just like asking for opinions about work practices, violates hierarchical allocations of power, since in many collectivist cultures, bosses are supposed to have the answers. Cultural differences also affect performance-reward systems: individual rewards for performance are out of place in societies where the group or collective effort is the primary driving force.

As seen in these examples, as in most of the areas discussed in this section, outcomes are often dependent on more than one cultural value.

## A QUESTION OF PRIORITIES: WHAT IS THE VALUE OF TIME?

Time factors also affect the approach to dealing with people from other cultures. For instance, in the specific situation at hand, will decisions be made and action taken quickly, or will many meetings be necessary just to get to know each other? Can the task be discussed directly or will it be necessary to socialize, avoid confrontations and talk about peripheral context issues first? Will the meetings proceed in an orderly, linear fashion, moving step by step toward a conclusion/decision or will a discursive, less task-focused discussion take place? Managing cultural differences requires prethinking and preplanning along these contingency lines. The specific situation requirements, and not theoretical, universal formulas, dictate how cultural differences are managed.

Such flexibility should not surprise any American who is familiar with the rural versus big-city lifestyles in the United States. Managers in New York City work on tight time schedules, hurrying from one meeting or task to another. On the other hand, managers living in smaller towns might be less controlled by tight time schedules and more accustomed to dealing with people they have gotten to know personally over the years. This can include shopkeepers, relatives, mail carriers—even the refrigerator repair person. Managers who can imagine, or have experienced, such different settings are aware that managing styles change in different environments. The same is true among national cultures.

When conducting training or other business in France, for example, times should be adjusted for lunch and breaks. For the French, lunch can be a two-hour event or longer, and time must be allocated to accommodate such habits. For the French, as for businesspeople around the world, lunch is not just a time to eat. It is also a time to conduct interpersonal business, carry out internal politicking, and clarify possible misunderstandings (Hatch 1995).

Even in societies that accept tight schedules, decisions may be made at a much slower pace. Other cultural traditions may intervene; these may be related to long histories that, perhaps, create the feeling that the near-term future is not very important and that other considerations such as society, respect for other members of the group, and the like are more important and therefore must be given equal time.

This same cultural perspective regarding time is also to be expected in São Paulo or Mexico City. For example, when Corning Glass joined forces with Vitro, a Mexican-based glass manufacturer, the American managers had a problem with the cultural time difference, finding that the Mexican workers would take hours for lunch and then work until 9 P.M. They were also often late when attending meetings. Such cultural differences, wherever encountered, must be taken into account by management (DePalma 1994).

As discussed in Chapter 4, monochronic cultures (such as in the United States) tend to focus on the present or immediate future and to believe that an individual can affect future outcomes. Polychronic cultures tend to be more futuristic and fatalistic—as in the saying, "Whatever will be, will be." This might lead to an attitude that since one cannot control tomorrow, why not make the best of today? In negotiations in such cultures, it can be difficult to adapt to a discursive, seemingly disjointed and random movement from topic to topic. Such randomness makes perfect sense, however, to someone with an agenda that includes group and consensus considerations within a broader perspective rather than just the task at hand.

Deadlines are also the victims of cross-cultural differences. For example, whenever a culture emphasizes other agendas, deadlines can give way to these. For example, while the French value efficiency, they also have great respect for quality. When problems arise, they may disregard the deadline in order to meet quality standards.

The action taken in these situations is often dictated by common sense: pay attention to complimenting others for what they do well (quality, for instance), take time to socialize with others before a meeting date, and above all, keep asking what is needed on both sides to help make each meeting work.

Cultural perspectives about time also affect training programs. Schedules have to be adjusted to allow for discussions of related contexts, which may not initially seem to a Westerner to be relevant to the task objectives. Times also must be allocated for interpersonal sessions where individuals are given the opportunity to get to know each other. While this sort of thing occurs at sessions in the United States, the amount of time allowed for breaks, and the function of meals (longer lunches, for example) may be different.

Another difficult adjustment across cultures is the difficulty of setting and following agendas and of "sticking to the subject" across cultures. Polychronic cultures have agendas that allow for the simultaneous discussion of related topics—at least those felt to be related according to their cultural perspective. Such discussions—which might include family matters, related social and group matters, or the need for information to make broader context decisions—may annoy and frustrate someone who is accustomed to narrowly focused tasks/decisions, tight time schedules and point-by-point agendas.

Monochronic cultures emphasize linear time and are concerned with causality.

Communication and argument are based on the need for logical, step-by-step activities. Polychronic cultures look for equilibrium. The emphasis on simultaneous activity, communications and argument is based on a need for balance. It is important to accept these differences and use them as a working premise when managing cross-culturally.

## OTHER FACTORS: CORPORATE CULTURE, INSTITUTION, BUSINESS AND INDIVIDUAL

An individual's personality may influence action. All of us have had to deal at meetings with people who were just contentious by nature, a character trait that may have been stimulated and conditioned by the individual's culture but may not be totally caused or explained by cultural influences. In other words, actions may not have a single cause or stimuli.

Institutional policies may stimulate and condition behavior. In Russia and other more controlled economies, approval policies may require different executive levels to approve the terms of a contract. The delays in these instances are related, not necessarily to cultural perceptions of time, nor to a reluctance to talk directly about controversial subjects; they are related to institutional policies. In similar ways, corporate cultures may also be the source of behavior.

In another negotiating situation, hesitancy and unwillingness to commit to longer-term plans, prices and deadlines was not related to cultural constraints, but rather to the country's high inflation rate, which was over 100 percent per month, prevent making long-term commitments. Cultural factors created a reluctance to talk about the problems immediately and directly, but the root cause was an economic/business condition.

Often, more than one factor generates and explains behavior. People do not always act based on one motive, nor can their behavior always be traced to a single stimulus—regardless of nationality. The five-point framework developed here, is therefore, useful for discussion, understanding, and recall purposes only. Such segmentation does not necessarily replicate reality, since in practice, events may work in a more integrated way.

## USING CULTURAL FACTOR ANALYSIS WHEN MAKING DECISIONS OR TAKING ACTION IN MULTINATIONAL CROSS-CULTURAL MANAGEMENT SITUATIONS

In light of the cultural and historical differences encountered in multinational cross-cultural management, it is necessary to be contingency oriented in interpersonal interaction situations, as it is in the other task situations described in this book. This is the common contingency framework was (discussed in Chapters 3 and 4), and which is the consistent underlying theme of this book.

As a first step in these situations, it is important to examine the situation context: both the individual and the culture being dealt with. Some factors to look at and be sensitive to have been discussed in this chapter (see also Chapter 4).

Those who are seriously interested in preparing to deal with business situations that cross cultural boundaries might consider preparing a chart similar to the one in Figure 10-1. The top of the chart would list the countries involved in the situation, both home and host (Egypt, Australia, United Kingdom, Norway, and India in the figure). The left side would list characteristics appropriate for the specific situation (responsibility, participation, relationship, achievement, time, and change in the figure). The task is described in the figure title (team management in this example).

While useful in many of the situations described in the following chapters, this is only one tool for analysis or decomposing a situation into its relevant components. Other tools are discussed in the following chapters. Being sensitive to cultural differences *in a systematic way* is a major first step in adapting to and managing perceived cultural differences.

Above all, when in doubt, ask questions gently, find out what situation context is being dealt with and where possible, explore alternative appropriate actions with those involved. With luck, the listeners will be very helpful—and appreciative.

## CONCLUSION: A DIFFICULT CULTURAL BALANCING ACT

Multinational cross-cultural management involves reconciling and balancing disparate factors in many different ways. Earlier chapters focused on balancing global and local factors, with rapid information transfer, when both planning and doing at the operational and enterprise-wide management level to meet present and longer-term future needs. This chapter focused on another area—balancing the cultural factors encountered during interpersonal interaction. An example would be balancing an American's desire to stick to task sequence agendas during a meeting with another person's culture-based desire to randomly discuss problem topics that might help develop deeper personal relationships and provide information on broader contexts.

The universally successful approach to balancing cultural factors seems to be to respect all cultures while adapting in interpersonal interactions to some degree, but not always, and focusing on the development of personal relationships and getting the job done as quickly as possible within this framework. This includes asserting oneself where necessary, being your own person, and avoiding confrontations. The secret, of course, is not so much *what* is done as *how*. The skills come largely from personal experience and, to a limited degree, from studying the experiences of others.

Personal experience can come from many sources. For one thing, it can come from your associations with other cultures within your own culture. The United States is a diverse melting pot, which provides many such opportunities. In

**Figure 10-1**
**Analysis of Cultural Differences: Team Management Decision**

## Cultural factors

## Countries

| Cultural factors | Egypt | Australia | UK | Norway | India |
|---|---|---|---|---|---|
| *Participation* | | | | | |
| Focus | Group | Individual | Individual | Individual | Group |
| Personal Space Needed | Less | More | More | More | More |
| *Relationship Focus* | | | | | |
| Task or Relationship | Relationship | Task | Task | Relationship | Relationship |
| *Responsibility* | | | | | |
| Authority Focus | Leader | Individual | Individual | Individual | Leader |
| Communication | Indirect | Direct | Direct | Direct | Indirect |
| *Time* | | | | | |
| Short/Long-Term Focus | Short | Long | Long | Short | Long |
| Punctuality | Less Important | Important | Important | Less Important | Important |
| *Change* | | | | | |
| Risk Taking or Avoidance | Avoid | Risk | Risk | Aviod | Aviod |
| *Achievement* | | | | | |
| Reward for Performance | Group | Individual | Individual | Individual | Group |

*Source:* Adapted from Odenwald (1996), p. 89.

addition, most Americans are, at most, third- or fourth-generation foreigners. In a sense, then, traveling and interacting overseas can be a kind of coming home, going back to other countries of origin—whether Europe, Asia, South America, or Africa. It is possible for many of us to examine the foreigner within ourselves and our families as a start in developing a cross-cultural perspective. In that way it will be not so much a chore in accommodating differences as a journey in enjoying and taking advantage of the richness of diversity and discovering the rewards arising from integrating global and local thinking and action. We and our country can in this sense be viewed as a microcosm of how this can be and is being done.

## WORKS CITED

Barnathan, Joyce, Pete Engardio, and John Winzenburg. "Asia's New Giants." *Business Week*, November 27, 1995, pp. 64–80.

DePalma, Anthony. "It Takes More Than a Visa to Do Business in Mexico." *New York Times*, June 25, 1994, p. 5.

Foster, Dean Allen. *Bargaining across Borders: How to Negotiate Business Successfully Anywhere in the World*. New York: McGraw-Hill, 1995.

Gargan, Edward. "From Chickens to Chemicals: Family Conglomerate Finds Fast Growth in China." *New York Times*, November 14, 1995, pp. D1, D4.

Gogan, Janis, Shoshana Zuboff, and Gloria Schuck. *Motorola-Panang*. Boston: Harvard Business School Publishing, 1994.

Handy, Charles. *The Age of Paradox*. Boston: Harvard Business School Press, 1994.

Hatch, Eric K. "Cross Cultural Team Building and Training." *Journal for Quality and Participation*, March 1995, pp. 44–49.

Kraar, Louis. "The Risks Are Rising in China." *Fortune*, March 6, 1995, p. 179.

Moran, Robert T., and William G. Stripp. *Successful International Business*. Houston: Gulf Publishing Company, 1991.

Mu, Dan Ping. "Culture and Business: Interacting Effectively to Achieve Mutual Goals." *East Asian Executive Reports*, March 15, 1995.

Naisbitt, John. *Global Paradoxes*. New York: Avon Books, 1994.

Odenwald, Sylvia B. *Global Solutions for Teams*. Chicago: Irwin Professional Publishing, 1996.

Pollack, Andrew. "Can the Pen Really Be Mightier Than the Germ?" *New York Times*, July 27, 1995, p. A4.

Riding, Alan. "To Parisians, Nice Is a Place, Not an Attitude." *New York Times*, August 6, 1995, Week in Review Section, p. 4.

Tyler, Patrick. "Forum on Women Agrees on Goals." *New York Times*, September 15, 1995, pp. A1, A3.

WuDunn, Sheryl. "Many Japanese Women Are Resisting Servility." *New York Times*, July 9, 1995, p. 10.

———. "In Japan, Even Toddlers Feel the Pressure to Excel." *New York Times*, January 23, 1996, p. A3.

# Chapter 11

# Staffing, Training and Communications

The common contingency process framework for multinational cross-cultural management implementation, which was discussed in Chapter 9's review of organization tasks, is shown in Figure 9-2. It provides a contingency perspective for the discussion in this chapter.

This chapter discusses three aspects of human resources management in multinational cross-cultural management situations: staffing, training and communication.

Staffing tasks can differ, depending on the situation. The staffing tasks for a new company or division will obviously differ from those at an established company. Staffing top-level management positions differs from staffing at the middle-management and operator level. Staffing needs and practices also differ by kind of company and industry involved, as well as according to many other situational factors (identified in Figure 9-2). Cultural diversity increasingly has come to have an impact on these decisions, although the impact may affect management action and decision making in different ways in international companies. This chapter focuses on managing a variety of international staffing task situations in the host (overseas) countries and home (enterprise headquarters) countries.

Multinational management training and development involves home country and host country operations, as well as the upper-management, middle-management and operational levels. Training is instruction directed at enhancing specific job-related skills and abilities. For example, it might involve how to manage cross-cultural teams, how to deal with cultural differences during negotiations, or how to speak a foreign language. Development is general education concerned with preparing managers for new assignments or higher-level positions. For example, a development program might be aimed at improving decision-making skills (Vanderbroeck 1992).

Communication skills are especially critical to successful management and leadership in an international enterprise because of the geographic distances and mix of cultures involved. They are, therefore, a key factor in staffing and in training and development. Communications are discussed within the perspectives of a situation's cultural and technology factors, especially in relation to the media used (and how to use them), nonverbal communication, using an interpreter, and face-to-face communications and negotiating.

## STAFFING MULTINATIONAL OPERATIONS

For some corporate leaders, staffing is considered the most significant enabler in multinational cross-cultural management. For example, when Colman Mockler became CEO of the Gillette Company in the 1970s, his first and, according to him, most difficult task was to ensure that he had in place a substantial number (initially, an estimated 60) of middle managers who were able to carry out his vision for the company. His requirements were that they be entrepreneurial thinkers and doers who could work within the Gillette culture. His new strategic vision involved focusing on what Gillette did best (personal-care and writing-instrument products) and eliminating a wide range of businesses (such as Welcome Wagon), which his predecessors had acquired. To him, such a staff would be the primary engine to drive his newly conceived Gillette Company. Simply put, he could not get the job done the way he felt it should be done without the right people.

Clearly, many of Gillette's existing managers already had the required profile, others had the potential, and still others appeared not to match the envisioned profile. Working within the Gillette cultural framework (which is very much a culture concerned with people), Mockler felt that he could not simply change the staff abruptly as corporate leaders in the 1990s are inclined to do when downsizing. Instead, he took over eighteen months to finally put in place, through rotation, training, and incentives (with no terminations directly related to the change in strategy), a staff that was judged able to do the envisioned job.

At the same time, Gillette had an even longer-term staffing need related to its attempts to succeed in the international market. It needed more than the products, operations, contacts, and a presence to succeed internationally; it needed a large, international group of expatriates. This would have to be a staff of seasoned expatriates who knew Gillette and its businesses very well, had the facility to move across cultures, and were free to move themselves and their families quickly and often during their careers (on average, every two to three years).

Gillette built that staff over a twenty-year period. In the view of Al Zeien, its CEO in 1996, Gillette had a twenty-year competitive advantage—a core competency consisting of some 350 trained expatriate managers who knew Gillette and its businesses, had worked in a variety of overseas locations, and could move quickly and easily to new assignments (Zeien 1995).

This same staffing and training process continues today at Gillette. It starts with hiring highly competent people who are familiar with an international area. They must have entrepreneurial skills yet be able to work within a corporate framework. They spend eighteen months to two years at the company's Boston headquarters and at various company sites. During this time, they are exposed to core company competencies and policies and meet a wide range of people in the company with whom they will interact over the coming years. In addition, they are expected to be able to move from country to country every three years or so, on very short notice when required.

For example, one candidate, Justyna Pisiewicz, a Polish recruit with a degree from a Beijing university, was first put through a trial run at the local operation in Poland and then went to Boston for an eighteen-month stay at Gillette's headquarters, also making visits to London and Singapore. Making her especially qualified was the fact that she spoke English and Russian, along with Polish and Chinese (Dwyer et al. 1994).

Gillette considered the management group, of which Pisiewicz was a part, as a group that knew both the global aspects of Gillette and the company's local markets, giving Gillette a major competitive advantage over competitors. The program focused on hiring people with existing and potential skills in specified areas, and on continual training, development, and feedback (Zeien 1995).

This is only one approach, which proved suitable to Gillette's specific situation. Other companies have been equally successful in staffing their organization in other ways appropriate to the different situation requirements they faced. The following sections review some of the tasks, decisions and actions involved in managing staffing for multinational operations in a wide range of companies:

- identifying needs,
- recruiting, screening, selecting and development,
- compensation and performance appraisal (evaluating, promoting, transferring or dismissing, and repatriating), and
- training and development.

### Identifying the Needs

In an international operation, most staffing is normally done at the *local* level—involving citizens of the countries in which the company operates. Locals obviously have the most knowledge about how the business can be effectively run in their region. Like the line in the famous American musical, *The Music Man*, "You gotta know the territory." The territory for a multinational company, however, is both local and international.

At times, therefore, *expatriates* (noncitizens) are needed. Expatriates are either home-country nationals (citizens of the country in which the company is head-quartered) or third-country nationals. The need for expatriates arises when special skills and expertise are needed at the host (overseas) company, when there is a significant need for integration with the multinational company and its other global divisions, when needs cannot be filled locally, and when qualified candidates are available for hiring.

The need for specialized skills may arise at the upper management, middle-management or operational levels. It might be a one-time need for a short period of time, or a continuing need to support a large and growing international presence over the long term. It might arise very quickly and so be an immediate need. It might be a need encountered by a company just entering an overseas market for the first time. In addition, situation requirements can change over time. Staffing changes, therefore, may be needed as the company grows globally and so has growing needs for developing expatriate managers in conjunction with changes in product mix, internal resources and the external competitive market. The variety of needs has led to a wide range of staffing approaches at international enterprises. Therefore, as in other multinational management task areas, a contingency approach is needed.

The following discussion focuses on *management* staffing, not on staffing operations within each functional unit.

### Recruitment, Screening, Selection and Development

In many companies, recruitment starts before the immediate need arises and includes recruitment and development in *anticipation* of the job need arising on a *continuing* basis.

The Coca-Cola Co., like the Gillette Company, has in place a major, continuing anticipatory expatriate program suited to its specific needs. Such a continuing program is to be expected at a company that in 1996 obtained 80 percent of its sales from non-U.S. operations and declared itself a "world" company (Collins 1996). The program maintains a pool of 500 expatriates who know the company well and are available on short notice to fill varying needs around the world (Anfuso 1994). For example, when Coca-Cola started operations in Eastern Europe, it sent in an expatriate from Chicago who was of Polish descent to fill the position of finance manager. Of its pool of 500 expatriates, Coca-Cola regularly transfers 200 each year, both to fill local needs and to enhance the pool's international experience.

The company has an international service group that supports this worldwide program. The group coordinates the transfer of international service people, taking care of such aspects as assuring that compensation is equitable no matter where and how quickly the expatriate is transferred.

Other continuing anticipatory approaches are used to fulfill short-term technical needs in foreign operations. As described in Chapter 9, many companies fulfill technical operating requirements with expatriate "SWAT" teams. For example, in 1994 Texas Instruments had some 200 professionals—dubbed the "Nomads"—who had set up chip-fabricating plants in Italy, Taiwan, Japan, and Singapore in the prior four years. U.S. West and Unilever also have such teams (Dwyer et al. 1994).

Molex, Inc., a 56-year-old American technology firm that derives more than 70 percent of its billion-dollar income from outside the United States and so has 70 percent of its employees outside the country, has a somewhat different anticipatory program suited to its specific needs. The company uses a combination of techniques, including extensive recruiting, training, and creation of *career paths*—recognizable paths for moving up in the company through working on international projects and jobs.

When hiring, Molex rarely seeks out potential managers among U.S. nationals. Instead, it looks for foreign-nationals who are studying in the United States for MBA degrees, who have engineering degrees, and want to return to work overseas. In that way, the potential expatriate managers have exposure to at least two cultures, are skilled in at least two languages, and have some technical training. Once hired, these managers are expected to spend two to three years with the company, principally in the United States, to learn about Molex's operations and culture before going overseas on a permanent assignment, often back to their own countries. In contrast, Gillette's program sends these new people to a third country. In addition, Molex has formal five-week classroom training programs. Training programs and international assignments are also offered to employees who were not initially hired specifically for the expatriate program (Solomon 1995a). Even if these employees do not eventually end up in the program, such training and foreign exposure acquaint them with the international aspects of Molex's operation.

These are selected examples of only a few staffing and development programs created to meet the specific needs of specific companies. Not all companies have the resources needed to create such anticipatory programs, not do they have the same requirements. For example, Tellabs, Inc., a Chicago-based designer and manufacturer of telecommunications products, faced a short-term and long-term staffing need in 1994 as it was opening a new operation in Germany. Tellabs developed a balanced solution to their situation's requirements in a much different way.

At the outset of international expansion, Tellabs believed that the best strategy was to staff overseas operations with locals. However, Tellabs learned, as have many companies, that while a good idea, hiring local managers was not enough. For example, when the company opened its Irish facility, staffed with locals, management of the parent company did not take the time to adequately communicate to the Irish staff Tellabs' corporate culture: informal, flexible and entrepreneurial. In Tellabs' culture employees call each other by first names, share information widely, and have direct access to senior management. As a result, the company found that when an American executive went to Ireland, the Irish would appear to agree with suggested changes yet would not always proceed in the anticipated manner. The problem was a major cultural and communication gap.

When Tellabs subsequently acquired Martis Oy, a Finnish telecommunications firm, in 1993, it wanted to maintain the entrepreneurial spirit that had made the company successful, but it also wanted to tie employees into the global parent corporation. In this situation, therefore, time was allowed for cultural training and frequent exchanges of executives for short periods to help make the transition work. These steps provided both the cross-pollination of resources and the imbedding of Tellabs' corporate culture that had been lacking at the Irish facility. The Finnish operation was very successful.

Tellabs drew on these experiences in 1994 when it sent Laura Bozich, its Central European regional director and one of the few expatriates working for the company, to Munich to start operations and staff a German branch. Her job was to introduce Tellabs' corporate culture while interviewing and hiring—before handing the office over to host-country nationals. In a sense, she was introducing the development phase during the selection process. Bozich faced many problems in a German society whose cultural values seemed completely contrary to the corporate culture that she needed to create. In addition, in Germany American companies had a reputation of having a hire-and-fire mentality.

Her approach was to search for Germans who had worked for American companies and so might understand the American informal entrepreneurial style that prevailed at Tellabs. In addition, she was careful to point out to those she interviewed that nationals would be promoted to top positions—a standard strategy at all of Tellabs' overseas facilities (Solomon 1995b). Each of these steps were clearly an effort to meet Tellabs' specific needs.

As seen from these experiences, in the staffing area, as in other multinational cross-cultural management areas, situational needs dictate the solution. Few universal formula solutions exist; there are only heuristic situational patterns that suggest solutions or unique situational solutions appropriate to the specific problem under study. The following discussion describes some of these situational patterns.

Many companies do not have the foresight, needs or resources of a Gillette Company, Coca-Cola, or Unilever to build an inventory of middle management and technical expatriates that can be tapped as new assignments arise. Because of the high cost (both in developing and compensating expatriates) and high failure rate of expatriates in general (especially among Americans), companies generally prefer hiring nationals. This was the short-term approach of Tellabs, but clearly it could not work without intensive supplemental development programs designed to create integrative global synergies.

In addition, although hiring, training, and developing locals is preferred, it is not always possible, since competent personnel are not always available on a timely basis. For this reason, where companies have not been able to follow the lead of firms such as Gillette, Coca-Cola, Unilever and Texas Instruments by creating a pool of available expatriates to fill local needs, they have had to select and train personnel now working for the company or hire experienced third-country or outside managers and technical people.

When recruiting, screening, and training and developing personnel for overseas operations, Gillette, Coca-Cola, and other experienced international companies expect candidates to:

1. know the company, its philosophy, people, processes and competencies,
2. know the country or countries where they are working,
3. be highly skilled at their jobs, and
4. be adaptable, mobile, innovative and entrepreneurial within the context of company guidelines.

The same common success profile of the expatriate manager has been used by other companies, which have nonetheless taken different approaches from those of Coca-Cola and Gillette in finding and developing local and expatriate managers. Both Tellabs and Molex were examples of companies employing different continuing anticipatory approaches.

Obviously, not all companies have major continuing needs. Some are just starting to internationalize operations. When searching for staff, it is important for them to assess an individual's qualifications and likelihood of success. As seen in the qualifications list, personal characteristics such as adaptability, innovative and entrepreneurial instincts, and mobility are essential to success in international management (qualification no. 4). Al Zeien, Chairman of the Gillette Company, described the persons he would like to hire as "pussy cats"—referring to the fact that if you throw a cat into the air, even upside down, it always seems to land on its feet. Zeien wanted to hire people who could get things done, overcome adversity and always land on their feet—no matter what problems the situation presented (Zeien 1995). Many companies, such as AT&T, give tests to measure these capabilities (Fuchsberg 1992).

Even after thorough testing, it is important to have trial periods during which to judge a person's capabilities at work in different company situations over several years. This was Molex's approach: it carefully observed and tracked candidates' performances during the first two or three years of employment. In addition, during this period the employee could get to know the company (qualification no. 1) and acquire more advanced technical skills (qualification no. 3). As for qualification no. 2, Molex most often hired foreign-nationals, but it also exposed other managers to international development opportunities by providing them with foreign assignments.

Molex had a flexible, multifaceted approach to building a strong enabling staff. While its approach was structured around a common, four-qualification framework, the specific tools used were appropriate for the needs of Molex and its competitive environment.

The problems arising from not paying careful attention to expatriate selection and training, as was done at Molex, Gillette, and Coca-Cola, can be costly. For example, when Beijing Auto Works (BAW) and American Motors Corporation (AMC) entered into a joint venture (named Beijing Jeep Corporation, or BJC) to produce jeeps and other four-by-four vehicles in 1984, American middle managers, because of their advanced technical know-how, were sent to China to manage day-to-day operations. In this instance, they were not given adequate cultural and language training, and so made many mistakes. The eventual solution was to establish a transition phase in which expatriate managers worked closely with Chinese managers to transfer technical expertise. After this transition period, the Americans returned home (Aiello 1991).

In contrast, Volkswagen (VW) entered into a joint venture with China Automotive (CA) during the same period, basing its approach on lessons learned from prior experiences abroad. From the beginning, host and home country managers were paired and shared decision-making authority. In addition, the German expatriate managers who were selected had technical expertise, prior overseas experience, knew the language and culture of the host country, and had voluntarily chosen to take the assignment (Clark 1995).

As seen in these company experiences, special technical or enterprise global business needs, costs, host country business and cultural needs, other existing and anticipated competitive market requirements, candidate qualifications, the amount of training required, company resources, and the urgency of the need are among the critical situation factors affecting this staffing decision. As in every situation described in this book, the successful solutions here were those tailored to the specific situation needs.

Evidence exists that the American educational system does not adequately prepare its students to meet the challenges of international business. Professor Dan Couger, who studied information technology professionals worldwide, summed it up in this way:

For an international position, American managers are still considered less prepared than others. Non-American managers are considered more attractive because they adapt more easily, coming from environments in which they were made aware of cultural and language differences very early in their education. (quoted in Dykeman 1995, p. 44)

The U.S. educational system is, of course, a major part of the problem, since international studies have only recently been emphasized. It is not the only cause, however.

One problem has been that many companies lack clear policies and action patterns that convey the message that international assignments, training and perspectives are major paths to success and advancement at the company. Such policies and practices can be a major factor in successful recruitment, especially when recruiting from within a company.

Studies have shown that success is most likely to occur where clear career paths and models of success exist for moving up in a company along an international track. These studies suggest that the following conditions can help create a believable international career path:

- giving each person a choice, so that the international career path or assignment is of his or her own choosing
- giving adequate preparation and training, either through rotating assignments, training and development programs, or thorough orientation programs that realistically preview the assignment
- providing, through commitments or other actions, a basis for realistic expectations about what is likely to happen after the international assignment
- providing a clear link between the overseas assignment and the long-term career paths of the expatriate within the company (Black and Gregersen 1991a; Feldman and Thomas 1992)

Molex clearly established a believable career path within its organization culture, as did Gillette and Coca-Cola. This is important when recruiting, since many problems may be associated with international assignments.

One problem is that in the absence of a well-defined international career path, the professional risks for an individual accepting or seeking out international assignments can be considerable. Second, educating dependent children overseas can be a problem. Third, if a person is married, the spouse will often have to find compatible employment at comparable salary rates, which can be very difficult. Strong career and monetary incentives, as well as extensive training and development programs, may be needed to help overcome such problems. Last, given the present U.S. educational system's lack of extensive cross-nation cultural training, it is difficult for Americans in general to adapt easily to other cultures, which increases the overall risk of failure.

### Compensation and Performance Appraisal: Evaluation, Promotion, Transfer or Dismissal and Repatriation

Compensation differentials can exist among countries and must be taken into account when assigning expatriates. For example, by one measure (the cost of living index), living costs in Japan are twice those of the United States. One would add to this cost differential housing costs, income tax differentials, moving and schooling costs, home leave, and in some instances, a foreign service premium. This can increase the cost to the company of using an expatriate by fourfold: for example, someone earning $100,000 might cost the company as much as $400,000 per year as an expatriate in Japan. Because Japan is probably the most expensive country in the world in which to live, this figure is probably represents the maximum. However, on average, costs will likely be two to three times higher than the home-country salary. This can be another major incentive to use expatriates only where the situation absolutely requires it.

The costs do not always have to be so high. Companies such as Coca-Cola have companywide expatriate programs with established policies for compensation. These programs, or those based on consultants' recommendations, are needed to provide benchmarks for the expatriate in deciding whether to take an overseas job and for the company in doing cost-benefit analyses.

In addition, performance evaluation criteria are needed for expatriates. These will vary considerably by situation. For example, they may involve standard Western measurements such as profits and profit margins or sales and market-share growth. They may also relate to technical projects and their successful completion. The criteria may relate to specific problems and whether they were overcome.

When searching for causes of, and remedies for, any below-standard performance, a situational diagnosis is needed. Of course, inappropriate selection and lack of training (which are management tasks) may cause performance problems. Expectations can be another problem. These and similar considerations are present in addition to the normal possible causal problems of lack of professional competence in international business areas. How the evaluation is handled, the criteria used, and the subsequent actions taken will define the nature of a company's international career path, the risks involved in pursuing it, and the expectations and rewards of pursuing it.

In some ways, the evaluation process can be culturally dependent, since performance is judged in different ways in different countries. For example, Table 11-1 gives the contrasting cultural biases inherent in the review processes in three cultures—American, Japanese, and Arab. Success in one culture is not always defined the same way in other cultures. The culturally dependent aspects of evaluating performance at the management level are discussed further in the section on management.

Repatriation is another staffing consideration. For example, at times, adjustments may be required for returning expatriates in areas such as financial (it is possible to have lived better abroad, for example, having servants and being able to save more); professional (the job abroad may have been more interesting, carried more responsibility, or had more diversity); or personal (old friends may be gone, old lifestyles may have changed). Again, problems can be reduced if there is a systematically organized career development program designed to take care of repatriation matters (Black and Gregersen 1991).

## TRAINING AND DEVELOPMENT

As seen from the company experiences discussed here, development for international managers can begin during the recruitment and selection phases. This section continues that discussion by focusing on more formal training methods and tools.

Like staffing, both training (job-related skills and abilities instruction) and development (generally, management education) involve assessing needs (both for the training and trainees), selecting methods or approaches, and managing

**Table 11-1**
**Cultural Contrasts: Performance Reviews**

| | American | Japanese | Arab |
|---|---|---|---|
| **Objective** | Review based on preset goals; identify personal strengths/weaknesses | Find out why performance is not in harmony with group | Set employee on track; reprimand for bad performance |
| **Structure** | Formal procedure; every 6 to 12 months in manager's office | Informal, ad-hoc with employee; frequent reporting to administration; in office, coffee shop, bar | Informal, ad-hoc; recorded in manager's office |
| **Interaction** | Two-way, both sides present openly own point of view; manager as leader/adviser; employee independent, self-motivated | Employee answers manager's concerns; manager gives advice as parent, mentor, senior employee; part of group/family; continuous feedback | One-way; manager guides subordinate; authority figure, mentor; random feedback; treated like child in family |
| **Evaluation** | Success measured by performance against stated goals | Success measured by contribution to group harmony and output | Success measured by major personal contribution |
| **Outcome** | Promotion; salary increase; bonus; commission; salary freeze; loss of title; loss of power | Mainly affects amount of semi-annual bonus; less important job; job rotation; dock bonus/salary | Bonus of 1/2-day salary; promotion; salary decrease |
| **Closing** | Openness; equality; fairness | Group achievement; relationship | Privacy; authority; parenthood |

*Source:* Adapted from Elashmawi and Harris (1993), p. 152.
Copyright © 1997 by R. J. Mockler.

and carrying out the process. A special focus on international operations is needed to prepare managers for international assignments and to prepare workers for assignments to international teams.

### Needs Assessment

Training and developing needs are arrived at through a matching process. For example, first, the basic job needs are defined. This was the case with the list of four qualifications identified for successful expatriate managers.

Such success profiles are then matched with individual profiles to determine areas where training is needed. The amount and kind of gap between desired qualifications and each individual's level of skills will determine the amount of training and the methods and approaches used, as well as how the training is managed. Examples of this matching process are given in the following sections.

### Training Methods and Approaches

Training decisions involve several different areas: kind and source, content, environment, methods and tools.

*Kind and Source.* The decision to use programs that are standardized or customized (meeting specific company requirements) can depend on:

- the size of the company and its international operations (large companies, such as Coca-Cola, tend to have their own customized training programs), and
- the content (standardized programs are available for language training, interpersonal interaction, and country-specific familiarization training, for example).

Whether the program will be developed and conducted in-house or outsourced (developed and conducted by someone outside the company) will be decided by studying:

- the training resources available in-house and outside (does the company have facilities appropriate for the program and people qualified to teach it?),
- the financial resources available,
- the perceived effectiveness of each (programs tailored to company needs and conducted by in-house personnel are favored by many),
- the timing, and
- the content to be covered.

*Content.* Both kinds of training—familiarization with the specific country or countries involved and managing or dealing with interpersonal interaction between cultures—are needed for expatriate mangers and technical personnel. The first is generally background for the second.

*Environment.* Training can be conducted on- or off-site, in classrooms or on-the-job, depending on the availability of facilities, resources and people, content and level of training. For example, machine operations are good on-the-job, on-site content-training candidates, as will be seen in the discussions of Motorola-Panang in the following chapter. On the other hand, country-specific information can be conveyed effectively in a classroom. Shadowing (working along with an experienced manager) and mentoring are also effective for management development.

*Teaching and Learning Methods and Processes.* Whether the passive lecturing method or the active, participative learning approach is used depends on both the content and the cultural environment. For example, participative learning methods, such as interactive discussions, work well in the American and Australian cultures, while more structured and passive approaches work best in Arab nations (Elashmawi and Harris 1993, ch. 6; Francis 1995). Exceptions exist, of course, depending on who is giving or taking the course. The authors have, for example, found that interactive methods work well in both China and Russia among more educated and cosmopolitan executives, even when working through an interpreter.

*Teaching and Learning Tools.* The selection of tools depends on such situation factors as the cultures involved (for example, writing and reading for Americans; group practice sessions and intragroup discussions for the Japanese) and the content or subject matter (country-specific information can be learned from readings, lectures, case studies and presentations, for instance, whereas interpersonal interaction is best learned through active learning tools such as team projects and incident/case studies).

## MANAGING THE STAFFING, TRAINING AND DEVELOPMENT PROCESSES

Managing staffing, training and development, as in managing other multinational cross-cultural management areas, involves balancing many disparate situation factors. First, there are the cultural factors. Whatever the specific goals of training and development—for example, interpersonal interaction across cultures—available techniques must be adapted to the cultural, content, facility, people, resources and business restraints within the situation being managed.

Table 11-2 shows some of the different approaches that are needed when dealing with three different cultures. This is an example of the contingency management process in action. As seen in the figure, the contingent adjustments made to suit the situation's cultural requirements can range from the timing of the sessions and training materials used to how the training is conducted.

The concept is not difficult to grasp when one studies cultural differences (such as those reviewed in Chapter 10) and then proceeds to manage a common business function, such as training and development, in a way appropriate for the situation at hand. For instance, because of the Japanese cultural bias in favor

**Table 11-2**
**Cultural Contrasts: Training**

| | American | Japanese | Arab |
|---|---|---|---|
| **Group Composition** | Medium-sized; mixed level acceptable | Smallest group; grouped for functional harmony | Largest group; very level-conscious |
| **Time** | 8-5 with breaks | 9-6 with breaks; may go until 8 or continue informally after hours | 9/10-3 maximum; no lunch break |
| **Preparation** | Individual reading; written homework | Group orientation | Not necessary or important |
| **Getting Started** | Self-introductions; randomly or by seating order | Introductions emphasizing company/belonging; senior member going last | Introduction by status; senior member going first |
| **International Process** | Emphasize "how to" and practical applications; self-reliance; specialization; ample reading | Emphasis on doing/discussion; sharing experiences; intragroup discussion; role play; rotation | Memorizing general skills; coaching; demonstration by leader; minimal reading |
| **Training Materials** | Written; self-explanatory | Visual with group discussion and practices | Visual; coaching by team leader |
| **Tests of Knowledge** | Direct questions to individual; spontaneous, open questions | Group questions; intragroup discussions; directed questions | No direct, individual questions; participants need preparation |
| **Cultural Values** | Self-reliance; competition; time conscious | Relationship; group achievement; group harmony | Seniority; reputation; individual achievement |

*Source:* Adapted from Elashmawi and Harris (1993), p. 133.
Copyright © 1997 by R. J. Mockler.

of group work, consensus, protocol and status, the teaching methods that work best for them are intragroup discussions and sharing experiences with the group (but not necessarily with the instructor).

In a sense, the management process for training sessions is the familiar contingency process—the methods chosen have to be adapted to the audience, subject matter and objectives. The major situational difference is the cross-cultural mix of the audience and required adjustments (listed in Figure 11-2) that must be made to accommodate that mix.

In the same way, cultural differences impact on other training tasks, such as motivation. This impact can also be identified and analyzed (as shown in Table 11-3).

An example of such culturally dependent management action is found in the experiences of Electronic Data Systems, Ltd. (EDS), a U.S. company with offices worldwide. The company introduced a new leadership strategy in 1992—a more team-, people- and vision-oriented strategy. In trying to implement this new leadership strategy in Japan, Larry Purdy, the leadership development manager, came to two conclusions based on the first year of leadership training. First, he discovered many shared leadership values among the Japanese and Americans. These shared values were designated the *core set of values* and included team orientation. Second, the company discovered that major cultural differences affected the way in which values were communicated and leaders were evaluated (Purdy 1995). For example, in Purdy's words:

1. As for the ways we teach our values generally Japanese workers spend much less time than Americans doing formal classroom training. Japanese workers are educated and developed by giving them frequent new assignments; by on-the-job training; and by establishing career-long mentor-like relationships with seniors who will help them assimilate the values and culture of the company. As our training program was based primarily on a classroom, lecture-style format, our Japanese middle managers (almost all of whom have only recently joined EDS from other companies) felt they could have understood our message more clearly, and put it into practice more effectively, if we have chosen a more culturally appropriate manner of conveying that message.

2. The second aspect of leadership that is culturally dependent concerns how we measure, evaluate, and select leaders in relation to our leadership value model. This involves judging how leaders demonstrate the behaviors associated with the identified leadership attributes or values: strong personal convictions, vision, emotional bonds, inspirational, team oriented, risk takers, and drive to excel. For example, EDS expects its leaders to be team oriented. The Japanese also place great value on teamwork. However, the motivation and the expectations of team members and manifestation of team spirit varies significantly between the two cultures. The Japanese find satisfaction in being anonymous contributors to group goals. Though Americans also value teamwork, they expect recognition for their individual contributions. American management in turn expects individuals to make recognizable, measurable contributions. Japanese managers would place much more emphasis on a team member's ability to harmonize with the group as a whole than they would on evaluating individual contribution and performance.

**Table 11-3**
**Cultural Contrasts: Motivation**

| | American | Japanese | Arab |
|---|---|---|---|
| **Management Style** | Leadership; friendliness | Persuasion; functional group activities | Coaching; personal attention; parenthood |
| **Control** | Independence; decision-making; space; time; money | Group harmony | Of others/parenthood |
| **Emotional Appeal** | Opportunity | Group participation; company success | Religion; nationalistic; admiration |
| **Recognition** | Individual contribution | Group identity; belonging to group; group contribution | Individual status; class/society; promotion |
| **Material Rewards** | Salary; commission; profit-sharing | Annual bonus; social services; fringe benefits | Gifts self/family; family affair; salary increase |
| **Threats** | Loss of job | Ouster from group | Demotion; damage reputation |
| **Cultural Values** | Competition; risk-taking; material possession; freedom | Group harmony; achievement; belonging | Reputation; family security; religion; social status |

*Source:* Adapted from Elashmawi and Harris (1993), p. 144.
Copyright © 1997 by R. J. Mockler.

As a simple generalization, we might say that though both cultures value teamwork, Japanese expect individuals to conform to the group by suppressing their individuality; Americans expect the group to conform to the needs of its individuals by accommodating and measuring everyone's individuality. Thus, we need a culturally relative way in which to interpret someone's ability to be team oriented. (Purdy 1995, pp. 13-14)

The EDS experience illustrates how difficult it is to balance the many diverse cultural differences encountered in multinational cross-cultural management situations. First, it is necessary to recognize the similarities and differences in order to provide a basis for action. Second, it is necessary to find a way that reasonably balances differences—in this case, differences in evaluation criteria used for judging leadership performance by two distinct cultural norms within the same worldwide company.

Before turning to that discussion in Chapters 12 and 13, one other aspect of training and development, communications, will be discussed.

## COMMUNICATIONS ACROSS CULTURAL BOUNDARIES

This section covers available communication tools and the way their effectiveness depends, in large measure, on cross-cultural factors as well as on other situation context factors, such as the task, the business and the individual media's inherent characteristics.

Four aspects of communications are covered: types of media and how to use them, nonverbal communication, using an interpreter or translator, and face-to-face negotiation.

### Media: Types and How to Use Them

Four types of media are discussed here: electronic mail, written (facsimile and postal), telephone, and videoconferencing.

*Electronic Mail (E-mail).* E-mail sent over Bitnet and the Internet is a familiar type of electronic media. The main advantages of this media is that it is immediately transmitted, saves time since it is entered directly, is generally less expensive than telephone calls, and enables time and place differences to be bridged. Its drawbacks are that it can be impersonal and terse. In addition, while it is formal—in writing—it is often not written or edited carefully. No visual feedback exists to verify and refine understanding. As a result, it is often incomplete, inaccurate, and lacking in the nuances necessary for exploring situation contexts and developing close personal relationships with people from different cultures.

Since computers and computer systems are needed at both ends to access and use it, e-mail (and the associated Web pages) are difficult to read and send without some introductory training. In addition, e-mail messages can be read by others, so that privacy is lacking.

Given these characteristics, e-mail can have limited effectiveness. It is certainly effective in communicating simple tasks and uncomplicated information quickly. This may include minor reporting and resolution of shipping delays, technical specifications for products, routine changes in assignments, orders that are repetitive or uncomplicated (for example, electronic retailing commerce), and any hard data that can be communicated by letter or fax (which is not too long and involved and does not need extensive explanation or feedback to understand).

Such media are not always effective ways to initially get to know someone personally, to amplify contexts of more complex decision and action situations, or to clarify ambiguities—all necessary steps in establishing relationships and communicating in many non-U.S. cultures. E-mail can best be used in such situations only after orientation and face-to-face trust building have occurred, though recent studies have shown that under special circumstances, personal relationships can be established through e-mail, just as they are, at times, through regular mail (Qureshi 1995).

Other potential problems also exist. For example, many Asian cultures regard off-the-cuff responses and intellectual banter, such as are sometimes found in e-mail communications, insulting and rude. Blunt, untempered criticism, which is common on e-mail systems, is particularly offensive in many cultures. Irony and sarcasm can often be misread. Moreover, electronic media lack reinforcement from other communication media, such as body language and eye contact. Certainly, more can be done through training and use to increase sensitivity to, and handling of, such problems, but electronic media nonetheless have built-in limitations.

Language differences can also create problems when using electronic media. To overcome such problems, new computerized digital-coding software systems are being developed to allow representation in, and translation into, any language, from Chinese ideographs and Russian Cyrillic to Sanskrit (Pollack 1995). Such new computer software systems will allow the Internet, the powerful information/telecommunications systems framework, to adapt to, and integrate, a major cultural difference—language.

Many computer-related telecommunications software systems not only enable using electronic media for correspondence purposes, but go beyond it. One example is *groupware*, the name for software systems that enable a group of individuals to interact through computers. Since groupware enables exploring, coordinating and reconciling different viewpoints, it provides a mechanism for developing interpersonal relationships. This can be reinforced by using groupware in combination with teleconferencing in conference-room settings (a group of people on one side of a four-sided conference room with television screens on the three other sides of the conference room showing people at similar conference tables in three other worldwide locations). The technology is still in the very early stages of development, however, so its use is extremely limited and costly.

*Written: Facsimile and Postal.* Postal communications are the most traditional and familiar forms of written communication. Facsimile machines are essentially faster ways of sending letters and other written communications. Since, like e-mail, they do not involve face-to-face contact, facsimile and postal communications share many of the following advantages and drawbacks of e-mail:

- facsimiles are transmitted instantly, like e-mail, though they require more time for preparation and sending (e-mail is typed and sent in the same media).
- facsimiles enable time and place differences to be bridged.
- there is no visual feedback to refine and verify understanding, making them, like e-mail, limited in effectiveness in developing the personal relationship necessary to work across some cultural boundaries.
- they are effective and efficient in conveying basic information.

There are also differences. Written communications such as letters and reports often are more carefully prepared and considered more formal when sent by facsimile or post than when sent through e-mail. Moreover, since these media are more familiar, they are also easier to use. Facsimile transmission is also more versatile: any printed material can be sent, including letters, reports, diagrams, spread sheets, financial statements and the like; whereas e-mail is more limited.

Cultural differences influence the use of written communications. For example, Tellabs found that the Finnish prefer written communications to face-to-face interaction. Consequently, whenever possible everything to Finland is sent by letter or by fax at Tellabs (Solomon 1995a). As with e-mail, neither of these media is a strong way to develop the personal relationships necessary when dealing with many cultures.

*Telephone.* Interpersonal oral communications are essential to enable organizations and people to work to maintain a balance among global efficiencies, local responsiveness, and rapid new information and technology transfer. The daily and weekly telephone conversations of CEOs J. Richard Stonesifer (GE Appliances in Louisville, Kentucky) and Richard J. Callahan (U.S. West International in London, England), described in Chapter 1, are only two examples of the need for a constant exchange of information among divisions and with a home office.

Telephone communications have the disadvantages of being more expensive, requiring one to work within the differences in time zones, being ineffective where there are language differences, and lacking the added visual dimension arising from supporting nonverbal communications.

Since telephone conversations involve oral conversations, successfully using them in business interactions requires understanding and being sensitive to the cultural differences described in Chapter 10. Telephone conversations have the advantage over e-mail and other written media in that they provide the means of instantly asking for clarification, exploring nuances, amplifying points, and pursuing new ideas that arise during the conversation. In this sense, they can be used more effectively than written communications to develop the personal relationships that provide a basis for working with other cultures. The impact of the cultural factors on oral communications is explored further in the face-to-face and negotiating sections that follow.

*Videoconferencing.* Videoconferencing is another way to bridge cultural communication gaps. In contrast to the media already described, it permits vision along with interactive voice communications. The format can save a considerable amount of travel time and expense in some situations. Videoconferencing is growing in popularity; for example, GE Medical Systems reportedly does 1,000 hours of teleconferencing a year worldwide (Dwyer et al. 1994). While it is now done over telephone lines, video capabilities are being built into computers and will be available generally in a short time.

One problem with videoconferencing, as with voice telephone communications, is that the time differences are sometimes encountered. Videoconferencing works only when both parties meet at the same time in different worldwide locations. For example, conversations between New York and Singapore offices—a twelve-hour time difference—require one party to keep inconvenient business hours.

A second problem is availability, since at present, facilities are available only in major cities. Videoconferencing is not yet as widespread worldwide as the telephone, however, although telephone companies are increasing their service in this area. The technology is also relatively new and emerging, so the problems may ease as the computer capabilities for video expand.

While not the same as face-to-face communications, videoconferencing is, in some ways, superior to telephone, facsimile or postal, and electronic media. It permits communication by body language and enables greater multilevel interaction, which is important in communicating across some cultures.

### Nonverbal Communication

Nonverbal communication is important in many cultures, especially those which are more relationship oriented. Since Americans depend largely on verbal communications in their culture, this is an area with which they are normally unfamiliar.

The Japanese, for example, depend, not just on words, but also on gestures, body language, and the use of silence and personal space to convey information. Information is also conveyed by status in those cultures where status is important. In order to participate and benefit from such information flows it is necessary first to understand them. When Japanese and Americans are communicating, it is likely that the Americans will be communicating mostly verbally, while their counterparts will be communicating on many levels. In this sense, nonverbal communication is another communication media.

Differences need to be learned situation by situation, culture by culture. For example, handshakes may be forceful and vigorous in the United States, limp in Asia, and quick in Europe. In Southeast Asia, direct eye contact should be avoided until you know someone well, but the French like to look directly and intently into one's eyes. As for embracing, Mexicans will want to at the end of a successful meeting, as will Central and East Europeans. If you touch the side of your nose in Italy, you will have indicated distrust, and in some cultures, beckoning to someone with the palm is considered polite, while beckoning with the forefinger is considered impolite.

These are all examples of the messages that nonverbal communication can convey in cross-cultural business situations.

## Using an Interpreter or Translator

In situations where there is not sufficient language fluency to communicate face-to-face, an interpreter is needed. A translator is one who translates written communications. The level of fluency needed of course depends on the complexity of the subject and the importance of nuances to communicating among parties.

When affordable, it can be helpful to have an interpreter who understands your situation, especially if the other party has one. Your interpreter should be acquainted with any special ideas or themes you may want to highlight or any special problems. An interpreter can function as your partner, who can further your goals along the way through the subtleties of language handled by one familiar with the other culture being dealt with. Additionally, the interpreter should have any special skills that may be needed, such as familiarity with your industry or subject matter.

When communicating through an interpreter, one should always talk and look directly at the person one is talking with, and not at the interpreter. Moreover, speaking in groups of words or complete units of thought assists the interpreter in communicating (interpreting) the *ideas* behind the words rather than just translating word by words. The most exciting aspect of using an interpreter is the time it gives one to think and regroup ideas as one observes the listeners' reactions to the interpreter. It is possible to switch paths, rephrase, rethink, and reinforce when the pace is slowed by the interpretation process.

## Face to Face: Negotiation

While face-to-face communications are effective and often preferred, they are not always possible due to cost and time limitations. When they are, careful attention should be paid to cultural differences in order to maximize the benefits of the meetings. This section will focus on one of the key face-to-face situations during which cultural factors have a major impact and where business interests are most often affected—business negotiations.

Intercultural negotiation consists of four major processes: preparing for the negotiation, establishing rapport, exchanging information and persuading. This list is not unlike the process one might go through when negotiating anywhere in the world. However, the way the process is carried out will vary considerably depending on the cultures, business tasks, time frame and stage of negotiations, and people involved.

The purpose of the negotiation should be determined when *preparing for a negotiation*. Whether price, joint ventures, distribution contracts, or any other business purpose, both sides should agree on the objective. During intercultural negotiations, subjects should be brought up in a culturally appropriate way. For example, Americans tend to move more quickly than Japanese, who need more time to get acquainted. Negotiators from non-Western cultures may withdraw from negotiations if they interpret the American fast-paced time frame as excessive pressure (Foster 1995).

Nonverbal communications are also important. These include seating arrangements, dress codes, and the presentation style—which may be indicators of status in other cultures. Protocols also can communicate messages such as a willingness to make concessions (for example, communicated by informal dress in some cultures). The number and identity of participants involve other cultural differences—the Japanese tend to prefer larger negotiating teams and often vary the members from meeting to meeting; in the Arab culture, senior members may attend only the first and last sessions.

*Establishing rapport* means different things in different cultures. Americans value directness and are action- and task-oriented. Therefore, they tend to give less emphasis to establishing personal relationships and focus directly on the task. They also consider time schedules important. The Japanese will spend considerable time in establishing a relationship, even to the point of mixing socially at dinner and on weekends. Latin Americans also consider this a most important phase.

*Exchanging information* will also vary by culture. For the Japanese, given their cultural bias, this will be the most important step, as they seek detailed information and ask for in-depth explanation, clarification, justification and evaluation. For others, for example in Latin America, it may be the least important step and the time will be used to develop personal trust as a contingency base for final decisions; technical people may also be involved.

*Persuasion* is the most important phase for Americans who often present offers directly, with time pressures indicating that the deal is not open-ended but rather will be a lost opportunity if not accepted quickly. The Japanese often work to quietly persuade behind the scenes rather than openly.

As seen from these brief examples, different cultures respond in different ways to each of the phases of negotiation. There are many examples. At the end of a successful negotiation a Mexican associate may wish to embrace, as will Central and East European associates. In Asia the age of negotiators makes a difference, with younger ones automatically considered to be less experienced.

Women are not accorded the same respect and position as men in Latin America, Spain, or the Arab countries, so they are not good choices to lead a negotiating team in those countries. The list of potential problem areas is a long one, and the list that applies to the country being dealt with should be studied thoroughly before any negotiation.

Everything being discussed in this section is well known to managers here and abroad. Times are changing rapidly, and many people are experienced in these processes. They are experienced to the point that the parties can, at times, play roles, manipulate perceived cultural differences, and play off expectations created by just such cultural discussions as the one here. For example, negotiators will sometimes claim they lack the authority to make a decision when they actually do, invent last-minute time restraints to extract last-minute concessions, and provide an unpleasant negotiating environment. These ploys do not have to be accepted or tolerated.

Ultimately, then, each situation dictates its own scenario and breaking rules or calling bluffs as judged appropriate for the situation may at times be the best solution.

## CONCLUSION

This chapter has discussed managing human resource enablers—the people and processes that get things done and get results from three perspectives.

First, the staffing of the organization was discussed. This is the major enabler: the people who do the work, triumph over difficult circumstances, handle emergencies, meet deadlines no matter what, satisfy customers one by one, adapt to changing competition, and generally make the future happen.

Second, ways to support this staff by training and development were discussed from several viewpoints, including training and development methods and environments. Managing these two processes in balanced, contingent ways appropriate for the specific situation at hand was also covered.

Third, communications, which serves as the lubricant for these processes and helps get the tasks done well, was briefly covered. Communications is an all-encompassing facility that impacts significantly on leading and management (discussed in the following two chapters).

## WORKS CITED

Aiello, Paul. "Building a Joint Venture in China: The Case of Chrysler and the Beijing Jeep Corporation." *Journal of General Management* (Winter 1991): 47–63.

Anfuso, Dawn. "HR Unites the World of Coca-Cola." *Personnel Journal*, November 1994, pp. 112–116.

Black, Stewart, and Hal B. Gregersen. "The Other Half of the Picture: Antecedents of Spouse Cross-Cultural Adjustment." *Journal of International Business Studies*, 3rd quar. 1991a, pp. 461–477.

————. "When Yankee Comes Home: Factors Related to Expatriate and Spouse Repatriate Adjustment." *Journal of International Business Studies*, 4th quar. 1991b, pp. 671–694.

Clark, Tanya. "Managing China's Challenge." *Industry Week*, July 17, 1995, pp. 31–36.

Collins, Glenn. "Coke Drops 'Domestic' and Goes One World." *New York Times*, January 13, 1996, pp. 35, 37.

Dwyer, Paula, Pete Engardio, Zachary Schiller, and Stanley Reed. "The New Model: Tearing Up Today's Organization Chart." *Business Week, Special Issue: 21st Century Capitalism*, November 1994, pp. 80–90.

Dykeman, John. "HR Takes An Active Role In Selecting Global IT Staff." *Managing Office Technology*, March 1995, pp. 43–45.

Elashmawi, Fadrid, and Philip R. Harris. *Multinational Management: New Skills for Global Success*. Houston: Gulf Publishing Company, 1993.

Feldman, Daniel C., and David C. Thomas. "Career Management Issues Facing Expatriates." *Journal of International Business Studies*, Spring 1992, pp. 271–293.

Foster, Dean Allen. *Bargaining across Borders: How to Negotiate Business Successfully Anywhere in the World*. New York: McGraw-Hill, 1995.

Francis, Joyce L. "Training across Cultures." *Human Resources Development Quarterly*, Spring 1995, pp. 101–107.

Fuchsberg, Gilbert. "As Costs of Overseas Assignments Climb, Firms Select Expatriates More Carefully." *Wall Street Journal*, January 9, 1992, p. 81.

Pollack, Andrew. "A Cyberspace Front in a Multicultural War." *New York Times*, August 7, 1995, pp. D1, D4.

Purdy, Larry [Manager, Leadership Development, Electronic Data Systems]. "Leadership: Is It Culturally Dependent?" Presentation at the Strategic Management Society annual national conference, Mexico City, October 15–18, 1995.

Qureshi, Sajda. "Meeting and Working on an Electronic Social Space: Behavioral Considerations and Implications for Cross-Cultural End User Computing." *Journal of End User Computing*, Fall 1995, pp. 12–21.

Solomon, Charlene Marmer. "Learning to Manage Host-Country Nationals: Multinationals Are Increasingly Committed to Hiring Local Managers; But the Greatest Challenge Is to Skillfully Link Their Native Expertise to the Company's Strategic Goals." *Personnel Journal*, March 1995a, pp. 60–67.

————. "Navigating Your Search for Global Talent: International Human Resources Managers Are Learning It Takes Years to Develop a Globally Aware Work Force; By Using Innovative Career Pathing and Training Techniques, and by Providing Handsome Compensation Packages, Companies Can Attract and Keep the Growing Cadre of Global Leaders." *Personnel Journal*, May 1995b, pp. 94–101.

Vanderbroeck, Paul. "Long-Term Human Resource Development in Multinational Organizations." *Sloan Management Review*, Fall 1992, pp. 461–477.

Zeien, Albert. "Gillette's Global Marketing Experiences." Talk given at St. John's University's Annual Colman Mockler Leadership Award Ceremony, New York, February 27, 1995.

# Chapter 12

# Leadership and Management

It is possible to distinguish between leadership and management in concept. *Leadership* involves leading or showing the way to some envisioned objective, whereas *management* involves guiding and controlling a project, person, or activity.

In practice, however, it is difficult to distinguish between managers and leaders. In general, managers guide, staff, and control an enterprise's operations; that is, they *manage* an existing enterprise or the start of a new enterprise. They are also required to plan and guide plan implementation, that is, at times they *lead* or show the way. Managers, therefore, need some leadership skills and perform leadership tasks.

Leaders, on the other hand, create visions and inspire (show the way), *lead* by example (show the way by going before), and energize a company and its people. They also have to *manage* (guide and control), for example, when management-related crises arise affecting enterprisewide policy.

Strategic management, for example, is both a *leadership* and *management* job, depending on the situation. This is clear from the mix of multinational cross-cultural management tasks (creating visions to intervening where appropriate) which are listed in Table 2-1 and from the discussions of the strategic management job in Chapter 2. The exact mix will depend on the kind of situation and the level and nature of the task involved.

For instance, enterprisewide corporate leaders generally are called chairman or president. As much as circumstances permit, they deal primarily with longer-term strategic visionary aspects of an enterprise—but not exclusively, as seen from the experiences of Whirlpool, where team management involved a corporate-level executive group that set policy and participated in managing an enterprisewide corporate cultural change. Managers are located throughout an organization's business units and operating areas, the top manager, often called the chief operating officer, working under the president or chairman. As seen from the company experiences described in this chapter, therefore, both leaders and managers in practice perform a diverse balanced mixture of leadership and management tasks, whatever in concept is supposed to be the major thrust of their jobs.

It is possible to distinguish between leadership and management in concept. Leadership involves leading or showing the way to some envisioned objective. Managing involves guiding and controlling a project, person or activity.

This chapter is divided into three sections. First, a leadership section deals mainly with the tasks involved in leading a multinational company or enterprise, as well as the values and character traits, knowledge and skills, and behaviors (leadership styles and actions) of successful leaders at all levels of a multinational business. The second section, which presents a contingent view of leadership and management, identifies contingency frameworks and contingency guidelines for determining which leaders to select and which leadership behaviors are more likely to work in different kinds of situations. The final section of the chapter discusses a major application area: managing and leading teams.

A more thorough discussion of integrative multinational cross-cultural management in a variety of other situations is discussed in Chapter 13.

## LEADERSHIP

The discussion in this section is in four parts. The first part gives an overview of the tasks or jobs of a multinational enterprise leader. The second part discusses the basic values and character traits found in successful leaders today—that is, the kind of people who generally make successful leaders. The third part discusses knowledge and skills—that is, what leaders are capable of doing and how their competencies have developed through education, training, and experience. The fourth part describes how successful leaders act—the behaviors (leadership styles and actions) that translate strategic visions into business realities.

In life it is not always possible to achieve the ideal: it is rare that anyone has all the qualifications needed to handle all complex situations. This is certainly true of leaders. The solution in each situation, therefore, will depend on balancing the leaders' individual characteristics and values, knowledge and skills, and behaviors with the situation requirements. Given the contingent nature of multinational management, what will work in each situation depends on the specific situation requirements.

### Leadership Tasks: An Overview

While good managers are usually leaders, and while leaders engage in management activities, leadership implies more than simply management. It implies the vision to lead into the future, not just manage what already exists. Those working for a company need this leadership vision context in order to meet the paradoxical demands of today's multinational cross-cultural environments.

Leadership is especially important in multinational management situations to achieve a day-to-day working balance, a balance that enables global centralization and efficiencies, local entrepreneurial initiatives and responsiveness, and the rapid dissemination and use of new knowledge. This is done through:

- Creating an overall strategic framework, including strategic vision and guidelines (described in Chapters 2 and 5).

- Stimulating and guiding the emergent development of specific plans (enterprisewide and in functional areas) over time through the enabling systems and processes (described in Chapters 5 and 6).

- Activating, guiding and energizing the enabling frameworks needed for achieving success in light of changing competitive environments. (Chapters 6, 7, 8 and 9 described this enabling framework from four perspectives: functional area operations, telecommunications and information systems, accounting and finance systems, and organization.)

- Ensuring that a core management staff, with appropriate interpersonal, communication, and leadership and management skills and potential (see Chapters 4, 10, and 11), is in place and functioning in order to achieve balance.

- Communicating and implementing the strategic framework, as well as cultural benchmarks that are needed to enable the core management staff to translate the desired balance into action. The actual processes involve leadership and management appropriate for both the manager and people or groups involved in the situation, as well as for the specific competitive market needs of the situation.

- Leaving managers relatively free to manage and pushing decision making as close to the customer as possible, but intervening where appropriate to make certain that integrative activities are operating efficiently and effectively to achieve company strategic short- and long-term objectives.

This chapter and the next go beyond the earlier discussions of these tasks and focus on the leadership and management involved in doing the tasks.

## Leadership Character Traits and Values

The following character traits (psychological, physiological and intellectual) that affect leadership success have been identified by researchers, business executives and consultants (Murray-Bethel 1990; Heller 1995; Kouzes and Posner 1995; Lord and Associates 1986).

*Adaptability.* Leaders today need to be able to deal with continuing change. For example, both IBM's CEO, Louis Gerstner, and Microsoft's CEO, Bill Gates, were actively transforming their companies to meet the challenges of the fast-growing world of networks in early 1996 (Gates 1995; Zuckerman 1995).

*Versatility.* Given the diversity of the marketplace, leaders also need the ability to employ whatever tools and techniques are appropriate to success. Lorenzo Zambrano, chairman of the board and chief operating officer (COO) of CEMEX, a multinational cement company headquartered in Mexico, explained that in general he runs his company using a supportive leadership style. At times, however, direct orders are required, such as when technology transfer was rapidly needed at the company's Spanish plant to respond to competitive market pressures (Zambrano 1995). Al Zeien at Gillette and Jack Welch at General Electric displayed similar versatility in the experiences cited earlier (Day and LeBarre 1994; Zeien 1995).

*Vision: Creative and Innovative.* When asked what it takes to succeed as a leader, Dean John McArthur at Harvard Businesss School commented that to succeed, "you have to dream really big dreams" ("Conversation" 1995). Louis Platte, chairman of Hewlett-Packard, showed this type of visionary outlook when he described H-P's new strategy involving information appliances and networks (Gillooly 1995).

*Risk Taker, Anchored with Good Judgment.* To realize dreams, leaders need to be risk takers, not gamblers. Anyone involved in planning has to be a risk taker, since planning deals with the future and the future is to some measure often uncertain. When Gillette introduced its "sensor razor" in the late 1980s (it was to prove the most successful product introduction of the decade), it risked making its then-best-selling razor obsolete; it was a prudent risk, however, backed by over $100 million in introductory advertising. Risks are especially necessary to move into major international markets. Large companies cannot afford not to be in major growth areas such as China and Russia, even though the risks are great. For example, in 1996 China was demanding the transfer of technology, which constitutes a long-term risk for major companies. However, this risk has to be balanced with the risk of losing position in a major market (Smith and Hamilton 1995).

*Intelligence.* Creating visions requires analytical as well as conceptual intelligence. Visions are concepts, so conceptual people are needed to create them. Organizing those visions also requires structured thinking.

*Practical.* A realistic person is also needed to turn visions into reality. This is another paradox, since effective leaders are also dreamers. However, their dreams have to be achievable. Practical instincts combined with intelligence are especially useful during crises: Perrier, for example, moved ahead quickly and simply to limit the damage to its brand image when traces of benzene were found in some of its bottles in February 1990; similarly, Goodyear Tire and Rubber Company in Mexico followed a series of very common-sense, aggressive steps in December 1994 to minimize the potential damage from the crash of the Mexican peso (Meyerson 1995).

Handling unusual situations is essential to international success, since problems continually arise around the world. In 1995, for example, when China exceeded its import limit to the United States for certain types of textiles, Chinese companies made deals with companies in other countries that had unused quotas for the United States, enabling it to continue to tap the U.S. market.

*People Oriented.* Getting things done in most instances involves working through and with people. The experiences of Jack Welch at General Electric and others (discussed in the following sections and in Chapter 11) provide abundant evidence of the importance of this leadership trait.

*Enjoys Seeing Others Succeed.* Sharing is as important as caring. Gil Amelio, CEO and chairman of National Semiconductor, revitalized the company between 1991, when the company was losing hundreds of million of dollars on several billion dollars in sales, and 1994, when it made $264 million on $2.3 billion in sales. One of his key beliefs was that we should value the worker who "helps others by contributing to their success" much more than the brilliant loner. Transformation, in his words, "demands people who can work in combined efforts" (Amelio and Simon 1996, p. 74).

*Performance Driven.* Al Zeien described what he liked most about his job: as he walked home each night, he could say, "Things are different because I went to work today." Zeien gets a "great deal of satisfaction from getting things done" (Zeien 1995)—a common trait among business leaders.

*Firm in Convictions, Flexible in Execution.* Successful adaptable and flexible leaders also have the courage of convictions. Both Coca-Cola and Gillette are firmly committed to globalization of their brands but they are extremely flexible in the way this is achieved from country to country. These company global policies are a reflection of the personalities of their leaders. Helmut Maucher, chairman and CEO of Nestlé S.A., was extremely firm in his commitment to ethical and moral values (that are, in his words, "consistent"), but at the same time was dedicated to "learning" and to having managers who were "change-able" and stimulated innovation (Maucher 1994, pp. 77-80).

*Balanced Orientation.* Given the diverse requirements of business leadership, a leader needs to balance many diverse, seemingly contradictory (paradoxical) situation factors. Richard Hackborn at Hewlett-Packard, who was responsible for the phenomenal growth of H-P's printer business, was described as having his "head in the air" and his "feet on the ground" (he was a practical thinker). Jack Welch felt the necessity of, so to speak, "clearing the forest so the trees could grow" by eliminating thousands of jobs at GE, but he has continually demonstrated great concern for people, even to the point of introducing leading edge compensation policies for laid-off workers.

*Values and Attitudes.* Given the growing interest in social responsibility concerns, leaders are required to be moral, ethical, and honest. Nestlé's Helmut Maucher considered being credible and consistent in word and deed the most significant values for him, since they are important enablers to generating trust among employees and customers (Maucher 1994).

From its founding in 1936, H-P has been ruled by a value that represents what is today a prevailing concept of people-oriented leadership, the belief that men and women want to do a good job, and that if they are provided the proper environment, they will do so (Sherman 1995).

Closely associated with values are personal principles or attitudes. Stephen Covey (1991) identified seven basic ones that seem to lead to success in general and are applicable to leadership:

- *be proactive*—respond in your own way.
- *begin with the end in mind*—always keep objectives in mind.
- *put first things first*—keep your priorities straight.
- *think win/win*—make sure everyone wins something as you negotiate through life.
- *seek first to understand*—learn to truly listen, put other people first.
- *synergize*—search for ways to make two and two equal five, by combining energies.
- *seek continuous improvement*—seek self-renewal and help others seek the same.

These are basic values of successful individuals, especially at the enterprise leadership levels. They are also human values important to success in business and in life. They are essential ingredients of a learning organization, the lubricants that enable it to function (Senge 1990).

This section has discussed the attitudes, values and traits that are imbedded in a leader. Whether they have been developed during childhood or from experiences along the way, these are the innate instincts that guide actions and responses to situation needs. They are, however, only one aspect of successful leadership.

### Leadership Competencies: Knowledge and Skills

More than just character traits, values, principles, and attitude traits are needed. A leader also needs knowledge and skills developed from education, training and experience. Knowledge required in today's international businesses includes financial acumen, international knowledge, technical knowledge, knowledge of company operations, and competitive market familiarity. Related skills include those involving communications, handling people, decision making, and building and managing teams. These capabilities to get things done are called *leader competencies*.

### Leadership Behaviors: Styles and Actions

While it is important to have the traits and values, and the competencies needed to succeed, the true test of leadership is in the doing. The essence of leadership in the 1990s, which has been described as "helping people find their way through adaptive challenges—problems without apparent solutions" (Sherman 1995)—is "influencing human behavior in an environment of uncertainty."

**Figure 12-1**
**General Electric Company Mission Statement**

### Statement: GE Values

*GE Leaders, Always With Unyielding Integrity:*

Create a clear, simple, reality-based, customer-focused vision and are able to communicate it straightforwardly to all constituencies.

Set aggressive targets, understanding accountability and commitment, and are decisive.

Have a passion for excellence, hating bureaucracy and all the nonsense that comes with it.

Have the self-confidence to empower others and behave in a boundaryless fashion. They believe in and are committed to Work-Out as a means of empowerment and are open to ideas from anywhere.

Have, or have the capacity to develop, global brains and global sensitivity and are comfortable building diverse global teams.

Stimulate and relish change and are not frightened or paranoid by it, seeing changes as opportunity, not threat.

Have enormous energy and the ability to energize and invigorate others. They understand speed as a competitive advantage and see the total organizational benefits that can be derived from a focus on speed.

**Industry Category:**  Diversified

**Corporate Description**
GE is a diversified technology, manufacturing and services company with a commitment to achieving worldwide leadership in each of its 13 major businesses:  aerospace, aircraft engines, broadcasting (NBC), electrical distribution equipment, electric motors, financial services, industrial and power systems, information services, lighting, locomotives, major appliances, medical systems, and plastics.  John F. Welch, Jr., is Chairman and Chief Executive Officer of GE.

**Size Revenues:**  $60,562,000,000 as of 1993

**Number of Employees:**  222,000 as of 1993

*Source*: 1993 annual report.

This modern concept of leadership is exemplified in the experiences of Jack Welch at General Electric.

*The Story of GE's Jack Welch.* In April 1981, Jack Welch became CEO at GE, a diversified worldwide technology, manufacturing and services company with a commitment to achieving worldwide leadership in each of its major businesses. The company's mission statement is given in Figure 12-1 (Abrahams 1995).

Initially, Welch moved decisively in a very directive and autocratic way to transform GE. In essence he "created his own crisis by delayering the management hierarchy, reducing corporate staff, and slashing 100,000 employees to focus on what he believed to be the core elements of the business." Once this period had passed, "he set about to release the organization's emotional energy and creativity to capitalize on the opportunities offered by changes in GE's environment" (Hurst 1995, pp. 112–113). He moved decisively and was firm in his convictions, yet he was flexible in their execution. He did not flinch at making hard decisions when necessary.

During and after this crisis phase, Welch exhibited his versatility and adaptability as a leader. In his words:

It was hard during that period. Today, people sort of get a badge of honor for 10,000 layoffs. It's terrible to take out people. It's the worst part of the job. But we had to get rid of anything that was getting in the way of being informal, of being fast, of being boundaryless. You can't say to a big bloated bureaucracy, "let's be boundaryless," because they've already got defined slots. Unless you clear the forest, you don't see anything. (Day and LeBarre 1995)

Welch clearly was people oriented, since his major focus was to release the untapped energy in people, so they would gain greater satisfaction from their jobs.

Welch's idea of "boundaryless" was that horizontally, between functions, people should be open—sharing with suppliers and customers. Thus, new products are designed with customers and suppliers in the room, in multifunctional teams. The quality of an idea does not depend on its altitude in the corporation, in his view (Day and LeBarre 1994). This was only one of the many ways in which Welch energized innovative thinking in GE.

Welch moved authority and decision making down as far as possible within the organization so that managers could participate with workers and work groups in managing and leading. Welch wanted to eliminate the "boss" factor. He encouraged participation by example: in the plastics business he led before coming to GE, his technician worked on the same project as a partner: "We had two people, then four people, then eight people, then 12 people, and now we're a $5 billion business. But it started that way. So that's my vision of how people should communicate. Everybody's involved. Everyone knows. Everyone's got a piece of the action. The organization's flat." Reflecting his background, he appeared to be a very practical, down-to-earth person (Day and LeBarre, 1994).

To achieve this participation, Welch defined his job in these words: "21st century leaders will forgo their old powers—to plan, organize, implement and measure—for new duties: counselling groups, providing resources for them, helping them think for themselves" (Heller 1995, p. 186). He perceived his job as supporting the participation of others in running the enterprise.

Welch "stressed the sharing of the facts and assumptions behind decisions" rather than the logic of decisions themselves. The "work-out" program he developed to increase communication, for example, was designed to expose business managers to the vibrations of their businesses—opinions, feelings, emotions and resentments, not abstract theories of reorganization and management (Hurst 1995, p. 113). The work-out sessions allowed GE to become innovative in many ways by removing barriers in order for the company to become faster and better. Reaching and stretching without punishment was a major breakthrough for Welch, and he achieved excellent results in very pragmatic ways.

Welch was also a risk taker in the worldwide markets. For example, when people told him he was taking a big risk in going into China, his reply was, "We may not make it in China, but there's no alternative to being in there with both feet, participating in this huge market" (Day and LeBarre 1994).

Welch also worked with common global frameworks adapted to local circumstances. For example, he was able to use his "work-out" sessions in Hungary, but only after adapting the concept to the cultural bias left over from the collective communist days, when workers were not used to thinking for themselves. Three very difficult years were required to make the transition. GE persisted, however, based on Welch's belief that on one level, people are the same: they want to be more involved—and involvement, not empowerment, was a key ingredient of GE's transformation (Day 1994; Perlez 1994).

One aspect of Welch's core values, loyalty, has stirred some controversy:

I think people have to understand that a business institution is here to provide economic values for the community and country in which it is located and for the employees who participate in it. Loyalty to excellence. Loyalty means giving people an opportunity. Our job is to provide an opportunity and an atmosphere where people can thrive and enjoy the fruits of winning. So the word "loyalty" per se has an old connotation. I think that trust in a company is a better word. You can trust that its values and yours are congruent. You can trust it to give you fair treatment. But in the end, you and your associates in that business have to create an atmosphere where customers want what you're delivering or all the speeches about loyalty won't mean a thing.

And that's the problem with bad leaders. One of the worst parts of this job is taking people out of jobs. But if you get a bad leader in one of our businesses, they take productivity down and decrease morale. Then what do you do? We bring in someone to create the shock treatment and lay them all off. An involved work force is what we are after.

But we do it fairly. For example, when we engineered the crisis in the 1980s when it was not apparent GE did need changing, we pioneered new lay-off benefits. We put in an early notice in the early 1980s, before anyone else did. We had broken all the ground for generous severance, because it was so foreign for us to take people out. Fairness and trust seem to be more significant value concepts.

The word loyalty is a difficult one. But I don't hear it much anymore. (Day and LeBarre 1994, p. 16)

Welch in many ways exhibited the leader's character traits, values, knowledge and skills. He also seems to have sensed what leadership's tasks are: to stimulate and guide, activate and energize, ensure a core staff is in place with adequate skills, create enabling organization mechanisms, and leave managers relatively free to manage. His view of the first leadership task, creating a strategic framework, went beyond his vision and mission statements. According to Welch, clear thinking and fast decision making at GE happened in part because he and his colleagues focused on the answers to a handful of basic strategic queries:

- What does your global competitive environment look like?
- In the last three years, what have your competitors done?
- In the same period, what have you done to them?
- How might they attack you in the future?
- How might you leapfrog them?

Several aspects of leadership styles and behavior observed in the experiences at GE and other companies can provide useful benchmarks for others. The most obvious is their situational context: as needs changed, so did the leadership style. The second is that the approach was a people-based, participative, and supportive orientation, which today is a very popular approach worldwide.

Such an approach is not that new, however. For example, according to Manuel Jorge Cutillas, chairman and chief executive officer of Bicardi Limited, a company based in Latin America, Bicardi has had such a flexible value-based approach for over a century. According to Cutillas, this approach has done much to help the company prosper and survive through very difficult times over that period. The key was to focus on the company as the ultimate creation, with the basic values being dedication to product quality, family unity, creativity, long-term vision and a commitment to the institution, the Bicardi company itself. The company's philosophy is to promote collaboration, teamwork and synergies to enable adapting to an ever-changing world (Cutillas 1995). Moreover, many European companies have had a similar worldwide orientation for many decades (Calori and Dufour 1995).

*Leaderships Styles.* Many leadership styles have been identified. Rowe identified four: analytical, conceptual, behavioral, directive (Rowe and Mason 1987); Bourgeois and Brodwin, five: commander, change, cultural, collaborative, and crescive (Bourgeois and Brodwin 1984); Fiedler, two: task oriented; relationship-oriented (Fiedler 1967); Hofsted, five: autocratic, consultative, persuasive, participative, and democratic (Hofsted 1983a, 1983b, 1984, 1992); and Gibson and House and colleagues, four: directive, participative, supportive, and achievement (House, Hanges and Angar 1993–94). Hofsted, as well as House and colleagues, extended this type of study to multinational company situations.

Each of these researchers analyzed and categorized different kinds of group and individual situations encountered, and attempted to develop a contingency framework to guide in selecting a leadership style most appropriate for the kind of group or individual situation under study. Welch's experiences illustrate this situational point. He effectively used several leadership styles—directive, supportive and participative—as situation circumstances dictated.

*Leadership Behavior: Imbedding Culture.* Additional lessons about how seasoned leaders, such as Jack Welch at GE and others discussed above, have acted effectively have been summarized often (for example, Kouzes and Posner 1995). The major points include:

1. Search out challenging opportunities to change, grow, innovate, and improve.
2. Experiment, take risks, and learn from the accompanying mistakes.
3. Envision an uplifting and ennobling future.
4. Enlist others in a common vision by appealing to their values, interests, hopes and dreams.
5. Foster collaboration by promoting cooperative goals and building trust.
6. Strengthen people by giving power away, providing choice, developing competence, assigning critical tasks, and offering visible support.
7. Set the example by behaving in ways that are consistent with shared values.
8. Achieve small wins that promote consistent progress and commitment.
9. Recognize individual contributions to the success of every project.
10. Celebrate team accomplishments regularly.

The cumulative effect of these actions is to create a new culture, to embed a cultural change—one consistent with the guiding principle articulated at the beginning of this section: helping people find their way through adaptive challenges. This cultural imbedding involves all the communication, management, organization, human systems, telecommunications and information systems, and other enablers, as well as charisma, the ability to inspire, and the tenacity to continually reinforce a company's new culture. The management and leadership processes discussed above work together to build a fabric of cultural values appropriate to the individual company involved—again, this is a contingency perspective.

## SITUATION APPLICATION GUIDELINES

While leadership generalities are helpful, their value comes from how well they are adapted and put to work by individual leaders in specific situations. The experiences of Jack Welch in adapting his style to meet situation requirements is just one example.

According to Setsuo Mito, former CEO of Honda Motors, Honda's leadership "is not precisely the same in every country." As it is put into practice in Europe, the United States, and Asia, it is tailored to specific needs and conditions. For example, while the company adopted the joint boardroom concept (within this boardroom executives are able to express their differences in a constructive manner), the sessions were run differently in each country. The U.S. sessions encouraged individual contributions, while the ones in Japan focused on consensus and subordinated individuals to the team effort. The experiences of EDS (described in Chapter 11) also showed how a common leadership framework was adapted in moving among cultures—in that situation, like in Honda's, between America and Japan.

Attempts to develop contingency guidelines for leadership style and behavior selection have been made. For example, Geert Hofsted had access to two IBM preference surveys of 116,000 employees at overseas location, one in 1969 and one in 1972, and a later survey of students in 23 countries. Based on these studies he identified characteristics useful in analyzing appropriate leadership styles. For analytical purposes, he measured each culture by five criteria, in a way similar to what was done in Chapter 10:

- *social orientation*, involving the relative importance of the interests of the individual versus the interest of the group and ranging from individualism to collectivism.
- *power orientation*, involving the appropriateness of power/authority within organizations and ranging from marginal tolerance to a great deal of respect for power and for the hierarchies having power.
- *Uncertainty orientation*, involving an emotional response to uncertainty/change and ranging from avoidance to acceptance of it.
- *Goal orientation*, involving what motivates people to achieve certain goals and ranging from a highly goal/achievement (masculine) interest to passive interest in goals and a more (feminine) interest in quality of life, social relevance and the welfare of others.
- *time orientation*, involving a short-term versus a long-term perspective and ranging from placing less emphasis on hard work to placing great emphasis on working hard as a means of self-fulfillment and success.

Some of the conclusions he drew, for example, were that in cultures, such as Mexico, that respect hierarchies, supportive leadership styles that include mixing with employees at social gatherings have to be carefully structured so as not to violate the culture's sense of superior/subordinate distance/power relationships. In autocratic societies as in Germany, a style that is more goal oriented is likely to be more successful than a behavioral one emphasizing caring and interpersonal concern. Robert House and colleagues were in the process of extending this type of study to additional countries and types of companies (House, Hanges, and Angar 1993–94).

Earlier, Fred E. Fiedler (1967) did a similar contingency study for leading small groups. He analyzed work groups by three measures:

- Leader-member relations—good to very poor
- Task structure—high to weak
- Power-position—strong to weak

Fiedler used two leadership styles:

1. A leader can take primary responsibility for the group; she or he can be autocratic, controlling, managing, directive, and task oriented.
2. A leader can share decision making; she or he can be democratic, permissive, non-directive, considerate of the group members' feelings, and offer therapeutic leadership.

Several of his contingent guidelines included the following:

Considerate, relationship-oriented leaders tend to perform best in situations in which they have only moderate influence, either because the task is relatively unstructured or because they are not too accepted although their position is high.

In situations where the leader has power, informal backing among group members, and a relatively well-structured task, the group is ready to be directed and the group members expect to be told what to, thus favoring a more directive leadership style.

A more recent study of European management styles had a dual conclusion (Calori and Dufour 1995). First, it identified traits that typified European managers: a greater orientation toward people; a high level of internal negotiation; greater skill in managing international diversity; and capability in managing in a more balanced way between extremes. Second, it pointed out that: leadership styles are changing and becoming less homogeneous across Europe. There are now, for instance, differences among European countries (the French are quite different from the Germans in many ways). Moreover, even where the leadership styles are ostensibly similar (people concern, for example), the manifestation is quite different (much less interpersonal caring in Germany, for example, but strong unions; strong support for women in Sweden, but not so much in Germany).

These studies conclude that, first, situation requirements are not always static, but rather (as seen at GE) can change over time and in relation to the level of management and leadership being exercised. Second, the cultural characteristics of each situation should be studied as one approaches leadership decisions. Third, in leadership tasks, as in other multinational cross-cultural management task areas, common frameworks can be adapted to meet local requirements. The EDS, Honda, and GE Hungary experiences are only three of many examples in the international environment.

Leadership pressures are substantial and are continuing in today's dynamic, rapidly changing multinational competitive market environment. Moving from analytical, rational, and conceptual planning tasks to sensitive, interpersonal day-to-day tasks requires a difficult-to-achieve mix of conflicting task-oriented and people-oriented leaderships styles. For instance, while it is good to allow entrepreneurial autonomy, it is also necessary to intervene as required in the business process in order to create and maintain the adaptable and flexible organization environment needed for successful multinational cross-cultural management. Leaders who can achieve such a balance, and who also have the charisma needed to communicate with and inspire people, are rare.

As some companies have learned from experience, alternative approaches are used when a perfectly balanced person and personality suitable for a company situation is unavailable. It is the one Coca-Cola chose; have two leaders whose combined traits, knowledge, skills, styles, and behaviors provide the sought-for balance. Roberto C. Goizueta, the introverted chairman of Coca-Cola, knew he could not rethink the company and run a sprawling multinational operation at the same time. He therefore insisted, when he took the job, that he pick his own president, since he needed someone like the extroverted Don Keogh to galvanize the operation in a way that Goizueta could never have managed (Heller 1995, ch. 5, sec. 1).

A leader does what she or he has to do to make things work within legal, ethical, moral and policy restraints. Success in this multinational cross-cultural management task area, as in other areas, then, depends on developing a creative solution that meets the requirements of each specific situation.

The following section discusses a major leadership/management area important in today's multinational cross-cultural businesses—team management.

## LEADING AND MANAGING TEAMS

A team consists of people doing something together. A team is more than just a group, however (Robbins and Finley 1995, p. 10). A team is generally a limited number of people with complementary skills who are committed to a common purpose, performance goals, and approach for which they hold themselves mutually accountable (Katzenback and Smith 1993, p. 45). Teams are also described as cohesive work groups that have interdependent tasks and common goals to outproduce and outperform any random collection of individuals (McIntosh-Fletcher 1996, p. 1). Teams can range from groups of two individuals with coordinated but independent tasks to whole integrated organizations.

Integration through cross-cultural teams is used widely in multinational corporations as an effective way to bridge cultural gaps and to effectively balance global efficiencies, respond to local differences, and transfer knowledge and information across cultural and corporate boundaries. Teams are used at many levels within multinational enterprises.

Companies often join together through mergers and acquisitions to develop synergies that enable them to compete more effectively. Such synergistic combinations are often referred to as "teaming up," even though they may involve entire companies (Odenwald 1996). Joint ventures are easy to conceive as team efforts, since they depend to a great extent on the people involved and so multiple team efforts throughout the businesses are often a means of achieving desired synergies. The success of mergers and acquisitions also can depend on the effective merging of corporate and national cultures through team efforts.

For example, Whirlpool, primarily a North American appliance maker, acquired the appliance division of N.V. Phillips Gleoilampenfabriekin, a Netherlands Corporation, in 1989 and was renamed Whirlpool International B.V. to reflect its new, global character. The union transformed two parochial, margin-driven companies into a unified, consumer-focused organization capable of using its combined talents to achieve breakthrough performance in markets around the world. It was the beginning of the creation of a new company. As a first step in this creation process, during the first two years after 1989, the company's goal was to concentrate on building trust and creating a common vision (Maruca 1994, p. 57). Whirlpool started with a team approach to integrate European and U.S. senior management.

In 1990 Whirlpool instituted an annual conference for its top executives from 16 different countries. Its objective was to:

- Advance a unified vision of the company's future,

- Instill the idea of embracing the future as one global company,

- Establish a keen sense of responsibility with the leadership group for creating the company's future,

- Identify and initiate explicit steps toward integrating various activities and ideas throughout Whirlpool worldwide, and

- Open communications links.

Through these team efforts, Whirlpool's managers were encouraged to mix culturally, participate actively and get to know each other as business-team partners. They were, for example, strategically seated with their counterparts from other countries. The objective of the meetings was for managers to share with their counterparts ideas, processes, and systems used and to evaluate how they could be integrated (Marquardt and Reynolds 1994, pp. 119–121). After focusing on getting its senior managers from the United States and Europe to integrate as a global team, Whirlpool concentrated on its employees throughout the worldwide organization.

Intel Corp. of Santa Clara, California, has teams for many projects. For example, teams formulate product sales strategies, develop new products, improve quality testing, and redesign manufacturer microprocessor elements. Typically, Intel's teams work together across geographic and cultural boundaries—for example, as many as six or seven of the company's locations in Ireland, Israel, England, France, and parts of Asia may be involved in specific team efforts. Many of the teams assemble quickly, do their work, and then disband and regroup with other team members.

A group of Intel intercultural managers formed a global team to determine what made high-performing teams successful. Their conclusion was: "It is very important to have very simple basic procedures and processes, to set clear expectations, and to have clearly defined goals, roles, and responsibilities." It was also important to have several face-to-face meetings early in the team's development. Cross-cultural training also made team members more adaptive, and so helped harness the synergies possible in cross-cultural and cross-functional exchanges. These preliminary steps make later long-distance communications, through such means as teleconferencing, videoconferencing and electronic mail, go much more smoothly. Clear agendas are needed for meetings, and written minutes of the meeting must be distributed immediately thereafter to ensure that everyone understands the tasks and decisions that were agreed on during the meeting. They provide a means of refreshing memories and monitoring progress.

According to Intel's study, before one can have effective global groups, it is also important to have enabling support that makes it easier for people to share information, get feedback from one another and communicate. "If the technology isn't in place—if team members don't have groupware so they can share documents, or e-mail and videoconferencing capabilities so they can communicate rapidly—people will be discouraged by physical barriers" (Solomon 1995). The study also showed that it is important to include in the global groups people with an appropriate mix of cultural, interpersonal and technical expertise.

In 1991, Honda Motor Co. was having problems with costs rising faster than the U.S. market could bear. (Miller 1993; Updike, Woodruff, and Armstrong 1995). Consequently, Ron Shriver, an engineer at the company's East Liberty, Ohio, plant (where Hondas are built for the U.S. market) put together a twelve-member team that would spend the next eighteen months scouring Honda's U.S. suppliers and its Ohio factory workers for ideas to make the next Honda Civic cheaper. Shriver did not know it, but back in Japan, Honda executives had reached the same conclusion. The rising yen meant that Honda could no longer overengineer. Consequently, Hiroyuki Itok, the Civic's chief engineer, began putting together his own team—one that, within months, merged with Shriver's U.S. crew to collaborate in a battle to wring costs out of the Civic.

Honda paid $500,000 each to move nearly 60 U.S. engine and production specialists to Japan with their families to spend two to three years at the Japanese research and design facilities. The Americans brainstormed with Japanese designers and reviewed preliminary sketches. The relationships in this cross-cultural (U.S. and Japan) and cross-functional (production and design) self-managed team were rocky at first. For example, the Japanese were shocked by their eager visitors, who had an avalanche of questions. Daijro Watanabe, a senior engineer at the company's Wako plant near Tokyo, said he thought the Americans had come merely for instruction.

The Americans did learn a few things: Avoid being forceful, avoid showing emotions, and if you request a design change, you must substantiate it. In spite of skepticism on both sides, after a break-in period, the partners got along well. The first new models based on this cross-cultural research and development team effort, which reduced costs substantially without reducing quality and performance, were produced in late 1995.

Texas Instruments Malaysia (TIM) was opened in 1974 in Kuala Lumpur, Malaysia's capital, to serve growing regional and global demand for integrated circuits for computers and related products. By 1990, TIM had more than 3,000 employees organized in different forms of self-managed work teams. TIM management believed that the development of teams would enable the company to reduce cycle time and increase output while improving overall quality. In the early 1980s, TIM installed quality circles and problem-solving teams at the worker/operational levels, which reaped modest cost savings and productivity improvements. However, they were not successful overall because the employees perceived them as temporary.

TIM persisted, however, managing in the late 1980s to create a pilot program of self-managed, employee-empowered teams, a concept in which it believed. This time around, they had more than 40 hours of training at the outset. In addition, the teams developed specific goals. Team responsibilities fell into two categories: maintenance (equipment maintenance and daily administrative activities, such as managing cost, delivery, safety, housekeeping equipment setup, tracking attendance, and assigning daily duties and responsibilities) and customer satisfaction. Job assignments were rotated within teams but only over the long run. Because automatic semiconductor fabricating equipment is so complex, most team members held specific jobs for at least one year. This gave members a sense of ownership of the job and its output, assigned responsibility, and enabled training for replacements.

Facilitators were assigned, as at GE's work-out sessions, to help teams develop schedules and learn how to perform other required management and leadership functions. Appraisals included both self-assessments and peer evaluations. Rewards for goal attainment were merit increases to the group, group gift certificates, and free lunches (Wellins, Byham, and Dixon 1994).

Motorola's experiences in Malaysia were somewhat different, not only in the way it developed team structures but also in the adaptations it made of the team approach to suit the Malaysian culture (Gogan, Zuboff, and Schuck 1994). The cultural mix in Malaysia is generally 50 percent Malays (generally Muslims), 35 percent Chinese, 10 percent Indian and Pakistanis, and 5 percent other; the plant reflected that mix. In addition, most of the employees were women. A number of differences arising from this cultural mix that led to adaptations and adjustments were noted by S. K. Ko, the first woman managing director of Motorola-Penang (MP) in Malaysia.

In Malaysia there is a desire to avoid decision making (whereas the Western ideal is active decision making), so shared decision making was initially not a part of team efforts (except for efforts with high technical requirements and more advanced personnel). As one manager said, "At home [women] are supposed to follow their husband's directions. We encourage them to speak out but their husbands don't want them to speak out." Therefore, a program for written recommendations was instituted with formal procedures.

Steps also were taken to stimulate group relationship building through "Dignity and Respect" program initiatives. There were also hierarchical structure problems, since initially Malaysians were uncomfortable with working on the same level as managers. Therefore, the program included a "training-the-trainers" program: engineers trained technicians, and managers trained supervisors, who in turn trained the operators (who considered themselves students). They also instituted a "Critical Thinking Skills" program aimed at strengthening operators' learning capabilities, which awarded advancements and certificates to participants. Another program involved improving cycle time.

While monthly IR were given to individuals, the awards arising from the "Total Customer Satisfaction" (TCS) program were team awards. Many operators belonged to TCS teams. Rewards and training also differed by the technical complexity of the specific process involved, with the more highly skilled, better educated and more capable workers being given more advanced training. In short, the training, awards, and team structures varied within different segments of the plants, depending on the situation specifics. In general, the higher the skill requirements of the job and the higher the operator skills, the more useful team approaches were.

Director Ko was very people-oriented. She believed that the chief should have a heart. In her words, "Treat your people with respect, as you would treat your own family; no yelling, no shouting, no finger pointing; give visible rewards for achievers; create enthusiasm; share every success story" (Gogan, Schuck, and Zuboff 1994, p. 13). This was an effective approach since production operators and some supervisors were women, while most managers and engineers were men, and since in the Malaysian culture gender differences are important.

At the same time, she had a very difficult task in translating her leadership initiatives into action in her culture and her business situation. She explained the vision at one meeting: "Today 2,820 employees produce $380 million. By 2000, 1,500 employees will produce $1 billion. The factory will be highly automated. We will make state-of-the-art systems. Our work force will look completely different" (Gogan, Schuck, and Zuboff 1994, p. 9).

While empowerment is a key ingredient of building a learning organization that may grow into the one envisioned, it was very difficult to do at MP. Ko and her managers, who had visited U.S. facilities, were convinced that at this time, the use of empowerment was limited. Up to 1994, only one small department (six women on one assembly line) and cross-functional teams working in limited areas, such as quality improvement and cycle time reduction, had been effective. The basic cultural orientation in Malaysia meant that self-managed or even cross-functional teams were almost impossible in any great numbers at that time and that empowerment was not possible to any great degree, a barrier that created major obstacles to meeting the challenges of the new vision.

Ko's job, therefore, did not appear to be an easy one. Over the short term she had to build a basis for the future company by putting in place more sophisticated organization and training approaches, such as those used at other companies (such as Intel) in situations where more sophisticated workers and tasks were involved. At the same time, she had to keep her factory running efficiently and effectively during the five-year transition period. The solution was a balanced compromise whose exact dimensions grew from the requirements of her particular situations.

Teams do not work in all situations. Rather, they generally work only when carefully planned and managed and in cases where the situation has tasks and people suited or trained for self-directed interpersonal work in a task-oriented work environment, or where sufficient time (as with GE in Hungary) and energy have been taken to train people in working in teams. Where circumstances favor team structures, a number of common approaches can help make team management more effective. The following appear to be useful guidelines for approaching team management. They should, of course, be read with the usual reminder that adaptation to individual situation requirements is required.

To be successful, teams need effective leaders (Solomon 1995; Zenger et al. 1994). Leadership is needed both to initiate and to manage teams. The initial task is to define the general objective and guidelines for the team, as well as the initial general structures. This might include the level on which the team will function, its main task, and the general organization in the following situations:

- merging corporate entities through a short-term formal team of top management heads of independent business units (Whirlpool);
- performing operating functions (product development, marketing, and technical production) that require cross-functional expertise from different cultures operating in a self-managed environment using advanced information technologies that are formed for both short-term (new product development, marketing plans) and long-term (continuing production units) purposes (Intel);
- carrying out long-term strategic projects involving cross-functional (production and design) and cross-cultural (Japanese and American) professional expertise; such projects affect overall corporate success or failure (Honda);
- performing functional tasks within different manufacturing departments in a high tech operating environment in an Asian country, using company facilitators to insure team functioning (TIM);
- introducing the team concept into a low-tech environment in an Asian country, using both intradepartment and cross-functional teams as a long-term means of eventually moving to a high-tech production environment in a mixed cultural environment (MP).

Leadership tasks also include ensuring that enablers are put in place (including staffing, technology, controls and organization) and then communicating, motivating, energizing, and guiding.

Managing teams involves the early tasks of actually selecting team members. This can be done by upper management before the team forms, and continued by the team members themselves on a self-renewing basis, depending on whether the teams are self-managed and continuing. Early on, it is best to have face-to-face meetings among all team members. In one instance, such meetings were not possible so it was necessary to allow a longer period of letting people work with small projects in order to get acquainted with using available electronic media.

At this point, in order for teams to function they need to be guided through tasks such as defining the leader/manager roles, team member responsibilities, team facilitator functions, and various other responsibilities and jobs assignments such as recorder/secretary, monitoring, meeting scheduling, and performance benchmark identification (Lundy 1994; Zenger et al. 1994). Working together effectively on a day-to-day basis may also require supplementary interpersonal interaction training for handling cross-cultural situations (Lundy 1994). Team meetings need to be managed, starting with planning them, establishing agendas and sticking to them as far as possible in the cultural setting involved, economy of presentation, balancing controlled and free-flowing exchanges, identifying specific action assignments and deadlines, recording the meeting, and promptly communicating minutes to all involved (McIntosh-Fletcher 1996, ch. 8). Self-learning exercises in team building can be found in workbooks by Maddux (1994), Hartzler and Henry (1994), and Myers and Barbato (1996).

These are only guidelines based on observed experience in a selected number of situations. As in other management task areas, the guidelines will evolve and be refined as emergent behavior finds new solutions to new problems in other types of team-management situations. The guidelines, therefore, are only a starting point, a baseline from which to develop one's own experienced-based rules of thumb.

## CONCLUSION

This chapter discussed common frameworks in multinational cross-cultural management leadership and management task areas, as well as adaptations needed to meet specific situation global, local, and knowledge transfer requirements. Special attention was given to team management, which is a critical aspect of today's multinational cross-cultural management (Marshall 1995). However, teams are useful only in selective applications and situations. Odenwald pointed out (1996, p. 52) that over the past five years, the use of teams has, in fact, dropped in popularity in U.S. businesses.

For example, in Malaysia at Motorola-Penang teams were not very useful at that particular point of time, given the nature of the work, the composition of the work groups, and the skills of the workers. In fact, teams functioned there mainly as a change agent to meet long-term strategic goals. At other companies the situations were different and various forms of teams were effective. Teams are, therefore, just one of many enablers which may be useful in some form in one's own situation.

The same is true for leadership. Different styles are useful in different situations. And while there are some heuristics contingency guidelines, ultimately the individual decides what is best for his or her situation. Even where there are common frameworks, such as leadership styles and guidelines for making teams work in general, the way the frameworks are perceived, communicated, and learned can vary by culture. Ultimately, then, as in the other multinational cross-cultural tasks areas described in Chapter 2 and discussed throughout this book, the major common framework at work in these situations is the one underlying the contingency orientation of the book: the basic entrepreneurial contingency process shown in Figure 3-3.

Chapter 13 continues this discussion of common management frameworks. In discussing a variety of management tasks, it examines some of the steps involved in adapting and applying common frameworks when responding to local differences arising from the crossing of national and cultural boundaries in multinational cross-cultural management.

## WORKS CITED

Abraham, Jeffrey. *The Mission Statement Book.* Oakland, CA: Ten Speed Press, 1995.

Amelio, Gil, and William Simon. *Profit from Experience.* New York: Van Nostrand Reinhold, 1996.

Bourgeois, L. J., III, and David Brodwin. "Strategic Implementation: Five Approaches to an Elusive Phenomenon." *Strategic Management Journal*, July-September 1984, pp. 241–264.

Calori, Roland, and Bruno Dufour. "Management European Style." *Academy of Management Executive*, August 1995, pp. 61–77.

"Conversation With Kim Clark, A." *Harvard Business School Bulletin*, December 1995, pp. 42–48.

Covey, Stephen. *Principle-Centered Leadership.* New York: Simon and Schuster/Fireside, 1991.

Cutillas, Manuel Jorge. "Managing Growth through Dramatically Changing Conditions." Presentation given at the Strategic Management Society annual national conference, Mexico City, October 15–18, 1995.

Day, Charles R., Jr., and Polly LeBarre. "GE: Just Your Average Everyday $60 Billion Family Grocery Store." *Industry Week*, May 4, 1994, pp. 13–18.

Fiedler, Fred E. *A Theory of Leadership Effectiveness.* New York: McGraw-Hill Book Company, 1967.

Gates, Bill. *The Road Ahead.* New York: Viking/Penguin Books, 1995.

Gillooly, Brian, "H-P's New Course: Hewlett-Packard Wants to Construct a Global Information Infrasructure and Supply All the Equipment That Users Will Need to Access It; The First Step—Converge Its Core Businesses." *InformationWeek*, March 20, 1995, pp. 45–56.

Gogan, Janis L., Shoshana Zuboff, and Gloria Schuck. *Motorola-Panang.* Boston: Harvard Business School Publishing, 1994.

Hartzler, Meg, and Jane E. Henry. *Team Fitness: A How-To Manual for Building a Winning Team.* Milwaukee, WI: ASQC Quality Press, 1994.

Heller, Robert. *The Leadership Imperative: What Innovative Business Leaders Are Doing Today to Create the Successful Companies of Tomorrow.* New York: Dutton/Truman Talley Books, 1995.

Hofstede, Geert. "National Cultures in Four Dimensions: A Research-Based Theory of Cultural Differences among Nations." *International Studies of Management and Organisation*, Summer 1983a, pp. 46–74.

————. "The Cultural Relativity of Organizational Practices and Theories." *Journal of International Business Studies* (Fall 1983b): 75–89.

————. "Cultural Constraints in Management Theories." Distinguished International Scholar Lecture, Annual Meeting of the Academy of Management, Las Vegas, Nevada, August 11, 1992.

————. *Culture's Consequences: International Differences in Work-Related Values.* Beverly Hills, CA: Sage Publications, 1984.

House, Robert J., Paul Hanges, and Michael Angar. *A Multi-Nation Study of Cultures, Leadership and Organizational Practices.* Vol. 1, *Prospectus.* Vol. 2, *Status Report.* Philadelphia: University of Pennsylvania, 1993–94.

Hurst, David, K. *Crisis and Renewal: Meeting the Challenge of Organizational Change.* Boston: Harvard Business School Press, 1995.

Katzenbak, Jon R., and Douglas K. Smith. *The Wisdom of Teams: Creating the High-Performance Organization.* Boston: Harvard Business School Press, 1993.

Kouzes, James M., and Barry Z. Posner. *The Leadership Challenge: How to Keep Getting Extraordinary Things Done in Organizations.* San Francisco: Jossey-Bass Publishers, 1995.

Lord, Robert G., and Associates. "A Meta-Analysis of the relationship Between Personality Traits and Leadership Perceptions: An Application of Validity Generalization Procedures." *Journal of Applied Psychology* 71, no. 3 (August 1986): 402–410.

Lundy, James L. *Teams: Together Each Achieves More Success.* Chicago: Dartnell, 1994.

Maddux, Robert B. *Team Building: An Exercise in Leadership.* Menlo Park, CA: Crisp Publications, 1994.

Marquardt, Michael, and Angus Reynolds. *The Global Learning Organization: Gaining Competitive Advantage through Continuous Learning.* Burr Ridge, IL: Irwin, 1994.

Marshall, Edward W. *Transforming the Way We Work: The Power of The Collaborative Workplace.* New York: Amacom, 1995.

Maruca, Regina Fazio. "The Right Way to Go Global: An Interview with David Whitwan." In *Global Strategies: Insights From the World's Leading Thinkers*, ed. Percy Barnevik. Boston: Harvard Business School Publishing, 1994, pp. 57–74.

Maucher, Helmut. *Leadership in Action.* New York: McGraw-Hill, 1994.

McIntosh-Fletcher, Donna [McFletcher Corporation]. *Teaming by Design: Real Teams for Real People.* Chicago: Irwin Professional Publishing, 1996.

Meyerson, Allen R. "Out of a Crisis, an Opportunity: After Peso's Fall, Goodyear Doing More in Mexico." *New York Times*, September 26, 1995, pp. D1, D4.

Miller, Karen Lowry. "How a Team of Buckeyes Helped Honda Save a Bundle." *Business Week*, September 13, 1993, p. 68.

Murray-Bethel, Sheila. *Making a Difference: Twelve Qualities That Make You a Leader.* New York: G. P. Putnam and Sons, 1990.

Myers, Scott A., and Carole A. Barbato. *The Team Trainer: Winning Tools and Tactics for Successful Workouts.* Chicago: Irwin Professional Publishing, 1996.

Naisbitt, John. *Global Paradox.* London: Nicholas Brealey Publishing, 1994.

Odenwald, Silvia B. *Global Solutions for Teams: Moving From Collision to Collaboration.* Chicago: Irwin Professional Publishing, 1996.

Perlez, Jane. "G.E. Finds Tough Going in Hungary." *New York Times*, July 25, 1994, pp. D1, D8.

Robbins, Harvey, and Michael Finley. *Why Teams Don't Work, What Went Wrong, and How to Make It Right.* Midland Park, NJ: Pacesetter Books, 1995.

Rowe, Alan J., and Richard O. Mason. *Managing with Style.* San Francisco: Jossey-Bass Publishers, 1987.

Senge, Peter. *The Fifth Discipline: The Art and Practice of the Learning Organization.* New York: Doubleday/Currency, 1990.

Sherman, Stratford. "How Tomorrow's Best Leaders Are Learning Their Stuff." *Fortune*, November 27, 1995, pp. 90–102.

Smith, Craig S., and David P. Hamilton. "Price of Entry into China Rises Sharply: U.S. Firms Face Growing Pressure to Transfer Technology." *Wall Street Journal*, December 19, 1995, p. A14.

Solomon, Charlene Marmer. "Global Teams: The Ultimate Collaboration: You Think Team-Building in the United States is Challenging? Companies Such as Maxus and Intel Have Gone Even Further. They've Built Cross-Functional Teams That Comprise Different Cultures, Languages, Locations and Time Zones." *Personnel Journal*, September 1995, pp. 49–58.

Updike, Edith, David Woodruff, and Larry Armstrong. "Honda's Civic Lesson: The Carmaker Learned to Listen to the Troops When a Key Model Faced a Cost Squeeze." *Business Week*, September 18, 1995, pp. 71–74.

Wellins, Richard S., William C. Byham, and George R. Dixon. *Inside Teams: How 20 World-Class Organizations Are Winning Through Teamwork.* San Francisco: Jossey-Bass Publishers, 1994.

Zambrano, Lorenzo. "CEMEX: An Emerging Multinational" Keynote Address, Strategic Management Society Conference, Mexico City, October 16, 1995.

Zeien, Albert. "Gillette's Global Marketing Experiences." Talk given at St. John's University's Annual Colman Mockler Leadership Award Ceremony, New York, February 27, 1995.

Zenger, John H., Ed Musselwhite, Kathleen Hurson, and Craig Perrin. *Leading Teams.* Burr Ridge, IL: Irwin Professional Publishing, 1994.

Zuckerman, Laurence. "From Mainframes to Global Networking." *New York Times*, December 18, 1995, pp. D1.

Chapter 13

# Integratively Managing Change and Diversity

Many aspects of the strategic management job (summarized in Table 2-1) have been discussed in this book. In the area of multinational cross-cultural management, they range from the leadership task of formulating enterprisewide vision statements to the management tasks involved in translating strategic visions into day-to-day operating realities throughout a company. Figure 2-1 gave a breakdown of these tasks.

Multinational cross-cultural management is a context-specific process; that is, it works from situations to solutions, as shown in the outline of the process in Figure 13-1. This process is an application of the basic, almost generic, entrepreneurial contingency focus of this book (outlined in Figure 3-3). This process is, based on extensive experience and research, a worldwide common framework in business, which is why it has been a core concept throughout the discussions in this book.

While for discussion purposes, multinational cross-cultural management has been broken into task segments (Table 2-1 and Figure 2-1) and depicted as a linear process (Figures 2-1 and 13-1), in practice it is not always segmented into discrete tasks, nor is it linear in execution. Rather, it is an integrative process, which is iterative and continuing, more like the process shown in Figure 2-2.

This chapter discusses several additional specific and overall perspectives on the integrative aspects of multinational cross-cultural management.

A central aspect of multinational management is *managing change*. In addition to briefly reviewing the earlier discussions of change management, this section discusses a key change situation of worldwide interest today—privatization.

Managing change and diversity in a rapidly changing environment often requires skills in *crisis management, improvisation* and *innovation*—three aspects of multinational management. These are discussed in the second and third sections of this chapter. Ways in which small companies can compete with larger firms in the multinational market are discussed next.

Ultimately, multinational cross-cultural management requires a *long-term future orientation*, which is discussed the following section. The chapter concludes with a summary discussion of the overall contingency processes involved in multinational management, which, in essence, involves *managing diversity within general, integrative, common concepts and frameworks.*

## MANAGING CHANGE

This section first briefly reviews some of the perspectives on managing covered so far in this book. It also focuses on a key change occurring now in the global environment with great frequency—privatization.

### Perspectives on the Management of Multinational Change

Many aspects of managing change have been covered in this book, including:

- becoming a multinational company
- meeting changing multinational competitive market needs
- assuring an enterprise's long-term global future prosperity

Chapters 1 through 6 described many experiences of companies wrestling with the management of change:

- Ford Motor's Alex Trotman's bet on a global car and reorganization of Ford in the shape of his global vision, in sharp contrast to the vision of General Motors.
- Hewlett-Packard's and Intel's long-term visions of networks.
- a wide range of companies meeting the needs of planning and new market entries, product modifications to meet local needs, shifting supply sources to meet changing trade patterns, and the like.

Chapter 7 describes management moves made to meet the growing opportunities and threats arising from advances in telecommunications and computer information-systems technology worldwide. Chapter 8 covers enabling finance and accounting systems that are useful in meeting the challenges of change worldwide. Chapter 9 describes the experiences of companies such as France's Alcatel Alsthom, which used an accelerated approach in managing the organization changes needed to meet changing market needs. Chapters 10 through 13 describe further examples of change management, especially those

Figure 13-1
The Overall Multinational Operations Approach to Making Strategic Management Decisions

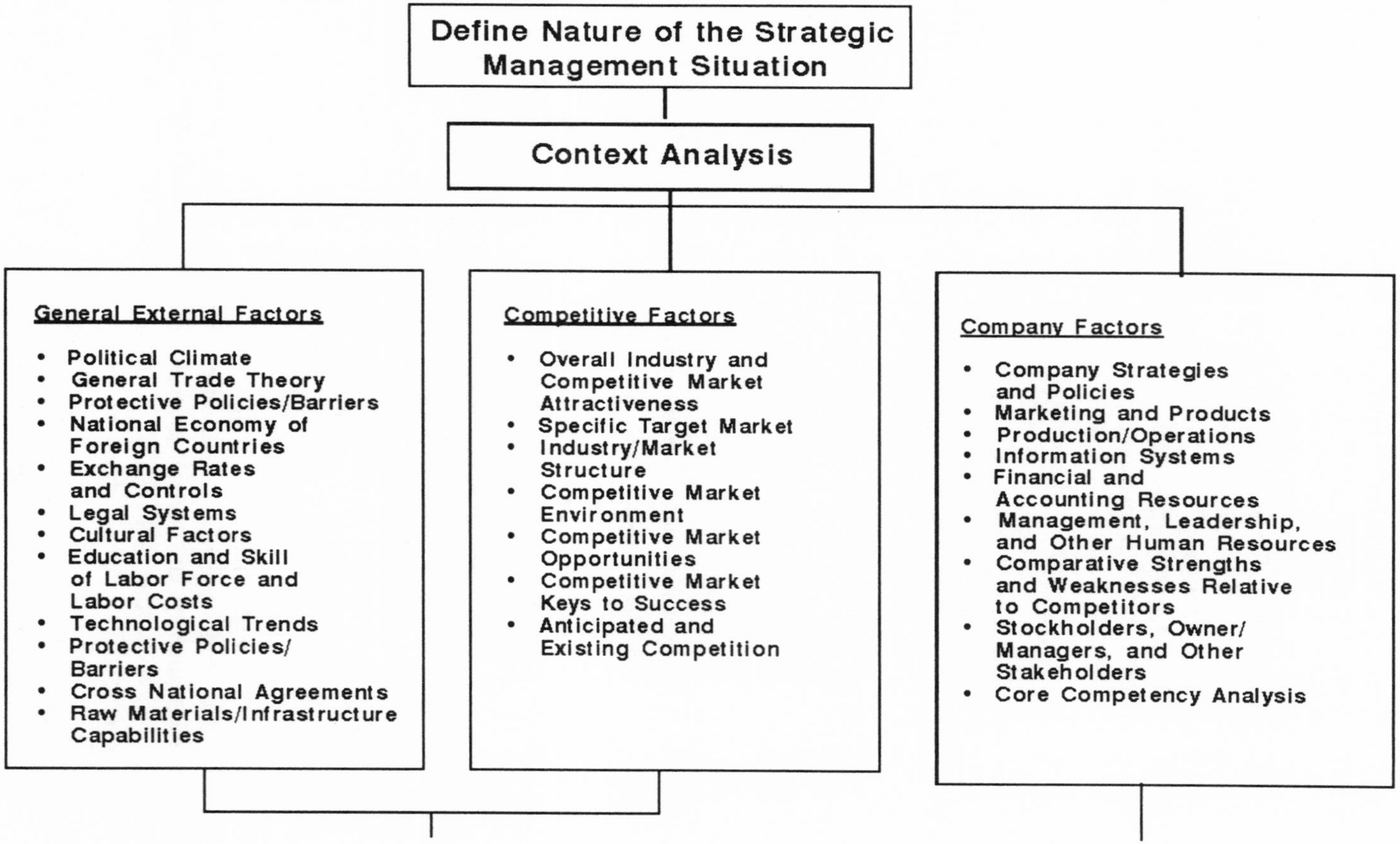

**Define Nature of the Strategic Management Situation**

**Context Analysis**

**Company Factors**

- Company Strategies and Policies
- Marketing and Products
- Production/Operations
- Information Systems
- Financial and Accounting Resources
- Management, Leadership, and Other Human Resources
- Comparative Strengths and Weaknesses Relative to Competitors
- Stockholders, Owner/Managers, and Other Stakeholders
- Core Competency Analysis

**Competitive Factors**

- Overall Industry and Competitive Market Attractiveness
- Specific Target Market Industry/Market Structure
- Competitive Market Environment
- Competitive Market Opportunities
- Competitive Market Keys to Success
- Anticipated and Existing Competition

**General External Factors**

- Political Climate
- General Trade Theory
- Protective Policies/Barriers
- National Economy of Foreign Countries
- Exchange Rates and Controls
- Legal Systems
- Cultural Factors
- Education and Skill of Labor Force and Labor Costs
- Technological Trends
- Protective Policies/Barriers
- Cross National Agreements
- Raw Materials/Infrastructure Capabilities

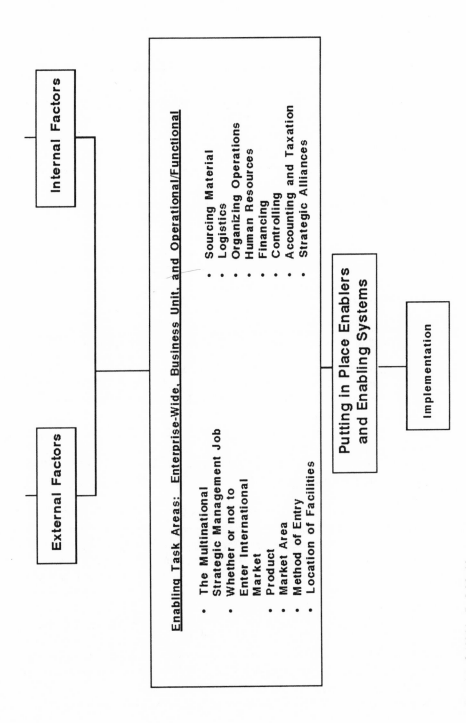

External Factors

Internal Factors

Enabling Task Areas: Enterprise-Wide, Business Unit, and Operational/Functional

- The Multinational
  Strategic Management Job
- Whether or not to
  Enter International
  Market
- Product
- Market Area
- Method of Entry
- Location of Facilities

- Sourcing Material
- Logistics
- Organizing Operations
- Human Resources
- Financing
- Controlling
- Accounting and Taxation
- Strategic Alliances

Putting in Place Enablers
and Enabling Systems

Implementation

Copyright © 1996 by R. J. Mockler.

285

involved in working within the diverse needs of different cultures. These included:

- General Electric in Hungary—changing work habits built up over years under communism,
- Coca-Cola in Eastern Europe and Ben & Jerry's in Russia—creating new marketing infrastructures and alliances that enabled them to successfully compete there,
- Motorola in Malaysia—trying to introduce new work structures that would enable realizing a new vision by the year 2000,
- Tellabs in Germany—opening a new operation using culturally appropriate recruiting approaches, and
- Whirlpool in Europe and the United States—using team management to make new mergers work.

Going beyond, and adding a new perspective to, these discussions of change management, the following section describes two experiences in privatization—a major international change management situation encountered throughout the global community.

### Privatization: A Rising Tide of Change in the Global Market

This section describes two contrasting approaches to change management (both initiated in 1989), one in Argentina, through privatization of a state-owned oil company, and one in Mexico through modernization at a state-owned oil company (Solis and Friedland 1995).

In Argentina, Yacimientos Petroliferos Fiscates SA (YPF) was a vast wasteland of patronage while it was wholly owned by the state. In 1995, however, two years after a large segment of the company was sold to the public, YPF's workforce was one-tenth of the former size and the company was a gusher of profits.

Several factors contributed to the firm's success. By the early 1990s the government had deregulated the energy sector (freeing up pricing and domestic oil trading) and the economy as a whole (for example, exploration properties were thrown open to the highest bidder). At the same time, privatization moves by the government allowed the company to sell non-core assets and use the proceeds to boost efficiency while placing it under competitive pressures. The government also quashed inflation.

A charismatic manager, Jose Estenssoro, was appointed. He first brought in a team of U.S. executives from Hughes Tool Co. He renegotiated contracts with independent Argentine producers and consumers that had invariably worked to YPF's disadvantage. He sold off one-third of YPF's oil and gas properties in 1993, raising $2 billion.

Several steps were taken to cut the workforce. First, several union leaders were given control of YPF's sizable shipping fleet. Other nonessential businesses—an air fleet, hospitals, supermarkets and movie theaters—were sold to other managers and employees on favorable terms. Finally, tens of thousands of workers were laid off with generous severance pay or one-year contracts. Remaining employees were promised 10 percent of YPF's equity to ensure that they would remain motivated. Since the company had been used for patronage and its refineries were environmental disasters, it was not difficult to explain to the public why a privatized, professionally managed company would be best in the long run for customers, suppliers, most employees and the country.

In June 1993, after the turnaround was well underway, 45 percent of the government's stake was sold to the public for $2.5 billion, which was used to repay government debts. Estenssoro used the $2 billion from asset sales and cost savings to modernize YPF's facilities and boost its long-neglected exploration and development program.

In contrast, in Mexico, where Petroleos Mexicanos SA (Pemex) remained owned by the government in 1995, oil reserves were actually declining because the company lacked the money needed to find new ones, and imports of natural gas were increasing, even though Mexico's underdeveloped reserves were among the biggest in the world. Ironically, all of this occurred five years into a program to modernize the company's operations.

In contrast to the way workers' unions were handled in Argentina, in 1989 Mexico's President Carlos Salinas de Gortari sent in troops to arrest the union's head on weapons charges; in 1995, the union leader was still in jail. This government show of force inaugurated the modernization program. Some progress has been made: the workforce has been cut in half, and Pemex planned to sell off some of its petrochemical properties for an anticipated $1 billion (Dillon 1995). Some private foreign investors have been allowed to build natural-gas pipelines. Mexico, however, has maintained a nationalist energy policy, heavy with regulation and skittish about foreign capital. Moreover, in Mexico, there is still considerable antiforeign sentiment, especially toward Americans.

The overall results of the modernization program at the state-owned Pemex have not matched results of privately-owned YPF in Argentina. Revenue per worker at Pemex is under $250,000 per year, about one-third that at YPF and far below the industry standard. Pemex still ran 21 hospitals, 21 clinics, 41 pharmacies, 100 medical offices, and even several elementary schools—services normally run by the state. Moreover, problems of inefficiency, poor maintenance, and ecological contamination persisted, as evidenced by protests and by accidents that have killed hundreds. While the profits are high ($10.8 billion in 1994), most of that goes to the government (close to 90 percent), leaving little for investment in the company. As a result of lack of capital for exploration, in 1994 Pemex reported a 3 percent drop in proven oil reserves, to 43.1 billion barrels. Exports dropped 2.2 percent to 1.3 million barrels daily (Solis and Friedman 1995).

As these two approaches to privatization in different situations indicate, in multinational businesses such change is managed in a wide range of ways. The following sections discuss some additional company experiences involving the multinational cross-cultural management of change.

## MANAGING CRISES

Crises can be expected to occur at any time in a rapidly changing worldwide environment. They may be triggered by political events, such as the Mexican peso crisis in late 1994 or the breakup of the Soviet Union in 1991. Crises may be technology-related, as in Chernobyl in the Soviet Union in 1986, or they may arise from human error, unexpected major competitor moves, or planned management moves to create a changed environment within a company.

Change, therefore, does not always come upon an enterprise gradually; it is sometimes thrust upon it in the form of a crisis. Crises must be managed, proactively if possible, in order, first, to minimize damage and, second, if possible, to turn adversity into triumph. As described by Laurence Barton in *Crisis in Organizations: Managing and Communicating in the Heat of Chaos* (1993) crises in business come in many forms and can be handled in many ways.

For example, in January 1990, Perrier bottled water had wholesale revenues of $640 million in the United States. In February of that year, however, abnormal traces of benzene, a natural byproduct, were reportedly found in Perrier. The French-based company reacted quickly by voluntarily recalling 70 million bottles of its water. It eventually traced the problem to a faulty filtering process. After repairs, shipments of the products were resumed three months after the incident, and the reintroduced bottles were labeled "New Production."

Crises are not always operational, or as survivable as the crisis at Perrier. For example, they may be caused by terrorists, such as the bombing of a Pan American flight over Scotland in December 1988, which led to the eventual bankruptcy of the airline, or they may be caused by technology failures, such as the Union Carbide disaster at Bhophal, India, which killed over 2,000 people in 1984, and the nuclear power plant explosion in Chernobyl in the Soviet Union in 1986, which is estimated to have killed or injured several thousand people.

The lessons learned from crises are varied (Barton 1993):

*Why do some companies do better than others at containing crisis?* Some proactively prepare for crisis by writing crisis management plans and rehearsing their response to problems well in advance. Others react in a vacuum of information and fail to contain the crisis.

*Which aspects of management are most helpful in preparing for an inevitable crisis?* Understanding the importance of public opinion in the marketplace is a good beginning. Equally relevant are public-relations skills, understanding organizational behavior and developing a sense of social responsibility.

*How can you test the crisis skills you have developed on and off the job so they will be ready to be used at the company for which you work?* A large number of corporations, particularly multinational ones, use role-playing sce-

ductions can also increase a firm's overall creativity (Freedman 1988). For example, Sony has had a policy informally referred to as "eating your young," which encourages product developers to work on making obsolete existing products starting from the day a new product is introduced (Kodamo 1995).

Because of cultural differences, the concept of creativity and innovation can vary from culture to culture (Ishida 1994; Rickards and Moger 1994).

## SPECIAL MULTINATIONAL MANAGEMENT PROBLEMS OF SMALL COMPANIES

It is possible for even small companies to tap into global alliances and become part of international networks. Rosabeth Moss Kanter has identified three key areas that can affect success when introducing and running successful international operations: concepts (innovative ideas, services and products—the thinking side of management), competencies (ability to get things done—the producers), and connections (the ability to work with partnerships, alliances and networks) (Kanter 1995). While generally, these three task areas are focused on most often in large-company international ventures, small companies considering going international may also find such a perspective useful.

For example, Cohen & Wilks International (CWI), a British apparel manufacturer/supplier with around $30 million in sales, is an example of how new forms of partnerships in today's global community can be created and used by a small company to succeed. CWI management oversees the manufacture of 2 million garments annually in ten stitching factories spanning six countries in East Asia and the Middle East. Today it is half owned by Mitsui & Co, a multibillion-dollar Japanese trading company with 189 offices worldwide and interests in steel, machinery, chemical products, foodstuffs and petroleum.

Initially, Mitsui's role in CWI was largely administrative and financial, with occasional introductions, such as enhancing CWI's image by connecting it with an important design firm with which Mitsui had worked in Japan. It also initiated introductions that led CWI to switch nearly all its trouser-manufacturing operations to the United Arab Emirates.

CWI also prospered by maintaining a very high competency in production and by close on-site supervision of its contract-production connections. In addition, it established very close supportive ties with major customers, such as BHS, a large apparel retail chain (Kanter 1995).

Another small company studied by Kanter, Tech Ridge, specializes in manufacturing identification (ID) cameras and components. Tech Ridge prospered first by creating new innovative concepts in ID cameras that met world-class quality standards. It provided extra services and reliable and fast service, with turnaround for repairs in 24 hours (compared to weeks for competitors). It also prospered because it formed alliances with both suppliers and customers, especially Polaroid, which was located very close to Tech Ridge. Through these alliances, Tech Ridge began selling to Mexico and worked out other alliances

nario games as a crisis management tool. A hypothetical crisis is announced to a group of corporate executives, and for the next several hours, or longer, they are asked to react and manage the crisis. Throughout this scenario, new information is continually provided by the game organizers, along with realistic surprises and turns in events. Just weeks before Iraq invaded Kuwait in August 1990, for instance, managers at Shell Oil used such a tool to rehearse how their company would respond to a war in the Middle East.

*What do those managers who have managed a crisis, and can discuss their responses, have to say about the predicaments they faced?* They regret not having been exposed to crisis management when they were formally trained in management. Some crises help the careers of executives if their judgments and actions are proven correct. In many other cases, however, lessons in effective crisis management come much too late and can produce a national embarrassment.

*How can a manager train a team that can cope well enough with crisis to minimize damage to the organization's future?* Balance, in terms of background and professional skills, is a good beginning.

*Why is a crisis management plan (CMP) important? Why should students pursuing a business management degree, and managers in almost every field of endeavor, care about crisis management?* A single crisis can alter your career and life. A CMP lets you test how you will treat people inside and outside your organization during moments of intense stress. It will challenge you to consider issues and individuals with whom you have had little contact. One day it could prove to be the tool you use to save lives, protect assets, and retain or even enhance your company's image.

While there is no guarantee that the right answer will be found during training to actually guide action in response to an event in the future, preparation does enable managers to plan for, and practice responding to, such situations.

For example, at one company such preparation led to establishing guidelines for handling emergencies, one of which was that whenever a crisis occurs involving a major health risk—for example, a defective product—the objective is to take the initiative and try to have the company be the first to make a public announcement of the problem. At the same time, if possible, the announcement should contain information on how the company has taken care of the problem and its impact, or potential impact, on the public.

This guideline was based on lessons learned from Johnson & Johnson's handling of the Tylenol recall in 1982 following the deaths of seven people who took the product (several packages had been tampered with and contained poison). Swift action by the company and its public relations advisers established a principle for crisis management: by taking the offensive and addressing the concerns, real and imagined, of key audiences, a company is more likely to be viewed as a responsible and responsive citizen rather than a recalcitrant or indifferent monolith.

Plans cannot fully cover all contingencies. An innovative, entrepreneurial, situational management orientation is needed to respond on short notice to un-usual and unexpected accidents, distribution and delivery problems, environ-mental problems, customer-service problems, product defects, manufacturing breakdowns, political upheavals and other crises.

Going beyond managing the crises that occur, it is argued that at times man-agers are advised to deliberately create crises by committing acts of "ethical anarchy" in order to break the constraints of past successes and renew their organizations. David Hurst has argued that even successful organizations be-come systematically vulnerable to catastrophe. In one sense, then, creating crises is a major way to prepare for the ultimate catastrophe, long-term failure in the marketplace (Hurst 1995).

Young organizations are often dedicated to learning and innovation. Much like a young person, they are natural learning organizations. As they mature and grow, they change and focus on performance and eventually become limited by their own success, as self-selected roles become designated tasks, flexible teams change into rigid organization structures, open networks become closed systems, and control replaces personal commitment. Such a maturation can render or-ganizations incapable of responding to changes in the market. Renewal, Hurst (1995) suggests, can come from creating crises.

One of the best examples of a planned "crisis creation" effort designed to revive a major organization is Jack Welch's attempt to transform General Elec-tric (GE) after he was appointed CEO in 1981 (described in Chapter 12). One of his first steps was to create his own crisis by delayering the management hierarchy, reducing the corporate staff, and slashing 100,000 employees in order to focus on what he believed to be the core elements of the business. He then set about to release the organization's emotional energy and to capitalize crea-tively on the opportunities offered by changes in GE's environment. In a sense, Welch moved from crisis management to orderly change management combined with charismatic leadership, an ideal path in successful management in the mul-tinational environment. In 1995, GE was reportedly the largest (and third most profitable) publically held company in the world (Symonds, Bremmer, Toy, and Miller 1996).

## IMPROVISATION, SITUATED ACTION AND INNOVATION

Other useful concepts in change management and crisis management are *sit-uated action* and *improvisation*. Studies in these areas examine and suggest ways to handle problem situations that arise in business (Lave and Wenger 1991; Perry, Stott, and Smallwood 1993; Suchman 1987).

Chapters 5 and 6 discussed more rational and systematic contingency planning processes at work in multinational management. This is only one level of mul-tinational cross-cultural management, and is sometimes considered a cultural phenomenon of so-called Western rational planning (Lave and Wenger 1991; Suchman 1987).

Management also involves another, more intuitive kind of con cess, which is less easily explained or mastered. Lucy Suchman an analogy with primitive navigators who sailed the seas in a purp to get to a specific destination—but were guided by their ability t the changing conditions encountered, based on experience or cor not guided by charts or planned itineraries.

Similarly, while plans and coordinated efforts underlie most ente ities, success can also depend on the ability of managers to take ac the context of particular, concrete circumstances—these are callec *situated* actions—where more than one alternative solution is avail national cultural management actions must often be improvisationa vative.

For example, Gillette's experiences at the inauguration of a ne Poland (described in the Chapter 1) demonstrated how planned crea manship and timing, plus entrepreneurial thinking and action, di achieved business goals effectively in crossing cultural boundaries (Ze Clearly, a combination of purposeful or planned action and innovativ neurial responsiveness to market situation needs has helped Gillette i tinational operations.

Such experiences explain in part why it is necessary to have entre skills when running multinational businesses—due to rapidly changin itive markets and a wide range of unusual incidents and happening cannot always be anticipated. Such skills are necessary to be responsiv needs, whether they be redesigning products for a Muslim country, int change at a Polish factory, negotiating a contract in Japan, or openin plant in China.

The ability to improvise and innovate can be improved by developing *ing organization*, that is, an organization that is flexible and adaptable able to learn and change as situation requirements change. Such an orga is described by Peter Senge in his book *The Fifth Discipline* (199( Welch's changes at General Electric created a learning organization the

Many other aspects of the learning organization have been discussed book. For example, teams are designed to enable an organization to lea so to change and grow with a changing environment. Leadership that de decision making and learns to listen can help create an adaptable, flexible ing organization. Staffing and training can also do this, as was seen experiences of Gillette in developing its group of 350 experienced exp managers.

Specific steps can also be taken to foster and stimulate innovation, wl the lifeblood of corporations today, especially in the area of technology. can involve encouraging individual creativity, not only through leadershi tiatives (Getz and Drozdeck 1994), but also through training (McGartland 1 Putting in place business processes and other organization enablers that stim and guide innovations through to successful cost reductions or product i

with Kodak (Dominican Republic) and IBM (also Mexico), as well as in Europe (Kanter 1995).

Kanter cites these and many other local companies and communities that have prospered by thinking and acting globally.


## MANAGING THE LONG-TERM FUTURE

It has been said that the best measure of a company's potential for success is not what it has accomplished, but how well it manages to continually improve its *prospects* for the future. Managing change, therefore, necessarily also involves planning for the long-term future.

Earlier chapters described the longer-term strategic visions of a number of companies, such as IBM, Intel, and Hewlett-Packard. Microsoft Corp. has a similar long-term vision, which is tied to global networks and a wide range of individualized utilities and appliances that will enable people to use these networks.

In an effort to manage the realization of that vision, Microsoft CEO Bill Gates used a variety of techniques (Clark and Rigdon 1995). For example, he wrote the following memo to his upper-level managers in late 1995, (entitled "The Internet Tidal Wave"):

Now I assign the Internet the highest level of importance. In this memo I want to make clear that our focus on the Internet is critical to every part of our business. The Internet is the most important single development to come along since the IBM PC was introduced in 1981. (quoted in Clark and Rigdon 1995, p. B7)

The memo went on to argue that all Microsoft products must be modified to exploit the broader Net or else face obsolescence. This is essentially a first, small step to realize the emerging vision of networks embraced by major computer companies, a vision that is responding to technological change and increased competitiveness.

The process continued in 1996 when Gates announced that he was reorganizing Microsoft by creating a division to develop Internet applications and other new advanced technologies (Markoff 1996) and intended to take the lead in developing Internet applications ("Gates Gets on the Net" 1996).

Much of this new thinking and action was triggered by the introduction of the World Wide Web, the graphical portion of the Internet, which makes it easy for people to publish information and sell goods and services without middlemen (Lohr 1995). Because key specifications are openly available, many companies and individuals have developed programs for creating and reading Web pages on different kinds of computer systems. This trend will likely lead to the development of an array of Internet appliances, both computer and other kinds. This expectation was reinforced by a Nielsen survey in late 1995 indicating that in the United States and Canada alone, already 37 million people aged sixteen and older (17 percent of the population) had access to the Internet. Moreover, 24 million had used the Internet in the past three months and spent an average of 5 hours, 28 minutes, on the Internet per week. Of these users, 34 percent were women, 66 percent reached the Internet from work, and 25 percent of Worldwide Web users had incomes over $80,000 (Dibbell 1995).

## CONCLUSION: SYNERGISTICALLY MANAGING DIVERSITY WITHIN INTEGRATIVE COMMON FRAMEWORKS

A central focus of this book has been to show how cross-cultural diversity can be managed within common frameworks in multinational enterprises. Contrary to some views, while multinational businesses vigorously pursue global solutions, they also have an interest in encouraging and managing diversity. These and other diverse aspects of multinational cross-cultural management, as well as the common frameworks within which they should be integratively and synergistically balanced, are discussed in this concluding section.

### Managing and Encouraging Global Diversity: Managing Paradoxes

Multinational cross-cultural management is, at the core, paradoxical, since it requires dealing with seemingly contradictory factors. This is not unusual today, since we live in an age of paradox. Charles Handy, in *The Age of Paradox* (1994), wrote about this in general terms. For example, from a personal viewpoint, there are paradoxes of success since success in business often can cause family difficulties. There are social paradoxes involving the desire to preserve differences (such as ethnic or personal customs and values) while also promoting common causes and country goals. Handy's book provides ways to balance these general paradoxes, which parallel the processes involved in handling the cultural differences, or seeming contradictions in business, discussed in this book.

John Naisbitt, in his *Global Paradox* (1994), dealt in general terms with the specific contrary trends among countries and cultures. For example, there is the search for alliances, like the European Economic Union and its goal of a common currency (Nash 1995). At the same time, smaller ethnic segments, such as the Slovakians in the former Czechoslovakia, who broke with the Czech Republic to form a separate country, are seeking ways to assert and maintain their independent character in some way, in spite of the resulting economic hardships. This is only one instance of a global paradox.

In the same way, multinational cross-cultural management carries the burden of

- recognizing, balancing and preserving each culture's special interests and needs
- the need to integrate some aspects of these diverse elements into a single successful business enterprise

• the end goal of enabling the enterprise to operate in a way that achieves global efficiencies and the rapid transfer of new technology at the same time that it serves the
needs of diverse cultures, interests and markets.

While not necessarily true of all enterprises, substantial evidence exists that
corporate managers and leaders, and their multinational enterprises, are a major
social mechanism for both respecting and encouraging diversity. This is evident
from examining business self-interest. For example, it is as much to the advantage of a business to encourage diversity in markets, and so create market niches,
as it is for businesses to encourage global frameworks and concepts where useful
and appropriate. In this regard, books such as *When Corporations Rule the
World* (Korten 1995), which argue that global trends in international business
are harmful to society, miss this key point about multinational businesses.

While multinational businesses are interested in global efficiencies, it is also
in their interest to maintain a balance and to selectively encourage and manage
diversity. It is in their self-interest, not only in order to create market niches,
but also because businesses and their products and services need to be different
in order to win in a competitive market. Survival of a business depends on
differentiation—that is, having a brand or product or service that is distinctive,
from that of competitors. If such differences and diversity did not exist, businesses would have to create them. Such a key paradox (being locally different
and globally efficient at the same time) is central to the theme of this book.

The concept of seeming contradictions is essential to understanding effective
multinational management. What at first may appear to be a contradiction, can
from the perspective of common frameworks, combined with integrative management skills, go beyond reconciling differences. If done well, it can produce
dynamic, synergistic benefits and yield significant competitive advantages.

### Managing Diverse, and Often Paradoxical, Factors within Common Frameworks: A Continuing Integrative Process

Many major integrative common contexts or frameworks at work in multinational cross-cultural management have been discussed in this book:

• contingency cognitive and behavioral frameworks
• strategic visions of each company
• global products and services
• telecommunications and information systems
• the organization and its culture—the company itself
• accounting and finance systems
• other human resource management approaches

This book focuses on these common frameworks, which make moving across cultural and national boundaries easier. Central to multinational management is managing cultural diversity across and within national borders in a balanced, integrative way. Many aspects of this synergistic, interactive balancing of diverse paradoxical elements—a process through which the total can equal more than the sum of the individual parts—have been discussed.

The book began by discussing common frameworks for diversity management, especially contingency management processes. These were discussed in terms of planning, enabling action, and management throughout business enterprises. Chapters 5 and 6 gave examples of how planning decision processes make use of common contingency processes to synergistically reconcile and balance different cultural and other situation factors in both enterprisewide and operational-level situations, and at the same time to promote the use of global products and services. Examples of these contingency cognitive processes are given in Table 2-1 and Figures 2-1, 2-2, 3-3, and 13-1.

As an example, the international affiliate of a pharmaceutical multinational company described in Chapter 6 used a well-defined contingency decision process to reconcile and balance different cultural and other situation factors when trying to decide how to introduce a new, differentiated product into Venezuela. This decision framework is shown in Figure 4-2 and discussed in Chapter 6. It is an extension and application of the basic underlying entrepreneurial contingency process outlined in Figure 3-3. Additional integrative planning decision frameworks and decisions are identified and defined in Chapters 5 and 6.

Gillette's computer system, which calculates the most efficient use of diverse production sources to make the Atra razor, is an example of another common enabling framework (discussed in Chapter 7) drawn from the computer information system area. Such common frameworks have proved useful in integratively managing diverse situation factors across cultures and national borders. The Gillette experience is another good example of how the synergy generated through integrative common frameworks can lead to the total solution being greater than the simple sum of all the parts.

Chapter 8 discussed how global finance, accounting and control systems and standards have been (and are still being) developed and used to help businesses function more easily across diverse cultural boundaries. While preserving the integrity of different individual currencies, for example, computer systems enable on-line individual transactions, which move money back and forth among different currencies. The control function was also shown to be a major integrative force within a company.

Chapter 9 discussed how organizations and their processes and cultures culture can also enable a more balanced management of diverse cultural forces. This was the purpose of Ford Motor Company's reorganization. The collaborative infrastructures (especially the human systems) within the proposed new organization structure—especially cross-cultural teams—were expected to be particularly useful in achieving the synergistic balance on a day-to-day basis and in stimulating the rapid transfer of knowledge. Chapter 9 presented another common contingency framework that is useful in the implementation of strategies and strategic plans (shown in Figure 9-2). It is also an extension and application of the underlying entrepreneurial process shown in Figure 3-3.

Success also depends on being able to creatively and innovatively deal with many situations on an ad hoc basis (as discussed in Chapters 10 through 13). It especially depends on interpersonal interaction, communication, staffing and training, leadership and management action. For example, Gillette hired and trained a group of 350 managers over a twenty-year period to effectively manage diversity in the field on a daily basis and within the framework of global efficiencies. This is an example of the balancing that must occur daily throughout the worldwide Gillette organization. It is enabled through a well-developed, systematic, synergistic worldwide staffing and training program (itself a common framework).

Based on the experiences of the many companies studied and described in this book, common frameworks are clearly a major means of reconciling local multinational differences and still achieving global efficiencies thus resolving the essential, continuing paradox in multinational cross-cultural management.

The management process described in this book is consistently context driven. It is a common contingency process: identify situation requirements, identify differences and commonalities, search for underlying reasons, and then build appropriate global, and locally responsive, hybrid solutions. This entrepreneurial process is deeply imbedded in all cultures, though not necessarily within every person. At the core, it is a human survival process, and so it provides a natural path into bridging cultures and managing cross-culturally.

Even in situations involving ad hoc interpersonal interaction, some common behavioral frameworks can be identified, for example, the search for understanding and managing cultural diversity within ourselves and our own origins as a starting or reference point, and the processes involved in finding the appropriate balance between adapting to, and asserting, differences during one-on-one exchanges.

Ultimately, no book can fully articulate the most important skill needed: the individual ability to find appropriate solutions on a minute-to-minute, day-by-day basis—to find just the right balance among the specific (and almost always unique in some aspect) factors faced in each situation. Finding that balance depends on both individual skill and, at times, luck.

Since reconciliation of, and respect for, diversity ultimately needs to be done daily on the job, multinational cross-cultural management is a very demanding task which can lead to early burnout for managers. This can be avoided.

In all diversity management situations, the key seems to rest with the individual manager understanding that balancing seemingly different or conflicting elements in a situation is a continuing process, in business as it is in life. It is not something that is done once and for all. It never seems to stop. There always seem to be new problem situations that need solving. The key, then, is both to become good at the work and to enjoy it. It can be fun to be the instrument of creating unity out of diversity, while still preserving diversity. If this core aspect of multinational cross-cultural management is not rewarding and fun for you then you had better get into another life pursuit.

## WORKS CITED

Barton, Laurence. *Crisis in Organization: Managing and Communicating in the Heat of Chaos.* Cincinnati: South-Western Publishing Company, 1993.
Clark, Don, and Joan E. Rigdon. ''Stripped-Down PCs Will Be Talk of Comdex.'' *Wall Street Journal,* November 10, 1995, pp. B1, B7.
Dibbell, Julian. ''Nielsen Rates the Net.'' *Time,* November 13, 1995, p. 121.
Dillon, Sam. ''Mexico's Lifeblood on the Auction Block: Workers Call the Selloff of Parts of Oil Monopoly Almost Unpatriotic.'' *New York Times,* November 4, 1995, pp. 37, 38.
Freedman, George. *The Pursuit of Innovation: Managing the People and Processes That Turn New Ideas into Profit.* New York: American Management Association, 1988.
''Gates Gets on the Net: Bill Gates Says Microsoft Is Dead Set on Taking the Lead in Exploiting the Internet [Interview].'' *InfoWorld,* March 18, 1996, pp. 1, 24.
Getz, Karl F., and Steven R. Drozdeck. *Empowering Innovative People: How Smart Managers Challenge and Channel Their Creative Employees.* Chicago: Probus Publishing, 1994.
Handy, Charles. *The Age of Paradox.* Boston: Harvard Business School Press, 1994.
Hurst, David. *Crisis and Renewal: Meeting the Challenge of Organizational Change.* Boston: Harvard Business School Press, 1995.
Ishida, Hiromi. ''Japanese and European Experiences of Creativity Compared: A Personal Case Study.'' *Creativity and Innovation Management,* December 1994, pp. 233–239.
Kanter, Rosabeth Moss. *World Class: Thriving Locally in a Global Economy.* New York: Simon and Schuster, 1995.
Kodamo, Fumio. *Emerging Patterns of Innovation.* Boston: Harvard Business School Press, 1995.
Korten, David C. *When Corporations Rule the World.* San Francisco: Berrett-Koehler Publishers, 1995.
Lave, Jean, and Etienne Wenger. *Situated Learning.* New York: Cambridge University Press, 1991.
Lohr, Steve. ''His Goal: Keeping the Web Worldwide.'' *New York Times,* December 18, 1995, pp. D1, D4.
Markoff, John. ''Microsoft Sets a Revamping to Gain Edge on Internet.'' *New York Times,* February 20, 1996, pp. D1, D7.
McGartland, Grace. *Thunderbolt Thinking: Transform Your Insights and Options Into Powerful Business Results.* Austin, TX: Bernard-Davis, 1994.
Nash, Nathaniel C. ''Europeans Agree on New Currency.'' *New York Times,* December 16, 1995, pp. 1, 49.
Naisbitt, John. *Global Paradox.* London: Nicholas Brealey Publishing, 1994.
Perry, Lee Tom, Randall G. Stott, and W. Norman Smallwood. *Real-Time Strategy:*

*Improvising Team-Based Planning for a Fast-Changing World*. New York: Wiley, 1993.

Rickards, Tudor, and Susan Moger, eds. *Creativity and Innovative Management* [Special issue on creativity variations in different cultures] (December 1994).

Senge, Peter. *The Fifth Discipline: The Art and Practice of the Learning Organization*. New York: Doubleday/Currency, 1990.

Solis, Dianne, and Jonathan Friedland. "A Tale of Two Countries: Argentina and Mexico Both Set Out to Modernize Their State-Owned Oil Companies; Only One Succeeded." *Wall Street Journal*, October 2, 1995, World Business Section, pp. R19, R23.

Suchman, Lucy. *Plans and Situated Action*. New York: Cambridge University Press, 1987. Reprint. New York: Wiley, 1987.

Symonds, William C., Brian Bremmer, Stewart Toy, and Karen Lowry Miller. "The Globetrotters Take Over: Worldwide Champions Outpace Domestic Competitors." *Business Week*, July 8, 1996, pp. 46–48.

Zeien, Albert. "Gillette's Global Marketing Experiences." Talk given at St. John's University's Annual Colman Mockler Leadership Award Ceremony, New York, February 27, 1995.

# Selected Bibliography

Abraham, Jeffrey. *The Mission Statement Book*. Oakland, CA: Ten Speed Press, 1995.

Akwule, Raymond. *Global Telecommunications: The Technology, Administration, and Policies*. Stoneham, MA: Butterworth-Heinemann, 1992.

Amelio, Gil, and William Simon. *Profit from Experience*. New York: Van Nostrand Reinhold, 1996.

Aslund, Anders. *How Russia Became a Market Economy*. Washington, DC: Brookings Institution, 1995.

Bartlett, Christopher A., and Sumantra Ghoshal. *Managing across Borders: The Transnational Solution*. Boston: Harvard Business School Press, 1991.

Barton, Laurence. *Crisis in Organization: Managing and Communicating in the Heat of Chaos*. Cincinnati: South-Western Publishing Company, 1993.

Brealey, Richard A., Stewart C. Meyers, and Alan J. Marcus. *Fundamentals of Corporate Finance*. New York: McGraw-Hill, 1995

Choi, Frederick D. S., and Gerhard G. Mueller. *International Accounting*. 2nd ed. Englewood Cliffs, NJ: Prentice-Hall, 1992.

Covey, Stephen R. *Principle-Centered Leadership*. New York: Simon and Schuster/Fireside, 1991.

Cox, Taylor. *Cultural Diversity in Organization Theory, Research, and Practice*. San Francisco: Barrett-Koehler Publishers, 1993.

Dewey, John. *Logic: The Structure of Inquiry*. New York: Putnam, 1938.

Dologite, Dorothy G., and Robert J. Mockler. *An Information Systems Plan (Strategic and Operational) for the Malaysian Agricultural Research and Development Institute (MARDI)*. Kuala Lumpur, Malaysia: MARDI, 1993.

Ehrenreich, Barbara. Review of Alvin Toffler and Heidi Toffler, *Creating a New Civilization* (Atlanta, GA: Turner Publishing, 1995). *New York Times*, May 7, 1995, Book Review Section, p. 9.

Eiteman, David K., Arthur I. Stonehill, and Michael H. Moffett. *Multinational Business Finance*. 7th ed. Reading, MA: Addison-Wesley, 1995.

Elashmawi, Fadrid, and Philip R. Harris. *Multinational Management: New Skills for Global Success*. Houston: Gulf Publishing Company, 1993.

Eng, Maximo V., Francis Lees, and Lawrence J. Mauer. *Global Finance*. New York: Harper-Collins College Publishers, 1995.

Engholm, Christopher. *When Business East Meets Business West*. New York: Wiley, 1991.

Evans, James R. *Creative Thinking: In the Decisions and Management Sciences*. Cincinnati: South-Western Publishing, 1991.

Fallows, James. *Looking at the Sun: The Rise of the New East Asian Economic and Political System*. New York: Pantheon Books, 1994.

Fatehi, Kamal. *International Management*. Upper Saddle River, NJ: Prentice-Hall, 1996.

Fiedler, Fred E. *A Theory of Leadership Effectiveness*. New York: McGraw-Hill, 1967.

Forester, Jay. "A New Corporate Design." *Sloan Management Review*, Fall 1965, pp 94–112.

Foster, Dean Allen. *Bargaining across Borders: How to Negotiate Business Successfully Anywhere in the World*. New York: McGraw-Hill, 1995.

Freedman, George. *The Pursuit of Innovation: Managing the People and Processes That Turn New Ideas into Profit*. New York: American Management Association, 1988.

Galbraith, Jay R. *Designing Organizations*. San Francisco: Jossey-Bass, 1995.

Gates, Bill. *The Road Ahead*. New York: Viking/Penguin Books USA, 1995.

Gates, Stephen. *The Changing Global Role of the Finance Function*. New York: Conference Board, 1994.

Getz, Karl F., and Steven R. Drozdeck. *Empowering Innovative People: How Smart Managers Challenge and Channel Their Creative Employees*. Chicago: Probus Publishing, 1994.

Goold, Michael, Andrew Campbell, and Marcus Alexander. *Corporate Level Strategy*. New York: Wiley, 1994.

Gray, Sidney J. *International Financial and Accounting Reporting*. New York: McGraw-Hill, 1995.

Griffin, Ricky W., and Michael W. Pustay. *International Business*. Reading, MA: Addison-Wesley, 1996.

Hagstrom, Robert G. *The Warren Buffett Way*. New York: John Wiley and Sons, 1994.

Hamel, Gary, and C. K. Prahalad. *Competing for the Future: Breakthrough Strategies for Seizing Control of Your Industry and Creating the Markets of Tomorrow*. Boston: Harvard Business School Press, 1994.

Handy, Charles. *The Age of Paradox*. Boston: Harvard Business School Press, 1994.

Helgesen, Sally. *The Web of Inclusion: A New Architecture for Building a Great Organization*. New York: Doubleday/Currency, 1995.

Heller, Robert. *The Leadership Imperative: What Innovative Business Leaders Are Doing Today to Create the Successful Companies of Tomorrow*. New York: Dutton/Truman Talley Books, 1995.

Hofstede, Geert. *Culture's Consequences: International Differences in Work-Related Values*. Beverly Hills, CA: Sage Publications, 1984.

House, Robert J., Paul Hanges, and Michael Angar. *A Multi-Nation Study of Cultures, Leadership and Organizational Practices*. Vol. 1, *Prospectus*. Vol. 2, *Status Report*. Philadelphia: The University of Pennsylvania Press, 1993–94.

Hurst, David K. *Crisis and Renewal: Meeting the Challenge of Organizational Change*. Boston: Harvard Business School Press, 1995.

Kanter, Rosabeth Moss. *When Giants Learn to Dance*. New York: Simon and Schuster, 1989.

Katzenback, Jon R., and Douglas K. Smith. *The Wisdom of Teams: Creating the High-Performance Organization*. Boston: Harvard Business School Press, 1993.

Kerr, Steven, and David Ulrick. *The Boundaryless Organization: Breaking the Chains of Organization Structure*. San Francisco: Jossey-Bass, 1995.

Kodamo, Fumio. *Emerging Patterns of Innovation*. Boston: Harvard Business School Press, 1995.

Korten, David C. *When Corporations Rule the World*. San Francisco: Berrett-Koehler Publishers, 1995.

Kouzes, James M., and Barry Z. Posner. *The Leadership Challenge: How to Keep Getting Extraordinary Things Done in Organizations*. San Francisco: Jossey-Bass, 1995.

Krugman, Paul R., and Maurice Obstfeld. *International Economics*. New York: Harper-Collins, 1994.

Lave, Jean, and Etienne Wenger. *Situated Learning*. New York: Cambridge University Press, 1991.

Lewis, Jordan D. *Crafting Strategic Alliances: Corporate Partnerships for Growth and Profit*. New York: Free Press, 1990.

Lewis, Michael. *Pacific Rift: Why Americans and Japanese Don't Understand Each Other*. New York: W. W. Norton, 1993.

Loden, Marilyn. *Implementing Diversity*. Chicago: Irwin/Professional Publishing, 1996.

Lundy, James L. *Teams: Together Each Achieves More Success*, Chicago: Dartnell, 1994.

Maddux, Robert B. *Team Building: An Exercise in Leadership*. Menlo Park, CA: Crisp Publications, 1994.

Madura, Jeff. *International Financial Management*. St. Paul, MN: West Publishing Company, 1995.

Marquardt, Michael, and Angus Reynolds. *The Global Learning Organization: Gaining Competitive Advantage through Continuous Learning*. Burr Ridge, IL: Irwin Professional Publishing, 1994.

Marshall, Edward W. *Transforming the Way We Work: The Power of the Collaborative Workplace*. New York: Amacom, 1995.

Maucher, Helmut. *Leadership in Action*. New York: McGraw-Hill, 1994.

McDaniel, George, ed. *IBM Dictionary of Computing*. 10th ed. New York: McGraw-Hill, 1994.

McIntosh-Fletcher, Donna. *Teaming by Design: Real Teams for Real People*. Chicago, IL: Irwin Professional Publishing, 1996.

McNair, C. J. *World Class Accounting and Finance*. Homewood, IL: Business One Irwin, 1993.

Mitroff, Ian I., and Harold Linstone. *The Unbounded Mind: Breaking the Chains of Traditional Business Thinking*. New York: Oxford University Press, 1993.

Mockler, Robert J. *Knowledge-Based Systems for Strategic Planning*. Englewood Cliffs, NJ: Prentice-Hall, 1989.

———. *Computer Software to Support Strategic Management Decision Making*. New York: Macmillan, 1992.

———. *Strategic Management: An Integrative Context-Specific Process*. Harrisburg, PA: Idea Group Publishing, 1993.

Mohrman, Susan Albers, Susan G. Cohen, and Allan M. Mohrman, Jr. *Designing Team-Based Organizations*. San Francisco: Jossey-Bass, 1995.

Mueller, Gerhard G., Helen Gernon, and Gary K. Meek. *Accounting: An International Perspective.* 3rd ed. Burr Ridge, IL: Irwin, 1994.

Murray-Bethel, Sheila. *Making a Difference: Twelve Qualities That Make You a Leader.* New York: G. P. Putnam and Sons, 1990.

Myers, Scott A., and Carole A. Barbato. *The Team Trainer: Winning Tools and Tactics for Successful Workouts.* Chicago, IL: Irwin Professional Publishing, 1996.

Naisbitt, John. *Global Paradox.* London: Nicholas Brealey Publishing, 1994.

Needles, Belverd. *Financial Accounting.* Boston: Arthur Andersen and Co. Alumni, 1995.

Nolan, Richard, and David C. Croson. *Creative Destruction: A Six Stage Process for Transforming Organizations.* Boston: Harvard Business School Press, 1995.

Odenwald, Silvia B. *Global Solutions for Teams: Moving from Collision to Collaboration.* Chicago, IL: Irwin Professional Publishing, 1996.

O'Hara-Devereaux, Mary, and Robert Johansen. *GlobalWork: Bridging Distance, Culture and Time.* San Francisco: Jossey-Bass, 1994.

Olmstead, Barney. *Creating a Flexible Workplace.* New York: Amacom, 1995.

Overholt, William H. *The Rise of China: How Economic Reform Is Creating a New Superpower.* Boston: Norton, 1995.

Perry, Lee Tom, Randall G. Stott, and W. Norman Smallwood. *Real-Time Strategy: Improvising Team-Based Planning for a Fast-Changing World.* New York: Wiley, 1993.

Pine, J. Joseph, II. *Mass Customization: The New Frontier in Business Competition.* Boston: Harvard University Press, 1993.

Porter, Michael. *Competitive Strategy.* New York: Free Press, 1980.

————. *The Competitive Advantage of Nations.* New York: Free Press, 1990.

Price Waterhouse Change Integration Team. *The Paradox Principles: How High-Performance Companies Manage Chaos, Complexity, and Contradiction to Achieve Superior Results.* Chicago, IL: Irwin Professional Publishing, 1996.

Rickards, Tudor, and Susan Moger, eds. *Creativity and Innovative Management* [Special issue on variations in creativity in different cultures] (December 1994).

Robbins, Harvey, and Michael Finley. *Why Teams Don't Work, What Went Wrong, and How to Make It Right.* Midland Parks, NJ: Pacesetter Books, 1995.

Rose, Peter S. *Money and Capital Markets.* 5th ed. Homewood, IL: Irwin, 1994.

Rowe, Alan J., and Richard O. Mason. *Managing with Style.* San Francisco: Jossey-Bass, 1987.

Senge, Peter. *The Fifth Discipline: The Art and Practice of the Learning Organization.* New York: Doubleday Currency, 1990.

Shim, Jae K., and Joel G. Siegel. *Encyclopedic Dictionary of Accounting and Finance.* Englewood Cliffs, NJ: Prentice-Hall, 1989.

————. *Barron's Accounting Handbook.* Happauge, NY: Barron's Educational Series, 1990.

Simons, Robert. *Levers of Control: How Managers Use Innovative Control Systems to Drive Strategic Renewal.* Boston: Harvard Business School Press, 1995.

Springate, David J. *Ampak International, Ltd.* Rev. ed. Dallas: University of Texas at Dallas, 1990.

Suchman, Lucy A. *Plans and Situated Actions.* New York: Cambridge University Press, 1987. Reprint. New York: Wiley, 1993.

Symonds, William C., Brian Bremmer, Stewart Toy, and Karen Lowry Miller. ''The

Globetrotters Take Over: Worldwide Champions Outpace Domestic Competitors.'' *Business Week*, July 8, 1996, pp. 46–48.

Wellins, Richard S., William C. Byham, and George R. Dixon. *Inside Teams: How 20 World-Class Organizations Are Winning through Teamwork*. San Francisco: Jossey-Bass, 1994.

Wurman, Richard Saul. *Information Anxiety: The Black-Hole between Data and Knowledge, and It Happens When Information Doesn't Tell Us What We Want or Need to Know*. New York: Doubleday, 1989.

Yergin, Daniel, and Thana Gustafson. *Russia 2010: And What It Means for the World*. New York: Vintage Books, 1995.

Yoshino, Michael Y., and U. Srinivasa Rangan. *Strategic Alliances: An Entrepreneurial Approach to Globalization*. Boston: Harvard Business School Press, 1995.

Zeien, Albert. ''Gillette's Global Marketing Experiences.'' Talk given at St. John's University's Annual Colman Mockler Leadership Award Ceremony, New York, February 27, 1995.

Zenger, John H., Ed Musselwhite, Kathleen Hurson, and Craig Perrin. *Leading Teams*. Burr Ridge, IL: Irwin Professional Publishing, 1994.

# Index

accounting: common global framework, 61; comparative control systems, 197; computer software, 61; costs, 197; and currency translation exposure, 183; currency translation in reports, 192; definition, 176, 186; as an enabling system, 59; financial, 187; Generally Accepted Accounting Principles (GAAP), compliance, 187, 188; impact of different report preparations, 188; information, uses of, 186; International Accounting Standards Committee (IASC), 189–190; international standards, 61, 190; standards, 35; standards, differences among, 188–189; systems, 37, 38; tax, 193

adaptability, 261

Aflaco (American Family Corporation Inc.), 126–127; market niche strategy, 84, 97

Airbus Industrie, 149

airlines: British Airways, 4; KLM, 28; Lufthansa, 28; partnerships, 23, 137; Singapore Airlines, 4

airplane manufacturers: export of product, 149; subcontracting, 150

Alcatel Cable S.A., and AT&T, 110, 160; organizational structure, 204–205; telecommunications in Africa, 169

American Accounting Association, 176

American Home Products, 125

American Motors Corporation, 242

Ameritech Corporation and Deutsch Telekon, as investment partners, 114, 160

Ametek, Inc., 195; mission statement, 21

Ampak International, Ltd., 181, 185

analysis, financial, 117–118, 148

Anheuser-Busch, 5; brand identification, 64; contingency process, 46

Apple, agreement with IBM, 110

ARPANET (Advanced Research Projects Administration Network), 160–161

AT&T, 4; and the Internet, 59–60; structural organization, 205; Telstar, 110; Telstar and other systems, 160

ATMs, 111

attitudes, cultural, 107

Bank of China, 179

banking, competition, 115

banks, investment, lending strategy, 178–179

basic contingency processes, 46–47

**About the Authors**

ROBERT J. MOCKLER is Professor of Management in the Graduate School of Business at St. John's University, and is Director of the Strategic Management Research Group. Dr. Mockler has written widely on the subject; his published works include thirty-eight books and monographs. He has consulted and conducted training programs in many developing and developed countries.

DOROTHY G. DOLOGITE is Professor of Computer Information Systems in the School of Business at Baruch College, City University of New York. Dr. Dologite has written twelve books and many articles on the subject, and has lectured in Russia, China, and several other countries.